*Conflicts in the North of Ireland, 1900–2000*

# Conflicts in the North of Ireland, 1900–2000

## FLASHPOINTS AND FRACTURE ZONES

Alan F. Parkinson and Éamon Phoenix

EDITORS

FOUR COURTS PRESS

Typeset in 10.5 pt on 13.5 pt AGaramond for
FOUR COURTS PRESS LTD
7 Malpas Street, Dublin 8, Ireland
www.fourcourtspress.ie
and in North America for
FOUR COURTS PRESS
c/o ISBS, 920 NE 58th Avenue, Suite 300, Portland, OR 97213.

A catalogue record for this title is available
from the British Library.

ISBN 978–1–84682–189–9

Printed in England
by MPG Books, Bodmin, Cornwall.

# Contents

# Contributors

B.E. BARTON taught at the Belfast Institute of Further Education and was a Research Fellow in Politics at Queen's University Belfast. He is currently working as a Tutor and Research Associate at the Open University. He is author of *Northern Ireland in the Second World War* (1995), *From behind a closed door: secret courtmartial records of the 1916 Easter Rising* (2002), and co-author of *The Easter Rising* (1999).

GEORGE BOYCE is currently Professor Emeritus at the University of Swansea. He has written extensively about British, Irish, imperial and military history/politics. His publications include *Nationalism in Ireland* (1993), *Nineteenth-century Ireland* (2005) and *The Falklands War* (2005).

FIONNTÁN DE BRÚN is a Lecturer in Irish at the University of Ulster and the editor of *Belfast and the Irish language* (2006).

PETER COLLINS is Senior Lecturer in History in St Mary's University College, Belfast. He is the author of *Who fears to speak of '98* (2004), a study of the commemoration of the 1798 Rising, and *County Monaghan sources in the Public Record Office of Northern Ireland* (1998), and is editor of *Nationalism and Unionism* (1994).

RICHARD DOHERTY has published and broadcast widely in the area of Irish military history. His publications include *Eighth Army in Italy, 1943–5: the long hard slog* (2007), *None bolder: the history of the 51st Highland Division in the Second World War* (2006) and *The Williamite War in Ireland, 1688–91* (1998).

AARON EDWARDS is Senior Lecturer in Defence and International Affairs at the Royal Military Academy (Sandhurst). He is the author of *Transforming the peace process in Northern Ireland* (2008) and *A history of the Northern Ireland Labour Party: democratic-socialism and sectarianism* (2009).

SEÁN FARREN is a former Senior Lecturer in Education at the University of Ulster and the author of *The politics of Irish education, 1920–65* (1995) and *The SDLP: the struggle for agreement in Northern Ireland, 1970–2000* (2010). A prominent member of the Social Democratic and Labour Party (SDLP), he was a negotiator of the Good Friday Agreement of 1998 and served as Minister for Higher Education and Learning and Minister for Finance in the first Northern Ireland Executive of 1999–2002.

JOHN GRAY was born in Belfast in 1947 and educated at Campbell College and Magdalen College Oxford. He has written and broadcast widely on many aspects of the social and cultural history of Belfast. Since 1982 he has been Librarian of the city's historic Linen Hall Library. His *City in revolt: James Larkin and the Belfast dock strike of 1907* (1985, 2007) is the only full-length account of the 1907 crisis.

INGER V. JOHANSEN lectures at the University of Copenhagen. Her PhD thesis was on the Northern Ireland Civil Rights movement. A media commentator on Irish affairs in Denmark, she has also written on the Northern Ireland peace process.

DENNIS KENNEDY is an experienced observer, both as a journalist and as a historian of the Irish political scene. He worked for the *Belfast Telegraph* and later became Deputy Editor of the *Irish Times* before serving as EC representative in Belfast. His publications include *The widening gulf: Northern attitudes to the independent Irish state, 1919–49* (1988), *Living with the European Union: the Northern Ireland experience* (2000) and *Climbing Slemish: an Ulster memoir* (2007).

JIM McDERMOTT taught history for thirty years and was formerly head of history in Corpus Christi College in West Belfast. He is the author of *Northern divisions: the Old IRA and the Belfast pogroms, 1920–22* (2001).

DOMINIC MURRAY has taught in universities in Northern Ireland and the Republic and is currently Emeritus Professor at the University of Limerick. He is the author of *Worlds apart: segregated schools in Northern Ireland* (1985). His two most recent research projects have studied initiatives supporting collaboration in education in Northern Ireland and also the degree of cross-border police cooperation in Ireland.

ALAN F. PARKINSON is Senior Lecturer in History and Education at London South Bank University. He is the author of *Ulster Loyalism and the British media* (1998), *Belfast's unholy war: the Troubles of the 1920s* (2004) and *1972 and the Ulster Troubles* (2010).

ÉAMON PHOENIX is Principal Lecturer in History at Stranmillis University College, Belfast. A frequent media commentator on modern Irish political history, he is the author of *Northern Nationalism: Nationalist politics, partition and the Catholic minority in Northern Ireland, 1890–1940* (1994) and editor of *A century of Northern life: the Irish News and 100 years of Ulster history* (1995). He is currently working on a biography of the Northern Irish Nationalist leader, Cahir Healy.

GRAHAM WALKER is Professor of Political History at Queen's University, Belfast. His latest book is *A history of the Ulster Unionist Party: protest, pragmatism and pessimism* (2004). He is currently working on a research project investigating the history of devolution in both Scotland and Northern Ireland, and also on a study of the Scottish Labour Party and the Union.

* Editors' Note: The views expressed by individual contributors are not necessarily shared by the editors.

# Abbreviations

| | |
|---|---|
| ANZAC | Australia and New Zealand Army Corps |
| AOH | Ancient Order of Hibernians |
| BBC | British Broadcasting Corporation |
| BLP | Belfast Labour Party |
| BPA | Belfast Protestant Association |
| BrLP | British Labour Party |
| CLP | Commonwealth Labour Party |
| DCAC | Derry Citizens Action Committee |
| DHAC | Derry Housing Action Committee |
| EC | European Community |
| GAA | Gaelic Athletic Association |
| GOC | General Officer Commanding |
| HC | House of Commons |
| IFA | Irish Football Association |
| ILP | Independent Labour Party |
| IPP | Irish Parliamentary Party |
| IRA | Irish Republican Army |
| IrLP | Irish Labour Party |
| IVF | Irish Volunteer Force |
| MLA | Member of the Legislative Assembly |
| NAD | National Archives, Dublin |
| NHS | National Health Service |
| NICRA | Northern Ireland Civil Rights Association |
| NIHC | Northern Ireland House of Commons |
| NILP | Northern Ireland Labour Party |
| NIO | Northern Ireland Office |
| NLI | National Library of Ireland, Dublin |
| NUDL | National Union of Dock Labourers |
| ODR | Outdoor Relief (esp. agitation/riots in Belfast, 1932) |
| PRO | Public Record Office, London |
| PRONI | Public Records Office of Northern Ireland |
| PSNI | Police Service of Northern Ireland |
| RIC | Royal Irish Constabulary |
| RUC | Royal Ulster Constabulary |
| SDLP | Social Democratic and Labour Party |
| SPO | State Paper Office, Dublin |

| | |
|---|---|
| UCDC | Ulster Constitution Defence Committee |
| UDA | Ulster Defence Association |
| UIL | Ulster Irish League |
| UN | United Nations |
| UPL | Ulster Protestant League |
| UPV | Ulster Protestant Volunteers |
| USC | Ulster Special Constabulary |
| UUC | Ulster Unionist Council |
| UUP | Ulster Unionist Party |
| UVF | Ulster Volunteer Force |
| UWC | Ulster Workers' Council |

# Introduction

ALAN F. PARKINSON & ÉAMON PHOENIX

Though dealing with specific and very different individuals and topics, the seventeen essays in this collection often overlap, sharing linked themes or trends. While the editors have used chronological order in the placing of essays, the contents exhibit shared links in terms of seven central themes. These are:

a) the doomed attempts to unify the working classes in the North of Ireland in terms of a trade union movement, political party or civil rights movement;

b) the efforts made by individuals and political parties to destroy either Home Rule or the new statelet which emerged after 1920;

c) the impact of international warfare on both military personnel from the North of Ireland on the Western Front and on Belfast's 'home' front during the early 1940s;

d) the significance of community and political divisions upon school provision and the development of the Irish language;

e) street disturbances in the northern metropolis during the earlier part of the century;

f) aspects of division and polarization overcoming momentary hopes of compromise and community cohesion during the inter-war period, illustrated by the clashing aspirations of fledgling governments and populations during the formative years of the two new Irish states, and the lack of political impact of a shared experience of poverty by Catholics and Protestants during the 'hungry thirties';

g) two essays dealing with different aspects of the modern conflict, namely the splits within Republicanism early in the 1968–94 Troubles and an analysis of one of the most spectacular 'own goal' instances of terrorism emanating from Republican groups during the IRA's 'long war' of the last three decades of the twentieth century.

Three essays have focused on various attempts to forge working-class unity across the sectarian divide in different ways and periods across the century. In John Gray's essay about Belfast's 1907 dock strike, attention is drawn to divisions between the unskilled and skilled sections of the city's industrial workforce and to the subsequent schisms within the Protestant community. The Unionist Party and other main political groups were to quickly distance themselves from the strikers, but this relative split would soon be remedied, particularly after the re-emergence of the Home Rule threat in 1910. Street violence broke out in the city's Nationalist Falls Road district, providing Unionists with an opportunity to reclaim the political initiative. Gray suggests that a lack of genuine support from the British trade union movement and infant Labour Party combined with growing constitutional fears to ensure a return to the more familiar world of sectarian-dominated Belfast politics by the eve of the First World War.

Graham Walker and Aaron Edwards focus on political divisions, both internal and external, and relate these specifically to one political party, the Northern Ireland Labour Party. Political groups in the North of Ireland had to endure several turbulent decades in the twentieth century and the NILP was actually founded and later experienced its demise in 'a climate of conflict and division'. The authors describe the impossible situation encountered by a party more concerned with class issues than ones of religion or ethnicity, and suggest it was the very different nature of Ulster's political scene which resulted in the NILP's marginalization. In particular, it was the perennial problem of the constitutional issue which would check the party's progress, evidenced by its own internal schism between those falling into the camps of Harry Midgley and Jack Beattie. Walker and Edwards argue that despite occasional electoral success in the late 1950s and early 1960s, the NILP crucially lost its middle ground support on account of the moderate policies adopted by Terence O'Neill and fell by the wayside, as it was unable to relate to the methods and street politics favoured by the Civil Rights movement. The party's attempt to provide a forum for cross-community debate was ultimately 'a noble failure'.

Inger Johansen's essay charts the origins of the Civil Rights movement and analyzes its degree of success in its short existence. Johansen maintains that the rise of such a popular movement was not simply the outcome of local develop-ments but was also the result of international influences and general change. She rejects the notion of a Republican 'conspiracy' within the Civil Rights move-ment, and instead stresses the impact of the radicalism of groups like the People's Democracy and the growing momentum of the Civil Rights movement itself. Johansen also examines the legitimacy of Civil Rights demands, especially in the context of Derry, 'the cradle of the Civil Rights movement'.

Though the essays of Éamon Phoenix and George Boyce focus on individuals and parties from very different backgrounds, there is commonality in the distinc-tion between the perception and actual nature of the threats posed respectively by Edward Carson's Ulster Volunteer Force and the IRB-inspired 1916 Rising. Boyce examines the unique situation where the North came close to civil war without the loss of a single life. He reminds us that Carson's 'respectable rebels' provided the first example of a clear move away from constitutional politics in modern Ireland, and suggests that it was to usher in an era of political violence and communal strife. Boyce draws attention to the solidarity of a movement which believed in its own 'moral force'. For him, the UVF provided a safety-valve for rising Protestant feelings, and the Unionist campaign constituted evidence of 'a community in defiance' rather than one which was simply a 'defence' movement.

In a parallel essay, Éamon Phoenix traces the development of the Irish Parliamentary Party's growing ascendancy over the mass of Catholics in the north of Ireland, especially under the influence of its charismatic Belfast leader 'Wee Joe' Devlin after 1900. Devlin's manipulation of the sectarian-based AOH to galvanize northern Nationalism is traced in the context of the introduction of the third Home Rule Bill in 1912. Phoenix examines the catalytic impact of 'Carson's Army' on Irish Nationalism in the shape of the IRB-inspired Irish Volunteers and the drift towards some form of exclusion or partition by 1914. The impact of the 1916 Rising on northern Nationalist opinion and the Ulster Question are probed, with the abortive Lloyd George negotiations of May–July 1916 viewed as a watershed in the eventual emergence of partition in 1920. The author shows how, for a large section of northern Nationalists, the desire to avert partition outweighed the broader ideological question of 'Home rule v. Republic'. By 1921, however, the divided Nationalist minority would find themselves facing permanent minority status and permanent partition in a Unionist-dominated state scarred by political and sectarian conflict – a far cry from the high hopes of 1912. Éamon Phoenix's essay on the major Nationalist figure, Cahir Healy, provides 'a focus for the study of the political history of the Nationalist community in Northern Ireland' over a fifty-year-period. Phoenix traces Healy's eventful career, including a spell as a member of Arthur Griffith's early Sinn Féin group, contrasting the nature of this brand of Republicanism with that of post-1916 Ireland. He also looks at Healy's spells as an internee on the *Argenta* prison ship in Belfast Lough in the early 1920s, his time as a Westminster MP, as well as his wider contributions to literature and the Irish language. Phoenix's essay is explicit in its identification of the non-violent nature of Cahir Healy's Nationalism, but also registers that this was in sharp contrast with his opponents' interpretation of his political thinking.

Divisions were not just the outcome of traditional, sectarian communal differences and disagreements, but were exacerbated by new, 'external' tensions provoked by two periods of global warfare in the twentieth century. Two essays exploring the varying experiences of Irish soldiers at the Western Front and Belfast's civilian population during the early years of the Second World War suggest that the negative perceptions of those from a different religious back-

ground or happening to live in the south of the island were extenuated by direct
experience of the horrors of global conflict. Richard Doherty examines the
contributions of two divisions – the 16th (Irish) and 36th (Ulster) – to the Allied
effort on the Western Front during the First World War and questions the 'myth'
that they represented distinctive religious and political communities which were
to unite in a spirit of mutual cooperation, as at the battle of Messines in 1917.
Doherty admits that there were some individual cases of generosity and inter-
divisional support, but points out that men from the respective divisions never
shared the same trenches. He also disputes the argument that the religious
composition of the divisions constituted a neat demarcation, pointing out that
the structure of 36th (Ulster) Division was altered markedly in terms of religion
and regional adherence post-1 July 1916, and shows that a significant proportion
of the supposedly predominantly Catholic 49 Brigade of the 16th (Irish) Division
were actually Protestants, some of whom had signed the Ulster Covenant.
Despite these differences, Richard Doherty believes that the Peace Park in
Messines is evidence of the common aim of Irish soldiers in defending wider
democratic principles.

Brian Barton's essay looks at the impact of direct experience of international
warfare upon the population of Greater Belfast. He points out that, despite the
ferocity and sustained nature of inter-communal violence, the damage inflicted
by a handful of Luftwaften air attacks was greater than in any previous bout of
sectarian disturbances in the city. Barton reminds us of the cruel irony that
Belfast's industrial prowess resulted in its direct targeting by the Nazi leadership
in 1941. In marked contrast to other UK cities, Belfast exhibited a comparative
lack of preparation for safeguarding against aerial attack. Though Brian Barton
concurs with other perceptions of Belfast's Forties' Blitz – the shared nature of its
citizens' suffering and the help provided in the aftermath of bombing by the
southern authorities – he has reservations. For Barton, prevalent sectarian attitudes in the city resulted in mutual distrust, and despite help which was
forthcoming after the Nazi attacks, he stresses the 'polarization' in attitudes
towards the war between the respective authorities in Belfast and Dublin.

Two essays deal with the development of faith schools in Northern Ireland
and look at how segregated education has resulted in community division, and
the potential role of integrated schools in helping to break down such barriers.
Dominic Murray's essay traces the development of faith schools in Northern
Ireland for both traditions. He notes how schools, even technically 'state' schools,
are regarded by most to be fundamentally 'Protestant' or 'Catholic' ones, and
stresses the importance of this distinction upon determining attitudes in an
already divided society. The results of this distinct separation between schools
have been the increase in mutual ignorance of what actually happens inside their

buildings, and the spread of unfortunate myths and stereotypes. Murray concludes that it will be economic factors rather than educational philosophies that will determine the future successful development of integrated education in an increasingly dominant white collar society.

Seán Farren investigates the inter-relationship between community division and education. While he concludes that educational issues did not directly provoke the modern Troubles, he makes it clear that a variety of educational controversies did underline the range and scale of the fissures within Northern Irish society. Initially, Farren traces the broad development of Irish education, stressing that divisions had more to do with an all-island based educational structure going back some 200 years, rather than simply being the outcome of late twentieth-century conflict. In doing so, he highlights the close relationship between educational institutions and political or religious allegiance and illustrates how key movements in the history of education in the North, including the assumption of control of schools by the Unionist administration, were to highlight Catholic sensitivities and concerns over ultimate control of their schools, especially in the sphere of Religious Instruction. Despite a gradual easing of some of these concerns (particularly those relating to state funding), Farren maintains that the distinct separation of Catholic schools from the state and the virtual homogeneous nature, in religious terms, of voluntary and state schools, resulted in a lack of knowledge of what actually went on in these educational establishments.

Another essay looks at the far-reaching impact of communal and political division, in this instance upon the cross-community development of the Irish language. Fionntán de Brún's essay pinpoints the pre-partition 'Carsonia' period as being pivotal in determining the subsequent rejection of the Irish language by Northern Ireland's political establishment. Acknowledging that the Irish language was primarily regarded by Unionists as 'the manifestation of Nationalist, anti-partition sentiment', de Brún argues that inevitably Loyalists had difficulties in expressing any existing feelings of Irishness in the post-partition period. Especially during the 1930s and 1940s, the Irish language was dismissed as having little commercial or practical value and was regarded as being 'a badge of dissent', which accounts for the alienation of the language and its speakers from the Northern Ireland state. De Brún also acknowledges the negative impact which the regional bias of the Ulster language movement had upon its potential appeal to members of the region's majority community and concedes that the national language was unfortunately associated with various aspects of political conflict in the North.

Two essays are set within the context of inter-war street-disturbances in the Belfast area. While Alan Parkinson's essay focuses mainly on the political causes and repercussions of a two-year conflict, Jim McDermott's contribution concentrates on the rather different social and economic factors surrounding the smaller scale disturbances that broke out in parts of Belfast for a short period in 1935. McDermott's essay deals in considerable detail with the semblance of working-class unity in various parts of the city during the early 1930s (including the Outdoor Relief Strike of 1932), as well as examining the changing responses of a range of the city's political and paramilitary leaders to this shared social deprivation and the more familiar one of sectarian discord which was to follow. The essay ends with an account and assessment of the 1935 Lancaster Street riots.

Alan Parkinson's essay on the Belfast Troubles of the early 1920s examines the causes and nature of communal violence in the city some half a century before the modern conflict erupted. He stresses the difficulty in defining the nature of this violence and questions whether the description of the conflict as a 'pogrom' is altogether appropriate. Instead, he stresses the 'unholy' nature of the violence and also focuses on its relative modernity. Parkinson argues that it was a combination of factors and incidents, especially those attacks on police in other parts of Ireland, the spread of disturbances to Derry and the increase in tension caused by the passage of the Government of Ireland Bill at Westminster, which precipitated the outburst of trouble in Belfast's shipyards during the mid-summer of 1920. The essay investigates how serious violence was averted at potentially dangerous moments of the crisis (such as the period around the middle of 1921, when there were elections for the new parliament and its opening shortly afterwards by King George V), largely due to a strong security force presence for shorter, concentrated blocks of time, but this was difficult to sustain for prolonged periods, such as the protracted treaty negotiations towards the end of 1921. The essay examines the atrocities carried out by both the IRA and Protestant groups, including some of the most atrocious incidents of the 1920s Troubles, such as the McMahon family murders and the killing of Catholic children in Weaver Street. A key feature of Parkinson's contribution is the emphasis given to the recollections of some of the last surviving 'child veterans' of this early twentieth-century conflict.

Two more essays focus on further aspects of division during the inter-war period. Peter Collins looks at the fusion of a number of economic, social and political factors or events within a single year, 1932, which he suggests might be regarded as 'a coming of age' for the recently created Northern Ireland. These included northern Nationalists' sense of abandonment by their co-religionists south of the border, the abstentionist policy adopted by Joe Devlin's group in the northern parliament, a religious furore over the perceived 'ownership' of Ireland's patron saint, the official opening of Stormont in east Belfast, and the city's 'Outdoor Relief' disturbances that year. Collins concludes that 'a deeply polarized' society was already in place barely a decade after the creation of the northern state and some four decades before the outbreak of full-blown civil disturbances.

Dennis Kennedy's essay looks at the peculiar mix of psychological and physical warfare conducted by southern Republicans against northern Unionists during the early years of the Northern Ireland state. Most of his essay is concerned with examining the 'malign' impact of political negotiation and uncertainty upon Unionist sensitivities, though Kennedy also looks in the latter part of his essay at the 'rhetorical Nationalism' of southern politicians later in the 1920s and also in the 1930s. The physical threat to Protestants both within the territory of the new Irish Free State and those living in border areas during the early years of the two states is also examined. Kennedy maintains that the threats resulted in Unionists adopting an ultra-defensive approach in the 1920s. The Nationalists' refusal to accept partition or to work with the institutions of the northern administration, and the gradual move towards Republican status in the Free State also meant that there was little scope for the development of broader, more tolerant views within the Unionist community. Kennedy concludes that the partition of Ireland was the product of 'a combination of territorial Nationalism' and the 'ignorance and bigotry that doubtless existed among Unionists'.

Two essays look at very different aspects of the modern Northern conflict. Jim McDermott's contribution on the critical Republican split of 1970 offers a detailed analysis of the reasons for such a split, and suggests that bitterness at such divisions was probably stronger among volunteers in both strands of the IRA than it was among the Official and Provisional leaderships. McDermott endeavours to unravel the reasons why these fissures within Republicanism at an early stage of the Troubles did not lead to renewed division towards the end of the conflict some thirty years later. Though McDermott does identify a number of factors which were very different to this situation in the mid-1990s, he also acknowledges some similarities, including the Republican movement's propensity for sharp treatment of dissenting voices.

Alan Parkinson's essay on the Enniskillen bombing of 1987, and especially the British media's coverage of this incident, looks directly at the impact made on both political policy and public opinion by one of the most serious terrorist attacks during the recent Troubles. Contextualizing the incident within the political climate of the time – the zenith of pan-Unionist opposition to the Anglo-Irish Agreement – Parkinson concludes that, despite the widespread condemnation of a bombing which appeared to insult the memory of Britain's war dead, this did not lead to increased sympathy for the wider plight of Ulster's Protestant community at whom this attack was aimed. This was because the 'Poppy Day' bombing was portrayed not as an outrage specifically aimed at the besieged border Unionist community, but rather as a cross-community attack, and consequently Loyalists were unable to derive any political leverage from this incident. Other themes raised in this essay include the powerful impact of 'human angle' news stories and the pivotal role of Gordon Wilson and his willingness to forgive the IRA who had killed his daughter. His remarkable response ensured that this Northern Ireland story would prove to be a 'long-runner', and it was also the difference between national and local media coverage of the bombing.

This collection of essays does not attempt to cover every aspect of the multifaceted conflict which has scarred the north of Ireland for much of the past century and more. There are clearly gaps, not least in regard to the recent Troubles of *c.*1968–94, the events of which are only now being subjected to serious historical research as primary sources become available. Previously confidential cabinet files on such key events as Internment in 1971, Bloody Sunday, the fall of Stormont in 1972 and the history of the 1974 power-sharing executive have only recently been released to researchers.

Conflict of one type or another has been endemic in the history of Northern Ireland since 1921. Indeed, a survey of its contemporary history reveals a number of conflicts and fracture zones not covered in these essays. Thus, the tradition of violent Republicanism, reflected here in the IRA campaign of 1919–22 and the Troubles after 1969, continued in the intervening decades. Though defeated by Craig's security measures in 1922–3, the anti-treaty IRA regrouped in the 1930s and managed to sustain a desultory campaign of violence against the RUC and military barracks during the early war years. In the end, the threat was neutralized by the introduction of internment, north and south, de Valera's ruthless measures and the receding prospect of Nazi assistance.

By 1945, the IRA was virtually extinct on both sides of the border. However, the failure of the post-War anti-partition campaign, supported by the Anti-Partition League in the North and the All-Party Mansion House Committee in the (newly declared) Republic, saw a recrudescence of militancy by the early 1950s. A series of spectacular arms raids and Sinn Féin's momentary success in winning 150,000 votes in the 1955 Westminster election in Northern Ireland was to set the scene for the abortive border campaign of 1956–62.

The Sinn Féin vote was largely a protest gesture by a frustrated Nationalist population, but it was seen by the 'new IRA' leadership as providing the necessary moral sanction for a renewal of terrorism along the border. The ensuing 'Operation Harvest', aimed at expelling 'the British army of occupation' from the six counties, had little real support outside a few border areas, but by the time it was finally abandoned in 1962 it had cost sixteen lives. The campaign's failure was guaranteed by vigorous security measures on both sides of the border, the strong condemnation of the Catholic hierarchy and, most importantly – and the factor stressed by the IRA itself in its valedictory statement – the striking lack of support from the Nationalist population in the North.[1]

This was partly due to the impact of the 1947 Stormont Education Act on middle-class Catholics, who were increasingly keen to secure equality within the Northern Ireland state while retaining their aspiration to Irish unity. A new generation of educated Catholics, epitomized by young professionals like John Hume and Austin Currie, now preferred 'to use their own efforts to achieve a tolerable present rather than wait behind the barricades for a heavenly Nationalist hereafter'.[2] Therein lay the germ of the Civil Rights movement of the 1960s.

Conflict flared over other issues in the war and post-War years. A source of inter-community and cross-border tensions during the early 1940s was the so-called 'Éire Workers' issue. With the intensification of wartime production, some 14,000 southern workers entered the North between 1942 and 1946 to avail of the ready employment and higher wages. The Unionist government became alarmed at the flood of migrants, partly on political grounds and partly to safeguard local employment. As the control of entry into Northern Ireland was a matter for Westminster, Stormont made representations to the British government to curb the influx. The result was the issue of a residence permit order by the Home Secretary, Herbert Morrison in 1942. The issue continued to rankle among the Unionist grassroots, however, and in 1944 the new Prime Minister, Sir Basil Brooke, moved to dispel complaints from leading Unionists at the employment of southern Catholics in the civil service. Such persons, a critic told Brooke, 'certainly will not work for the strengthening of our imperial connection'.

The issue was temporarily shelved when the Finance Minister, Maynard Sinclair, informed Brooke that a shortage of suitably qualified technical staff made recruitment from the south unavoidable. Towards the end of the war, however, the Brooke cabinet decided to ask the Imperial government to empower the Unionist administration to introduce legislation to regulate southern migration. In a memo to cabinet colleagues, the Minister of Home Affairs, Edmund Warnock, felt that Stormont might hope to capitalize on British resentment at Éire's neutrality during the war. It might be pointed out to the British government that 'Ulster's soil and ports' had been vital to Britain's defence, while, 'if free entry from Éire is permitted, it is probable that the political complexion of Ulster would change … and the result would be an Irish Republic embracing all Ireland'.[3] Despite the concern of the Attlee Labour government at the crude political motivation of the Stormont authorities on the issue and its negative

1 John Bowyer Bell, *The secret army: a history of the IRA, 1916–1970* (London, 1970), pp 269–70, 333–4. 2 Desmond Fennell, *The Northern Catholic: an inquiry* (Dublin, 1958). 3 Memo by Edmund Warnock, 'Control of entry of labour from Éire into Northern Ireland' PRONI CAB9C/47/2; Russell Rees, *Labour and the Northern Ireland problem, 1945–1951: the missed opportunity* (Dublin, 2009), pp 65–75.

impact on relations with de Valera, the necessary powers were granted in 1946. This enabled the Northern Ireland government to introduce the Safeguarding of Employment Act (1947) to Nationalist protests.

The perennial conflict which marked the development of the education system in Northern Ireland was mirrored in the National Health Service after 1945. Here, the fracture lines converged on the Catholic-controlled Mater Infirmorum Hospital in north Belfast, a respected acute and teaching hospital which chose to remain outside the new state health service to preserve its religious ethos. The Mater's decision was prompted by key differences between the Stormont health proposals and the British Act of 1946. In particular, the Stormont Act dispensed with the guarantee to preserve the 'religious character' of any such hospital joining the NHS. In Britain, an 'exempted hospital' (such as the Mater became) could enter into a contractual relationship with the state for the use of its facilities. However, this option was not available in Northern Ireland where the Minister of Health, William Grant, insisted that the Mater must choose between being '100 per cent in or 100 per cent out' of the state health service.[4]

As a direct result of the attitude of the Unionist government, the Mater opted out and was 'deemed not to be a hospital for the purposes of the act'. Only a resourceful fund-raising operation ensured the hospital's survival as the 'unofficial' acute hospital for north Belfast.

The 'Mater' issue was to sour relations between northern Catholics and the Unionist government for almost twenty-five years after 1948. The fact was that the Mater was the only acute hospital outside the NHS anywhere in the United Kingdom, though it catered for all sections of the community. The issue continued to generate conflict until 1972 when, following prolix negotiations between the Stormont government and the Mater's trustees, the hospital finally joined the state system as a 'bright star in a bright constellation'.[5]

Since the 'Affray at Dolly's Brae' in south Down in 1849, the issue of parades or party processions had been a recurring source of conflict in the North. The issue had faded somewhat in the 1920s and 1930s as the Unionist government used the Civil Authorities (Special Powers) Act (1922) to regulate the right to march, particularly by Republicans. In November 1939, for instance, the government prohibited an anti-partition meeting in the mixed border village of Newtownbutler, Co. Fermanagh, sparking a Nationalist outcry.

The anti-partition campaign of the post-War years saw a series of clashes between Nationalists and the RUC over the display of the Irish Tricolour. The

---

**4** Martin Wallace, *Northern Ireland: fifty years of self-government* (Dublin, 1971), pp 112–13; *Belfast Telegraph*, 1 Feb. 1967.  **5** *Belfast Telegraph*, 1 Dec. 1971 for William Fitzsimmons's speech.

regional government responded by introducing the Flags and Emblems Act (1954), which made it an offence to interfere with the Union Jack and gave the police powers to remove any other flag likely to lead to a breach of the peace. Further clashes flared at Nationalist demonstrations in Pomeroy, Co. Tyrone, while in Newtownbutler in 1955, serious violence erupted when the RUC tried to prevent the flying of the Tricolour at a Nationalist Feis. The early fifties also witnessed clashes between police and anti-partition demonstrators in the centre of Derry.

The marching crisis intensified in the late fifties over the Stormont government's decision to permit an Orange parade through the Nationalist Longstone Road district in south Down. At Easter 1958, an Orange parade was again forced through the district by the RUC and, that July, an Orange march in the overwhelmingly Nationalist town of Dungiven generated Nationalist anger and a boycott of local Protestant shops.

The spreading community polarization caused by the marching issue against the backcloth of the IRA border campaign alarmed the moderate-minded Inspector General of the RUC, Sir Richard Pym. In a blunt memo to the Minister of Home Affairs on 8 August 1958, Pym placed the impact of processions in a broad historical perspective, noting:

> Past experience in Ireland has shown that a recurrence of such incidents … can lead in the end only to serious sectarian riots and communal disorder in which the whole country will eventually become embroiled. The riots of 1935 are perhaps the clearest example of what can happen.[6]

Pym felt that the recent disturbances at Dungiven and the Longstone Road had set a dangerous pattern. He pointed out that such conflict often occurred 'where what might be called "ultra-Loyalists" wish to march through a Nationalist district carrying their flags'. In response to criticism from Unionists that 'no man should be prevented from exercising their right [to march] and that the Union Flag should he honoured', he wrote that 'These are admirable principles but, unfortunately, they cannot always be adhered to in Ireland.' Pym went on to bewail the lack of 'give and take' between leaders of the two communities and to warn that such brinkmanship, if wantonly pursued, might lead to communal disaster.

Marches and parades would continue to form a fracture zone between the two communities into the 1960s, when Civil Rights marches would face Loyalist counter-marches. By 1971, the Unionist government of Brian Faulkner was forced

---

6 Memo by Sir Richard Pym, 8 Aug. 1958, PRONI HA/33/2/5.

to ban all parades for six months. The issue emerged again in serious form in the aftermath of the Anglo-Irish Agreement (1985) and again in the 1990s, when the seemingly intractable Drumcree dispute brought Northern Ireland close to civil war as violence and intimidation spread across the region.

Conflict of a different sort erupted over the BBC's remit from the early 1920s to include both parts of Ireland in its programming. The Corporation's Northern Ireland director, the Scots-born George Marshall, was openly hostile to neutral Éire in the Second World War, declaring that 'there is no such thing as an Irishman ... Irishmen as such ceased to exist after partition'. Marshall's anti-Éire views were shared by the Unionist government and press during the Second World War. When a regular 'Irish' magazine programme was mooted by the BBC in 1941, the Prime Minister, J.M. Andrews, protested strongly to the station's director: 'This, in my view, would be an insidious form of propaganda which would slur over the neutral and most unhelpful attitude Éire has taken up during the war.'

Conflict over BBC programming continued in the post-War years. In 1958, a special *Tonight* programme on the North by Alan Whicker, which focused on armed police and betting, drew criticism from Unionist politicians, resulting in the withdrawal of the remaining *Tonight* special reports on Northern Ireland. In April of the same year, a television interview with the Belfast-born actress, Siobhán McKenna, in which she attacked partition and voiced sympathy with the IRA, which had killed four policemen in its ongoing border campaign, prompted a Unionist outcry.[7]

The theatre had been uneventful in the North since the heyday of the pro-Nationalist Ulster Literary Theatre in the Edwardian period. In 1960, however, Sam Thompson's mould-breaking play, 'Over the Bridge', which dealt with the issue of sectarianism in Belfast shipyard, precipitated an outburst of indignation among Unionists. Thompson's message was a stark one:

> Davy: There's nothing civilized about a mob, Warren, be it Protestant or Catholic. They can store their bigotry for a long time. Then they spew it out in violence.[8]

Such was the furore that the play was cancelled by the Ulster Group Theatre only to be produced by the rising young Ulster actor, James Ellis, at another Belfast venue.

Inevitably, sectarian and political divisions manifested themselves in the

7 Rex Cathcart, *The most contrary region: the BBC in Northern Ireland, 1924–1984* (Belfast, 1984), pp 118–20, 190–5.  **8** Seán McMahon and Jo O'Donoghue, *Brewer's dictionary of Irish phrase and fable* (London, 2004), p. 791.

sphere of sport. Soccer, by far the most popular sport in Ulster, fell victim to the political tensions surrounding partition in 1921, when the Dublin-based Leinster Football Association seceded from the Irish Football Association to form the Football Association of the Irish Free State. Sectarianism remained a factor in Northern Ireland after partition and in 1949, following a serious mob attack on one of its players during a match, the Nationalist-supported Belfast Celtic decided to withdraw from the Irish League. Though the Northern Ireland team contained players from both religious traditions, the vast majority of its supporters were Protestants who resisted moves towards the establishment of an all-Ireland side on the lines of teams in other sports, especially rugby and cricket.

The Gaelic Athletic Association (GAA), with its Nationalist commitment and all-Ireland structure, had emerged by the 1930s as the premier sporting body for northern Nationalists. However, its ban on 'foreign games' (until 1971) and exclusion of members of the Northern Ireland security forces from membership did little to attract Protestant involvement. The Patton reform of policing after 1999 saw Gaelic games opened to all, including the new Police Service of Northern Ireland. However, the 2005 case of the sectarian intimidation of a young Fermanagh Protestant player showed that the GAA, like the IFA, was not immune from the impact of ancestral prejudice.

During the Troubles after 1968, the ongoing violence often competed with moral force protests. The introduction of internment in August 1971 by the last Unionist government evoked a major civil disobedience campaign among the Nationalist population. Initially endorsed by the SDLP and the Civil Rights movement, the campaign involved a rent and rates strike which, at its height, involved two-thirds of Nationalists. Ironically, it fell to the SDLP in the ill-fated power-sharing executive of 1974 to impose a punitive levy on those still in conflict with the state over internment.

The H-Block protest in the Maze Prison was marked by mounting conflict between sentenced Republican prisoners, protesting against the removal of Special Category status after 1976, and the British authorities, both Labour and Conservative. The 'dirty protest' spilled onto the streets, with regular marches by Republican sympathizers, led by blanket-clad figures representing the prisoners. This movement reached a crescendo during the hunger strikes of 1980 and 1981, which culminated in the deaths of ten Republican hunger-strikers. Paradoxically, the surprise by-election victory of the dying Bobby Sands in May 1981 was to see a portentous shift by the Republican movement towards electoralism, while continuing with the IRA campaign.

On the Unionist/Loyalist side, there were moments of conflict with the British government during the Troubles. In February 1973, a one-day Loyalist strike was organized by a 'United Loyalist Council' to protest at the internment of two Loyalists. The stoppage lacked widespread Protestant support and was accompanied by considerable street violence, but the accompanying electricity blackout demonstrated that Loyalist workers had the industrial muscle to bring Northern Ireland to a standstill. The same tactic was successfully employed in May 1974 by the Ulster Workers Council to overthrow the power-sharing Executive.

A final strike, organized by Revd Ian Paisley with the support of the UDA in May 1977 with the aim of restoring a majority rule Stormont, was a spectacular failure however. This was due to a firm line by the tough Labour Secretary of State, Roy Mason, the government's absorption of the lessons of the UWC strike and the fact there was no 'sitting target' for popular wrath, unlike in 1974.

This collection of essays, therefore, does not cover every expression of conflict and division in Northern Irish society over the last century. Yet it does reflect a wide range of conflict situations and seeks to analyze the origins and outworkings of sectarian, political and community divisions. In many cases, there is clear evidence of a commonality of experience, especially that of extreme emotional trauma. In others, the two communities are separated by a gulf of distrust and misunderstanding.

These essays fully illustrate the perennial, deep-rooted and many-faceted nature of the problems facing the elected leaders of both sections of Northern Irish society and the two sovereign governments as they endeavour to translate the historic compromises of the Good Friday and St Andrews agreements of 1998 and 2006 into a workable and sustainable framework.

# The 1907 Belfast dock strike

## JOHN GRAY

The Belfast dock strike of 1907 emerged from the twilight of history in 2007 when its centenary commemoration was a central feature of the annual May Day celebrations and a wider programme of events organized by the Northern Ireland Committee of the Irish Congress of Trades Unions. The accompanying brochure described the dock strike as 'arguably the most significant event in the history of the trade union movement in Northern Ireland'.[1] A permanent memorial to those events in the form of a fine stained glass window by John McLaughlin and featuring James Larkin centre stage[2] was unveiled in the City Hall, a development that would have been inconceivable a decade earlier, and reflecting a wholly new balance of power in city politics.

Commemoration, and our particular penchant for centenaries, is as much about now as it is about the past. Two very clear assertions can be made about the events of 1907, however. The first is that, thanks to the appearance in the public domain during 2007 of the extraordinary photographs of Alex Hogg,[3] we can now actually see that a mass working-class mobilization extending far beyond the 3–4,000 strikers was involved. Secondly, it is an incontrovertible fact that the Irish administration viewed this as a major crisis; the 6,000 troops rushed to the city in August 1907 far exceeded any re-enforcement either planned, let alone undertaken, at any time during the Home Rule crisis up to 1914.

Belfast seemed to be the last centre where a major labour challenge could spark events of this kind. The grandiose new City Hall completed in 1906[4] was a symbol of the city's overweening pride in its industrial success. Edwardian Belfast could claim the world's largest shipyard, linen mill, rope-works and tobacco factory.[5] Over the course of the 1890s, the city's population had grown by almost a third, rising from 256,000 to 349,000.[6] In a city so heavily dependent on linen and latterly and increasingly on shipbuilding and engineering, all parties freely acknowledged the benefits of late imperial expansion. When in 1898 the Lord

---

1 Irish Congress of Trades Unions, Northern Ireland Committee, *May festival 2007: centenary celebrations of 1907 dockers and carters strike* (Belfast, 2007).   2 John Gray, *City in revolt: James Larkin and the Belfast dock strike of 1907*, 2nd ed. (Dublin, 2007), p. x.   3 There are approximately 70 photographs of the 1907 strike in the remarkable album owned by Mr Frank Boyd of Killultagh Estates. Some of these were reproduced as postcards at the time, and wide use was made of them in commemorative publications during 2007.   4 Gillian McIntosh, *Belfast City Hall: one hundred years* (Belfast, 2006).   5 Jonathan Bardon, *Belfast: an illustrated history* (Belfast, 1982), p. 156.   6 Ian Budge and Cornelius O'Leary, *Belfast: approach to crisis* (London, 1973), p. 28.

Mayor told delegates to the Irish Trades Union Congress that the city was 'an elysium for the working-classes',[7] no-one contradicted him.

Certainly skilled workers shared in the prosperity, enjoying rates of pay governed by the British market and unequalled outside London.[8] Doughty defenders of their own rights, they had helped make Belfast the leading centre for labour organization in Ireland,[9] albeit in a movement that had as yet barely touched the unskilled. William Walker, the most prominent Belfast labour leader of the period, had served as President of the Irish Trades Union Congress in 1904 and hardly foreshadowed any new era of industrial militancy when he argued that 'surely it is a wiser policy to spend £1,000 on the return of a member to the House of Commons than to spend ten times that amount on a strike which is often not successful'.[10] On a programme of social reformism combined with opposition to Home Rule, he came close to winning the North Belfast seat in three elections in 1906 and 1907.[11]

James Larkin's arrival in the city on 20 January 1907[12] arose precisely because of Belfast's breakneck growth and sudden arrival in the first rank of British industrial cities. It was now a natural venue for the first ever conference of the British Labour Party, one buoyed up by parliamentary successes elsewhere in Britain in the 1906 General Election.[13] Larkin was an obscure delegate representing the Liverpool-based National Union of Dock Labourers (NUDL), who supported this impetus. He was no Irish evangel yet – as a subsequent Irish critic put it, he looked like 'a big burly docker from Liverpool or London' and spoke in the 'approved manner of an English slum'.[14]

Larkin had other work to do in Belfast – to see if he could organize the Belfast dockers, work of a kind that he had already undertaken with modest success in Preston, Aberdeen and Govan.[15] There were no indications in this trajectory of what was to occur in Belfast. No reports survive of Larkin's early street-corner speeches in Belfast. All we have is anecdotal memory of mesmerizing effect, a new sense of empowerment. William Long heard 'as fine a speech as ever I heard' at the corner of Corporation Street.[16] The response was extraordinary: by the begin-

7 James Henderson, *A record year in my existence as Lord Mayor of Belfast in 1898*, p. 200. 8 *Report of an enquiry by the Board of Trade into working-class rents, housing, retail prices and standard rates of wages in the United Kingdom* (1908, Cd. 3864 cvii), p. xxxix. 9 J.W. Boyle, 'The rise of the Irish Labour movement, 1880–1907' (PhD, TCD, 1961), p. 228. 10 J.D. Clarkson, *Labour and Nationalism in Ireland* (New York, 1925), p. 350. 11 Gray, *City in revolt*, pp 36–9. 12 Irish National Archives SPO CSORP 1908 20333. District Inspector Clayton, 'Report on Belfast Strike', par. 8. 13 *The forgotten conference* (Belfast, 1982). 14 E.W. Stewart, *The history of Larkinism in Ireland* (Dublin, 1912), p. 1. 15 For Larkin's life generally, see Emmet Larkin, *James Larkin* (London, 1965); Donal Nevin (ed.), *James Larkin: lion of the fold* (Dublin, 1998). For the National Union of Dock Labourers, see Eric Taplin, *The Dockers' Union: a story on the National Union of Dock Labourers, 1889–1922* (Leicester, 1986). 16 PRONI, D3358/12.

ning of April, Larkin had recruited over two thousand men,[17] and both the police
and the press were beginning to take notice.

There is no doubting Larkin's power as an exceptional mobilizer of men, but
why did he find such fertile ground in Belfast? The tinder that he set alight lay in
the abyss that separated a skilled labour aristocracy from the far larger mass of the
unskilled. The pay differential between skilled and unskilled workers in Belfast
was wider than that in any other centre in the British Isles. It is no accident that
Belfast's most successful industries, shipbuilding and linen, were labour-intensive
with a high proportion of unskilled labour.[18] They were in significant measure
dependent on a frontier labour economy and that very Irish factor, the never-
ending tide of cheap labour flowing in from a collapsing countryside.[19]

While the frontier in Belfast has usually been defined as that between
Catholic and Protestant and between British and Irish, and the city's unenviable
reputation for accelerating sectarian violence was well established by the end of
the nineteenth century, and itself served as a grave obstacle to labour organization, that other unnoticed frontier, between the haves and the have-nots, was far
less discriminating. Although Catholics were relatively disadvantaged, Protestants
remained a majority at every level of degradation. Poverty was shared, and that
created the possibility of organization across the sectarian divide.

It could only do so if a new, confident and powerful message emphasized the
immediate potential gains that could be won with united action. Larkin was the
most effective conceivable exponent of such a new departure. New because in the
Belfast labour market every minimal advantage could be contested on sectarian
grounds, and that contest had been at its fiercest among the unskilled. Early
efforts in the 1890s to organize the dockers had run foul of such divisions,[20] and
in 1907 the demarcation between Protestant cross-channel dockers and Catholic
deep-sea dockers was a clear one.

Typical of those caught in the low wage trap were the 3,100 dockers, mainly
casual workers, often earning no more than 10s. a week.[21] Lindsay Crawford,
Grand Master of the Independent Orange Order, but also a radical journalist as
editor of the Liberal *Ulster Guardian*, estimated the minimum cost of keeping a
family at 22s. 5d.,[22] so women and children too were pressed into service in the
low-wage economy of the mills as a matter of necessity.[23]

**17** *Forward*, 13 Apr. 1907. **18** For shipbuilding, see Alistair Reid, 'Skilled workers in the shipbuilding
industry' in Austen Morgan and Bob Purdie (eds), *Divided nation; divided class* (London 1980), p. 127. For
linen, see D.L. Armstrong, 'Social and economic conditions in the linen industry', *Irish Historical Studies*
(1950–1), 265. **19** A factor identified by Richard McGhee, one of the founders of the NUDL, during his
attempts to form an Ulster Labourers Union for rural labourers in 1892 (see *Irish News*, 8 Aug. 1892) and
confirmed in 1905 in government statistics (see *12th Abstract of Labour statistics* (1908, Cd. 4413 xcviii), p.
lxxxxviii). **20** Linen Hall Library. John McKeown, 'Autobiography', p. 105. **21** *Irish News*, 6 June
1907. **22** *Ulster Guardian*, 24 Aug. 1907. **23** Report of Miss Martindale, a factory inspector, in *Ulster*

Tommy Carnduff, a young unskilled worker at the time and later the 'ship-yard poet', remembered how the 'labouring classes … were bordering on starvation',[24] and yet starvation did not make mobilization easier. Efforts by skilled workers to encourage unskilled organization had signally failed, and the strategies they suggested – essentially the humble petitioning of employers – led to nothing but humiliating reverses.[25]

Larkin was to be given no opportunity to steadily build the new NUDL branch. Employers had soon noticed the impact of his early organizing efforts, and rapidly embarked on their own counter-offensive. On 26 April a coal-importer, Samuel Kelly, dismissed union members among his coal-heavers because 'a union … should not embrace such a class of employment'.[26] Almost his entire work-force walked out. Simultaneously, the Belfast shipping companies were contacting the Europe-wide Shipping Federation, warning that they might need 'free' labour.[27]

Rank-and-file union enthusiasm made restraint difficult. On 6 May, Belfast Steamship Company men walked out rather than work with a non-union man. Larkin conceded that this 'was a mistake' and instructed the men to return to work. When they sought to do so they were locked out and found that they had been replaced with Shipping Federation scabs imported from Liverpool.[28] The Belfast dock strike was under way.

Thomas Gallaher, owner of Belfast Steamship Company, was one of Belfast's self-made businessmen, with a fortune founded on his great tobacco factory. He was to prove an inflexible and single-minded opponent. He may have banked on an early climb-down by his men, but humble petitioning was suddenly out of style; the following day, union men stormed both Kelly's coal quay and the Steamship Company's sheds and chased the scabs.[29]

Kelly promptly capitulated, granting union recognition and a pay rise. A victory march, led by a Union Jack with the men singing 'Britons never shall be slaves', passed through the town.[30] Gallaher, by contrast, spurned an intervention from the Lord Mayor, who relayed Larkin's willingness to go to arbitration.[31] Only when this overture was rejected did Larkin fight back, denouncing Gallaher as 'an obscene scoundrel' and on 16 May urging the mainly women workers at Gallaher's tobacco factory to join a union and declaring in millennial terms: 'There was a strike of quay labourers at New York and Montreal, and before long

---

*Guardian*, 27 July, 3 and 10 Aug. 2007. 80% of the 51,000 employees in Antrim and Down were women and 4,000 were half-timers (children).  **24** John Gray (ed.), *Thomas Carnduff: life and writings* (Belfast, 1994), p. 72.  **25** During the major 1906 textile strike, Belfast Trades Council sent a delegation to the Lord Lieutenant, Lord Aberdeen, who advised the strikers to go back to work. Linen Hall Library, Belfast Trades Council minutes, 3 Aug. 1906.  **26** *Belfast Newsletter*, 29 Apr. 1907.  **27** *Irish News*, 9 May 1907.  **28** Ibid.  **29** *Northern Whig*, 10 May 2007.  **30** *Irish News*, 11 May 2007.  **31** Ibid.

it was not improbable that there would be a general strike all over the United Kingdom'.[32] Gallaher dismissed seven girls for attending this meeting, and a thousand promptly walked out; and yet they had to return the following day: the NUDL had no means of supporting them.[33] Sailors in the coastal trade were threatening to come out, and an unrelated strike by 500 iron-moulders led to the laying off of thousands of men in the shipbuilding and engineering industries. With time on their hands, they proved ready recruits for increasingly rowdy strike activity on the streets.

Rumours that an attack would be made on Donegall Quay led the Lord Mayor, Lord Shaftesbury, to requisition 200 soldiers from Victoria Barracks to help defend Belfast Steamship Company's quay. No attack materialized and the use of troops at this stage was condemned by the *Northern Whig* 'as a serious mistake',[34] and viewed with disgust by the military authorities.[35] What was clear was that Thomas Gallaher, in pursuing a hard line with the NUDL, could pull other key forces in behind him, however unwillingly.

Larkin initially pursued entirely legal means to try to disrupt the ongoing blackleg operation at Donegall Quay. To the consternation of the Harbour Commissioners, the new Trades Disputes Act entitled union representatives to pass through cordons and to speak to those within. Only when these tactics failed did Larkin dismiss the new act as 'the Trades Act folly'.[36]

What Larkin and the newly founded branch of the NUDL could not afford was a continuing impasse with their men locked out. Accordingly, Larkin moved elsewhere and in early June presented all of the coal-importers with demands for union recognition and pay increases, as already granted at Kelly's coal quay, and by 17 June all had conceded.[37]

Buoyed up by this success, Larkin played for the highest stakes yet with a general demand to all the cross-channel shipping companies on 20 June.[38] A key objective was no doubt to isolate the obdurate Thomas Gallaher, but Larkin was also taking on other far more formidable opponents than the purely local shipping companies. The great British railway companies had a key stake in cross-channel shipping.[39] These were also companies that had consistently refused recognition in Britain to the members of the Amalgamated Society of Railway Servants. Larkin's Belfast ultimatum was undoubtedly timed to encourage ASRS members, who were simultaneously meeting in Birmingham, to take industrial

**32** *Belfast Newsletter*, 16 May 1907. **33** *Belfast Newsletter*, 17 and 18 May 1907. **34** *Northern Whig*, 17 May 1907. **35** NAD SPO CSORP 1908 20333, General Dawson to Sir A. MacDonnell, 17 May 1907. **36** *Northern Whig*, 1 July 1907. **37** *Belfast Evening Telegraph*, 17 June 1907. **38** *Belfast Newsletter*, 21 June 1907. **39** Thus the Fleetwood route was owned by the London and North West Railway Company and the Lancashire and Yorkshire railway, while the Barrow and Heysham routes were owned by the Midland Railway Company (*Northern Whig*, 27 June 2007).

action.[40] They failed to do so, and the Belfast men were left to go it alone on 26 June. Seven smaller local firms gave in; but the larger companies held out.[41]

More scabs arrived, and soldiers and the RIC guarded an extended perimeter on the quays. Strikers stormed the monthly meeting of the city corporation; a cry from the gallery, 'The Lord Mayor is no use. I'd shoot the Lord Mayor'[42] confirmed the angry mood but did nothing to resolve the new and extended impasse in the dispute. But Larkin had another powerful card to play.

Almost overnight, the NUDL had recruited most of the city's carters, and indeed persuaded them to defect from the semi-defunct Carters' Association, and now an ultimatum was issued on their behalf.[43] For some, it was a step too far: Robert Gageby, a veteran moderate labour leader, urged the carters 'to carry on their work'.[44] At the same time, the Presbyterian *Ulster Echo* made the first sectarian attack on the union leadership – they were 'extreme and rabid Nationalists and Roman Catholics'.[45]

Disagreements about strategy precipitated a crisis marked by Larkin's dramatic resignation as strike-leader at a mass meeting on 2 July and his nomination of Alex Boyd, an Independent Orangeman and leader of the Municipal Employees, as his replacement. Larkin emphasized that Boyd was a Protestant and sought to vindicate himself in the face of two charges: that 'he was the great dictator' and that he was 'a hindrance to negotiations'.[46] His willingness to step down provided an immediate answer to his critics behind the scenes.

The following day, moderate strategy collapsed in ruins when the Lord Mayor sought to intercede with the employers and met a flat rebuff. At Dublin Castle, the Under Secretary, Sir Anthony MacDonnell, sent a memo to the Chief Secretary, Augustine Birrell, observing that 'you will notice deadlock is due to refusal of employers to consult Trades Union leaders'.[47] The effect on the trade union movement was electrifying. Alex Boyd declared that it was now 'war to the knife' and denied that Larkin had ever resigned the leadership. There was, however, a new, wider organizational framework, with a strike committee involving other unions[48] and inevitably curtailing Larkin's powers of independent action.

Now, on 3 July, Larkin's instruction that 'no carter's wheel of any union man would turn on the streets of Belfast' was enthusiastically obeyed. It no longer mattered if scabs were free to work at the quays behind military guard if no carts

**40** *Northern Whig*, 22 June 1907 and *Belfast Evening Telegraph*, 28 June 2007.   **41** *Belfast Evening Telegraph*, 27 June 1907. NAD SPO CSORP 1908 20333, Clayton Report, paras 24, 26.   **42** SIPTU. William McMullen typescript history of 1907 strike, ch. 6, p. 3.   **43** *Northern Whig*, 1 July 1907.   **44** *Northern Whig*, 2 July 1907.   **45** *Ulster Echo*, 2 July 1907.   **46** *Irish News*, 3 July 1907.   **47** NAD SPO CSORP 20333 1908, Sir Anthony MacDonnell to Augustine Birrell, 4 July 1907.   **48** Linen Hall Library. Belfast Trades Council minutes, 4 July 1907.

could get through to them. The *Northern Whig* reflected gloomily: 'We are on the eve of an experience something akin to that which has paralyzed Russian cities during the last couple of years'.[49]

And this was on the eve of the Twelfth of July, so often a season of working-class division in Belfast. At the Independent Orange Order demonstration, £80 was collected for strike funds.[50] Even within the more conservative 'old' Orange Order there were many supporters. Walter Savage, now a dockers' delegate to Belfast Trades Council, wrote to the newspapers claiming that he could get

> 1,000 Old Orange Order Orangemen who belong to the union to sign this letter. Our fervent prayer is that James Larkin may long be spared – to work for the emancipation of the unskilled workers in his native land.[51]

Tactically, the strike leadership now sought to enlist support throughout the city and beyond the immediate dispute arena. Mass meetings were organized in all the working-class areas of the city. Larkin was well received on the Shankill Road;[52] Alex Boyd and others from Sandy Row were enthusiastically received on the Falls Road.[53] All culminated in a massive march on 26 July, possibly involving more than 100,000 demonstrators,[54] which passed through the main working-class areas, and in doing so crossed all those sectarian dividing lines that normally so disfigured the life of the city.

The *Irish News* noted the new contrasts in the movement, as:

> the older established societies preceded by banners, many of which were designed with much taste ... marched two and two with almost military precision, whilst members of the more recently organized unions were collected in an irregularly formed but solid body, sometimes twenty abreast, rendering a computation of the total number taking part ... out of the question.[55]

Four platforms were needed at the City Hall to address the multitude. What was once a purely industrial dispute, and indeed one that was never to involve more than 4,000 men directly, was now a popular mass mobilization.

Yet, by late July, problems were crowding in apace. Threats to further extend the strike movement came to nothing; thus Alex Boyd as leader of the Municipal Employees, threatened to 'leave Belfast in absolute darkness',[56] but it did not

**49** *Northern Whig*, 4 July 1907. **50** *Irish News* and *Northern Whig*, 13 July 1907. **51** *Irish News*, 10 Aug. 1907. **52** *Irish News*, 16 July 1907. **53** *Irish News*, 18 July 1907. **54** James Sexton later claimed 200,000. See *Report of the select committee on employment of military in cases of disturbance* (1908, 236, vii), para. 400. **55** *Irish News*, 27 July 1907. **56** *Belfast Newsletter*, 4 July 2007.

happen. Mass meetings were often substantially devoted to a new spirit of social transformation: as Police Commissioner Hugh Hill noted, there was much talk of 'socialism and generalities', but this could not disguise tactical inertia. Instead, the coal quay employers took the initiative and locked their men out. Meanwhile, the carters' strike led to the laying off of thousands in industry. In this war of attrition, the strikers faced starvation.

Increasing desperation was reflected in growing militancy on the streets. Critical here was the capacity of flying pickets of dockers, carters and their supporters to prevent any blackleg carting. It was an easy enough matter to 'coup' a horse-drawn cart,[57] but larger and more determined forces were required to wreck traction engines hastily imported by the employers,[58] at locations as far afield as the Antrim Road[59] and the Newtownards Road.[60] On occasions, these skirmishes developed into mini-riots.[61]

Growing violence on the streets ensured that the employers presented an ever more united front in demanding increased security but, following the earlier premature call out of troops at Donegall Quay, Dublin Castle delayed over providing re-enforcements.[62] That left the RIC severely over-stretched, unable to protect strike-breaking operations on the quays themselves beyond Donegall Quay, and also unable to protect any significant scab carting in the city as a whole. The employers had their vulnerabilities too, but starvation was not one of them.

For Larkin and the strikers, external assistance from the British labour movement was now essential. There were no doubt some who hoped that the august authority of the British trade union movement could extract them from all-enveloping crisis. James Sexton, General Secretary of the NUDL, arrived on 19 July to pledge his support and 'every penny of their reserve fund of £20,000',[63] but brought only £200.[64] Delegates from the General Federation of Trades Unions arrived too; they were to provide a mere £1,692 throughout the strike, and their priority from the outset was always damage limitation.[65]

The employers, offered the prospect of piecemeal settlements, listened, and in short order both the iron-moulders' and coal quay disputes were settled in negotiations from which Larkin and the Belfast strike-leaders were excluded. At the

**57** Sketch in *Irish Independent*, 7 Aug. 1907, reproduced in Gray, *City in revolt*, p. 88.  **58** *Irish News*, 10 and 11 July 1907.  **59** *Irish News*, 25 July 1907.  **60** PRONI D 3358/1, John Hunter.  **61** *Belfast Newsletter*, 20 July 2007.  **62** Lord Shaftesbury requisitioned 500 cavalry on 1 July (*Belfast Evening Telegraph*, 1 July 2007), but only 120 were eventually supplied and not immediately used (NAD CSORP 20333, Clayton Report, para. 35).  **63** *Northern Whig*, 20 July 1907.  **64** *Belfast Newsletter*, 22 July 1907. **65** General Federation of Trades Unions, *Report of the eighth annual general council executive*, 4 and 5 July 1907. In this, Alderman Allen Gee, now to be one of their representatives in Belfast, saw their role as being to settle disputes rather 'than that we should have to pay out of funds for the purposes of disputes and lockouts'.

great rally on 26 July, Larkin announced that the coal quay men 'had won a great victory,' including increases of 11s. per week.[66] Only on 5 August was it admitted that 'nothing had been committed to writing'.[67]

It was Lindsay Crawford writing in the *Ulster Guardian* who pointed up the moral of the story: 'It would be disastrous for the cause of Labour in Ulster were the impression to be created in the minds of employers here that, in cases of dispute, they could go behind the backs of local officials to headquarters officials in England'.[68] Larkin was left to bitterly concede that they had 'withdrawn one of the wings of their army and allowed the employers to surround the rest'.[69]

Meanwhile, that other peril so feared by all, the raising of political and national as opposed to purely industrial issues, surfaced, and as a direct consequence of the non-sectarian mass-mobilization of the strike movement. Pressures on the RIC in the city brought about by long hours of strike duty in the face of universally hostile working-class communities[70] led to the emergence of a 'more pay' movement within the force, and insensitive leadership[71] provoked virtual mutiny. On 27 July, between 500 and 800[72] out of the RIC force of 1,000 seized control of Musgrave Street Barracks and admitted civilian strikers to an almost night-long meeting. Larkin was not in the city, but other labour leaders advised the policemen to petition for redress and return to barracks, the course that was eventually adopted.[73] If in this way civilian strike-leaders hoped to win kudos for their role in maintaining law and order, they were to be cruelly disappointed.

As were the mutinous police! The Liberal government had been happy to allow Belfast employers to stew in their own juice; it was another matter when law and order in Ireland as a whole was threatened – the events of 27 July provoked a Dublin Castle reaction nothing short of panic. Six thousand troops were hurried into place, the greatest military concentration in Belfast up to 1914, and one undertaken without observance of the legal necessity of prior requisition by the Lord Mayor.[74] The leaders of the police mutiny were dismissed, and 208 men now viewed as suspect were transferred post-haste out of the city.[75]

Unionists denounced the mutiny as a Nationalist conspiracy, although the RIC dissidents had included eighty-three Protestant deportees as well as

**66** *Belfast Newsletter*, 26 July 1907. **67** *Belfast Newsletter*, 6 Aug. 1907. **68** *Ulster Guardian*, 3 Aug. 1907. **69** *Belfast Newsletter*, 6 Aug. 1907. **70** PRONI D3358/1. Recollections of Bob Getgood: 'They were getting into trouble at home, at the barracks, and on the job.' **71** A 1906 enquiry had found 'a deep and widespread feeling of discontent in the force'. It was suppressed. See NAD SPO CSORP 1908 5541. **72** The lower estimate was that of the Unionist *Belfast Newsletter*; the higher that of the Nationalist *Irish News*. Sir Anthony MacDonnell gave a government estimate of 600; see *Report of the select committee on the employment of military in civilian disturbances* (1908, 236, vii), para. 513. **73** *Northern Whig*, 29 July 1907. **74** *Report of the select committee on employment of the military in cases of disturbances* (1908, 236, vii), para. 513. See also NAD CSORP 1908 20333, Gambell to Chamberlain, 29 July 1907. **75** NAD CSORP 1908 20333, Commissioner Hill to Neville Chamberlain, 20 Nov. 1907.

Catholics. Nationalists, including Joe Devlin MP and the Dungannon Clubs, precursors of Sinn Féin, who had ignored the dock strike, now denounced the introduction of the army reinforcements.[76] Meanwhile, British trade union delegates from the GFTU saw the continuance of the civilian strikes as a security risk and sought to force a settlement on the carters. As one of the GFTU delegates, a Mr Appleton, put it, 'I felt that it would be of the greatest use to remove one of the elements of danger'[77] – a bizarre reflection on the men he was supposed to represent. At the last moment, the carters repudiated his proposal on a technicality: they were not yet prepared to 'blackleg' on the dockers.[78] Once again, it was a 'fight to a finish', but this time with a real army.

The decisive Assistant Inspector-General Gambell, now commanding the RIC in the city, and working with General Dawson, drew up a scheme for 'showing the turbulent classes how easily we can cover the city with military pickets'.[79] This was put into effect with overwhelming force on 7 August. At a stroke, the strike pickets lost their month-long dominance of the streets, and blackleg carting got under way.[80] The angry rhetoric of the strike-leaders was in inverse proportion to their ability to do anything about the new situation. Larkin told the men that 'he was not a believer in bombs, but if a bomb would settle the matter he would not hesitate';[81] more prophetically, Joseph Harris asked, 'Were they [the strikers] to be blamed if riots resulted?'[82]

They did indeed, and yet stemmed from a moderate and parliamentary tactic – a mass meeting on Saturday 10 August to which all the city's four MPs were invited. The expectation was that only two would attend, that is Joe Devlin, Nationalist MP for West Belfast, and Tom Sloan, the independent Orange MP for South Belfast. At the last moment, Sloan, ever a weather vane of opportunism within Independent Orangeism, cried off,[83] and although he was replaced by Lindsay Crawford, Grand Master of the Independents, only Devlin carried the parliamentary imprimatur.

He had little to say about the strike to the crowd of in excess of 10,000 and instead used the opportunity to denounce the military presence.[84] It was an intervention that heightened tensions in his Falls Road heartland, a process that accelerated with the assistance of provocative military tactics which were now running beyond any political control and involved 'special treatment' of the Nationalist heartland.[85]

---

**76** *Belfast Newsletter*, 2 Aug. 1907.  **77** *Irish News*, 17 Aug. 1907.  **78** *Belfast Newsletter*, 6 Aug. 1907. **79** NAD CSORP 1908b 20333. Gambell to Chamberlain, 4 Aug. 1907.  **80** *Belfast Newsletter*, 9 Aug. 1907.  **81** *Belfast Newsletter*, 2 Aug. 1907.  **82** *Irish News*, 9 Aug. 1907.  **83** A letter from Sloan appeared in the *Northern Whig* on 15 Aug. denying that he had had any contact with Larkin. Larkin replied on 19 Aug. quoting a letter of apology from Sloan.  **84** *Irish News*, 12 Aug. 2007.  **85** NAD SPO CSORP 1908 20333. Sir Anthony MacDonnell to Augustine Birrell, 12 Aug. 1907.

The following day, minor disturbances in the Lower Falls were exacerbated by the heavy-handed introduction of the military in force. Full-scale rioting broke out, in what was essentially a battle between a working-class Nationalist community and the army, a pattern that was even more violently repeated the following day.[86] The Riot Act was read and troops shot dead three innocent bystanders.[87] Calm was only restored the following day when priests and laity persuaded the Lord Mayor to arrange for a military withdrawal.[88]

Certainly, labour leaders were able to play a significant part in subsequent peace-keeping, but William Walker's uncharacteristically overblown claim that these efforts 'spelt the downfall of capitalism and the dawn of a new era for the working men of Belfast'[89] missed the critical point smugly noted by Fred Crawford, the future hero of the Unionist gun running at Larne. He observed 'what a blessing all the rioting took place in the Catholic quarter of the city. This branded the whole thing as a Nationalist movement'.[90] Larkin, certainly, was under no illusions about the branding effect as 'the masters rejoiced at the rioting because it gave them the opportunity of asserting that this was a party [sectarian] struggle'.[91]

Although the English left mourned the Belfast riot victims as martyrs,[92] mainstream labour's inclination to distance itself from the Belfast strikes intensified. Philip Snowden, a future Chancellor of the Exchequer, condemned 'that portion of the Belfast population which is almost as much accustomed to rioting as a savage tribe is to constant warfare'.[93]

Larkin, recognizing the changed climate and the growing weakness of the strikers' position, now directly sought government arbitration.[94] Official arbitration was indeed a new possibility ushered in by the election of the Liberal government in 1906, but it was usually to be exercised in circumstances favourable to the employers. The government was now desperately anxious to close the whole Belfast episode, and agreed to intervene, provided that the employers consented.

The employers saw the opportunity to put further pressure on the carters, who had only at the last minute pulled out of the earlier prospective settlement. By 16 August, the men had grudgingly accepted terms available weeks before,[95]

**86** All the Belfast papers gave very full accounts of the rioting on 11 and 12 Aug.   **87** Birrell as reported in the *Northern Whig* on 16 Aug. lamented the death of one victim, Maggie Lennon. The inquest, while inconclusive on the matter, at least cast doubt on the need to open fire (*Irish News*, 5 Sept. 1907), as did the subsequent 1908 enquiry into the use of the military in such circumstances. See *Report of the select committee on employment of the military in cases of disturbances* (1908, 236, vii), paras 14 and 104.   **88** *Northern Whig*, 14 Aug. 1907.   **89** *Northern Whig*, 20 Aug. 1907.   **90** Patrick Buckland, *Irish Unionism 1885–1923* (Belfast, 1973), p. 215.   **91** *Belfast Newsletter*, 13 Aug. 1907.   **92** *Labour Leader*, 30 Aug. 1907. **93** *Scottish Co-Operator*, 23 Aug. 1907.   **94** NAD SPO CSORP 20333 1908, Larkin to Birrell, 13 Aug. 1907.   **95** *Northern Whig*, 17 Aug. 1907.

though James Sexton, who was after all General Secretary of their union, was sufficiently fearful of the decisive mass meeting in St Mary's Hall that he went armed with two pistols![96]

Now, as the employers had hoped, the dockers were isolated. There was no question of employer consent to arbitration in their case, and hence there was no arbitration for them. It was a return to the bad old days of humble petitioning. As one veteran put it, 'I felt a pity about the fate of the men I knew – they were never again employed by the shipping company'.[97]

By the middle of September, it appeared that the strike was over. There was a final bitter flourish, provoked by the efforts of the coal quay employers to form a bogus union and eliminate the NUDL.[98] In November, the men came out on a final desperate strike; but any little chance they had was scuppered by the NUDL leader, James Sexton, who paid a one-day visit from Liverpool, denounced the action, spoke to the employers on his own, assured the men that 'all would be plain sailing' and departed. The following day, union men found they had been permanently replaced by scabs.[99]

For all its pioneering heroism, the Belfast dock strike was, then, for most of its participants, a defeat, despite its enormous potential. The creation of the real possibility of change owed everything to Larkin, not as the espouser of any developed revolutionary theory, but as a visionary speaking from the heart and bringing new tools to Ireland in the form of the sympathetic strike. The concept of a solidarity that made the individually weak strong suddenly had meaning, and a particularly potent meaning in Belfast, where otherwise the bargaining position of unskilled labour was profoundly weak. Certainly, a new syndicalist intention can be read into Larkin's challenge to the great British railway companies; but, as even James Sexton pointed out, these were also the tactics that had marked the original formative struggle of the NUDL in Liverpool in 1889. The existing labour leadership in Belfast certainly had misgivings at first about Larkin, but they were soon swept together with him by the force of events. The critical distinction between Larkin and others at this time was that he did not flinch from the discovery that the tactics of English militancy had revolutionary implications in Ireland.

It was the misfortune of all that in Belfast they were faced by a particularly malevolent conjunction of forces. A confident and obdurate employing class never shrank from the toughest strategies, including, increasingly, the playing of the sectarian card. They may have been in some measure pariahs in the British body politic, and especially to a Liberal government, but when issues of Irish law

**96** Sir George Askwith, *Industrial problems and disputes* (London, 1920), pp 112–13.  **97** Letter from James Wilson in the author's possession.  **98** The Amalgamated Coalmen and Carters' Union. See *Belfast Evening Telegraph*, 14 Sept. 1907.  **99** *Irish News*, 28 Nov. 1907.

and order came to the fore, Liberals had vice-regal priorities, even if that meant using overwhelming force. Meanwhile, the British labour movement, the most obvious source of support, was unprepared for explosive developments of the kind seen in Belfast. From an early stage, their interventions were all about resolving the disputes, regardless of the interests of the strikers, while for some, the violence in Belfast provided an excuse for a retreat into narrow English chauvinism.

Thus, the would-be progressives of British society abandoned their exemplars in Belfast; but in Belfast the consequence was not merely a temporary reverse. The defeat of the dock strike, which weighed particularly heavily on the mainly Protestant cross-channel dockers and coal-heavers, played into the hands of resurgent Unionism, and by 1912 all strands of the movement that had contributed to the 1907 strike, whether in the new unskilled unions, in moderate or left-wing Labour, or in the Independent Orange Order, had been virtually eliminated in the course of the Unionist counter-revolution.

Certainly, Larkin left no coherent rearguard, armed either with theory or with rhetoric, with which to resist Belfast's counter-revolution. He was not that sort of man: rather he moved restlessly onwards to wherever the flame burned brightest. Even as Belfast's coal-heavers faced their final defeat, a sympathy strike in Newry was taking on a momentum of its own. Belfast had shown what was possible elsewhere in Ireland; indeed events in Belfast foreshadowed the later dramatic breakaway of the Irish Transport and General Workers' Union and the road to the great Dublin lock-out. The tragedy was that Belfast was left behind.

# Respectable rebels: Ulster Unionist resistance to the third Home Rule Bill, 1912–14

## GEORGE BOYCE

The Ulster Unionist campaign against the third Home Rule Bill seems like a watershed in the history of modern Ireland. When set within the context of the previous fifty years – or even the previous century – it stands in stark contrast to what was, on the whole, deeply contested but essentially constitutional politics. Looking forward, it seems to usher in an era of political violence, bloodshed and, in the north, communal strife, enshrined in the partition of Ireland. It is hard to find an account of this three-year period that does not lay some, most or all of the blame for this changed world of Irish politics on the Ulster Unionists. One historian who did not put Ulster Unionism in the dock and who, on the contrary, wrote with some sympathy towards the Ulster rebellion, Dr A.T.Q. Stewart, has been criticized for his point of view. Timothy Bowman, writing about Stewart's 1967 publication, suggests that it 'would not have been published, one imagines ... if it had appeared five years later, when the recent Northern Ireland troubles were raging'.[1]

Certainly, the spectacle of Unionists marching, drilling and eventually bearing real, instead of wooden, rifles suggests that a new era had dawned; one that typifies, and reinforces, the notion that not only Ireland and the rest of the United Kingdom, but Europe as a whole had lost its faith in reasoned argument and was willing to embrace the belief that bloodshed was a cleansing and sanctifying thing. Patrick Pearse's endorsement of Ulster Unionist militancy reinforces the argument that bloodshed in Ireland was only stopped – temporarily – by the outbreak of the greater European conflict in which the battlefields were given enough 'red wine' to satisfy the most romantic exponent of the virtues of warfare.[2] The resurrection of the title 'Ulster Volunteer Force' on the eve of the modern conflict seems to cement this connection between past and present, between the UVF and the paramilitary army of recent decades.

The Ulster Unionist resistance between 1912 and 1914 presents the historian with an intriguing methodological issue. It is an essential aspect of writing history that the researcher enters, as far as possible, into the minds of those who lived in

---

1 Timothy Bowman, 'The UVF, 1910–20' in D.G. Boyce and Alan O'Day, *The Ulster crisis* (London, 2006), pp 247–58. 2 Patrick Pearse, 'The coming revolution' (Nov. 1913) in P.H. Pearse, *Political writings and speeches* (Dublin, 1924), quoted in A.C. Hepburn, *The conflict of nationality in modern Ireland* (London, 1980), p. 80.

a different era and whose ideas must be empathized with, but not of course
endorsed. But to set aside all judgment on the behaviour of past generations can
lead the historian into a kind of moral wilderness, when all opinions have equal
value. Despite the latter danger, the only useful starting point for the student of
the past is to set out the beliefs and motives of the generation whose behaviour is
under scrutiny. And for the Ulster Unionists, the third Home Rule Bill was not
an exercise in a modest redistribution of governmental arrangements in the
United Kingdom, but a real and permanent threat to their existence. This was a
material and moral threat, for it was held that a Dublin parliament, dominated
by the agrarian interests of the south and west, would bring about the ruination
of Ulster's prosperity. Yet there was also behind this rational argument a real and
deep vein of dislike for the very notion of Catholic domination; for Home Rule
would place Protestants – progressive, modern people – under a priest-ridden
ascendancy; and one, moreover, in which the former predicament of the Catholic
(real or perceived) would make his ascendancy all the more dangerous and
unbearable. In *The making of modern Ireland*, Prof. J.C. Beckett wrote that 'what
Protestants of all ranks were preparing to fight for, though they might not have
admitted it, was the maintenance, in some form, of the threatened Protestant
ascendancy in Ireland'.[3] But this was not the ascendancy of 1700 or 1800; it was
one deeply undermined, politically, socially and economically, not least by British
policy in Ireland since Catholic Emancipation in 1829. This is not to lump all
Ulster Protestants into the shape of some kind of 'Herrenvolk'; but to tell the
truth about the genuine prejudices and real fears of a people who, if Nationalist
rhetoric was to be taken at its word, would be given short shrift by Nationalists
in the new Ireland. As Michael Wheatley has demonstrated in his thorough
examination of the provincial Nationalist Press, the favourite epithet to describe
Unionists was 'carrion crows'.[4]

   Ulster Protestants comprised different religious denominations which had by
no means been always comfortable with each other. Presbyterians rejoiced in the
disestablishment of the Anglican Church of Ireland in 1869. Small sects vied with
each other to save souls and denigrate their rivals in that worthy cause. Some
Presbyterians (the largest denomination in Ulster) took pride – from a safe
distance – in their dissenting past and their role in the 1798 rebellion in Cos
Antrim and Down. The past was not quite forgotten. A General Assembly of the
Presbyterian Church in 1913 voted against Home Rule by 821 to 43, but there were
165 abstentions.[5] The Church of Ireland was troubled by dissension, this time a

**3** J.C. Beckett, *The making of modern Ireland, 1603–1923* (London, 1966), p. 428.   **4** Michael Wheatley,
*Nationalism and the Irish Party: provincial Ireland, 1910–11* (Oxford, 2005), p. 159.   **5** Finlay Holmes, *Our
Irish Presbyterian heritage* (Belfast, 1985), p. 136.

geographical one, reflecting the different strengths of Protestantism throughout Ireland. In September 1912, the Bishop of Down, without consulting the other Ulster bishops, announced that there would be special services in the churches of his diocese on Covenant Day (when Ulster Protestants would pledge themselves to resist Home Rule by all means at their disposal). The southern bishops, fearing Nationalist reprisals, were unhappy with this, but the five bishops whose dioceses covered Ulster signed the Covenant. Also, a future Bishop of Down included the names of two retired bishops to strike an historical chord: seven bishops had come together in 1688 in the last great 'Ulster crisis'.[6]

Fear is a great unifier of disparate peoples. And two important organizations emerged as the axis of Ulster Unionist resistance in 1912, one of them traditional, the other modern. The traditional organization was the Orange Order, which until the first threat of Home Rule in 1886 was a relatively marginal phenomenon, consisting mainly of urban and rural workers whose activities in the countryside posed difficulties for landlords in the 1870s, when land reform became one of the central political issues of the time. When the Order came to prominence in the Home Rule crises, it brought both conviction, but also instability to the Unionist cause. It was a sectarian organization, but also a democratic one, but if Ulster Unionism was to win the hearts and minds of the British people, as it must, then the Order could prove to be a liability. The modern organization, the Ulster Unionist Council, helped harness a variety of Protestants in one democratic body. This was a direct consequence of Unionist anger at the British Unionist Party's dalliance with the possibility of giving Ireland some form of devolved government, but short of Home Rule: the creation of an Irish legislative and financial council.[7] Ulster Unionists felt that they had to stand on their own feet if need be. Their UUC, which rose from a meeting of Ulster Unionists in Belfast on 2 December 1904, and assumed the name Ulster Unionist Council in March 1905, comprised Ulster Unionist MPs and peers, and all local Unionist associations, Unionist clubs and Orange lodges in Ulster. Its delegates were appointed by every polling district and drawn from all classes and Protestant creeds, with a democratic method of election.[8] Its potential was not realized until the coming of the Home Rule crisis in 1911, but once the last barrier against Home Rule – the House of Lords' veto on Commons' legislation – was breached in the 1911 Parliament Act, its true value as a focal point for resistance was realized. On 25 September 1911, 400 delegates to the UUC agreed to set up a committee to submit a constitution for an Ulster provincial government to take

6 R.B. McDowell, *The Church of Ireland, 1869–1969* (London, 1975), p. 104.  7 Alvin Jackson, *The Ulster Party: Irish Unionists in the House of Commons, 1884–1911* (Oxford, 1974), pp 253–73.  8 Patrick Buckland (ed.), *Irish Unionism, 1885–1923: a documentary history* (Belfast, 1973), pp 201–2.

over the province when the Home Rule Bill became law; this was approved on 24 September 1913 in an enlarged UUC.[9]

For Sir Edward Carson, who assumed the leadership of Ulster resistance to Home Rule in 1911, the purpose of this campaign was simple: 'If Ulster succeeds, Home Rule is dead.'[10] His partner in this great enterprise, Sir James Craig, had a less ambitious project, which was to save Ulster from Home Rule. But Ulster Unionism was not an easy movement to lead. Carson urged Craig – if he needed urging – that this resistance must not be a game of bluff; that they were embarking on a dangerous path that must be followed to the end. But resistance can take several forms. It might be passive resistance, which the distinguished Unionist writer and thinker, A.V. Dicey urged on the Ulster Unionists, though he wondered if they had the 'self-control necessary for carrying out the very difficult policy of passive resistance within the limits of the law'.[11] It might take the more specific form of refusing to pay taxes to a Dublin government. But it might go down the ultimate road of armed defiance. This defiance need not spill over into violence; after all, the armed citizenry that constituted the Irish Volunteers who won legislative and economic concessions from the British in 1782 without a shot being fired, relied more upon the threat of force allied with parliamentary pressures and, most importantly, a British government that had initially lent public sympathy to Ireland's case for reform.

Much depended upon the nature of the citizen army and the way in which it was controlled by political leaders, and perceived by British public opinion. The idea of a military response to oppose Home Rule was not new; it had been floated in 1886 and 1893, but with no results. The Ulster Volunteer Force was as spontaneous as the Irish Volunteers of the 1770s had been. But whereas the Irish Volunteers had sprung into action in the first place to defend Ireland against a possible French attack, and only then turned their minds to political action, the UVF emerged as a direct consequence of the dangers of Home Rule. Drilling by members of the Orange Order and Unionist Clubs took place in 1911, and the expansion of the force was the result of a series of local initiatives, sometimes on the part of gentry, but often more by ex-soldiers.[12] But the question of what the UVF was founded to do was a difficult one to answer. Citizen militias could be taken as representing the best of a society, being tainted neither with the usual image of soldiers as drunken and irresponsible louts, nor as men from another country whose welcome by local people was mixed: regular soldiers spent money but also broke the law when on a spree. On the other hand, citizen militias did not have the discipline and training of regular soldiers. The vast majority of them

**9** Ibid. **10** Ian Colvin, *The life of Lord Carson*, vol. II (London, 1934), p. 104. **11** R.A. Cosgrove, *The rule of law: A.V. Dicey, Victorian jurist* (London, 1980), pp 242–3. **12** Bowman, 'The UVF', pp 250–2.

had not handled weapons before; and in the tense, sectarian atmosphere in Ulster during the Home Rule crisis (with Nationalist triumphalism knowing no bounds) the UVF might quickly turn from a respectable citizen army to a dangerous paramilitary force.

Fortunately for the Ulster Unionist movement as a whole, the UVF managed to maintain its image as a citizen army, dedicated to the defence of Ulster, but also representing a law-abiding people. Nothing could be more important than the maintenance of this feature of the UVF. The solidarity of the Ulster Unionist movement at this time, following its partial fragmentation before 1910, helped prevent the UVF from disintegrating into disparate groups, or degenerating into Loyalist gangs, like those of the 1970s. But the success of the UVF was also due to the determined efforts of local commanders to retain their discipline and therefore their preferred reputation as a loyal, defensive, orderly force. No doubt, ex-army commanders revelled in the chance to transfer their parade ground skills into their post-army lives. However, retaining discipline required more than the shouting of orders. Indeed, an incident at Bessbrook in October 1913 showed that instructors could be a liability in a tense situation. The adjutant to the 2nd Battalion South Down UVF regiment explained that a contingent of the Newry Volunteers were marching behind a band to Bessbrook when they were met by a Royal Irish Constabulary officer who said that the principal Unionist and Orange leaders had requested him not to let the band march to the 'Pump', as it was regarded as 'out of bounds' to both Nationalists and Unionists. The band ignored this request and marched on, but the UVF men (except for the front rank) did not follow. The contingent's instructor called on the rest of the men to fall out and follow the band, but they did not. The adjutant, Mr Nesbitt, wrote that he was 'proud to say when I called the Vols to stand steady and obey my orders not a single Volunteer fell out, showing splendid discipline of which any Line Regiment might feel proud'. The incident, he concluded, 'appears to have been a pre-arranged affair by the Band and we would be well rid of them and also any others refusing to obey orders'.[13] Efforts were also made by the Unionist Clubs Council to prevent sectarian disturbances.[14]

Their disciplined appearance and their appreciation of the need to keep within the bounds of order were summed up in Sir Edward Carson's call in September 1912 for defence not defiance.[15] Some UVF commanders insisted not only that they were respectable people – which fitted the general image which Protestants had of themselves as very different from the cattle-houghing, moon-lighting, secret murderers perception they and others had of the Land League and

---

**13** Buckland, *Irish Unionism*, pp 233–4.  **14** Ibid., pp 215–17.  **15** Harford Montgomery Hyde, *Carson* (London, 1953; 1987 ed.), p. 230.

Nationalists in general – but that they might do their bit to enforce the law, in alliance with the RIC. Mr R. Hall, commander of the 2nd Battalion County Down regiment, wrote on 14 June 1914 that the UVF were not to 'mix themselves up in riot or street fights unless to protect themselves or other Protestants, who may be assaulted, or when called upon by Police to assist them'. No rifles or revolvers were to be used 'until the last extremity'.[16] This image underlay and reinforced the general Ulster Unionist campaign in Great Britain, where the core of Unionist protest was that a loyal, peace-loving and God-fearing people were to be placed under the heel of their traditional enemies; of Nationalists, who were also (whatever the professed moderation of their aims) enemies of the British state and empire.[17] But when Sir Edward Carson reluctantly agreed to the demand by more militant-minded Unionists that the UVF be armed, and that guns should be bought and run into Ulster,[18] it was harder to maintain the line that Carson drew between defence and defiance. Unionism's defender, A.V. Dicey, wrote to the *Times* in March 1914, arguing that the Home Rule Bill, if passed solely by virtue of the Parliament Act, 'would be a political crime' lacking 'all moral and constitutional authority': the voice of the present House of Commons was not the voice of the nation.[19] However, he was alarmed by the 'Curragh incident', when officers of the British army said they would resign rather than moving north to coerce Ulster (deprecating Carson's 'repeated references to the conduct of officers of the Army, in case of disturbances or civil war in Ireland'); and he was 'filled with unbearable anxiety' about the Larne gun-running.[20] Colonel G. Hackett Pain, Chief Staff Officer of the UVF, was so concerned about the dangers of losing the moral ground so far gained in the anti-Home Rule battle that he wrote a memorandum setting out 'precautionary measures' should the RIC 'seize or search'. It was

> of the utmost importance that the UVF should not be responsible for any violence which can be avoided, and that there should not be on their part any firing or extreme measures, except so far as is necessitated by the attacking force having commenced firing, or such extreme measures.

Instead, the preferable method of defence by the UVF should be their 'sheer weight of numbers', which should be used to 'overpower the attacking force'. If

---

**16** Buckland, *Irish Unionism*, p. 261.   **17** R.D. Jackson and D.M. McRaild, 'The conserving crowd: mass demonstrations in Liverpool and Tyneside, 1912–13' in Boyce and O'Day, *The Ulster crisis*, pp 229–46. **18** Andrew Gailey, 'King Carson: an essay in the invention of leadership', *Irish Historical Studies*, 30:117 (May 1996), pp 66–87 at p. 79.   **19** *The Times*, 9 Mar. 1914.   **20** Ian C. Fletcher, 'The zeal for lawlessness: A.V. Dicey, the law of the constitution, and the challenge of popular politics, 1885–1915', *Parliamentary History*, 16:3 (Oxford, 1997), pp 309–29 at pp 325–6.

sheer weight of numbers should fail, and if the police produced arms in opposing the UVF, then 'a superior number of armed Volunteers will take the place of the unarmed men in opposing them, and intimidation will be given to the officers in charge of the Constabulary that their armed attempt will be promptly and firmly resisted'. Every means would be used to 'point out to the Constabulary officers in charge that responsibility for any action they may take and its consequences will rest with them. Only if and when the Constabulary commit the first act of aggression by firing will the Volunteers fire in reply.'[21]

It is surely surprising that these instructions came from a senior officer of the British army. The notion that there could be a carefully calibrated action of this kind, in the middle of a confused and tense encounter between Volunteers and police is hardly credible. Indeed, by 14 May 1914, when Hackett Pain's memorandum was written, it was late in the day for the UVF commander to set his mind to working out a military strategy that would best serve the Ulster Unionist cause. However, it is hard to conceive of any circumstances in which a trained British regular army force, if fired on by the UVF (however that fire was carefully calibrated) would fail to decimate their UVF opponents. The chief value of the UVF was not what it would or would not do in a fire-fight, but that it retained order and did not fall into the trap of fulfilling its Nationalist and Liberal opponents' presentation of the UVF as dangerous Orange bigots. The UVF presentation of themselves as peace preservers rather than aggressive enemies could not have looked like that to Irish Nationalists and to Ulster Catholics in particular.[22] Paul Bew has written that Carson approved of the founding of the UVF as a way of keeping Unionist hostility to Home Rule within orderly bounds. Timothy Bowman has not found any evidence for this,[23] but it seems that, whatever Carson's intentions, the organization did work to contain Protestant sectarian tensions. A Church of Ireland bishop wrote in 1914 that it was 'certainly true that we should have had anarchy in Ulster long ago but for the splendid order and constant watchfulness of the Volunteer force'.[24]

This, though important, was not the primary aim of Ulster Unionists and their UVF, but a means to an end. That end was, as declared in Ulster's Solemn League and Covenant, to defeat Home Rule for the whole of Ireland. But this ambitious purpose, which was central to Sir Edward Carson's decision to place himself at the head of Ulster Unionist resistance, was not shared by Sir James Craig, though there were still strong resonances of the assumption that a

**21** Buckland, *Irish Unionism*, pp 259–60.   **22** For an example from Co. Tyrone, see Éamon Phoenix, 'Northern Nationalists, Ulster Unionists and the development of partition, 1900–21' in Peter Collins (ed.), *Nationalism and Unionism: conflict in Ireland, 1885–1921* (Belfast, 1994), pp 107–22 at p. 114.   **23** Bowman, 'The UVF', p. 249.   **24** Patrick Buckland, 'Carson, Craig and the partition of Ireland, 1912–21' in Collins (ed), *Nationalism and Unionism*, pp 75–89 at p. 84.

Protestant Ulsterman could also define himself as an Irishman.[25] As the Home Rule crisis deepened, the idea of defusing it by some special treatment for Ulster counties was never lost sight of. This proved to be both a weakness and a strength for the Ulster Unionist cause: a strength, since it promised to reprieve at least some Ulster counties from Dublin rule; a weakness, since no-one could agree on how long special treatment (exclusion of some Ulster counties) should last, nor even what counties should come under any such arrangement. Once again, the fight for the moral high ground in the Ulster crisis exercised some influence. When on 13 June 1912 the House of Commons debated an amendment by the Liberal M.P. Agar-Robartes that four Ulster counties be struck out of the Home Rule Bill, James Craig was in a dilemma. He would vote for the motion, not because he liked it, but because he would be faced at public meetings by those who would point out that they had failed to take the chance of excluding Ulster, 'whatever Ulster is arranged to consist of'. And, he added a few days later in the debate on exclusion, 'how can we face the British electors in the uphill task we have before us if we do not show our sincerity in this matter?'[26] A fight to the finish to block Home Rule for most of Ireland, and a large portion of the province of Ulster, could not be justified.

Craig's cautious note reflected a real, if concealed, weakness in the Ulster Unionist case. Unionists liked to speak of 'Ulster' as if it were a homogeneous religious and political entity, whereas in three of the nine counties that comprised the province, Catholics were in a substantial majority, and were in a small but significant majority in another two. Even if Ulster Unionists were prepared to abandon their fellow Protestants in the south and west (whom they pledged to stand beside in the Covenant), they could still not comfortably defend those in Donegal, Cavan and Monaghan. And it was significant that the strongest areas where the UVF initially took root were in Fermanagh and Tyrone,[27] where Catholics held the numbers advantage, which also suggested that, whatever the Unionists said about their intentions not to attack or threaten Nationalists, this could not be set aside as a real and present danger. Carson, whom not even his worst enemies could label sectarian,[28] nonetheless warned in July 1913 that, just as there was a minority (Protestant) in the south, so there was a Catholic one in the north; though he added that northern Unionists hoped to live in amity with them.[29] Then there was the question about what Ulster's 'Provisional

**25** See, for example, Brian M. Walker's 'John Lonsdale, Unionist party leader 1916–18' in Boyce and O'Day, *Ulster Crisis*, pp 128–45. **26** Craig's speeches of 13 and 18 June 1912, in *House of Commons Debates*, vol. 39, cols 1115–17, 1562. **27** Bowman, 'The UVF', p. 253. **28** See Carson's spirited defence of Irish Catholicism, even during the Home Rule crisis, on 13 June 1912, *House of Commons Debates*, vol. 39, col. 1086, when a British MP who declared himself a Home Ruler said that the Bill would 'proceed to destroy the Catholic clergy of Ireland'. Carson said he had no sympathy with this view, 'none whatever'. **29** Paul Bew, *Ideology and the Irish question: Ulster Unionism and Irish Nationalism, 1912–16* (Oxford, 1994), p. 97.

Government' would do if their large Catholic minority – or more correctly
majority – refused to obey that government's 'laws'.

There was also the question of how the British Unionist Party would respond
to the danger of violence in Ulster, and how it would formulate policy as the
Liberals and Unionists sparred with each other over ways in which the crisis
might be resolved to the satisfaction of both parties. British Unionists had been
deeply divided on the issue of tariff reform; and when the Marquess of Salisbury
complained in April 1910 that there were those in his party who were 'willing to
sacrifice everything they value rather than the cause should be damaged by a
single act of weakness', he was referring to tariff reformers, not the Irish
Unionists. Moreover, he feared that even the Union was in danger from the tariff
reformers' intransigence.[30] Andrew Bonar Law rallied his party behind the battle
for the Union. But not all Unionists were pure in heart: some favoured a 'Home
Rule all round' settlement of the whole constitution of the United Kingdom; and
even Sir Edward Carson confessed to the leading federalists (as they were called)
that some scheme of 'all round' Home Rule with English, Scottish and Irish
parliaments, might be worth consideration: 'he would certainly, if any scheme of
this kind was proposed by the other side, bring it before his own friends'.[31] Law
was reluctant to open up a new front of dissension in his party, not all of whom
were in favour of federalism; and he was fully alert to the depth of feeling in his
party over tariff reform. He openly supported the Unionist plans for resistance;
but he knew that he could not push this too far, for he too had to keep an eye on
British public opinion. Hence his decision to adopt a tactic that held grave
dangers for the Ulster Unionists: to accept that if the Liberals held an election on
the Home Rule Bill, and that alone, the British Unionist Party would accept the
verdict of the electorate.[32] The Earl of Selborne, though a Unionist to the core,
acknowledged in May 1914 that 'I do not think that we should be strong enough
to repeal the whole of the Government of Ireland Bill unless we secured such an
overwhelming verdict at the polls in our favour as I for one certainly do not
expect.'[33] But the question was whether or not Ulster Unionists would accept the
verdict at the polls if it went against them. If they did not, then they might be
left to fight alone. And even in the Ulster Unionist Council there was division,
which emerged in May 1913, between those who favoured dialogue and those who
wanted to fight it out.[34] The furthest that the Liberals would go in conceding an
election was to promise that there would be one after the Home Rule Bill was

30 Salisbury to Lord Selborne, 29 Apr. 1910, in D.G. Boyce (ed.), *The crisis of British power: the imperial
and naval papers of the second Earl of Selborne, 1895–1910* (London, 1990), pp 428–9.  31 J.E. Kindle,
*Ireland and the federal solution: the debate over the United Kingdom constitution, 1870–1921* (Montreal, 1984),
p. 175.  32 R.J.Q. Adams, *Bonar Law* (London, 1999), p. 134.  33 Selborne to Lord Lansdowne, 1 May
1914, in Boyce, *The crisis of British Unionism*, pp 108–9.  34 Bew, *Ideology and the Irish question*, pp 91–2.

passed, and before a Dublin parliament met. Sir Edward Grey was in a relaxed mood when he wrote to Lord Selborne in April 1914, just before the Larne gun-running, that while the government had pledged that no force would be used to 'make Ulstermen submit to Home Rule, till after an election', yet

> if in the face of that, Ulster takes upon itself meanwhile and before an election to displace the Imperial Government and shoot Imperial Officers who try to carry out their duties in Ulster and refuse to obey its Provisional Government, we shall use force and, pace Bonar Law, be obliged to do so.[35]

It is probably true to say that, had it come to a crisis, the Ulster Unionists could at least have posed grave problems for those who wanted to govern them – they were simply there in large numbers, as was their UVF, and those numbers would be hard to overcome – but neither could they easily govern others, that is, the large Roman Catholic and Nationalist population of five of the nine Ulster counties (and pockets of resistance in the remaining four). To aspire to do so would have required the substantial police and army presence of 1920–3, and the special constabulary which was raised to defend the truncated 'Ulster' six-county state of Northern Ireland. The UVF, as one of its founder members acknowledged in 1915, amounted to no more than a 'very fairly efficient force of Volunteer infantry', whose chief strength lay in its ability to turn the attention of 'Englishmen and Scotchmen towards Ulster' and in 'materially assisting our political leaders'.[36] Then there was the divided and uncertain temper of their British political supporters, the British Unionist Party. On 25 July 1914, L.S. Amery warned Bonar Law:

> The fact is that everything I see and fear makes one feel strongly every day, that the policy of excluding Ulster, and inferentially accepting Home Rule for the rest of Ireland, has been absolutely detested by the rank and file of the Party and, if it had succeeded, would have led to something like an open explosion.[37]

It is not surprising, then, that Ulster Unionists felt more inclined to rely on their own strong right arm, more driven into themselves; and while Sir Edward Carson prepared gloomily for the worst, their own man, James Craig, 'went on quietly preparing for the coup to take control of Ulster, and for the blockade and

---

**35** Grey to Lord Selborne, 12 Apr. 1914, in Boyce (ed.), *Crisis of British Unionism*, p. 107. **36** Buckland, *Irish Unionism*, pp 261–3. **37** David Dutton, *His Majesty's loyal opposition: the Unionist Party in opposition, 1905–15* (Liverpool, 1992), pp 236–7.

military action which might follow: food supplies had been stored, emergency hospitals made ready and plans drawn up to evacuate refugees to England'.[38] The strength of the UVF was that, contrary to Carson's claim, it represented a community in defiance rather than defence: defence would come if and when defiance failed. Unionists set the law at defiance, but no dock in the land was large enough to hold them all – any more than it could hold all the Catholics who were driven by events into protest and defiance in the late 1960s.

Where the Ulster Unionist rebellion would have led cannot be more than speculation. However, the events of 1912–14 look backwards as well as forwards. The most extraordinary aspect of the crisis was that it led to no considerable or sustained outbreaks of violence between Catholic and Protestant in Ulster. There were no 'pogroms', no flight of local people from attacks by their enemies on either side, as there were to be between 1920 and 1922. Nor did the Ulster Volunteers (and for that matter their Nationalist opponents, the Irish Volunteers) resemble modern paramilitary organizations, with their balaclavas, their terrorism, their assassination of their political and religious foes. It is impossible to say how long this would have lasted, but the fact that it did meant that the crisis remained political and constitutional, though both the Ulster Unionists and the British Conservative Party played dangerously near the boundaries. In their preparations for 'defence', the Ulster Unionists and their UVF in some ways were not unlike their Nationalist counterparts of the previous century. Young Irelanders and Fenians conceived of their rebellions as those in which the 'people' would rise in support of the cause, and they assumed that the fight that ensued would be a regular battle with the government forces. The spectacle of a whole people defying the law for the sake of their lives and liberty revealed that by 1914 there had been a major slippage in the British government's control of events in Ireland, and that the rule of law was more tenuous than could have been imagined before 1912. The Ulster Crisis stands out as the attempt by the Unionist leaders to take and hold the moral high ground, and – paradoxically – to threaten to use force in order to keep it. As Craig put it in the House of Commons in June 1912:

> The Prime Minister wishes to drive us from here under the present shattered Constitution. Who are the government that they should talk about constitutional means when it is impossible for us to secure our ends by constitutional means, seeing as there is no Constitution.[39]

**38** A.T.Q. Stewart, 'Craig and the Ulster Volunteer Force' in F.X. Martin (ed.), *Leaders and men of the Easter Rising: Dublin 1916* (London, 1967), pp 67–80 at p. 77.   **39** *House of Commons Debates*, vol. 39, 18 June 1912, cols 1560–1.

This ambiguous Moral Force Unionism, however, reached its high point by July 1914. It took the cataclysmic events of the First World War to transform radically the British, Ulster Unionist and Irish Nationalist perspectives and behaviour, and usher in a more violent and divisive era in the history of modern Ireland, of which the Ulster Crisis was but an overture.

# Northern Nationalists in conflict: from the third Home Rule crisis to partition, 1900–21

ÉAMON PHOENIX

The conflict in the north of Ireland over the third Home Rule Bill occurred at a time when Irish men and women, regardless of religious or party outlook, were more highly politicized than ever before. The Third Reform Act of 1884 had extended the vote to the agricultural labourer and urban worker alike. This act of a Liberal government was to pave the way for both an Orange and a Green political resurgence in Ireland and to set the mould of Irish politics until the end of the First World War.

Until the emergence of Home Rule as a live issue in the 1880s, Protestant voters in the north had been divided into supporters of the two main British political parties, Conservative and Liberal, while a small section of extreme Loyalists identified with Orangeism. Most Ulster Catholics, on the other hand, looked to the Home Rule Party of Charles Stewart Parnell, particularly from 1885, when Parnellites captured seventeen of the province's thirty-three seats in what their adversaries dubbed 'the invasion of Ulster'. But as the tar-barrels blazed in West Belfast and other Nationalist strongholds at this signal triumph, the mass of Ulster Protestants were determined to thwart any attempt by the Liberal Prime Minister, William Gladstone, to grant Ireland self-government.

Parnell's dramatic electoral victory finally convinced the 'Grand Old Man' of the essential justness of the Home Rule cause. His first Home Rule Bill of 1886 failed, however, in the teeth of a combined 'Unionist' opposition in the House of Commons. A second bill in 1893 was thrown out by the Tory-dominated House of Lords, which now became the greatest obstacle to Nationalist aspirations.

The more dramatic result of the Home Rule Crisis in the north of Ireland was the revival of the Orange Order. Formed in north Armagh in 1795 against a background of sectarian faction-fighting, the Order's sectarian overtones had tended to repel the better-off during the nineteenth century. From the 1880s, the gentry and middle-class returned to its banner, realizing its potential as a powerful cross-class alliance against an all-Ireland Home Rule scheme. Led by the redoubtable Cavan landlord, and Unionist MP, Colonel Edward Saunderson, the Ulster Unionists declared their determination to use force rather than submit to 'Rome Rule'.[1] In their campaign against an Irish parliament, the northern Loyalists were

---

1 Patrick Buckland, *Ulster Unionism* (Dublin, 1973), pp 1–19.

assured of the powerful support of the British Conservative Party, now re-named the 'Unionist Party'.

From 1885, therefore, until the treaty settlement of 1921, the 'Union' was the single transcendent issue in Irish politics. Apart from a faithful band of Protestant Home Rulers centred on the fearless Presbyterian divine, Revd J.B. Armour of Ballymoney, the mass of Ulster – and indeed Irish – Protestants took their stand against any form of Home Rule.[2] Catholic Unionists were equally in short supply, with the eminent lawyer and Unionist MP for South Derry, Sir Denis Henry being a rare example.

The Parnellite Split of 1890–1 led to the break-up of the party he had welded into a disciplined phalanx. The next decade was to witness a bitter 'civil war' within the Home Rule movement. Such internecine feuding, together with the Conservatives' long ascendancy at Westminster (1895–1905) ensured that the Home Rule Question was placed firmly on the 'back burner' of British politics.

Conservative governments, meanwhile, sought to undermine the popular groundswell for Home Rule by a policy of 'kindness'. The policy was always doomed to failure, but two of its fruits deserve special mention. The Local Government Act of 1898 swept away the old landlord-oriented 'Grand Juries' and placed local power in the hands of the people. A second measure of revolutionary significance was the Wyndham Land Purchase Act of 1903. By enabling the tenants to buy out their farms, this measure amounted to a bloodless social revolution and finally solved the vexed Land Question.

The ending of the period of Conservative rule coincided with the reunification of the various strands of constitutional Nationalism under the chairmanship of John E. Redmond. Redmond, a Wexford barrister and unrepentant Parnellite, believed passionately in the concept of 'Home Rule within the Empire'. His early career as a clerk in the House of Commons had instilled in him a deep attachment to the British parliamentary tradition. As Dennis Gwynn has observed in the first sentence of his life of Redmond, 'John Redmond's entire life was centred in the House of Commons'.[3] As such, he was strongly opposed to the separatist stirrings which marked the dawn of the new century. The Gaelic League had from the 1890s steadily promoted the idea of a separate Irish cultural nation. Of a similar stamp was Arthur Griffith's tiny Sinn Féin party, whose novel policy of an Anglo-Irish 'dual monarchy' even attracted some northern Protestants like the essayist Robert Lynd. In the background too flickered the 'Fenian Flame' of the militantly separatist Irish Republican Brotherhood, revived in Ulster after 1904 by two young men, Bulmer Hobson, a Quaker journalist, and Denis McCullough, a Falls Road Catholic.

---

**2** See J.R.B. McMinn, *Against the tide: J.B. Armour, Irish Presbyterian minister and Home Ruler* (Belfast, 1985).   **3** Denis Gwynn, *The life of John Redmond* (London, 1932), p. 15.

The Irish Parliamentary Party (IPP), however, still reigned supreme. Redmond's co-leaders in the regenerated movement were the astute John Dillon, former leader of the anti-Parnellites, and the young Ulster barman turned journalist, 'Wee Joe' Devlin. Devlin was the most significant Nationalist politician to emerge in the north during the first half of the twentieth century. Born in 1871 into a working-class family in West Belfast, he rose from humble beginnings as a pot-boy in a local public house to become a Home Rule MP and finally, in 1903, holder of the key post of general secretary of the United Irish League (UIL), the main organization of the Irish Parliamentary Party. For the next thirty years, Devlin's name was synonymous with northern Catholic politics. Small and thick-set with a large head, coal-black hair and a deep resonant voice with the hard intonations of his native city, he had emerged in the strife-ridden 1890s as the leader of the Dillonite 'Irish National Federation' in Belfast. He was a superb organizer and soon gained a reputation as a combative and captivating orator, skilled in the cut and thrust of political debate. Moreover, as a later Sinn Féin critic put it, 'No man knew Nationalist Ulster, its conditions and particularly its prejudices, better than Mr Devlin'.[4] His standing in the reunited Irish Parliamentary Party was further enhanced by a series of fund-raising tours in the United States and Australasia during 1902–6. For some twelve years from 1904 until 1916, this 'pocket Demosthenes' (as his enemy T.M. Healy once dubbed him) dominated the Ulster Nationalist scene by the sheer weight of his personality and his consummate political intellect.

Devlin was driven by a fixed hatred of dissent within the Home Rule ranks. Along with John Dillon he was an opponent of the moderate Nationalist, William O'Brien's policy of conciliation towards the landlord element. Already in the early 1900s, he had shown a characteristic ruthlessness in crushing the 'Belfast Catholic Association' (BCA), the political machine of the local bishop, Dr Henry Henry. His hostility to Henry's clericalist party was influenced by two factors: the first was the potential threat which such a 'factionist' vehicle posed to the official party in Belfast, but another was undoubtedly the close identification of Nationalism with Catholicism which the BCA seemed to portray.[5]

Devlin's growing ascendancy was cemented in 1906 when he captured the 'cock-pit' of West Belfast from the Conservatives by the narrow margin of sixteen votes. His success in that election was partly due to an unwritten pact between Devlin, T.H. Sloan, the radical Independent Orange leader, and the Labourite William Walker. Devlin, always a populist, declared the Belfast contests to be 'a fight of the workers and toilers against intrigues, political machines and combi-

---

**4** Memo by Kevin O'Sheil (Irish Free State's legal adviser), Jan. 1932 (NA, S2027).   **5** D.W. Miller, *Church, state and nation in Ireland, 1898–1921* (Dublin, 1973), pp 97–9.

nations'. Both Devlin and Sloan were elected in what was the greatest reverse ever sustained by official Unionism in the city.[6] It was this peculiar blend of populism and Nationalism that marked Devlin off from the rest of the Home Rule leadership, and especially Dillon, who feared that social innovation would undermine the demand for self-government.[7] Devlin's rise to power, however, was closely associated with the revival of the Ancient Order of Hibernians (AOH), a sectarian secret society which he converted into a personal power-base within the Home Rule movement after 1905.

The AOH traced its historical origins to the Defenders, an agrarian banditti which surfaced in Ulster in the 1790s as a sectarian corollary to Orangeism. As such, it fed on the intrinsic religious bitterness which characterized rural parts of the province. It saw its role as twofold – to give protection to both the Roman Catholic faith and the Roman Catholic population in Ireland. In a real sense, therefore, the 'Hibs' claimed 'to do for the Catholic community what the Orange Order claimed to do for the Protestants'.[8] Given the traditional importance of the religious factor in Ulster politics, the AOH provided Devlin with a potential power-base. The United Irish League, with its essentially agrarian programme, had little appeal in the industrial north-east. Devlin shrewdly realized that a revived AOH, firmly harnessed to the Home Rule movement, could provide the social cement that the IPP badly needed in Ulster.

In 1905, he established the Board of Erin as the controlling council of the organization, with himself as national president, a post he retained until his death in 1934. In his cultivation of the expanding order, Devlin was assisted by his close ally Bishop Patrick O'Donnell of Raphoe, who succeeded in persuading the hierarchy to lift its long-standing ban on Hibernianism. The attraction of the AOH was partly increased by the National Insurance Act of 1911 and, by 1915, it was strong within most 'chapel areas', particularly in Ulster and, with 122,000 members, it formed the grassroots of the Nationalist Party in the north of Ireland. Devlin's control of the AOH – the 'Molly Maguires' to their Nationalist critics – has led to the somewhat distorted image of the Ulster Home Rule leader as a 'ghetto boss', assiduously cultivating an atavistic sectarian vote. This view, however, is unfair to a politician who, despite his shortcomings, did much to improve the lot of the Catholic and Protestant working-classes of Belfast.

The truth is that he was, in some ways, like his great adversaries, Craig and Carson, an enigmatic figure. As the leading Nationalist in Ulster during the period 1902–18, it was inevitable that his speciality should be in organizing and

---

**6** J.W. Boyle, 'The Protestant association and the Orange Order, 1901–1910', *Irish Historical Studies*, 13 (Dublin, 1962), 117–52 at 142. **7** F.S.L. Lyons, *The Irish Parliamentary Party, 1890–1910* (London, 1951), pp 104–5. **8** For a study of the AOH, see M. Foy, 'The AOH: an Irish political pressure group, 1884–1975' (MA, QUB, 1976).

'getting out' the Catholic vote, especially in West Belfast, which, after 1906, became 'virtually his own little kingdom'. This role, however, which is really a reflection of his strong sense of political pragmatism, given the realities of the time, does not detract from his deep-seated hostility to every form of religious intolerance. His own humble origins, his personal experience of the bitter sectarian rioting in Belfast in 1886, and the leavening effect of his travels in America and Australasia, had convinced him of the common interests of the Protestant and Catholic working-classes. Moreover, his proletarian apprenticeship left its imprint in a sharpened social conscience, which did not go unregarded among sections of the Belfast Protestant working classes. Devlin was not a socialist, but he inveighed against the social evils of unemployment, sweated labour and insanitary housing conditions, and saw state intervention as the only solution. His successful exposure of the sweated conditions in the Belfast linen mills resulted in the application of the Trade Boards Act to the industry after 1909, with a consequent improvement in the lot of the workers.[9] Indeed, it was a criterion of his uniqueness in Irish politics in the twentieth century that he evoked a genuine affection and admiration that transcended class or creed. He was a tireless worker for the Belfast working-classes, and was remembered for his total accessibility to supporters of every party. In the words of his political adversary, James Craig, with whom he had a good personal rapport, 'he was ... an outstanding figure beyond politics in the way in which he strove unremittingly for the underdog ... throughout the Ulster area'.[10]

How then does this image of Devlin as the champion of working-class harmony and the enemy of religious intolerance square with his reorganization of a sectarian, semi-secret society? For Devlin, the answer was a simple one: there was no contradiction between his egalitarian principles and his *alter ego* as 'Grand Master' of the Board of Erin; he had demonstrated his antipathy to the sectarianization of Nationalist politics by his wilful destruction of the 'Catholic Association' in 1905. As a fervent Catholic, Devlin could find nothing objectionable in the professed objects of Hibernianism. Indeed, he could argue that by gaining control of such an unpredictable body, he had salvaged it form the morass of sectarianism: by connecting it with the UIL, he had secured its firm support for an organization which contained Protestants, and which lent its support to a parliamentary party, with Protestant MPs in its ranks. But in this defence, Devlin was arguably too simplistic. He failed to comprehend the exaggerated image of an insidious Catholic power which his reinvigorated AOH conjured up in the minds of Ulster Unionists. Apart from its sectarian nature, Hibernianism became

---

**9** F.J. Whitford, 'Joseph Devlin', *Threshold*, 1:2 (1957), p. 27.   **10** *Northern Ireland Parliamentary Debates*, vol. 16, cols 279–80.

associated with machine politics in the 'Tammany Hall' mould, fuelling the hatred of both James Connolly and the separatists. Moreover, its clandestine nature continued to incur the censure of the Catholic Primate, Cardinal Logue.

By the advent of the Third Home Rule Bill, Devlin was at the high-point of his political power in Ireland. Lovat Frazer, an astute observer from the *London Times*, who heard the northern Home Rule leader address a great Nationalist demonstration in Limerick in 1913, informed his editor:

> One thing struck me very much indeed. Devlin had a distinctly bigger reception than Redmond. He woke up the people more, although his speech was very brief … It was most instructive to mark his effect upon the people. He is evidently the coming man, and even here, the Ancient Order of Hibernians was more in evidence than the United Irish League.[11]

The Liberal landslide in the British general election of 1905 and the subsequent constitutional crisis in Britain over the powers of the House of Lords conspired by 1911 to bring Redmond, Dillon and Devlin within sight of the promised land. The Liberals' failure to win an outright majority in the two general elections of 1910 forced the Prime Minister, Herbert Asquith, back to the 1886 position of reliance on the votes of the Irish Nationalists. One immediate result was the 1911 Parliament Act, which effectively removed the veto power of the House of Lords. With this last constitutional obstacle to Irish self-government now removed, the much-heralded Third Home Rule Bill was introduced in the House of Commons in April 1912. Nationalist Ireland confidently predicted that 1914 would be the 'Home Rule Year' and that John Redmond would preside over an all-Ireland parliament in Dublin's College Green. But the two years between the introduction of the third Home Rule Bill and the outbreak of the First World War in August 1914 were to see the emergence of determined Ulster resistance to the Liberals' policy.

The Ulstermen were led by Sir Edward Carson, a Dublin lawyer and compelling orator and Captain James Craig, a Belfast stockbroker who, in his massive, blunt features seemed to personify 'the soul of Ulster intransigence'. Carson's aim was not to get special treatment for the Protestant north, but rather to maintain intact the Union of Great Britain and Ireland. He hoped to use the solid resistance of almost 900,000 Ulster Protestants as a weapon in this battle, convinced – wrongly, as it turned out – that 'Home Rule without Ulster would be impossible'. Craig, the authentic representative of the Belfast business class, had one idea; to preserve the character and integrity of the province he knew and

11 Fraser to Robinson, 12 Oct. 1913 quoted in *Lovat Fraser's tour of Ireland in 1913* (Belfast, 1992), p. 18.

loved. To this end, he had been instrumental in setting up the Ulster Unionist Council (1905), which gave northern Unionism a more militant focus. From the outset, the Unionist campaign was supported by powerful interests in British society, in the Conservative Party (now led by Bonar Law, a ruthless political antagonist and the son of an Ulster Presbyterian minister), in the army, in the aristocracy and in big business. 'There are things stronger than parliamentary majorities', declared Law darkly at Blenheim Palace in 1912, underling the extra-parliamentary nature of the Unionist campaign.

Tensions rose in Ulster with the introduction of the Third Home Rule Bill in April 1912. It seemed virtually certain that Home Rule would be enforced by 1914. The climax and supreme demonstration of Ulster Protestant feeling was the public signing by over 200,000 Loyalists of the Solemn League and Covenant in September 1912 at various centres throughout the north. This document pledged its signatories, 'humbly relying on God' to use 'all means which may be found necessary to defeat the present conspiracy to set up a Home Rule parliament in Ireland'. The Covenant was signed by the Presbyterian Moderator, the northern Church of Ireland bishops and leading Methodist clergy. The Moderator, Dr Montgomery, had appointed the previous Sunday as a day of 'humiliation before God and supplication for deliverance'. But prayer, he insisted, did not mean 'discarding of the sword'. Indeed, the leading Presbyterian journal, *The Witness*, declared that resistance to Home Rule, even in arms, was 'a sacred duty'.[12]

Against this backdrop of mounting rhetorical violence, groups of Orangemen throughout the north had commenced drilling with dummy rifles in halls or on the estates of sympathetic landowners. In January 1913, the Ulster Unionist Council decided to weld all these strands into a single disciplined force. This 'citizens' army' was to be known as the Ulster Volunteer Force. It was to be limited to 100,000 men who had signed the Covenant. Committees were set up in each of the nine counties of Ulster, and drilling and semi-military exercises became the norm.

At first, the UVF was dismissed by the Home Rulers as 'Carson's Comic Circus', while the Belfast *Irish News* ridiculed the claim of the Unionists' Provisional Government to 'conquer Ulster', a feat which even 'that brawny and valiant warrior', John de Courcy had failed to achieve in Anglo-Norman times.[13] Yet the decision of the Ulster Unionist Standing Committee in December 1912 to abate their opposition to Home Rule for all Ireland and Carson's subsequent demand on 1 January 1913 to exclude the whole province of Ulster from the operation of the act marked a significant watershed. Government concern at the turn

12 R.F.G. Holmes, '"Ulster will fight and Ulster will be right": the Protestant churches and Ulster's resistance to Home Rule, 1912–1914' in W.J. Sheils (ed.), *The church and war: studies in church history*, 20 (Oxford, 1983), pp 321–35.  13 *Irish News*, 25 Sept. 1913.

of events in Ulster in the autumn of 1913 was increased by disturbing reports of disaffection within the armed forces. Devlin, for his part, assured ministers that the danger of bloodshed was 'grotesquely exaggerated' and regarded by the northern Home Rulers 'with absolute contempt'.[14] But – never a Gladstonian Home Ruler – Asquith was unconvinced and warned Redmond in October 1913 of the need for a compromise to defuse the deepening crisis. The Nationalist leaders reluctantly acquiesced 'as the price of peace'.

The upshot was the 'County Option Scheme', drawn up by the pragmatic Lloyd George and unveiled in February 1914. The proposals allowed any Ulster county to opt out of Home Rule for a six-year period by means of a plebiscite. The Nationalists had little difficulty in securing the necessary local and episcopal support for such a measure, since it would have ensured the inclusion of Fermanagh, Tyrone and Derry City under a Dublin parliament, while virtually guaranteeing that the expected 'four-county bloc' would be forced to merge with Home Rule Ireland at the end of the statutory period. Carson's outright rejection of such a 'stay of execution' ended any hopes of a settlement. Lloyd George had, however, succeeded in introducing the idea of partition – or 'exclusion' as it was then known – into the public debate. A precedent had been created which would be built upon in the years ahead.

From the moment that Carson spurned 'temporary exclusion', the whole of Ireland began a lurch into anarchy that was only arrested by the onset of the First World War in August 1914. For a brief moment, the government considered a show of force against the 'Carsonites', but the Larne gun-running of April 1914, together with the 'Curragh Incident' destabilized an already beleaguered Asquith government. Military supremacy now lay with 'Carson's Army'. This factor, more than any other, was to ensure that the British government would introduce some form of partition to deal with the Ulster problem.

The impact of the UVF was no less dramatic on Irish Nationalism, however. As Michael Laffan observes, by blatantly challenging the authority of the sovereign parliament and by re-introducing the gun as the final arbiter in Irish politics, 'Carson rekindled the Fenian flame'.[15] The revolutionary Irish Republican Brotherhood, watching in the wings, was quick to take advantage of 'Carson's Army' and by late 1913, had called into existence a Nationalist counterweight in the shape of the Irish Volunteers. Patrick Pearse, who saw war as a means of national redemption, found an Orangeman with a rifle 'a much less ridiculous figure than a Nationalist without one'.

By the eve of the First World War, the IVF – now under Redmond's nominal

**14** Gwynn, *Life of John Redmond*, pp 258–9. **15** Michael Laffan, *The partition of Ireland, 1911–1925* (Dundalk, 1983), p. 32.

control – had mushroomed to some 170,000 men, a quarter of them concentrated in the north. The Nationalist army's main concern was to ensure the
implementation of all-Ireland Home Rule. The mood of the Nationalist majorities west of the Bann in the middle of the crisis was captured by the RIC County
Inspector for Tyrone in his report for March 1914: 'The Nationalists are disqui-
eted by recent events and think they must have an army of their own ... It is
alleged that the Catholic clergy have sanctioned the movement and ... it is likely
to spread'.[16]

Meanwhile, the Home Rule Bill had undergone drastic amendment in the
Lords, so as to exclude the whole province without either plebiscite or time-limit.
In a final effort to break the impasse, George V convened the abortive
Buckingham Palace Conference on 21–4 July 1914. This involved Redmond and
Dillon in protracted negotiations with Asquith and Lloyd George, for the govern-
ment, Bonar Law and Lansdowne, and Carson and Craig, representing the Ulster
Unionists. In this event, the discussion focused on the question of 'acreage; while
the more critical issue of 'temporary v. permanent exclusion' was never addressed.

It was, perhaps, too much to have expected agreement on the Ulster Question
at such a juncture. Arguably, feelings were running too high for either of the Irish
protagonists to make the necessary concessions. Redmond, straining under pressure from the restive anti-exclusionists of west Ulster, took his stand on 'county
option'. To have settled for less would have drastically undermined his credibility
in Nationalist Ireland. Carson's hands were similarly tied with his pledges to the
scattered 'Covenanters' of Cavan, Monaghan and Donegal compelling him to
demand the 'clean cut'. Between these two entrenched positions, the quest for a
compromise seemed futile. For Nationalists, Carson's argument that the exclusion of the whole province, with its large Catholic minority, was the best
guarantee of eventual Irish unity, had much to recommend it. Practical politics,
however, dictated otherwise.

As a result, much of the conference became bogged down in what Churchill
termed 'the muddy by-ways of Fermanagh and Tyrone'. In an effort to define the
'excluded area', Carson revealed his 'irreducible minimum': the proposition that
a six-county bloc – the area which was later to comprise Northern Ireland –
should be precluded from the operation of the Home Rule Act.[17] Though firmly
repudiated by the Nationalist leaders, this was a portentous development in the
evolution of the partition debate. Among Ulster Unionists, it marked the beginning of a rethink which, in subordinating principle to pragmatism, sought to
salvage the maximum possible area from the operation of Home Rule, while
projecting an image of 'reasonableness' in the eyes of the British public.

**16** RIC County Inspector's Report for Mar. 1914 (PRO, CO 904/92).   **17** Denis Gwynn, *The history of
partition, 1912–25* (Dublin, 1950), pp 130–2.

The outbreak of war was marked by what the Royal Irish Constabulary (RIC) termed 'a mutual cessation of political strife' in Ireland as both Redmond and Carson pledged unequivocal support for Britain's war effort.[18] As the storm clouds gathered, the Irish leader's success in forcing a reluctant Asquith to place the Home Rule Act on the Statute Book proved something of a hollow victory. Not only was its operation suspended for the duration of the war, but Asquith made it clear that any final settlement must include partition. In a desperate effort to win British goodwill for the future, Redmond – ever the imperialist – was to make his great mistake at Woodenbridge, Co. Wicklow, in September 1914 in urging Irishmen to enlist in the British army. In advocating such a course, the Home Rule leader – ever the imperialist – revealed his lack of touch with grassroots opinions which remained deeply distrustful of the British government. The effect was to split the Irish Volunteers. A small radical section – by far the most active militarily – broke away under Prof. Eoin MacNeill, Antrim Glensman and Gaelic Leaguer. This element now passed into the hands of the IRB, which was to use it as the strike-force of the Rising it was determined to stage before the end of the war. Thousands of Irish Volunteers joined the rush to the colours in the first two years of the war and fought bravely alongside their former UVF adversaries on the battlefields of Europe. Among the Irish contingent were several thousand members of Devlin's National Volunteers from West Belfast. 'We have succeeded in making national self-government the law of the land', Devlin assured them as they marched off to the front in November 1914. James Connolly, the leader of the Irish Citizen Army and a supporter of a separatist uprising, expressed a rather different view, however, in his paper, the *Workers' Republic*:

> Full steam ahead, John Redmond said,
> And everything is well chum.
> Home Rule will come when we are dead
> And buried out in Belgium.[19]

Redmond's political standing was further weakened in May 1915 when the Liberal administration was replaced by a War Coalition which included such Nationalist *bêtes noires* as Carson and Bonar Law. Home Rule, it seemed to many Nationalists, was now at the mercy of its implacable foes. In such circumstances, it required only the 'blood sacrifice' of the Easter Rising and the crop of martyrs it produced to seal the Home Rule Party's fate. The Rising was the climax of careful planning by the Supreme Council of the IRB. It had been originally intended as a successful national revolt by the anti-war Volunteers and the small

---

**18** RIC 'Precis of information', Apr. 1915 (PRO, CO 904/120/2). **19** *The Workers' Republic*, 8 Apr. 1916.

but elite Irish Citizen Army, formed by the Ulster Protestant 'misfit', Captain
Jack White during the 1913 lock-out. But, in the event, with the struggle
narrowed to Dublin, Pearse, Tom Clarke and the secret cadre of revolutionaries
realized that they had no prospect of military success. Nonetheless, they calcu-
lated that an armed stand – however futile – would almost certainly provoke the
British into harsh reprisals; by their 'martyrdom', they might give their cause –
an Irish Republic instead of anaemic Home Rule – its elixir of life.

The insurgents judged accurately. The Rising had at first engendered feelings
of strong hostility among Irish Nationalists, many of whose relatives were
fighting on the Western Front. Redmond's hasty condemnation of the Rising as
a 'wicked German plot' reflected the characteristic reaction of middle-class
conservative Nationalism. It was faithfully echoed by the *Irish News*, a paper
closely controlled by Devlin. On 1 May 1916, the paper rejoiced that an attempt
by 'German agents' to create a diversion had been thwarted. 'Happily', the editor
observed, 'the Irish people were not duped. We say nothing of the unhappy
instruments of Teutonic duplicity who have fought Germany's battle in the
capital of this country.'

The British response to the insurrection, involving internment, martial law
and, above all, the execution of sixteen of the leaders, served to transform Irish
public opinion. As one observer, Colonel Maurice Moore, the Inspector-General
of the Redmondite National Volunteers, wrote, 'A few unknown men, shot in a
barrack yard, had embittered a whole nation.' Unionist opinion, on the other
hand, was bitter at what was seen as 'a stab in the back' and 'a sample of what
might be expected if Home Rule came into being', as the Belfast RIC
Commissioner put it.[20]

In a final effort to salvage the Home Rule Act, the Nationalist leaders allowed
themselves to be stampeded in May 1916 into the disastrous Lloyd George scheme
for six-county partition. The resourceful 'Welsh Wizard' led Redmond to understand that the 'exclusion' would be temporary. Home Rule would apply
immediately in 'five-sixths of Ireland'; there would be no 'Orange parliament' in
Belfast, while the interests of the northern Catholics would be safeguarded by the
continual presence of eighty Irish Nationalist MPs at Westminster.[21] To Carson,
however, Lloyd George gave a contrasting written guarantee that partition would
be permanent, a factor which helped ensure the support of the pragmatic 'six-
county' Unionists. For the first time, however, Redmond and Devlin found
themselves confronted by virulent hostility of the Ulster Catholic bishops, whose
fears for the future of Catholic education in the north-east was only matched by

**20** RIC Report for Belfast, 1916 (PRO, CO 904/120/3).  **21** Devlin to Editor, *Irish Independent*, 29 June
1916.

a desire to avoid – in Logue's phrase – 'going down to posterity as the destroyers of the country'.[22]

The proposals fell through in July 1916, sabotaged by the southern Unionists in the cabinet, but not before the Home Rulers, and Devlin in particular, had become tarred by the brush of partition in the Irish Nationalist mind. The 'Black Friday' conference in St Mary's Hall, Belfast, which endorsed the Lloyd George scheme in June 1916, was to split northern Nationalism irrevocably and paved the way for the rise of the anti-partitionist 'Irish Nation League' with a power base in Tyrone, Fermanagh and Derry City. Beginning as a reformist Nationalist party, the new league gradually became separatist, finally merging with Sinn Féin in the middle of 1917. As such, it provided the bulk of the revolutionary movement's northern leadership. Revd Philip O'Doherty, PP, a leading Ulster Sinn Féin cleric, attacked the beleaguered IPP leadership for 'abandoning the Catholics of the six counties to … their unsleeping and relentless hereditary enemies'.[23] As a result of the Nationalists' endorsement of the Lloyd George scheme and charges that Devlin had 'packed' the Belfast Conference, the traditional AOH and IPP machinery in Ulster began to disintegrate while, as in the south, many of the younger clergy identified themselves with the advanced Nationalists. Only in east Ulster, where Devlin's influence remained strong, and among the older generation, did the Home Rule movement retain a substantial following.

Support for the insurgents and their cause soon crystallized around the new Republican Sinn Féin party, embracing Griffithites, Republicans and Nation Leaguers and dedicated to a policy of abstention from the British parliament. Its president from 1917 was Eamon de Valera, a young mathematics teacher and the sole surviving commandant of the Easter Rising. The new movement's growing popularity was reflected in a series of by-election triumphs in the south. In the north, however, the burning issue for Nationalists remained partition rather than 'Home Rule v. Republic'. Many Ulster Catholics opposed the abstentionist tactic, arguing, with much force, that such a policy would make the 'naked deformity of partition' more likely. This fear on the part of Ulster Nationalists largely explains the decisive victories of Home Rulers over Sinn Féin in the South Armagh and East Tyrone by-elections held in January and April 1918, respectively. They may also have hoped that the Irish Convention, which the IPP had attended along with the northern and southern Unionists, might yet produce a workable all-Ireland solution.

British policy during the last months of the war and particularly Lloyd George's threat to impose conscription in April 1918 gave an immense impetus to

**22** Logue to Bishop O'Donnell, 7 June 1916 (Armagh Archdiocesan Archives: Logue Papers). **23** Revd P. O'Doherty ('Red Hand'), *Through corruption to dismemberment: a story of apostacy and betrayal* (Derry, 1916), pp 2–3.

the revolutionary party. All over the country, tens of thousands declared their defiance to his 'blood tax' by signing the strongly-worded Anti-Conscription pledge, issued by Cardinal Logue. The fictitious German plot of May 1918 merely consolidated Sinn Féin's ascendancy over Nationalist Ireland. Though it brought de Valera and John Dillon (Redmond had died in March) together in temporary alliance, the conscription crisis enabled Sinn Féin to project itself as the champion of Nationalist Ireland. As Dillon wryly put it, 'the Sinn Féin tiger emerged from the conference with the constitutional party inside'.[24]

This was the background to the post-War general election of 1918. Sinn Féin, campaigning on a policy of abstentionism and an all-Ireland Republic, swept 73 of the 105 Irish seats. The old Home Rule party was reduced to half a dozen seats in Ulster thanks to a 'Green Pact' with Sinn Féin to avert the dangers of a split vote.[25] Edward Carson – symbolically switching from Trinity to 'a slum constituency in Belfast' (Duncairn) – demanded partition for the north-east, and assisted by a redistribution, now led the largest Irish grouping at Westminster with twenty-six seats, twenty-three of them in Ulster. However, northern Nationalists remained fatally divided between constitutional adherents of Home Rule and those who supported Sinn Féin until at least the late 1920s.

The three years between the 1918 election and the Anglo-Irish Treaty of 1921 form a watershed in modern Irish history. This period witnessed the setting up of Dáil Éireann as the effective government of much of the south, the Anglo-Irish War, partition and the conferring of Dominion Status on twenty-six Irish counties. In accordance with their election manifesto, the Sinn Féin MPs ignored Westminster and met in Dublin as Dáil Éireann ('the Assembly of Ireland'). Among other things, the new assembly reaffirmed the declaration of an Irish Republic 'in arms' in 1916, appointed delegates to the post-War Paris Peace Conference and set up an alternative government to that of Dublin Castle, headed by President de Valera. But while the new cabinet achieved striking success in such areas as the Dáil courts and local government, its hopes of raising the question of Irish self-determination at the post-War peace conference at Versailles were slim. As the peace strategy faded, an astute Devlin could predict gloomily in May 1919 that 'Things must come to a fierce conflict between the government and Sinn Féin'.[26]

Indeed, that conflict had already erupted at Soloheadbeg, Co. Tipperary, in what slowly crystallized into an Anglo-Irish War between the Volunteers, restyled the IRA and the RIC, soon to be reinforced by the notorious 'Counter-Terror' forces, the Auxiliaries and the Black and Tans. Though the relationship between the Dáil and the IRA was a confused one, the Volunteers might claim a certain

---

**24** F.S.L. Lyons, *John Dillon: a biography* (London, 1968), p. 424.  **25** Devlin to Dillon, 28 Nov. 1918 (TCD, Dillon Papers, 6730/201).  **26** Devlin to Dillon, 15 May 1919 (TCD, Dillon Papers, 6730/224).

legitimacy as the military arm of a democratically elected order. The struggle
between the IRA and the RIC and Crown Forces was to continue with accelerated ferocity until the Truce in July 1921.

At Westminster, the return of a Tory-dominated coalition government,
headed by Lloyd George, ensured that partition would become a 'fixed idea' of
British policy. In a joint manifesto issued on 21 November 1918, Lloyd George
and Bonar Law firmly rejected both Irish separation and the 'forcible coercion of
the six counties of north-east Ulster to a Home Rule parliament against their
will.'[27] Sinn Féin's 'blessed abstention' from Westminster – to borrow Churchill's
phrase – meant that the balance of power now shifted from Irish Nationalists to
the Ulster Unionists. Joe Devlin and his tiny band counted for little in the overwhelmingly Tory House of Commons. Craig, a junior minister in the
administration, was therefore well placed to influence the shape of the forthcoming Home Rule Act – the only one to be even partially enforced.

The cabinet committee which drew up the 'Partition Act' in late 1919 was
tempted to include the historic nine-county province in the new 'Northern
Ireland'. Liberals argued that the large Catholic population (43 per cent) might
make eventual Irish unity more probable. In the end, however, the Lloyd George
cabinet gave way to Craig's pragmatic view that a six-county bloc would provide
a more viable 'ethnographic area' for permanent Unionist control.[28] The scattered
Unionists of the three 'lost counties' of Cavan, Monaghan and Donegal felt
betrayed and deserted but had to face the toils alone.

The Government of Ireland Act (1920), as finally passed, divided Ireland into
two areas, each having its own regional parliament and government with control
over domestic affairs. At the same time, the measure seemed to envisage Irish
unity by providing a 'bond of union' in the shape of a low-powered Council of
Ireland. The 1920 act represented a major triumph for the Ulster Unionists. In
the words of James Craig's brother, Captain Charles Craig, MP, it placed them
'in a position of absolute security, for the future'.[29]

On the Nationalist side, only Devlin, a solitary figure at Westminster, saw the
dangers of the 'Partition Act'. He railed against it as portending both 'permanent
partition' and 'permanent minority status' for northern Catholics.[30] Not without
justification, the West Belfast MP attacked the glaring lack of safeguards in the act

---

**27** Ian Colvin, *Life of Carson*, vol. 3 (London, 1936), pp 365–6. **28** On 4 November 1919, the cabinet
committee charged with drafting the Partition Act (the Long Committee) recommended a nine-county
Northern Ireland. A week later, however, James Craig, then a junior minister in the Coalition, informed
the Committee of his preference for the six-county unit on the grounds that 'Protestant representation in
the Ulster parliament would be strengthened and … six counties would be … easier to govern than the
whole province'. By February 1920, the parliament had capitulated to this view (PRO, CAB 27/68). **29**
Laffan, *Partition of Ireland*, p. 65. **30** Devlin to Bishop O'Donnell, 13 Feb. 1920 (Armagh Diocesan
Archives: O'Donnell Papers).

for the minority. In particular, he railed against the government's failure to provide Nationalists with weighted representation in the northern Senate, and contrasted this with the treatment of the southern Unionists, who were to enjoy the protection of a strong effective voice in the Dublin Senate. The need for such a system of checks and balances, he told the Commons, was underlined by the tragic sectarian bloodshed in north-east Ulster in the summer of 1920 against the backcloth of the Anglo-Irish War. The worst episode occurred in Belfast in July 1920, when the assassination of a northern-born RIC officer in Cork resulted in the mass expulsion of some 8,000 Catholic workers from the shipyards and other industries.[31] These events were a foretaste of the serious sectarian disturbances which were to scar the face of Belfast and other northern towns during the next two years. In Lisburn, the assassination of District Inspector Swanzy by the IRA in August 1920 was the signal for what the police described as 'a crusade against all members of the Catholic faith'.[32] The effect of these 'pogroms', as Catholic Church leaders described them, was ultimately to create a strong anti-Unionist feeling in Britain, where the Liberal and Labour Press represented them as a sectarian assault upon defenceless people by those who claimed that Home Rule would lead to persecution.[33] The Dáil responded to northern Nationalist pressure with the 'Belfast Boycott' (1920–2), but this tended merely to reinforce the incipient border. It was not until late 1922 that murder, arson and expulsion from homes ceased to be a daily occurrence. Over 450 people, the majority of them members of the minority community, died violently during the black days of 1920–2. In a reference to these events, and the failure to prevent their monotonous recurrence, Lloyd George was to admit to Churchill: 'Our Ulster case is not a good one'.[34]

The upsurge in violence had important effects. First, it seemed to confirm Nationalist fears of being subjected to the rule of the Unionist majority in a separate state. Secondly, the mounting unrest led Lloyd George to endorse Craig's scheme for a new auxiliary police force. Formed in October 1920, the Ulster Special Constabulary – formed largely from ex-UVF members – was to play a crucial role in the creation of the new Irish border. In Nationalist eyes, however, this sectarian force was viewed – in the words of a British official – 'with a bitterness exceeding that which the Black and Tans inspired in the South'.[35]

**31** RIC Inspector-General's Report, July 1920 (PRO, CO 904/112); G.B. Kenna, *Facts and figures of the Belfast pogrom, 1920–2* (Dublin, 1922), pp 18–20 ('Kenna' was the pseudonym of a Belfast priest, Revd John Hasson). **32** RIC County Inspector's Report for County Antrim, Aug. 1920 (PRO, CO 904/112). **33** See, for example, *Daily Herald*, 31 Aug. 1920. **34** Martin Gilbert, *Winston S. Churchill*, vol. 4, 1916–22 (London, 1975), p. 729. The fatality figures for the Belfast troubles of 1920–2 were: 267 Catholics, 185 Protestants and 3 unascertained. For a detailed discussion of the subject, see Éamon Phoenix, 'Political violence, diplomacy and the Catholic minority in Northern Ireland' in John Darby, Nicholas Dodge and A.C. Hepburn (eds), *Political violence: Ireland in a comparative perspective* (Belfast, 1990), pp 29–47. **35** S.G. Tallents to Sir J. Masterton-Smith, 4 July 1922 (PRO CO 906/30).

In May 1921, following elections in the six counties, the new northern parliament was established, with Sir James Craig as its first Prime Minister. 'From that moment', wrote Churchill perceptively, 'Ulster's position was unassailable'. The Nationalists and Sinn Féin, cooperating on a platform of anti-partition and abstention from the 'Partition parliament', secured a total of twelve of the fifty-two seats and one-third of the popular vote.[36]

In general, during those vital years, the Sinn Féin leadership failed, in the words of the northern Republican, Louis J. Walsh, 'to grapple with the Ulster Question'.[37] The 'naked deformity of partition' came a poor second to National Status in the revolutionary scheme of things. This was certainly the case during the treaty negotiations between Sinn Féin and a formidable British delegation in London in the autumn of 1921. Arthur Griffith and Michael Collins, the leaders of the Irish delegation, tried to secure the 'essential unity' of Ireland, but were forced in the end to settle for Dominion Status for the twenty six counties. A Boundary Commission was to revise the 1920 border. The prospect of the Commission and the belief that it would so reduce the North's territory as to produce Irish unity to 'contraction' largely explains why Griffith and Collins signed the treaty of 6 December 1921.[38]

Northern Nationalists were shocked and bitterly disappointed at the treaty terms. Most supported them, however, in the hope that some form of 'essential unity' might yet be achieved. For the border Nationalist majorities of Fermanagh, Tyrone, Derry City and South Armagh in particular, the Boundary Clause (Article 12) was the crucial one. The wording of the clause, however, was fatally flawed. The point here was that while it referred to 'the wishes of the inhabitants' – implying large-scale gains by the new Free State – this was made subject to 'economic and geographic conditions'. Four years later, in 1925, the much-vaunted Boundary Commission collapsed, leaving the Northern Ireland state intact and partition more deeply entrenched. For the northern Nationalists, the disunity and disenchantment of the Parnell Split had been replaced thirty years later by an even deeper sense of isolation and betrayal. For the Ulster Unionists, their new state had survived despite Nationalist non-recognition, IRA attacks and British pressure. The minority problem, however, remained unaddressed and would continue to fester in the years ahead.[39]

---

**36** *Irish Independent*, 8 Apr. 1921. **37** *Irish Weekly*, 12 Apr. 1919. The speaker, the Antrim Sinn Féin leader Louis J. Walsh, urged the Sinn Féin Ard Fheis to treat the 'Ulster Question' more seriously. **38** See Collins' statement to the Newry Nationalist deputation on 1 Feb. 1922, *Frontier Sentinel*, 4 Feb. 1922. **39** For a full analysis of the impact of partition on the northern Nationalists, see Éamon Phoenix, *Nationalist politics, partition and the Catholic minority in Northern Ireland, 1890–1940* (Belfast, 1994).

# Some thoughts on the Island of Ireland Peace Park

## RICHARD DOHERTY

On 11 November 1998, President Mary McAleese, HM Queen Elizabeth II and King Albert II of Belgium took part in a moving ceremony at Messines in Belgium to dedicate a memorial to Irish soldiers, sailors and airmen who lost their lives during the First World War.[1] The site at Messines was chosen since it was on the Messines-Wytschaete ridge on 7 June 1917 that men of 16th (Irish) and 36th (Ulster) Divisions fought alongside each other in the first major British victory of the war. It was thus identified by those who had initiated the project as a suitable site on which to create the memorial as an example of Irishmen setting aside their differences in a common cause.[2]

That memorial, which forms part of the Island of Ireland Peace Park and takes the form of an Irish round tower, 110 feet high and built, partially, from material from a former British military barracks in Co. Tipperary, is the outcome of the work of the Journey of Reconciliation Trust.[3] The Trust was a cross-border and cross-community body, with diverse membership, established by Paddy Harte, from Co. Donegal, and Glenn Barr, from Londonderry. Harte is a former Fine Gael TD, while Barr was one of the organizers of the 1974 Ulster Workers' Council strike that brought down the first power-sharing regional government in Northern Ireland.

Inspired by the ancient site at Newgrange, the interior of which is lit by the sun's rays at the winter solstice, the tower's interior is illuminated by the sun only at the eleventh hour of the eleventh day of the eleventh month – 11am on 11 November, the anniversary of the beginning of the armistice in 1918 that brought the fighting in the First World War in western Europe to an end.[4] At the entrance to the Peace Park there is a bronze tablet on which is inscribed a 'peace pledge' which reads:

> From the crest of this ridge, which was the scene of terrific carnage in the First World War, on which we have built a peace park and round tower to commemorate the thousands of young men from all parts of Ireland who fought a common enemy, defended democracy and the rights of all nations, whose graves are in shockingly uncountable numbers and those

1 *Daily Telegraph*, 12 Nov. 1998.  2 http://en.wikipedia.org/wiki/Island_of_Ireland_Peace_Park, accessed 10 June 2010.  3 Ibid.  4 Ibid.

who have no graves, we condemn war and the futility of war. We repudiate and denounce violence, aggression, intimidation, threats and unfriendly behaviour. As Protestants and Catholics, we apologise for the terrible deeds we have done to each other and ask forgiveness. From this sacred shrine of remembrance, where soldiers of all nationalities, creeds and political allegiances were united in death, we appeal to all people in Ireland to help build a peaceful and tolerant society. Let us remember the solidarity and trust that developed between Protestant and Catholic Soldiers when they served together in these trenches. As we jointly thank [sic] the armistice of 11 November 1918 – when the guns fell silent along this western front – we affirm that a fitting tribute to the principles for which men and women from the Island of Ireland died in both world wars would be permanent peace.[5]

To what extent is the rationale of this Peace Park true? Did the men of the two Irish divisions fight 'shoulder to shoulder' in common cause voluntarily? Or is this a case of the organizers trying to make past events fit a template that suits their modern, laudable, purpose?

The assault on the Messines ridge was an outstanding example of a carefully planned operation for which exhaustive arrangements were made and which met with success, the objectives of the attacking forces – to seize the ridge from which the Germans had been able to dominate the Allied lines since early in the war – being achieved quickly and at relatively low cost to the attackers.[6] German losses were much greater, however.[7] It is certainly true that 16th (Irish) and 36th (Ulster) Divisions advanced together, but that was a matter of military happenstance rather than of any choice on the part of the personnel of the divisions. By this stage of the war, both divisions had been placed in the same corps for the first time; this was IX Corps, in which 19th Division also served. With II (ANZAC) Corps and X Corps, this was part of General Sir Horace Plumer's Second Army. Plumer's dispositions for the attack on the ridge placed the Anzacs on the right of the line, IX Corps in the centre and X Corps on the left.

We are reminded often that among the casualties of the day was Major Willie Redmond MP, who had earlier commanded a company of 6th Bn Royal Irish Regiment but who had been transferred to divisional headquarters.[8] Although

---

**5** Ibid.   **6** An account of the battle may be found in Tom Johnstone, *Orange, green and khaki* (Dublin, 1992), pp 269–81. The casualties were 748 killed and wounded in 16th Division and 700 killed and wounded in 36th Division.   **7** German losses can only be estimated as they did not record casualties in the same manner as the British armies. However, H.E. Harris, in *The Irish regiments in the First World War* (Cork, 1968), p. 108, suggests that from three regiments with a nominal strength of 11,500 no more than four men from one regiment, 'only a few' from a second and none from the third survived.   **8** Terence

simply too old to be in the front line, Redmond insisted on going forward, was wounded and succumbed to those wounds, from which a younger and fitter man would probably have made a full and speedy recovery.[9] Redmond's fate has been one of the factors that has led to the Messines battle being exemplified as a day of Nationalist and Unionist cooperation; the ill-fated brother of Irish Party leader John Redmond was also a member of that party at Westminster.

Willie Redmond was picked up by a party of stretcher-bearers from 36th (Ulster) Division and carried back from where he had fallen to be taken for treatment to that Division's Main Dressing Station (MDS).[10] In recent years, we have learned that he was attended to in the MDS by an Anglican chaplain of 36th (Ulster) Division, the Revd Jack Redmond.[11] This, we are told, was a clear case of cooperation across the political and religious divides of Irish society. However, a contemporary eyewitness account of Redmond's treatment in the Ulster MDS was also provided by a Catholic chaplain of 49 Brigade, one of the component formations of 16th (Irish) Division. That chaplain, Fr Edmund Kelly, wrote to the Senior Catholic Chaplain, Monsignor Ryan, to tell him how Major Redmond had 'received every possible kindness from the Ulster soldiers'. This, according to Kelly, had caused some surprise to an Englishman attached to the Ulster Division, although Fr Kelly considered it normal, as 'the Ulstermen are Irish too'.[12] Kelly's account suggests that the divisions of home persisted on the battlefield, even though the men of 16th Division considered those of the Ulster Division to be of the same race. Redmond received the Last Rites from Fr Barrett, the Catholic chaplain of 36th (Ulster) Division.[13]

In a sense, Willie Redmond had already contributed personally to the creation of what might be described as the myth of Messines. On 4 June, officers of the Leinster Regiment[14] held a dinner at the hospice in Locre, to which French and Belgian officers were invited as well as those of 16th and 36th Divisions. Among the guests were Lieutenant-Colonel Jourdain, commanding officer of 6th Connaught Rangers, which had recruited a large proportion of its personnel from West Belfast, and Major Willie Redmond MP. The latter was asked to reply to a toast and, in so doing, 'made an eloquent speech praying for peace and prosperity for Ireland and the consummation of peace between North and South'.[15] Redmond also told men of an Irish Fusiliers' battalion in 49 Brigade that they

Denman, *A lonely grave: the life and death of William Redmond* (Dublin, 1995), p. 97. **9** Ibid., p. 119. **10** Cyril Falls, *History of the Ulster division* (London, 1922), p. 101. **11** Denman, *A lonely grave*. p. 120. UTV's Paul Clark also featured the involvement of the Ulster Division stretcher bearers and the Revd Redmond in a series of programmes entitled 'We Were Brothers', broadcast to mark the 90th anniversary of the outbreak of the First World War; the Revd Redmond's story had featured in a news programme some years before. **12** Johnstone, *Orange, green and khaki*, p. 278. **13** Denman, *A lonely grave*, p. 121. **14** Ibid., p. 116; NA, Kew, WO95/1970, war diary, 7th Leinsters; Harris, *Irish regiments in the First World War*, p. 105. **15** Harris, *Irish regiments in the First World War*, p. 105.

would be fighting 'shoulder to shoulder with the men of the North', regardless of the fact that the Royal Irish Fusiliers were recruited in Ulster.[16]

But did this amount to 'the solidarity and trust that developed between Protestant and Catholic soldiers when they served together in these trenches' referred to in the Peace Pledge above? Indeed, there is an implication in that pledge that those soldiers had made a decision that they would work together irrespective of the differences that existed between them at home. This is an essential part of the myth that provides the foundation for the Peace Park. But even the statement that Protestant and Catholic soldiers 'served together in these trenches' is open to question. In the context of the Peace Park and the Peace Pledge, this is a reference to soldiers of 16th (Irish) and 36th (Ulster) Divisions sharing trenches. One must ask the twin questions: did they share trenches?; and is it accurate to describe them as Catholics (16th Division) and Protestants (36th Division)?

To the first question the answer is clear: they did not share the same trenches. Although the two divisions might have been deployed alongside each other in the period prior to the attack on the Messines ridge, they were in discrete forming-up positions. It made no sense to have two divisions sharing the same positions as there had to be clear inter-divisional boundaries to ensure that command, control and communications, the critical C3, remained properly defined so as to give the plan its best chance of success. While some soldiers and sub-units on either side of the boundary might have strayed into the neighbouring divisional area, this is not quite the same as serving together in the same trenches.

Nor is it correct to assume that 16th (Irish) Division was Catholic and 36th (Ulster) Protestant, that one represented Nationalist Ireland and the other Unionist Ireland.[17] Once again, this is part of the myth that has been created, although this is not a recent creation but one that has been extant almost since the war ended. While it is accurate to define the original 36th (Ulster) Division as representing the anti Home Rule movement, this applies only to the main body of the Division, its infantry and some support elements. However, the divisional artillery was raised in England, largely from the London area, and did not reflect Sir Edward Carson's political line. The infantry battalions, of which there were twelve, plus a pioneer battalion, were born out of Ulster Volunteer Force (UVF) units and had recruited the bulk of their personnel, about 13,000 men, from the UVF. The Royal Irish Rifles provided eight of those infantry battalions, as well as the pioneer battalion, and it is interesting to note that surviving registers of the personnel of the service, or war-raised, battalions indicate that their

---

**16** Denman, *A lonely grave*, p. 118. The source is the battalion's Catholic chaplain. **17** For example, Terence Denman entitles a chapter of his history of 16th (Irish) Division 'Nationalist Ireland on the Somme' in *Ireland's unknown soldiers* (Dublin, 1992), pp 78–103.

religious affiliation was predominantly Protestant.[18] However, the division did not fill the ranks of its infantry battalions exclusively from the UVF. At the regimental depot in Omagh, many Royal Inniskilling Fusilier recruits who ought to have gone to either 10th or 16th Divisions were diverted by Captain Ricardo DSO to 36th.[19] And other recruits were taken from north-east England and Scotland, with one group of 300 Glaswegian Orangemen giving the officer and NCO in charge of their draft more trouble than the pair had ever experienced in their respective military careers.[20]

After the losses sustained by 36th (Ulster) Division on 1 July 1916, the nature of that formation changed considerably. The original UVF element had suffered great loss and the Division absorbed 2,375 reinforcements, of whom 193 were officers, during July. Even though Falls could recount that the bands played 'King William's March' as they accompanied their battalions to a training area on 12 July, and officers and men wore marigolds in their caps to mark the day,[21] the early image of the Division as exclusively Unionist had died on the 1st; future reinforcements would be more representative of the overall populations of Ireland and Great Britain than hitherto.

In contrast to 36th (Ulster) Division, 16th is generally portrayed as a Nationalist formation. This was largely due to John Redmond's part in the creation of the division, his appeal for Irishmen to answer the call to arms and his further request that one of the three brigades of the division be an 'Irish Brigade'.[22] That third point surely indicates that Redmond was aware that 16th (Irish) Division was not Nationalist Ireland in khaki but was more representative of the overall population of the country. Indeed, the use of the descriptor 'Irish' in the divisional title was never intended to have any political resonance – unlike the use of 'Ulster' in that of 36th Division – but merely indicated the fact that the division was created out of the Army's Irish Command. This had also been true of 10th (Irish) Division. Table 1 shows how New Army divisions were formed within the Army's home commands.

These volunteer armies were known as Kitchener's armies (hence the use of the letter K). In K1, the divisions were formed from the Scottish, Irish, Northern, Eastern and Western Commands, with an additional non-territorial division formed from light infantry units. It will be seen that the pattern was repeated in K2.

Although both John and Willie Redmond encouraged their fellow coun-

---

**18** Royal Ulster Rifles Museum, Waring Street, Belfast. The Royal Irish Rifles were renamed Royal Ulster in 1921 so that each province might have a regiment bearing its name: the others were represented by the Connaught Rangers, the Leinster Regiment and the Royal Munster Fusiliers. **19** Johnstone, *Orange, green and khaki*, pp 12–13. **20** F.P. Crozier, *A brass hat in no man's land* (London, 1930), p. 45. **21** Falls, *History of the Ulster division*, p. 63. **22** See Denman, *Ireland's unknown soldiers*, ch. 2, pp 38–58.

**Table 1** New Army divisions within the Army's home commands.
K1 represents the first New Army and K2 the second.

| K1 | K2 |
| --- | --- |
| 9th (Scottish) Division | 15th (Scottish) Division |
| 10th (Irish) Division | 16th (Irish) Division |
| 11th (Northern) Division | 17th (Northern) Division |
| 12th (Eastern) Division | 18th (Eastern) Division |
| 13th (Western) Division | 19th (Western) Division |
| 14th (Light) Division | 20th (Light) Division |

trymen to join the units of 16th (Irish) Division – with the latter famously commenting that he preferred to exhort people to come rather than go[23] – neither man would have doubted that the division would have had a base broader than that of their own political followers. Unlike the Ulster Division, neither 10th nor 16th Divisions were born out of private armies, although many members of the Redmondite National Volunteers would have been in the ranks of the latter. In deference to John Redmond, the senior brigade – 47 – of 16th Division was designated the (National) Volunteer Brigade, but the Division also had an Ulster Brigade; this was 49 Brigade, which was formed of two battalions each of Royal Inniskilling Fusiliers and Royal Irish Fusiliers.[24] Although the division's GOC, Lieutenant General Sir Lawrence Parsons, averred that the vast majority of the men of 49 Brigade were Catholics, he also wrote that he kept no detailed figures on religious affiliation.[25] Since Sir Lawrence was responding to a criticism made only a day earlier, one suspects that his assertion might not have been based on hard evidence of the variety that would bear harsh forensic scrutiny.

This suspicion is heightened by a study of the relevant sections of *Soldiers died in the Great War*, covering 7th and 8th Battalions, the Royal Inniskilling Fusiliers and especially of those who died in 1915 and 1916.[26] The very few casualties of 1915, who died 'at home' and presumably from accidents in training or from illness, and the considerable losses of 1916 can be argued to have occurred to a division that was still very much as it had been formed; thereafter the influx of casualty replacements would have begun to alter its character (the 1916 losses include those who died at Hulluch in April as well as the dead of the Somme in September). Thus, of 220 killed in 7th Inniskillings in 1915–16, a total of 167 are shown to have been born in Ireland[27] and from that number it would appear that sixty-seven were Protestant. It has to be said that this is but a crude analysis, for which reason it is probably best to refer to these men as 'presumed Protestants'.

**23** Denman, *A lonely grave*, p. 84. **24** Denman, *Ireland's unknown soldiers*, p. 50. **25** Ibid., p. 51. **26** *Soldiers died in the Great War* (War Office, 1920), pt. 32, 'The Royal Inniskilling Fusiliers', pp 34–40, 7th and 8th Battalions. **27** Ibid.

Since the majority of soldiers' records from the First World War no longer exist, having been destroyed by German bombing in the Second World War, recourse was had to deducing religious affiliation through reference to forenames and surnames, as well as places of birth or residence. For example, it was accepted that Walter Edmond Aiken, born in Ballymacarrett, Co. Down, John Arthur, born in Brookeborough, Co. Fermanagh, Charles Bell, born in Larne, Co. Antrim, Bertie Blakely, born in Belfast, and Robert Criglington, also born in Belfast, were all Protestants, while Henry Peter Brennan, born in Dublin, George Byrne, born in Newtown, Co. Wicklow, Patrick Connell, born in Kilrush, Co. Clare, and Michael Feely, born in Kinlough, Co. Leitrim, were all Catholics. Of the battalion's dead, no fewer than sixteen are shown as having been born in the Shankill area of Belfast,[28] although four of these have names that suggest an affiliation to Rome rather than to Canterbury or Geneva. A similar picture emerges with 8th Inniskillings, whose fatal losses totalled 185, of whom 146 were Irish-born,[29] sixty-one of whom appear to have been Protestants. Of the 405 deaths in the two battalions to 31 December 1916, Irish-born soldiers numbered 313,[30] with 128 of those men being Protestants.

An attempt was made to cross-reference the names of the 'presumed Protestants' with signatories to the Ulster Covenant of 1912.[31] In the case of 7th Inniskillings, fourteen of the sixty-seven appear to have signed the Covenant. It must, however, be pointed out that there is insufficient information in *Soldiers died* to verify all fourteen beyond doubt. The same caveat applies to the twenty-five Covenant signatories among the sixty-one 'presumed Protestants' of the 8th Battalion.

Although the foregoing is not presented as being definitive – the lack of soldiers' records alone would preclude such a claim – it does provide sufficient basis for arguing that Sir Lawrence Parsons was wrong to state that the vast majority of 49 Brigade was Catholic. That so many men from two of its battalions – half its strength – can be shown to have been Protestant, and with more than a significant proportion having signed the Ulster Covenant – it is clear that Sir Lawrence's claim was mistaken, if not mischievous. This also chips at the myth that 16th (Irish) Division represented Nationalist Ireland. It would appear that it may have been more representative of all views in Ireland than has generally been accepted. On the other hand, this does lend a certain credence to the claim of the Peace Pledge that Protestants and Catholics had developed 'solidarity and trust' while serving on the Western Front. Against this, it must be remembered that any group of soldiers, especially frontline infantrymen, must develop a sense of solidarity and learn to trust each other if they are to survive. However,

---

28 Ibid.   29 Ibid.   30 Ibid.   31 www.proni.gov.uk, accessed 10 June 2010.

there is no evidence to support any thesis that such solidarity and trust developed at an inter-divisional level.

There is some evidence that 36th (Ulster) Division's units strove to retain their original ethos as the war progressed. In his history of 10th Royal Inniskilling Fusiliers (The Derrys), Mitchell notes that the battalion celebrated the anniversaries of the shutting of the gates of Derry in 1688 and of the relief of the city after the siege of 1689, the former by burning an effigy of Governor Robert Lundy.[32] Likewise, Canning records celebrations for 12 July 1917 in 11th Inniskillings (Donegal and Fermanagh).[33] References to such celebrations by Falls have already been noted. In addition, the writer was also able to interview several veterans of 36th (Ulster) Division, some of whom recalled Orange Order and Apprentice Boys' celebrations being held in France. Others, however, had no recollection of such events.

In contrast, there is little to suggest that such Nationalist celebrations as 15 August – the Feast of the Assumption, on which the Ancient Order of Hibernians (AOH) parade – were marked in any way by the battalions of 16th (Irish) Division. However, in December 1916, Major General Hickie, who succeeded Parsons as GOC, issued a special order of the day to mark the first anniversary of the Division's arrival in France. In that document, Hickie noted that the division was the successor to the Irish Brigade that had fought for France and, as such, would assume the title of 'the Irish Brigade' together with the motto of Louis XIV's Irish Brigade – *Ubique et Semper Fidelis* (Everywhere and Always Faithful).[34] Interestingly, Hickie wrote to Brigadier Pat Scott, who commanded 38 (Irish) Brigade in Italy in 1944–5, to pass on to Scott's command the traditions and motto of its First World War predecessor.[35]

The June 1917 battle of Messines was the first occasion on which 16th (Irish) and 36th (Ulster) Divisions served in the same corps. That action was followed by the campaign that became known as Third Ypres, in which both divisions were included in XIX Corps, which formed part of Sir Hubert Gough's Fifth Army. According to Hickie, Gough had asked for 16th Division to be included in his command.[36] Both divisions were to take part in what was effectively a follow-through to Messines which had delivered half of the arc of high ground dominating the Ypres salient into Allied hands. During July, the soldiers of the attacking formations underwent intensive training to prepare them for the offensive with 16th (Irish) Division selected for training as storm-troopers.[37]

The subsequent battles were not, however, planned with quite the same

**32** Gardiner Mitchell, *Three cheers for the Derrys* (Derry, 1991), pp 47–9.   **33** W.J. Canning, *Ballyshannon, Belcoo, Bertincourt* (Antrim, 1996), p. 107.   **34** WO95/1957, War diary A and QMG, HQ 16th (Irish) Division.   **35** Scott, *Account of the Irish Brigade in Italy, 1944–5*, in writer's possession.   **36** Denman, *Ireland's unknown soldiers*, p. 115.   **37** Ibid.

degree of skill and foresight as had been the case with Messines. Gough was simply no Plumer, although in differing circumstances this might not have been a major factor. However, the ground over which Fifth Army was to fight was low-lying and the drainage system had been destroyed by constant shelling so that the ground on which both divisions were to fight was liable to flood and become a morass in heavy rain. Although the offensive was planned for late-July/early-August, the summer months when it could be expected to be dry, rain came down heavily.

From this concatenation of circumstances comes the popular image of Third Ypres, often referred to as Passchendaele, from the ridge that the Allies sought to take, which includes foolish generals continuing to throw men into a senseless offensive. However, this image fails to take account of the fact that the British armies had to continue fighting to keep the pressure off their French allies who had suffered horrendously in the ill-fated Nivelle offensive and whose armies were close to breaking. Many French divisions had suffered mutinies, the army was temporarily not effective and, hence, the pressure was on the British to keep up the fight.

In circumstances where the soldier on the ground was unaware of the strategic imperatives that governed the tactical situation in which he found himself, it is hardly surprising that he placed the blame for his predicament on his own generals rather than on the strategic situation. Few soldiers would have been aware of the mutinous state of many French formations and of the overall low morale that followed Nivelle's failure to deliver the decisive victory that he had promised to his government and to his soldiers.[38]

Fifth Army opened its offensive on 31 July 1917, with General Anthoine's First French Army on its left flank.[39] In the initial stages, both armies met with considerable success and it seemed as if the objectives had been gained. However, the new German form of defence in depth, with lightly held forward positions, engendered a false sense of success. Local counter-attacks, a critical element of the new German tactics, recaptured much of what had been lost to the Allies,[40] although the Pilckem ridge remained in Allied hands. It was then that the weather started to play its notorious part in the battle. On the afternoon of the 31st, it began to rain very heavily, and by the morning of 1 August the ground had been transformed into what Falls described as 'a sea of mud'.[41] This ground had been turned over time and again by relentless shellfire and its drainage system had been destroyed.[42]

38 Gordon Corrigan, *Mud, blood and poppycock* (London, 2003), pp 333–8.   39 Harris, *Irish regiments in the First World War*, p. 114, who also notes the delay occasioned by the French insistence on deploying 'a small, elite force' in the coastal sector.   40 Ibid., p. 117; Denman, *Ireland's unknown soldiers*, pp 121–2; Falls, *History of the Ulster division*, p. 110.   41 Falls, *History of the Ulster division*, p. 110.   42 Ibid.

Hickie's division deployed first and suffered heavily. It was to assault the village of Langemarck on 14 August, but its suffering began even before that date. Since the division was XIX Corps' reserve until 4 August, battalions were used either as reinforcements in the battle areas or to provide work details. These latter duties also led to many casualties as they were often carried out in full view of enemy artillery observers or machine gunners. By the time that 16th Division was due to attack Langemarck, its strength had already been eroded by about a third through casualties or illness. The attack had been delayed by two days until 16 August and 36th (Ulster) Division was to advance alongside as at Messines.[43]

Both divisions lost heavily at Langemarck, with 16th (Irish) being forced back to its start line. When the corps commander asked the GOCs of both divisions to resume their attacks, the two men responded by stating that such would be impossible since none of the original assaulting brigades could now muster more than 500 men. Between 1 and 20 August, Hickie's command had taken 4,285 casualties, of whom 221 were officers, while in the period since the assault on 16 August, 2,167 (almost half) of those casualties had been sustained. Although 280 bodies were recovered, another 718 were missing, most of whom had been killed and many of whose bodies were never recovered (among them was one of this writer's great uncles, Patrick McCarron of 6th Royal Irish).[44] A similar picture existed in 36th (Ulster) Division: Falls recorded that 3,585 of the division's number became casualties in the period 2–18 August. Of those, 144 were officers with four commanding officers among them: Pratt of 11th Inniskillings and Somerville of 9th Royal Irish Fusiliers were killed, while Maxwell of 13th Rifles and Macrory of 10th Inniskillings were wounded severely.[45] This was the only attack launched by the division that 'suffered complete reverse'.[46] The same could be said for 16th (Irish) Division.

In the post-battle analysis, Gough attempted to blame 16th Division for the failure of his attack, but XIX Corps' commander did not agree, praising the performance of the division which left his corps shortly after Langemarck.[47] Although 36th (Ulster) Division had done no better, there was no attempt by Gough to attribute blame to that formation, which creates the suspicion that Gough placed more trust in the loyal Ulstermen than he did in the men of the Irish Brigade. However, it can be argued that the two divisions as originally formed ceased to exist at Langemarck, such were their casualties. Although many original members were still in the ranks, the nature of both divisions had changed completely and this was especially so in the case of the Ulster Division. Both were to see much more action, with 16th (Irish) being destroyed in the German spring

43 Denman, *Ireland's unknown soldiers*, pp 116–21.  44 Ibid., p. 123.  45 Ibid., p. 119.  46 Ibid., p. 120.  47 Denman, *Ireland's unknown soldiers*, p. 123.

offensive of March 1918 – Operation MICHAEL. Their days of fighting 'side-by-side' were over.

Thus, the time that 16th (Irish) and 36th (Ulster) Divisions spent 'side-by-side' was restricted to a brief few months in 1917 when, as part of the same corps, they were committed to two major offensives, one of which concluded in great success but the other in tragic failure. Both offensives were in the same sector of the front and so the Peace Park can help focus the attention of the visitor on Langemarck as well as Messines.

In telling its story of the Irish servicemen who died in the First World War, the Peace Park does not paint the entire picture. Whether a complete picture can ever be made is a subject for debate, given that so many of the returning Irishmen of 16th (Irish) Division remained silent about their experiences in the post-War years. This was understandable, given the conflict that began in January 1919 and continued into and beyond the creation of the Irish Free State with the Irish Civil War. Nor was the situation much different in Northern Ireland. Although many men of 36th (Ulster) Division joined the Ulster Special Constabulary (USC), those of 16th (Irish) Division were in a limbo, with the ranks of the USC seemingly closed to them (even though some Catholics joined in the early days, they were intimidated to resign by the IRA)[48] and their military past causing suspicion among physical force Republicans. Local newspapers of the period carry reports of Catholic former soldiers being shot dead during civil disturbances with, in some cases, those who fired the shots being former members of the Ulster Division.[49] Thus it was that the story of 16th (Irish) Division never received the same prominence as that of its fellow formation.

This writer has been able to interview a number of veterans of the First World War, almost all of whom were members of 36th (Ulster) Division. Few were aware of the formations alongside them – which is typical of the experience of the ordinary soldier in any war – or even of the units[50] that neighboured them. Their stories differed greatly, from the engineer who helped create the mines under Messines Ridge, to the infantryman wounded in the opening minutes of the battle of Albert on 1 July 1916, to another infantryman wounded at Cambrai in November 1917. In at least one case, that of Private Leslie Bell of 10th Royal Inniskilling Fusiliers (The Derrys), the personal story seems to have changed over the years to suit the prevailing popular conception of the First World War. Bell was first interviewed by Martin Middlebrook for his book *The first day on the Somme* when he recalled his thoughts as Zero Hour approached on 1 July 1916 as

**48** Arthur Hezlet, *The 'B' Specials* (London, 1972), pp 22–3.   **49** See, for example, the files of the *Derry Journal* (1921) in the Central Library, Londonderry.   **50** The term 'unit' refers to a battalion of infantry or regiment of cavalry or artillery; the term 'formation' refers to a body formed from several units, such as a brigade or division.

being of the peaceful farming community from which he came in the foothills of the Sperrin Mountains. In fact, he was specific that it was milking time and that the cows on his father's farm would be coming in from the meadows.[51] Since Middlebrook's seminal work was published in 1971 the interview with Bell would have taken place some time before that, perhaps as early as 1969.

The writer was present when Leslie Bell was interviewed for Mitchell's *Three cheers for the Derrys*, published in 1991, twenty years after Middlebrook's book. This interview took place in 1989 and no reference was made by the interviewee to thoughts of home on that July morning in 1916. Instead, he said that he had thought of the stupidity of officers in general and of some of his battalion's officers in particular. In 1991, the writer presented a BBC Radio Ulster programme to mark the 75th anniversary of the battle of the Somme, during which he interviewed Bell as one of the, then, few surviving veterans. On this occasion, the interviewee was asked about his thoughts before going over the top. Again he was critical of officers. When pressed on the question and asked if he had thought of home and what might be happening on the farm he replied that he 'wouldn'a had time for that'.[52]

It would seem that Leslie Bell had absorbed much of the popular imagery of the First World War that became prevalent from the late-1960s and is exemplified in the work of writers such as John Laffin and Alan Clarke. In Bell's view, Haig was a butcher, as was almost every officer who served in the British armies of the era. A marked contrast was provided in an interview with another veteran of 10th Inniskillings, Thomas Gibson, who was interviewed on 7 December 1988 for the Radio Ulster series 'the Sons of Ulster'. Contact was made with Thomas Gibson through Mr Ivan Glendenning of the Limavady Branch of the Royal British Legion, but Gibson was a reluctant interviewee, claiming that he had no experiences that would be of interest to any radio listener. He agreed to the interview, however, when it was stressed that the presenter and producer were interested as much in his day-to-day life as a First World War soldier as in his experiences of battle. What followed was an interview of surprising clarity, which was one of the most memorable that the writer has conducted.

Thomas Gibson spoke of his experiences from the day he attempted to enlist in the Army as an under-age youth at the railway station in Garvagh, Co. Londonderry. Having been sent away by one sergeant when he stated his true age, he joined another line of eager would-be recruits. However, there was a train at the platform waiting to pull out for Londonderry with enlistees, and many of his friends had already boarded. As the guard blew his whistle, those friends called to

**51** Martin Middlebrook, *The first day on the Somme* (London, 1971), p. 117. **52** Interview with Leslie Bell, Moneymore, June 1991.

Thomas Gibson to join them and he boarded the train hurriedly. Eventually, the group found itself in Finner Camp in Co. Donegal, where the Derry Volunteers were training. After some time there, it was discovered that Gibson and a number of others had not been enlisted formally and so the anomaly was rectified. Thus did Gibson explain for the writer the listing of 'enlisted Finner' in *Soldiers died* for many of the dead of his battalion.

The interview continued with Thomas Gibson recalling his training; his hospitalization with shingles, which kept him out of the carnage of the battle of Albert; the battle of Messines, at the start of which his commanding officer hoisted him by 'the scruff of my neck and my belt' as he tried to scramble out of the trench in which his battalion awaited the order to advance; the head wound that he suffered at Cambrai and which took him back to hospital in November 1917 – and the remarks of his comrades as he was stretchered away that 'you're a quare lucky fella'; and his eventual discharge from the Army in 1919. This 'uninteresting' interview had taken some seventy-five minutes but one of the interviewee's most telling comments was made as the writer and his producer left. As they thanked Thomas Gibson for his agreeing to be interviewed he told them that they were the first people to whom he had ever related his experiences. And yet those recollections were so strong, they commented. 'I can see them like they happened yesterday,' was his response, 'but I wouldn't know either of you boys if I met you again tomorrow' (members of his family later confirmed to the writer that the radio programme and the subsequent book based on the series were the first details they had ever known of their father's wartime experiences apart from the fact that he had been wounded in the head, since a cranial X-ray some years earlier had shown the presence of metal fragments from the round that caused the wound: this was seventy years after he had been injured).[53]

Neither Leslie Bell nor Thomas Gibson had any recollection of soldiering shoulder-to-shoulder with 16th (Irish) Division. In Bell's case, this is not surprising, since he was wounded in the opening minutes of the battle of Albert on 1 July 1916 and never returned to the Ulster Division; he finished the war in the Army Service Corps.[54] Thomas Gibson survived both Messines and Langemarck, however, and had no recollection of the divisions on his flank. The same was true of other soldiers of 36th (Ulster) Division that the writer was able to interview. As with most enlisted men, their world was that of their own unit or sub-unit and rarely did it encompass anything wider than that. For officers it could be different, although most subalterns and captains tended to be as constrained as were the soldiers.

**53** Interview with Thomas Gibson, Limavady, Dec. 1988.   **54** Interview with Leslie Bell, Moneymore, June 1991.

There thus seems little evidence on which those who established the Peace Park can base the claim of the pledge that the men of 16th (Irish) and 36th (Ulster) Divisions developed trust and solidarity while serving together in the trenches. In fact, we have seen that they did not serve together as Divisions of Catholics and Protestants as the Park's creators claim, although Catholics and Protestants served together in the ranks of 49 Brigade, the Ulster Brigade of 16th (Irish) Division. We have also seen that 16th (Irish) Division was not a Catholic and Nationalist formation as commonly believed and that it included many Protestants from the nine counties of Ulster. The immediate post-War period of violence and distrust also suggests that there was no legacy of 'trust and solidarity'.

Does this mean, therefore, that the Peace Park has no validity, that, since it is based on a flawed understanding of the history of the First World War and a lack of understanding of military organization, it has no lessons for the present generations? The writer does not believe this to be so. While there is a myth of Messines at the heart of the Peace Park, it should be remembered that myths may be categorized as being either malignant or benign. That of Messines falls into the latter category as it is one from which positive growth may come, whereas a malignant myth might lead to distrust and destruction. The positive growth from the Messines myth may be seen in the International School for Peace Studies, which is an integral part of the Peace Park concept.[55] This school has a valuable role to play in the education of young people from either side of the border in Ireland and from elsewhere. There is another clause in the Pledge in which it is noted that the Park commemorates the thousands of young men from all parts of Ireland 'who fought a common enemy, defended democracy and the rights of all nations' and, in this, the Park finds its true role. It is in remembering those many young men, and some not so young such as Major Willie Redmond, that today's and tomorrow's generations will learn the true price of peace, the value of democracy and the cost of war. In so doing, the Park aims to bring together young people from all over Ireland who might otherwise have had no exposure to the ideas and culture of their fellow students and thereby open their minds to a shared past and enlighten their thinking on the future. This is a noble aim and one that is to be encouraged. Thus, while the organizers may have tried to make the events of the First World War fit a modern-day template, they have done so with admirable rationale and their efforts deserve to meet with success. Should that happen, then the men who are commemorated in the Island of Ireland Peace Park will have found an even greater memorial than the replica round tower atop the Messines ridge.

55 www.schoolforpeace.com, accessed 10 June 2010..

# Belfast's unholy war: the 1920s' Troubles

## ALAN F. PARKINSON

### INTRODUCTION

The 'unholy' war which was fought mainly on Belfast's streets between the summer of 1920 and late 1922 occurred during a pivotal period in wider Irish history. The scale of the Belfast conflict was considerable. Nearly 500 people lost their lives, over 2,000 suffered serious injury and over £3 million worth of damage was inflicted upon the city's commercial centre. In addition, over 10,000 people, mainly Catholics, were forced from their workplace and over 20,000 were intimidated from their homes during these Troubles. The legacy of such bloodshed was also significant. Nationalists' suspicions of the Special Constabulary endured for years after the last conflict killing, while Unionists believed that the IRA campaign in the north justified the continuation of the emergency security arrangements that had been established during the bloodiest phase of these disturbances. Yet little has been written about this conflict, which is regarded by some as Belfast's 'forgotten war'. Why is this so? Writers have tended to focus upon other events in wider Irish history and on personalities of the period, such as Collins and de Valera, and those who have written about the 1920s' Troubles have focused on one specific aspect of the conflict, such as the IRA's campaign, the prison-ship *Argenta*, or the Ulster Special Constabulary. The depressing nature of the disturbances and the unavailability of clear evidence have certainly deterred others. No matter what the reason, the dearth of research in this important area of Irish historiography is undoubted.

Interpretations of the conflict tend to be one-dimensional, concentrating on simplistic notions of a 'pogrom'. While fundamental features of a 'pogrom' were evident, including the disproportionately high Catholic fatality rate, there is little evidence to suggest that state culpability for violence extended beyond the realm of neglect. Other underlying characteristics of the conflict include the significant involvement of the IRA and Loyalist assassination gangs, and the impact of events elsewhere in Ireland upon the city of Belfast. The causes of the city's violence during this period will be summarized and their inter-relationship with political events analyzed. The nature of this violence will also be examined and an account of the incident which is most closely associated with the conflict, the murders of several members of the McMahon family, is provided. The final part of this essay contains some of the childhood memories of 'veterans' of this conflict.

## 'SHIPYARD CONFETTI'

The outbreak of the Belfast disturbances was the result of a fusion of separate factors, resulting in bloodshed on an unprecedented scale. Apart from the ongoing passage of the Government of Ireland legislation introduced by Lloyd George earlier in 1920, the increasing threat posed by the 'flying columns' of the IRA, the killing of Ulster-born police personnel and Protestant civilians elsewhere in Ireland, the growing frustration of Loyalist workers in Belfast's shipyards, the gradual build-up of arms caches and fiery political speeches by Unionist leaders, combined to produce a significant increase in tension during the early summer of 1920. Such attacks on Protestants, especially in Ireland's south and west, led to increasing concern for co-religionists, typified by a successful Presbyterian Church resolution, expressing 'sympathy with all loyal citizens who reside in those parts of Ireland where they are exposed to terror and outrage'.[1]

Empathy was more easily experienced when terror attacks spread to Ulster itself. Nationalist gains in local elections led to increasing tension in Derry and street riots, accompanied by the intimidation of families in the city's Waterside and Bogside districts. Increased military deployment was necessary and nearly forty people lost their lives in disturbance covering a two-month period. These Derry disturbances prompted calls for the cancellation of the Twelfth parades in Belfast, which was feared would prove to be the 'match' to light the powder keg. Though Orange leaders resisted such calls, extra deployment of military and police helped result in a trouble-free parade. However, the political temperature was raised by Edward Carson's fiery Finaghy speech. Unionism's veteran leader again had his finger on the Orangeman's pulse and exploited Loyalist fears about Republican violence. Reminding Lloyd George that the Loyalists had an alternative weapon to political action, Carson warned that

> We in Ulster will tolerate no Sinn Féin … [to the government] We tell you this – that if, having offered you help, you are yourselves unable to protect us from the machinations of Sinn Féin, and you won't take our help … we will tell you that we will take the matter into our own hands. We will reorganize.[2]

Anxiety engendered by Carson's speech was compounded by the shooting in Cork of the RIC's Munster Divisional Commander, Gerald Smyth. Banbridge-born Colonel Smyth was probably targeted more on account of his outspoken

---

1 *Belfast Newsletter*, 9 June 1920.   2 Carson, quoted in Michael Farrell, *Northern Ireland: the orange state* (London, 1976), p. 27.

criticism of Republicanism than for his northern Unionist background, but his killing undoubtedly added to Loyalist discontent. Though there is a dearth of evidence for suggesting high-level coordination of disturbances by the Unionist establishment, it would be misleading to dismiss them as merely spontaneous outbursts against Republican violence elsewhere in Ireland. Build-up of UVF arms caches, calls for the reorganization of this force into a special constabulary and the timing of the trouble (the first working day after Ulster's annual holiday) indicate that Loyalists were, at the very least, cognisant of the need to be prepared for an immediate outbreak of communal fighting.

Sparks of communal violence had been lit and were soon to be applied to 'firewood', Belfast's religiously mixed industrial workforce, mainly in the east of the city. Large numbers of Protestants had failed to regain employment in the shipyards after their war service, and a meeting called by the Belfast Protestant Association at the Workman and Clark yard was attended by over 5,000 workers who demanded the expulsion of 'non loyal' workers. They then proceeded to the larger yards of Harland and Wolff where, armed with banners, iron bars, wooden staves and allegedly revolvers, they forced their way into the locked premises. They roamed the vast concourse searching for potential victims. Catholics were quickly identified and forced to seek escape by jumping into the Musgrave Channel, where they were pelted by 'shipyard confetti' – a mixture of iron nuts, bolts, rivets and pieces of sharp steel. Inevitably many received injuries, with over twenty being treated in hospital. One Catholic worker later recalled that

> The gates were smashed down with sledges, the vests and shirts of those at work were torn open to see if the men were wearing Catholic emblems and then woe betide the man that was. One man was set upon, thrown into the dock, had to swim two or three miles, to emerge in streams of blood and rush to the police in a nude state.[3]

Not surprisingly, shipyard workers became the targets of stone-throwing Catholic crowds at the end of the working day when trams from the city's industrial heart-lands made their way into the city centre. Within hours, stone-throwing and fist-fighting were replaced by gunfire, resulting in the first fatalities of what was to become a two-year conflict. Both Loyalists and the IRA had access to a comparatively sophisticated range of weaponry which produced the disturbances' 'modern' nature. Therefore, snipers utilizing high velocity rifles and frequently machine-guns, selected easy targets on neighbouring streets, including children and the elderly as well as members of the security forces, and bombs were either

3 Ibid., p. 28.

hurled into these streets or lobbed into workers' trams. Also, industrial intimidation soon spread from the shipyards to several other industrial and commercial premises. 'Vigilante' committees demanded that 'disloyal' workers, including socialists (or 'rotten Prods') as well as the Catholics, should leave their place of work. While many workers who had been intimidated from their workshop or factory were to eventually return to their jobs, this frequently took months or even years, especially in large firms like Harland and Wolff. Intimidation was not restricted to the workplace. Those living in interface areas or in a district dominated by residents of a different religious persuasion, were most at risk. Such intimidation occurred throughout the two years of conflict and 'flitting' was reported in several areas across the city, with victims seeking sanctuary in relatively safe Catholic areas such as the Falls Road and Short Strand. Many others left Belfast to find refuge in the south of Ireland (especially Dublin), or further afield, including Glasgow.

POLITICAL PACTS AND STREET SQUABBLES

Trying to measure correlation between intense political activity and levels of civil unrest is not always a precise science. This is partly due to a lack of clarity about which activity provoked the other, and also the likelihood that the degree of tension on the streets was not always reflected in actual security incidents or outrages. Often elaborate security arrangements resulted in an uneasy calm in the city for a short while, though this did not necessarily lead to a reduction in community tension. Thus, by temporarily deploying an increased number of military and constabulary in the greater Belfast area during the run-up to the elections for the new Northern Ireland parliament in May 1921 and for the royal visit which ended in the formal opening of this new institution the following month, Craig's administration was successful in offsetting politically damaging and embarrassing disturbances. However, it was also true that the tension created by prolonged political negotiation and uncertainty could result in an intensification of violence on Belfast's streets. This was evident during the period of treaty negotiations, when over thirty people lost their lives in the city during November 1921. Indeed, a bout of excessive blood-letting occasionally produced an, albeit short-lived, atmosphere favouring political compromise, rather than the more familiar climate of fear and distrust. This was probably the case with the orgy of violence in March 1922, which culminated in the horrific attack on the McMahon family and which led to the signing of the second Collins-Craig agreement within days of the Kinnaird Terrace incident.

The level of political activity in Ireland between 1920 and 1922 was unprece-

dented and it unquestionably constituted a 'backdrop' to the Northern disturbances. British Prime Minister David Lloyd George, who believed that Irish
Nationalists would be more likely to accept the creation of two regional parliaments, rather than Ulster's exemption from a Dublin-based parliament, was the
architect of the Better Government of Ireland Bill (better known to its
Nationalist opponents as the 'partition' bill) which became law on 23 December
1920. The new act transferred significant, but not absolute, powers from
Westminster to the new administrations in Dublin and Belfast. Loyalists were
initially apprehensive about a political package which appeared to offer what they
had consistently opposed, and their concerns over the plight of over 100,000
southern Protestants were gradually replaced by a sense of 'duty' which persuaded
them to accept this new legislation. Captain Charles Craig had voiced his support
for the Bill early in its parliamentary passage, when he claimed that Ulster
'without a parliament of its own would not be in nearly as strong a position as
one in which a parliament had been set up, where the executive had been
appointed and all the paraphernalia of government was already in existence'.[4] The
response from Nationalists was unequivocal. Open hostility to its political
proposals was expressed by politicians, church leaders and newspaper editors. The
key charge against the British premier was one of 'abandoning' the new area's
Catholic minority. At Westminster, Joe Devlin expressed the fears shared by
many of his constituents about the potential impact of likely Unionist domination of such an assembly:

> What will we get when they are armed with Britain's rifles, when they are
> clothed with the authority of government, when they have cast round
> them the Imperial garb; what mercy, what pity, much less justice or liberty,
> will be conceded to us then?[5]

The election campaign was lengthy and bitterly contested. The close relationship
between the Orange Order and the Unionist Party ensured that election 'fever'
would prevail in the Loyalist heartlands. Apathy was a genuine fear among the
Unionist leadership and Loyalist icon Sir Edward Carson made a significant
speech in the city on the eve of polling, in which he declared that those who failed
to vote would be 'aiding and assisting our opponents to destroy all that has been
handed down to us and which we are bound to preserve'. Nationalists and
Republicans were also aware of the need for electoral unity in their opposition to
the legislation. The Bishop of Down and Connor, Dr Joseph MacRory, claimed
that 'the character of your children's education and with it, perhaps, their eternal

4 HOC Debates, 5th series, vol. 127, col. 98, 29 Mar. 1920.   5 Ibid., vol. 134, col. 1455, 11 Nov. 1920.

welfare' would 'depend on the result of this election'.[6] Although a pre-election pact was agreed between Devlin's United Irish League and Sinn Féin, separate campaigns were mounted and street disturbances were reported between the rival anti-partition parties in Belfast's Short Strand district. Several leading Republicans, including Eamon de Valera, Michael Collins and Arthur Griffith, stood in border constituencies, and Sinn Féin sustained a lively campaign. An impressive 89 per cent of the 380,000-strong electorate voted for seventy-eight candidates on Tuesday 24 May 1921. Instances of intimidation and personation were reported, especially in the east of the city, but the election result was decisive. All forty Unionist Party candidates were elected, with Sinn Féin and the UIL equally sharing the other twelve seats (however, the former group failed to return a candidate in Belfast).

The formal opening of the new parliament was arranged for 22 June. Following an upsurge in violence leading up to the election and during the first part of June, fears spread that the protection of the royal party could not be guaranteed. However, the king's political advisors believed that such a visit and the monarch's delivery of a carefully-scripted plea for reconciliation would offer a modicum of hope for all of Ireland and not just Ulster. The respective communities had contrasting expectations for the visit. Ulster Unionists saw the royal trip as an indication that the British connection had actually been strengthened by the recent legislation. On the morning of their trip, the *Belfast Newsletter* confidently proclaimed that the visit would signal to 'the whole world that our acceptance of the new status in no way weakens the link between us and the Crown, and also the connection with Great Britain and the Empire'.[7] Loyalist Belfast, deprived of a visit from their monarch for nearly twenty years, eagerly awaited the royals' arrival. Nationalist Belfast, however, had different feelings about the visit. Concentrating on the plight of Catholics made homeless following violent attacks in West Belfast the previous week, the *Irish News* argued that the city's authorities had got their priorities wrong:

> Belfast today is beflagged and festooned. Streamers are flying from many houses and shops, bunting yields to the breeze and gives colour to a city which boasts of its loyalty to the king – and yet gloats at its bigotry. But if today Belfast is a beflagged city, it is also a besmirched one. For them [the Catholic homeless], Wednesday will pass as one more day of suffering and anxiety.[8]

---

6 MacRory, quoted in *Irish News*, 23 May 1921.   7 *Belfast Newsletter*, 22 June 1921.   8 *Irish News*, 21 June 1921.

Amid this frenetic atmosphere of fervour and anxiety, the Royal Yacht sailed up Belfast Lough during the mid-morning of Wednesday 22 June. The city's industrial centre came to a standstill and tens of thousands thronged central thoroughfares hours before the arrival of King George V and Queen Mary. Addressing the parliamentary representatives – with the boycott by Nationalists and Republicans, an exclusively Unionist audience – the king made a stirring plea for peace and reconciliation in Ireland as a whole. He implored the assembled representatives:

> I speak from a full heart when I pray that my coming to Ireland today may prove to be the first step towards the end of strife among her people, whatever their race or creed. In that hope, I appeal to all Irishmen to pause, to stretch out the hand of forbearance and conciliation, to forgive and forget, and to join in making for the land they love a new era of peace, contentment and goodwill.[9]

With the shadow of violence hanging over the whole occasion, the visit lasted a mere five hours. Despite the colossal security presence, fear was deeply etched on the faces of the main participants. Consequently, when the brief visit passed off without major incident, Unionist joy was unsurpassed. This was understandable, given the considerable apprehension among the king's advisors. This was certainly warranted. Barely forty-eight hours after the pageantry and joyful celebrations in the city, the IRA exhibited its response to the pleas of George V. Realizing that the heavy security presence in the Belfast area mitigated against the staging of a spectacular attack on the royal party, Republicans organized a low-risk operation aimed at relaxing military personnel, returning from Wednesday's ceremony in Belfast. A military train carrying nearly 120 soldiers and over a hundred horses, was destroyed by an IRA 'team' led by Frank Aiken, at Adavoyle in Co. Armagh, close to the new border. Four soldiers from 10th Royal Hussars, who had formed part of the cavalry escort during the king's visit, were killed, along with two civilians and eighty horses.

It was the continuation of the 'external' threat to northern Unionists which arguably did most to harden Loyalist anger and mistrust, and which led in turn to further alienation of Belfast's Catholic minority throughout the two years of the conflict. Growing Loyalist fury over attacks on Ulster-born policemen and southern Protestants during the Anglo-Irish War, concern about the growing political success of Sinn Féin, and what was believed to have been the clandestine activities of the Collins-backed Northern Division of the IRA, which continued

9 King George V, quoted in Harford Montgomery Hyde, *Carson* (London, 1953), p. 458.

to be active after the signing of the Truce by Republicans and British forces in July 1921, explains this curtain of hostility between north and south. A further example of southern ill-feeling towards Ulster Unionists was the boycott of northern goods, which operated, in practice, between the late summer of 1920 and the early summer of 1922. Initially devised as a strategy to persuade Ulster Loyalists to facilitate the return of Catholics to Belfast's industrial centres, the boycott involved the confiscation and destruction of northern-produced goods and the intimidation of customers and bank staff with northern connections. The action was monitored by southern-based members of the IRA, who boarded trains and confiscated or destroyed a large amount of produce, ranging from newspapers and bread to whiskey and linen goods. A report of an attack on a train near Drogheda in May 1921 provides some idea of the nature of such attacks:

> While the train was slowly proceeding up the incline, a number of armed men appeared and jumped on the engine. They compelled the driver and fireman to halt and stand by, and then approached the guard and procured from him his wage bill of invoices showing the forwarding station of the goods carried ... the raiders went systematically through the fifty-odd wagons of the train, and removed oil, cart wheels, drapery and tea.[10]

Such a concerted and sustained campaign did not result in economic disaster for the north. Though there was significant disruption in banking services and several smaller firms experienced considerable financial losses, the larger commercial and manufacturing concerns in Greater Belfast, which tended to trade with Great Britain and further afield, rather than with the rest of Ireland, were considerably less affected by these southern sanctions. The real damage was psychological, both in terms of the further poisoning of relations between northern Unionists and southern Nationalists, and also on account of it leading to increased persecution of Belfast's beleaguered Catholic minority.[11]

The six-month period between the end of 1921 and the middle of 1922 proved to be frenetic both in terms of the levels of street violence and also in the scale of political activity in London, Dublin and Belfast. Preliminary talks about Ireland's political future, involving de Valera and Lloyd George, but significantly excluding Craig, had started during the summer of 1921, with formal negotiations between the British government and the Sinn Féin delegation, led by Michael Collins and Arthur Griffith, commencing on 11 October. Lloyd George cleverly played on internal Republican divisions and put increasing pressure on the

---

**10** *Irish News*, 10 May 1921. **11** Unionist traders and businessmen formed an Ulster Trades Defence Association in May 1921, and this operated a counter-boycott campaign which was aimed at damaging the southern economy.

delegation to accept an agreement early in December. The Anglo-Irish Treaty was signed during the early hours of 6 December. It would, of course, divide Republicans and lead within months to civil war, and Collins' own assessment of its personal implications was chillingly accurate:

> Think – what have I got for Ireland? Something which she has wanted these last 700 years. Will any one be satisfied at the bargain? Will any one? I will tell you only this – early this morning, I signed my death warrant.[12]

Northern interest in the Downing Street Agreement differed from that in the rest of Ireland, where emphasis was more on the issue of sovereignty. In Ulster, attention turned to the question of partition, with Nationalists perceiving that their interests would be best represented by the pro-treaty lobby, which had gained a narrow victory in the Dáil on 8 January 1922. The *Irish News* wrote that 'Ireland as a whole has welcomed the Agreement with a spirit of hope and goodwill'.[13] Loyalist responses to the treaty negotiations and debates were mixed ones of curiosity and bewilderment, smug indifference, bullish condemnation and a growing acceptance of the treaty's terms. Some Unionists were, however, increasingly aware of the apparent inter-relationship between the tensions caused by ongoing political debate in London and Dublin and events on Belfast's streets, especially as political negotiations peaked in November and December. Republican attacks on workers' tram-cars and a spate of shootings carried out by both Loyalist and Republican gunmen, were clear evidence of the increasingly raw and reflex nature of these gunmen to prolonged political uncertainty.

    Given the violent atmosphere in Belfast during the first half of 1922, a remarkable series of meetings took place between Collins and Craig, resulting in two pacts, however ill-fated. It was Colonial Secretary Winston Churchill who brokered these meetings and for a while the fulcrum of the Irish question moved from Belfast's desolate, volatile streets to the calm, salubrious surroundings of Whitehall. The first of these agreements was signed on 21 January, following two days of intense negotiations. It offered Unionists the termination of Dublin's boycott of northern goods in exchange for the restoration of expelled Catholic workers and for the removal of religious and political tests by Belfast workers. The pact committed both leaders to compromises which, in reality, they had little chance of delivering, due to the prevailing increase in Belfast's level of violence. Within a fortnight, there had been a substantial increase in levels of violence in the city, which prompted the arrangement of another fruitless meeting between Collins and Craig at Dublin Castle on 2 February.

**12** Michael Collins, 6 Dec. 1921; quoted in Leon O'Broin, *Michael Collins*, p. 113.   **13** *Irish News*, 8 Dec. 1921.

Following the McMahon murders on 23 March and the escalation in sectarian violence throughout the city, Churchill and Lloyd George called Craig and Collins to London. After another forty-eight hours of talks, the 2nd Pact was signed at the Colonial Office on 30 March, in a bid to suppress this escalation in terror and also as an attempt to boost Catholic confidence in Northern Ireland's new institutions. The document reflected increased sympathy for Catholics, with its ethos underlining the need for encouraging Catholic participation in the local security forces. The first statement of the Pact – 'Peace is today declared' – epitomized Churchill's over-optimism. Radical it certainly was. Two committees were established to advise on the selection of Catholic recruits to the Special Constabulary and also to investigate specific sectarian outrages in the city.

There was a broad welcome for this pact, especially from Belfast's Nationalists. Bishop MacRory paid a rare compliment to the city's Unionist leadership, suggesting that the agreement had been 'conceived in a new spirit which does them credit', though Loyalists were more guarded in their responses. This pact also floundered on account of the real lack of powers invested in both committees, as well as the lack of trust between individual committee members. Both pacts represented the growing desperation felt by the three administrations and a belief that violence and the resulting political instability could be defused by negotiation. Desperation led to meetings and apparent compromises, but the degree of commitment on both sides was debatable.

## ARMAGEDDON BECKONS

The intensity of violence in several areas of the city, and not just the traditional battlefields of West Belfast, was a particular feature of these disturbances. It was especially evident during the first half of 1922 when over 40 per cent of the conflict's fatalities occurred. A disproportionately high number of victims were Catholics, either the targets of Loyalist gunmen – the Belfast Protestant Association was especially active in east Belfast – or the victims of security force shootings. Loyalist snipers and invading gunmen and bombers were particularly active on the sectarian interfaces in the city's western, eastern and northern areas. The most vulnerable members of society, the young, infirm and elderly, were particularly prone to warranting the attention of snipers and bombers. Also, people travelling to and from work, or indeed, going about their normal business, especially carters and pub workers, were favourite quarries of the gunmen. Though undoubtedly many attacks were premeditated, the majority of the conflict's fatalities were the tragic victims of fate, people who simply happened to be in the wrong place at the wrong time. There were many cases of children, teenagers and old people losing their lives just outside their homes, visiting local shops, or as they played games in the street. Perhaps the most infamous instance of this type of terror was the bomb-attack in Weaver Street in February, in which over twenty children who had been playing games at the time were wounded, four of them fatally. A cousin of one of these victims recalled her family's loss:

> My cousin Katie had just started working in a mill. She lived in Weaver Street where sometimes we visited her and the rest of the family. One night she was skipping in her street when a bomb was thrown from North Derby Street. She and several other children I had met were killed or seriously injured. Her father John was a fine, big, religious man but despite his faith, he never got over the waste of such a young life.[14]

Though the suffering of the Catholic community was deep, anguish and pain was experienced across most of Belfast's community, especially its working-class. This was particularly so when the IRA's Third Northern Division shifted from a low-key strategy primarily concerned with targeting police officers, to a more proactive approach, especially in the post-Truce period. Indeed, the IRA's role during the conflict proved to be a mixture of defending their threatened community and being reluctantly dragged into a sectarian dog-fight. Despite being initially ill-equipped and poorly prepared, the Third Northern planned and executed several blatantly sectarian attacks, including bombings on the tram-cars of Protestant workers. An IRA officer, Seán Montgomery, later described his role in an attack on a shipyard workers' tram, which had been transporting them back to their homes on the Shankill Road in November 1921:

> Things were getting very bad so orders were given to bomb two shipyard trams ... In Lancaster Street, I was approached by Alf Mullan. He could not get anyone to cover him, as he had orders to do two trams. I asked him if it was an order and he said it was so I went with him ... we went off to Berry Street and in front of the Grand Central Hotel he did the job. I covered him ... Well there was a bit of a stink about it.[15]

The IRA was also involved in several attacks on police personnel, the most spectacular of which occurred in May 1922, when they temporarily took control of Musgrave Street Barracks in central Belfast. As the conflict peaked in the late spring and early summer of 1922, the IRA employed relatively new strategies,

---

**14** Interview with Sarah O'Hare in Alan Parkinson, *Belfast's unholy war: the Troubles of the 1920s* (Dublin, 2004), p. 215. **15** Seán Montgomery; quoted in Jim McDermott, *Northern divisions* (Dublin, 2001), p. 130.

such as a systematic arson campaign directed mainly at commercial properties, and the assassination of leading political opponents. Over eighty business premises were seriously damaged or destroyed in Belfast in May and June. The 'Falls firebugs', as they were nicknamed, certainly kept the city's Fire Brigade at full stretch, and although most instances of arson involved commercial premises, there were a number of other serious fires, notably at schools and picture-houses. This arson tactic was used elsewhere in Ulster, with attacks on several 'Big Houses', belonging to wealthy Anglo-Irish families, including Shane's Castle and Crebilly Castle. Political assassination was another approach adopted by increasingly desperate Republicans. Unionist MPs William Twaddell and General Sir Henry Wilson were shot dead in street attacks in Belfast and London respectively.

The intense and barbaric nature of the conflict was unparalleled in Belfast's history. Evil men on both sides competed with each other in their depravity. A young Catholic, Jack O'Hare, was beaten up by a Loyalist gang on the Albert Bridge and subsequently thrown into the River Lagan, where he drowned, while the Catholic house-keeper of a Donegall Pass doctor was beaten and set alight by another gang. Carters were singled out by snipers as they travelled through dangerous areas, and workers, many of them Protestant, were shot as they travelled to and from the shipyard, or even at their workplace, such as the three coopers who were shot dead in Little Patrick Street.

The atrocity which most appears to personify the sectarian savagery of the early 1920s was, to a degree, atypical of other violent encounters. The apparently systematic targeting of the male members of one Catholic family had not been previously experienced during the city's disturbances. Nor was the setting and social background of the unfortunate family typical of other violent incidents. Owen McMahon was a successful publican who lived in a sprawling Victorian mansion off the Antrim Road. Following the fatal shooting of two police officers in the city centre hours before, a group of five men in police uniform, wielding sledgehammers and firearms, broke their way into the McMahons' home during the early hours of 24 March 1922. Mr McMahon, his six sons and a lodger were ushered into the downstairs living-room where, after being told to 'say your prayers', they were shot by the gunmen. Owen McMahon, four of his sons and Edward McKinney, his Donegal-born bank manager, succumbed to their wounds. The youngest son, Michael (12) recalled his horror at the inquest:

> The man in the fawn coat fired. When I saw him lift his revolver I fell under the table and began to moan and pretend to be shot. There was a number of other shots but I don't know who fired them; the result was that all the others were killed or wounded.[16]

**16** PRONI H828/508.

Press condemnation of such a horrific attack was universal. Describing the scene at Kinnaird Terrace as resembling a 'slaughterhouse', the *Belfast Telegraph*'s reporter graphically recorded that

> The house smelt of fresh blood – it seemed scarcely cold as it spread in large pools and small rivers all over the room...On the other side of the fireplace lay large pools of blood – thick, heavy coagulated stuff that turned one sick with horror. In places, it was rubbed and disturbed as if someone had macerated fresh bullocks' liver and strewn it about.[17]

Yet again the Catholic community bonded in their preparation for the funerals of the victims. Kinnaird Terrace proved to be a Mecca for the city's Catholics. Patrick O'Donnell recalls that there was a constant stream of people lining Belfast's streets as the cortege set off from St Patrick's Church.[18] Political reaction to the murders was also swift. A substantial reward was offered by the Craig administration for information leading to a successful prosecution of those responsible and the furore precipitated the second Collins-Craig Pact a few days later. Although no one was ever prosecuted for these killings, persistent rumours linked them to a group of 'rogue cops' allegedly led by District Inspector William Nixon and County Inspector Richard Harrison. While evidence against individuals remains inconclusive, it is likely that such a group was responsible for the McMahon murders and several other killings, as it is impossible to explain the easy access of gunmen to renowned trouble-spots during period of curfew restriction. Certainly, the enormity of the crime's impact upon the city's Catholic community cannot be doubted. In a devout, home-loving society, the sanctity of the family home had been breached and a deliberate attempt was made to eliminate the male line of an innocent family. If anyone had doubted the depth of menace stalking the city's streets during those dark days of 1922, the events at Kinnaird Terrace on 24 March soon reminded them of their own vulnerability.

The suffering of Belfast's population eased during the autumn of 1922. This was due to a combination of factors: the internment of Republican suspects following the introduction of emergency powers legislation and the continued threat of the USC; the declining morale of IRA volunteers especially after the start of civil war in the rest of Ireland during August; and the reduced threat posed by Loyalist assassins as the Republican campaign petered out in the city.

---

17 *Belfast Telegraph*, 24 Mar. 1922.   18 Patrick O'Donnell interview; in Parkinson, *Belfast's unholy war*, p. 233.

'MIND YOURSELF ...'

The relatively brief duration of the city's conflict and the intermittent periods of calm meant that, apart from those experiencing personal tragedy, the Twenties' Troubles would not have had a life-defining impact upon Belfast children. Yet few of them, especially those growing up in the city's predominantly working-class areas, would have been unaware of the unique crisis unfolding in their midst, given the heavy military presence, police patrols and searches, the constant rattle of gunfire and thud of explosions, emergency curfew regulations and the endless warnings of anxious parents. Certainly, Belfast in the early Twenties was undeniably a dangerous place in which to grow up. Inevitably, young people were especially vulnerable in an atmosphere of civil unrest, and incidents involving the young were exceedingly frequent. More often than not children became ensnared in the violence, falling victim to indiscriminate gunfire. They could be deliberately targeted, as in the Weaver Street bombing. Many would have been aware of neighbours or friends being shot or bombed in their districts and specific incidents would live long in their memories. Everyday social movement was seriously affected during these troublesome times. Even elementary school pupils experienced the harrowing experience of being intimidated and threatened by gangs of older boys. Patrick O'Donnell, who later became a priest, recalls one such occasion:

> I remember being stopped by a gang of older Protestant boys as I left my school in Donegall Street. They took me round a corner and told me that if I didn't say 'To hell with the Pope!' I would be duffed up. I'm afraid I had to agree to their demand, though I can now only laugh at the irony.[19]

Trams, exhibiting distinctive destinations and transporting, in the main, people of one particular religious group through hostile districts, were easy and regular targets for those determined to maim and kill. Even a Saturday afternoon tram trip to the safety provided by 'neutral' city centre stores tested the nerves of schoolboy Jimmy Kelly:

> The old red and yellow coloured tramcar swayed, whined and groaned over the rails down the Falls Road. There were certain danger points when it passed Cupar Street, Northumberland Street and Dover Street, long streets leading from The Falls to the Shankill. Across these streets, at moments of tension, the reports of rifle fire rang out, as snipers on both

19 Patrick O'Donnell interview; in Parkinson, *Belfast's unholy war*, p. 180.

sides opened up. The tram speeded and clanked past these streets, as the driver crouched down on the floor which the Tramways department thoughtfully provided with a carpet of straw. There were always audible sighs of relief when the neutral Castle Junction hove in sight.[20]

Despite the disturbances raging in the city at this time, children were still able to exhibit a degree of normality in their everyday lives, managing to play together in comparative harmony. Eddie Steele and John Parkinson remembered playing together, sometimes with Catholics, on the Bog Meadows or in the Falls and Dunville Parks. They enjoyed long summer evenings on the Meadows, playing football and cricket and catching stickleback in jam-jars.[21] For many young people, the spread of street disturbances meant that they had to reassess what they did in their spare time. Sarah O'Hare, at an age when she was keen to go to dances and the music-hall, found herself restricted by the disturbances. With an abundance of free time, she soon perfected her crocheting techniques.[22]

Summer was an exciting time for children old enough to ride a bicycle and escape the dangers of Belfast for a while. A youngster could hire a bike for 6*d.* an hour in a shop in McDonnell Street and head off on a Saturday, either down the Lagan towpath to Lambeg or even Lisburn, or along the Antrim and Down coasts to Whitehead, Carrickfergus, Groomsport or Bangor. Christy Robinson often enjoyed such rides. One of his friends was Jacky Kelly, a Catholic who played with him in the streets off the Grosvenor Road and on the Bog Meadows, where his chum earned a reputation for his culinary skills, roasting welcome sausages for his exhausted mates. Christy fondly remembers his bike rides:

> I remember waiting one Saturday, rather anxiously I'll admit, outside the Clonard Monastery where Jacky was attending Mass. We eventually got together and set off cycling on two-speed gear bikes to Kilroot. Mind you, some of the hills were steep, and on a hot summer's day, the sweat would fairly lash off us.[23]

Due to the nature of their fathers' work, some children found their movement curtailed. Yet sometimes their immediate environment could more than compensate for such restrictions. Sam Jamison's 'home' was the Whitla Street Fire Station, where his father was Assistant Chief Officer. Sam attended Bingham's School in Duncairn Gardens and when there was trouble, he had to travel in an ambulance based at the station. Sam recalled that

**20** Jimmy Kelly interview; in Parkinson, *Belfast's unholy war*, p. 181. **21** Interviews with John Parkinson and Eddie Steele in Parkinson, *Belfast's unholy war*, pp 187–8. **22** Ibid., p. 188. **23** Christy Robinson interview; in Parkinson, *Belfast's unholy war*, p. 189.

> The fire station was an exciting place to be at this time, what with fire engines rushing to put out fires and the ambulances bringing in the bodies of those shot or blown up in the disturbances. They used the station as a temporary morgue and our mothers frequently had to chase us youngsters away when they were laying out the bodies.[24]

The effect of the 1920s' Troubles on the lives of ordinary people was undoubtedly profound. Obliged to carry on with the rigours of everyday life, working-class people in the city's ghettoes had to cope with a mixture of sectarian street-fighting, evictions from work and home, bombs on trams, arson attacks upon homes and business premises, and sniping attacks on their own districts. They tended to adopt a pragmatic response to the ongoing terror, combining an approach which minimized the risk of injury with one of avoiding the interruption of the routine of their everyday lives. Clearly there is a deep resonance between such experiences and feelings with those experienced by subsequent Belfast generations. One experiences an eerie déjà-vu on taking a stroll down similar Belfast streets today. Neat two-up, two-down Housing Executive properties with charming patio gardens have taken the place of the kitchen-houses of the 1920s. However, women still chat over garden walls and treat strangers with caution in Little George Street, a long narrow street linking North Queen Street and York Street. One can imagine the trepidation of policemen patrolling in the street, ever wary of preying Nationalist snipers, and of anxious mothers, concerned that the innocent play of their children would be suddenly broken by spying Loyalist gunmen in York Street. Perhaps the last word on the similarities between past and more recent conflicts in Belfast should belong to a 'veteran' of both. John Parkinson recalls that

> A lot of things then were the same as during the recent Troubles. You know, people standing around in groups on their street, discussing what had happened, who had been shot the previous evening. As youngsters we generally obeyed our parents but sometimes we couldn't help sneaking out to see what all the fuss was about. The big difference about the Twenties' Troubles was that they were over much sooner; we knew they were hard times but we didn't expect them to last for ever. But we also used to wish all the trouble would be over so we could get on with our normal lives. That hasn't really changed, has it?[25]

---

**24** Sam Jamison interview; in Parkinson, *Belfast's unholy war*, p. 187.   **25** John Parkinson interview; in Parkinson, *Belfast's unholy war*, p. 316.

# Border trouble: Unionist perceptions of and responses to the independent Irish state, 1921–39

## DENNIS KENNEDY

Intransigent Unionism and perfidious Albion have taken most of the blame for everything that has gone wrong in Northern Ireland, but it was Irish Nationalism which brought Northern Ireland into being, and Irish Nationalism was a significant factor, perhaps even the determining one, in the shaping of politics and society within the province.

James Stephens, the novelist and poet and leading figure in the Irish literary renaissance, wrote in 1916, when dramatic actions were being taken in the name of Ireland, that before Irishmen could talk of Ireland as a nation, they had to make her one: 'A nation, politically speaking, is an aggregation of people whose interests are identical; and the interests of Ulster with the rest of Ireland rather than being identical are antagonistic.' The key to bringing Ulster into an Irish nation, he argued, 'will be a watertight friendship with England, and anything that smells, however distantly, of hatred for England, will be a true menace to Ulster. We must swallow England if Ulster is to swallow us, and until that fact becomes apparent to Ireland, the Ulster problem cannot be even confronted, let alone solved.'[1]

In the five years that intervened between the writing of those words and the birth of Northern Ireland, the Ulster problem was not confronted and, among Nationalists, hatred for England reached unimaginable heights. The partition already envisaged in 1916 became inevitable, and the depth of the division between the two parts of the island proved far greater than the Government of Ireland Act had proposed.

Dark clouds were on the horizon in 1921, but were not sufficiently threatening to exclude all optimism as the people of the new province[2] went to the polls in May to elect their first parliament. The Unionist leader, Sir James Craig, however, had seen them. In an article headed 'Ulster's Last Word', he told the English readers of the *Pall Mall and Globe*, that the shuttlecock had come to rest:

> Our province has for so long been a shuttlecock in the game of English and Irish politics that even our friends have difficulty in realizing that the shuttlecock has come to rest and will fly no more. They are reluctant to

1 James Stephens, *The insurrection in Dublin* (Dublin, 1916), pp 109–10.  2 The term is used to designate Northern Ireland as a province of the United Kingdom, not to equate the six counties of Northern Ireland with the Irish province of Ulster.

adjust their minds to new conditions in which concessions by Ulster are no longer the natural escape from every Irish deadlock, and they persist, therefore, in the belief that Ulster has some magic card, some hidden card, which she can produce at the psychological moment and with it "settle the Irish question". This is pure delusion, and it would be well if that were understood at once. We have reached the limit of our concessions. There is nothing more that we can offer.[3]

The article conveys well the mixture of hope and fear with which Unionists greeted the creation of Northern Ireland as a devolved region of the United Kingdom, with its own parliament and government. The hope was that they would now, finally, be masters of their own fate. A year earlier, Captain Charles Craig had told the House of Commons at Westminster that, while Unionists had originally not wanted a regional parliament, they now saw their safety in having a parliament of their own, 'for we believe that once a parliament is set up and working well ... we should fear no one, and we feel that we should then be in a position of absolute security'.[4]

In May 1921, Sir James still shared some of his brother's hope, but he realized that while the shuttlecock seemed momentarily at rest, the game was not over. He knew that secret negotiations had started between London and the Dáil leadership – he himself had been persuaded to go and meet de Valera in Dublin in early May. He feared that the outcome of such talks would be significant alterations to the Government of Ireland Act, and therefore to the terms under which Irish self-government would come about, with, inevitably, serious implications for Northern Ireland.

He continued to hold out some hope of a peaceful settlement; Ulster Unionists, he wrote, were as anxious as anybody to work in agreement with the rest of Ireland. They would be the first to stretch out the hand of friendship, cooperation and goodwill, if violence stopped and certain other conditions were met. But in the circumstances of May 1921, he was setting a very high bar for Sinn Féin to jump:

> Cease to kill, to outrage; and learn to do well. Instead of destroying, create. Rid your borders of violence. You claim to love freedom; then allow freedom to others. You clamour for liberty; prove that you understand the meaning of the word. Work instead of agitating ... Respect the laws of God and of civilization; establish justice, civil and religious, within your borders and in your government. While controlling your own affairs, proclaim your loyalty to king and empire.

---

**3** Conclusion of *Pall Mall* article quoted in *Northern Whig*, 25 May 1921.   **4** *HC fifth Series*; vol. 127, cols 989–90.

The spectacular manner in which those hopes were dashed must have surprised even Craig. The truce of July 1921 between London and the Dáil leadership led to an immediate and serious rise in violence inside Northern Ireland and in the activity of the IRA within the boundaries of the new province. The refusal of Nationalists to take their seats in the new parliament, and of Nationalist-controlled local authorities to recognize the new administration, or to work with it, was a stark rejection of the settlement under the Government of Ireland Act. The continuation of the economic boycott of Belfast and other Northern towns, instigated, organized and financed by the Dáil ministry, and enforced by the IRA, was an assault on the commercial life of the province.

The Catholic Church's public endorsement of Nationalist rejection of Northern Ireland, through, for instance, the call by Bishop MacRory of Down and Connor in a pastoral address of May 1921 to all Catholics to vote, effectively, against the establishment of Northern Ireland,[5] Archbishop Logue's boycott of the opening of the Northern parliament and of the Lynn Committee on Education, and the refusal of Catholic teachers to accept salaries from the new administration, hardened the already clear sectarian division between Unionism and Nationalism.[6] After the establishment of the Northern state, MacRory continued to urge a policy of non-recognition.[7]

The perception of Irish Nationalism as intrinsically Catholic – and therefore anti-Protestant – was nothing new among Unionists. Home Rule had long been denounced as Rome Rule, but the events of 1921 and 1922 provided horrific evidence of the danger that a tide of militant Nationalism could pose for people whose religion identified them as its enemies. The first half of 1921 had seen a rising number of IRA atrocities against individual Protestants, particularly in the south and west of the island, widely reported in the Belfast newspapers under headings such as 'War on Protestants', or 'Reign of Terror'.

In May 1921, Archbishop D'Arcy told the Church of Ireland synod in Dublin that members of 'our church, and others, in several parts of the country – quiet, defenceless farmers for the most part – have been most cruelly killed … because it was believed their political opinions were not acceptable'.[8] Later, the Catholic Bishop of Killaloe, Dr Fogarty, deplored the fact that their Protestant fellow-countrymen had been persecuted and dealt with in a cruel and coarse manner.[9]

Far from proclaiming their loyalty to king and empire, the Sinn Féin leaders repeatedly made it clear that their demand was for total independence, for the sovereign Irish republic they had proclaimed in 1916. Their refusal to contemplate

5 Éamon Phoenix, *Northern Nationalism* (Belfast, 1994), p. 128.  6 The Lynn Committee on education reform was established in 1921 by the Minister of Education, Lord Londonderry.  7 Dennis Kennedy, *The widening gulf: northern attitudes to the independent Irish state, 1919–49* (Belfast, 1988), p. 92.  8 Ibid., p. 55.  9 *Irish Times*, 8 May 1923.

a subsidiary parliament in Dublin, with continued Irish representation at Westminster, threatened to make the Government of Ireland Act unworkable, and therefore cut at the very foundations of the new Northern institutions, which rested on that act.

Two further shocks awaited Craig and his fellow Unionists immediately after the creation of Northern Ireland. The first was Lloyd George's invitation in June to de Valera to join himself and Sir James Craig in a conference. Some sort of negotiation to end the violence had been contemplated a year earlier, and indeed Craig, then a junior member of the government in London, had been involved in discussion of such a move, but the formal invitation to the leader of what up to then had been denounced as a murder gang, to an officially convened peace conference at which he would participate alongside the Prime Minister of the United Kingdom and the Prime Minister of Northern Ireland constituted a sudden and startling bestowal of legitimacy on the leadership of insurrection. De Valera was invited as 'the chosen leader of the great majority in Southern Ireland'.

As Churchill commented, this was a sudden and complete reversal of policy, and it greatly undermined Unionist confidence, not least in the British government. Even worse was to follow when word of the proposed Boundary Commission emerged from the treaty negotiations, carrying the very real threat that Northern Ireland could be dismembered. After much soul-searching, the northern Unionists had fixed on a Northern Ireland of six counties, and this became an article of faith in the negotiations on the Government of Ireland Bill and a cornerstone of the partition settlement. Now it was brought again into question, and there were real fears that using the county boundaries as the defining units might rebound, given the Nationalist capture of Fermanagh and Tyrone county councils in the local elections of January 1920.

The depth of anger and despair among Unionists was captured by an English observer, Lilian Spender, wife of Sir Wilfrid Spender, in her diary on 16 December 1921. Having written earlier that she had felt physically ill at newspaper speculation on the contents of the treaty, she continued:

> I think the past week since the publication of the treaty has been the most depressing I have ever known over here. Up to the last, I don't think we ever really believed England would do this thing – would reward murder and treachery, treason and crime of all kinds, and penalize loyalty ... And now we know that worse is to come, and further pledges are to be broken, for two of the six counties may be taken from us. Tyrone and Fermanagh.[10]

10 Lady Spender's diary, 16 Dec. 1921. PRONI D1633/2.

The conclusion of the negotiations, the signing of the treaty and its ratification, followed by the creation of the provisional government in Dublin, brought little respite for Northern Ireland. The Boundary Commission was to hang over Unionists for another three years, like a suspended death sentence, while Nationalists regarded it as a means to the desired end of dismembering Northern Ireland and making its continued existence impossible. While the Commission still seemed to offer hope of such an outcome, Nationalists within Northern Ireland had no motive for cooperating with the new institutions, or indeed of contemplating the implications of permanent partition.

After partition, these factors continued to have a malign influence on the internal development of Northern Ireland, and, in particular, on relations between the majority Unionist community and the Nationalist minority. In addition, the events and circumstances surrounding the actual establishment of Northern Ireland and its early years had a profound impact on the Unionist psyche, and on the evolution, or lack of it, of any broader Unionist political philosophy.

The first half of 1922 saw the worst violence the region had suffered. Inter-communal sectarian fighting was part of it and, in fact, more Catholics than Protestants were killed. But there was also a sustained IRA campaign of boycott, arson and murder, backed by Collins and the new Dublin administration, explicitly aimed at the destruction of Northern Ireland.[11]

As the south slipped towards confrontation between the Irregulars of the anti-treaty faction and the forces of the Provisional Government, the violence on and in the North increased, to be halted later in 1922 only by the outbreak of full-scale civil war south of the border. Three particular elements of what was seen as a full-scale assault on the very existence of Northern Ireland had enormous impact on the Unionist community. These were the mass-kidnapping of border Loyalists in February, the sustained campaign of arson, culminating in the burning of the 'Big Houses' of Ulster in May, and, the occupation by the IRA of the Belleek-Pettigo salient in June.

The major kidnapping took place on the night of 7–8 February 1922, when gangs of armed IRA men in Fermanagh and Tyrone seized a substantial number of prominent Loyalists. Newspaper accounts said that 200 prominent Protestants, Orangemen and Special Police were kidnapped and taken across the border, though the actual figure later turned out to about one quarter of that. The news was presented dramatically, not least so in the *Tyrone Constitution* of 10 February, which required twelve separate headlines to give due weight to the events:

11 For an account of this period, see Kennedy, *The widening gulf*, ch. 5.

> Onslaught on Northern Loyalists; Dreadful Happenings on Frontier Border; Rebel Outrages on Extensive Scale; Violation of Truce and Treaty; Murders, Woundings and Wholesale Kidnappings; Tyrone, Fermanagh and Donegal Loyalist Victims; Imported Assassins from Cavan, Leitrim, Longford; Wild Night in Clogher Valley; Monaghan Moonlighters Busy; Desperadoes Captured at Enniskillen; Unionist MP's House Attacked; Tyrone Grand Master Seized.

The numbers seized, and the people they were, meant that the affair was seen as a concerted attack on the Unionist establishment. It was also clearly an act of war against the territory of Northern Ireland, something much more significant than just another 'outrage', and the *Northern Whig* headlined it 'The Invasion of Ulster'.[12] The *Newsletter* commented:

> It is difficult to express in terms of restraint the indignation which every Loyalist in Northern Ireland feels at the audacious act of war committed by armed Sinn Féin bands all along the Ulster frontier from the Clogher Valley in the east to the Donegal-Fermanagh line in the west ... [these] constitute an act of war against the British Crown of the most offensive and heinous sort, an act which, if perpetrated by an alien people, would be visited with retaliatory violence.[13]

Reports that the kidnappings were probably the work of anti-treaty units in the IRA, not authorized by Collins, did nothing to lessen Unionist anger.

The IRA campaign of arson against business premises, particularly in Belfast, continued in the first half of 1922, and was significantly extended in May to include many of the mansion residences of the gentry and aristocracy of Ulster. In a period of a few days, some eight or nine such residences were destroyed, including historic buildings like Shane's Castle at Randalstown, Garron Tower on the Antrim coast, Old Court at Strangford and Crebilly Castle near Ballymena. Many of these were owned by leading Unionist figures. Shane's Castle was the home of the O'Neills. When it was burned, the IRA ordered 82-year-old Lord O'Neill and his wife from the house at gunpoint. As their son, Sir Hugh O'Neill, was Speaker of the Northern Ireland House of Commons, the firing of the O'Neill castle was doubly significant.

The destruction of such well-known historic landmarks was shocking to the entire Unionist population, and constituted an assault on the very fabric, physical and political, of Northern Ireland. A few days later, an even more serious incident

**12** *Northern Whig*, 9 Feb. 1922.   **13** *Belfast Newsletter*, 9 Feb. 1922.

occurred, when Republican forces seized and occupied the villages of Pettigo and Belleek, and the triangle of Co. Fermanagh around them known as the Belleek salient, which shared a long border with Donegal, but was cut off from the rest of Northern Ireland by Lower Lough Erne. London played down the incident, and Churchill told the House of Commons that he did not think anything in the nature of an invasion had taken place,[14] but in the end, he and the government had to treat the incursion as 'war', and despatch artillery from Enniskillen to retake the village of Pettigo on 4 June, though a portion of Northern territory still remained in IRA hands. On 8 June, 200 men of the Manchester Regiment advanced on Belleek from Enniskillen with artillery and retook the village.

The cumulative impact of all these dramatic events was that one year after Northern Ireland came into being, the shuttlecock was again flying about, and any confidence Unionism had that the creation of a new parliament and government in Belfast meant the Irish question had been settled and Northern Ireland made permanent, was shattered. Both Craig and Carson in the run-up to the May 1921 election had begun to address publicly the question of how Northern Ireland would develop, and how relations between majority and minority might be handled, but by mid-1922, Unionism was again totally on the defensive. Its only concern was to confront and defeat the forces of Nationalism.

This chronic insecurity over the survival of the province was to remain the dominant influence on Unionist political development at least up until the Second World War. That first dramatic year cemented various Unionist perceptions of the nature of the threat, and where it might come from.

The IRA remained the obvious menace, but the new Provisional Government in Dublin, and hence the new Irish state, were now identified in Unionist minds with the IRA, both in ideology and in method. Nationalists inside Northern Ireland had given their allegiance to the Dublin regime, so too had the Catholic Church and Catholic teachers. Hence the equation that Nationalist equals Catholic equals IRA was persuasive to many within Unionism, particularly those most personally exposed to IRA violence in the border areas, and in working-class confrontation spots in Belfast and Londonderry.

Certainly, the equating of Catholicism with political if not violent Nationalism was inescapable. Nationalism was much more than a matter of identity or cultural distinctiveness – it was a rejection of the state, and a refusal to recognize the legitimacy of the province and its institutions, and to work with or participate in them.

Nationalism was disloyalty, and the consuming objective of Unionist political activity had to be its defeat. At one level, this was pursued through the Special

14 *HC Fifth series*; vol. 154, col. 1892.

Constabulary and the use of exceptional powers, but this very early period in the life of the state also indicated the extent of Unionist fear of conceding any ground at any level to Nationalists. The real threat to Northern Ireland was more probably that of piecemeal dismantling rather than physical assault. It was this which prompted the Craig government to move rapidly in 1922 to abolish proportional representation in local government elections. The Nationalist victories in Cos Fermanagh and Tyrone in 1920 had been a lesson too well learned.

The establishment of the Free State, the defeat of its Republican opponents in the Civil War, and the agreement in 1925 to bury the Boundary Commission, should, it might be supposed, have offered an opportunity for a fresh start, both within Northern Ireland and in relations between the two parts of the island. The first Nationalists to take seats in the Belfast parliament had done so in 1925, Dublin had formally accepted the border, and the governments in Dublin and Belfast had agreed to meet 'as and when necessary' to consider matters of common interest. Craig told the Commons in Belfast that he felt cordial relations had been established between north and south.[15]

But the governments never met, relations were not cordial, and the border remained the overwhelmingly dominant issue in Northern politics, and its removal the prime objective, rhetorically at least, of all southern politics. Why? Part of the explanation is that the Tripartite Agreement of December 1925 was an agreement to leave the actual line of the border unchanged, but not, certainly as far as Dublin was concerned, to accept the reality and the permanence of partition. Inside Northern Ireland, large sections of Nationalism felt that the Agreement was a massive betrayal, and were reinforced in their view that the ending of partition had to be the defining goal of their political involvement. Also, by the end of 1925, the pattern of politics on the Unionist side had already set firm. Unionism's one objective was to defend Northern Ireland, and keep it in the Union. Its internal debates and tensions, often bitter, focused on how effectively this was being managed by those newly charged with the task – the government of Northern Ireland. In a parliament in which Nationalists refused to sit, the *de facto* opposition came from those who felt Ulster was not being defended strenuously enough, who wanted tougher security measures, and who saw an enemy of the state in every Nationalist (and a Nationalist in every Catholic). With the pressure constantly from the hard-line end of the spectrum, the centre of gravity of Unionism was inevitably moving in that direction.

Despite Dublin's acceptance of the proposal for meetings of the two governments to consider matters of mutual interest, in fact to take over some of the limited functions of the now abolished Council of Ireland, there was a

---

**15** *Northern Ireland Parliamentary Debates*, vol. 6, cols 1856–63.

fundamental unwillingness in Dublin to treat Northern Ireland and its institutions as in any way on a level with it. This view lay behind the South's failure to operate the Council of Ireland, and its readiness to see it abolished. During the Tripartite negotiations, the Cosgrave government rejected a British proposal for a new joint north-south legislative body to replace the Council, on the grounds that it would constitute a limitation on the Free State's independence. This ideological reservation about treating the Northern state and its government as anything like an equal partner was no doubt one reason why the two governments never did meet.

Relevant to all these issues was the shadow of de Valera, which from the setting up of Fianna Fáil in 1926, was to loom over Ireland, north and south, for decades to come. The two general elections of 1927 demonstrated that Fianna Fáil was not just going to be a powerful political force, but that it would inevitably, one day, be in government. As it represented that considerable section of the country which had rejected the treaty, on the grounds that it did not grant a sufficient degree of independence to the Irish state, this had serious implications for Northern Ireland.

Under Cosgrave, the Free State had already begun to show its intention to use the treaty as a stepping stone to full independence and, while doing so, progressively to undo those bits of it which it could. The arrival of Fianna Fáil meant increasing pressure on Cumann na nGaedheal to follow that line, and promised yet more radical moves if and when it came to power. For Unionists, this meant that the trauma of seeing the foundation on which Northern Ireland had been built – the Government of Ireland Act – dismantled by the treaty, was now being repeated as the treaty settlement was in turn dismantled. Fianna Fáil was already promising a new constitution that would 'recognize the independence and unity of the country'.[16]

While the latter part of the 1920s and the 1930s were, compared to the early 1920s, a period of quiet and stability on the island of Ireland, they were not without their periodic shocks and alarms for Unionists. IRA attacks in November 1926 on twelve Garda stations in the Free State, resulting in the deaths of two Gardaí, followed by the proclamation of a state of emergency, and the assassination of Kevin O'Higgins the following July, were powerful reminders that the violent tradition of Irish Nationalism had survived the treaty, the Civil War and the Tripartite Agreement.

Cosgrave's firm measures to deal with the IRA were noted, and welcomed, in the North, making de Valera's freeing of IRA prisoners and abolition of military courts on coming to power in 1932 all the more shocking. Unionist concern at

**16** *Northern Whig*, 20 Aug. 1927.

the apparent resurgence of the IRA under the eyes of a sympathetic government in Dublin turned to alarm in October 1933 when Belfast experienced its first significant IRA activity for almost a decade. A policeman was shot dead, and a Unionist MP was shot and wounded.

The IRA was active in the sectarian violence of 1935 in Belfast. Twelve people died, some of them, it was widely believed, shot by the IRA. By 1936, IRA activity in the south had reached such a level that de Valera's government was obliged to abandon its sympathetic stance towards the organization, and proscribe it. Even so, IRA gunmen and bombers continued to operate in Northern Ireland. In the course of 1938 there were, according to official figures, thirty-five IRA 'outrages' in the province.[17] In January 1939, the IRA launched its bombing campaign in Britain, culminating in the Coventry bicycle explosion, which killed five people and injured sixty.

While the IRA posed no real threat to the survival of Northern Ireland, it was a constant reminder to Unionists of the murderous lengths to which Nationalism, or the more ardent proponents of it, would go to in pursuit of their goals. Nor was the IRA an external threat – it drew its Northern membership from the Nationalist areas of Northern Ireland, particularly Belfast and the border districts. Unionists did not have to be entirely paranoid to wonder if, possibly, their Catholic neighbour might be a member.

Alongside the obvious rise in IRA activity, there was also in the 1930s a significant rise in the volume of rhetorical Nationalism. In March 1934, Seán T. O'Kelly was reported in the *Belfast Newsletter* as declaring that Dublin would use every effort to establish a Republic for the thirty-two counties of Ireland: 'That is our aim and if the gun is necessary, the people have the government to direct the army, and they have the volunteer force behind them.'[18] This was not the bravado of an IRA agitator – O'Kelly was vice-president to de Valera in the Free State executive; in other words, he was the deputy head of government. The explicit claim to the territory of Northern Ireland in de Valera's new Constitution of 1937 was a formal reiteration, at the highest level, of Irish Nationalism's refusal to accept the legitimacy of Northern Ireland. While such claims could be treated with contempt, Craig, now Craigavon, told the Unionist standing committee in January 1938 that 'at the same time, they provide an object lesson as to the lengths which Republican leaders are prepared to go if they had the authority and power'.[19] The following week, the same paper carried the headline 'de Valera's new bid for All-Ireland Republic' over its report of the news that de Valera had already started negotiations with London, and that he would be in London for a formal conference with Chamberlain to discuss 'outstanding questions which

**17** *Northern Whig*, 15 Dec. 1938.   **18** *Belfast Newsletter*, 28 Mar. 1934.   **19** *Northern Whig*, 7 Jan. 1938.

affect relations between the two countries' with partition definitely on the agenda.[20]

Craigavon's response was to call a general election as a means of publicly reasserting Unionist rejection of any such claims, and its determination to resist them. Every election held during his long premiership was a 'border' election; that is, it was called to answer some real or perceived threat to Ulster – whether it was the Boundary Commission in 1925 or the advent of de Valera in 1933. A bonus of such an approach was that it put his right-wingers and other dissenting Unionists on the defensive, and enabled him to see off any opposition from within.

It also meant that the minority community's political involvement was regularly refocused on the issue of partition, and developed little beyond disgruntled Nationalism. In 1932, Nationalist members again boycotted the Northern parliament and, for the rest of the decade, they pursued a policy of what has been called 'intermittent and erratic abstentionism'.[21] Many Nationalists, another historian has commented, continued to flaunt their disloyalty, and at best their attitude was one of surly resentment.[22]

When the Belfast parliament presented Craig with a silver cup in 1925 to congratulate him on the Tripartite Agreement, it was inscribed 'Not an Inch'.[23] The obvious reference was to 'not an inch' of territory lost to Northern Ireland, but the term is a fitting description of what was often the Unionist mindset towards the minority community and its complaints, requests and demands.

It was seen right at the beginning, in the abolition of PR for local elections in 1922, a move which in some instances hurt Unionists more than Nationalists, but which was motivated by a determination to do everything possible to preserve, or recapture, Unionist advantage at every level of representation. The same mentality later manifested itself in reorganization of local electoral boundaries to maintain Unionist control of, for instance, Londonderry, and in retaining the restricted franchise and property votes, and in the abolition in 1929 of PR for elections to the Northern Ireland parliament.

There was little echo in all this of Craig's more statesmanlike approach in 1921, when he had urged Unionists, at a meeting in the Ulster Reform Club, to 'remember that the rights of the minority must be sacred to the majority ... it will only be by broad views, tolerant ideas and a real desire for liberty of conscience that we here can make an ideal of the parliament and the executive'.[24] A week earlier, Carson, in a farewell speech as Unionist leader, had told a meeting

20 *Northern Whig*, 13 Jan. 1938.   21 Jonathon Bardon, *A history of Ulster* (Belfast, 1992), p. 511.   22 Michael Laffan, *The partition of Ireland, 1911–1925* (Dublin, 1983), p. 108.   23 St John Ervine, *Craigavon*, p. 507.   24 *Belfast Newsletter*, 8 Feb. 1921.

in Duncairn, in north Belfast, that he would be 'ashamed to lead a party which persecuted any man for his religion'.[25]

In the event, the refusal of both northern Nationalists and the new southern state to accept the partition settlement, or to recognize its institutions and work with them, coupled with the violent assault on people and property inside Northern Ireland in the early months of its existence, and the real threat posed by the Boundary Commission, left little room in Unionist thinking for broad views and tolerant ideas towards those they saw as the enemy within.

What they failed to recognize was that their real long-term interest, the security and stability of Northern Ireland, depended as much on winning the assent of a least a portion of the minority as it did on defeating the IRA, or frustrating the machinations of Dublin.

Apportioning blame is not the business of history, and over-concern with it can often obscure the real nature of long-standing problems. The United Kingdom, and in the process Ireland, was partitioned in 1921 by a combination of territorial Nationalism – a preoccupation with the physical island of Ireland – and blind devotion to a concept of Irishness almost entirely defined as the negation of Britishness, or more precisely Englishness, just as much as, if not more than, by the ignorance and bigotry that doubtless existed among Unionists.

**25** *Belfast Newsletter*, 4 Feb. 1921.

# 1932: a case-study in polarization and conflict

## PETER COLLINS

### INTRODUCTION

This essay looks at 1932, a year which in many respects may be seen as a coming of age for Northern Ireland, which had been in existence for just over a decade. It considers critically the major issues which arose during the year, all of which were contentious and indicators of how relations stood between the two major communities and both parts of the island. These include the first electoral victory of Eamon de Valera, religious controversy surrounding the 1,500th anniversary of St Patrick's mission, and the government's response to the Depression, including the Outdoor Relief Riots. It was also a year of tremendous celebrations for each community, with the Eucharistic congress and the opening of Stormont. We begin with a snapshot of the two communities in 1932. The picture that emerges is of a society that continues to be deeply polarized.

### UNIONISTS

Craigavon and his government had weathered the storms of partition, insurgency, and inter-communal strife in the early 1920s, but by the 1930s Unionists were masters in their own house. The Westminster government had given them what amounted to carte blanche with internal matters. The Government of Ireland Act of 1920 and the Anglo-Irish Agreement of 1921 were designed to finally banish the conflict in Ireland from the Westminster agenda. Indeed, 'hands-off Northern Ireland' had become a de facto convention for the Imperial government. Northern Ireland was financed by an annual Westminster subvention in return for an 'Imperial Contribution', which had dwindled to £10,000 by the 1930s. This, along with step-by-step social provision, meant that the North was better off economically than the rest of Ireland. Unionists had at first been lukewarm about being ruled differently from the rest of the UK. They feared that this would weaken the link with Westminster and in time lead to a drift into a united Ireland. However, they now realized that security was better in their own hands, with the RUC, the B-Specials and control of appointments to the judiciary. The draconian Special Powers Act, introduced in 1922, and renewed annually, was made permanent in 1933 by the Minister of Home Affairs, Dawson Bates. In 1963, the Justice Minister of South Africa, Hendrik Verwoerd, when introducing a new coercion bill, said 'he would be willing to exchange all the legislation of this sort for one clause of the Northern Ireland Special Powers Act'.[1] Craigavon, himself, did not exercise tight control over his government. Over the years, he became less willing to rein in members of his own government who were openly anti-Catholic. Unionists were still concerned about the threat from the IRA. They feared being eventually outnumbered through the higher Catholic birth-rate and migration from the Free State, and ultimately being voted into a united Ireland. As well, they were never fully confident that the British government would not sell them out.

Government and the Unionist-dominated media were hand in glove. The *Belfast Telegraph*, the *Northern Whig* and the *Newsletter* were effectively government organs, and their proprietors and editors were part of the Unionist establishment. Thomas Moles, editor of the *Telegraph*, was an MP in both parliaments and was Northern Ireland Deputy Speaker. He was succeeded in that office in 1937 by Sir Robert Lynn, editor of the *Whig* until 1929.[2] Like the Unionist provincial weeklies, English papers were generally sympathetic to the government. BBC radio in Northern Ireland invariably was supportive of the status quo. Its second Regional Director, Gerald Beadle, wrote

> I was invited to become a member of the Ulster Club, where almost daily I met members of the government ... and Lord Craigavon ... was a keen supporter of our work. In effect, I was made a member of the Establishment.[3]

He wrote to Lord Reith, in 1927, that the BBC's position would be 'strengthened immensely if we can persuade the Northern Ireland government to look upon us as their mouthpiece'.[4] His attitude continued with his successor, from 1932, George Marshall: 'Influenced by the local political situation ... Marshall, adopted an unfriendly attitude to the state south of the border.'[5]

With the election victory in 1932 of de Valera, the Unionists' bête noire, it seemed that their worst nightmare had come true. Elements of the IRA had supported Fianna Fáil in the election. The inclusion of Ulstermen Seán MacEntee and Frank Aiken, former 'gunmen', in the cabinet and the release of IRA prisoners seemed only to confirm this. Graphic newspaper reports in March 1932 of

---

**1** Campaign for Social Justice in Northern Ireland, *Northern Ireland: the plain truth*, 2 ed. (Dungannon, 1969), p. 3. **2** Dennis Kennedy, *The widening gulf: northern attitudes to the independent Irish state, 1919–49* (Belfast, 1988), p. 14. **3** Gillian McIntosh, *The force of culture, Unionist identities in twentieth-century Ireland* (Cork, 1999), p. 71. **4** Ibid. **5** Rex Cathcart, *The most contrary region: the BBC in Northern Ireland, 1924–1984* (Belfast, 1984), p. 5.

IRA platoons openly parading in the streets of Dublin, the enlisting of volunteers, and 30,000 people welcoming the released IRA prisoners, all spread alarm in the North.[6] Unionists feared that de Valera would next move against partition. His dismantling of the treaty, with the removal of the Oath of Allegiance, the downgrading of the status of the Governor General, the refusal to pay land annuities to Britain and the resulting Economic War, all appeared to justify these fears. The two-way imposition of duties between Ireland and Britain, arising out of the Economic War, affected north-south trade, especially along the border. Most hard hit were Protestant farmers in Donegal who appealed for help to the northern government. But there was nothing they could or would do for their abandoned brethren.

NATIONALISTS

The realization that partition was permanent finally dawned on northern Nationalists around the mid-1920s. Fr Philip O'Doherty's 1917 prophesy that they would be abandoned 'to the hands of our unsleeping relentless hereditary enemies' had come to pass with a vengeance.[7] The death of Collins and the turning inwards of the southern government, after the civil war, had left northern Nationalists to their own devices. This was abruptly brought home to them with the suppression of the Boundary Commission report. Nationalist non-participation in the Belfast parliament and the reform of local government and education had only given their opponents a free hand. The gerrymandering of local government closed off the well-spring of jobs and housing to Nationalists, even in areas where they were in a majority. At central government level, a systematic discrimination and a glass ceiling operated for Catholics in the civil service. G.C. Duggan, a Protestant former Northern Ireland Comptroller and Auditor-General, wrote that as Dawson Bates harboured

> such a prejudice against Catholics that he made it clear to his Permanent Secretary that he did not want his most juvenile clerk or typist, if a Papist, assigned for duty to his ministry, what could we expect when it came to filling posts in the judiciary, clerkships of the crown and peace and crown solicitors.[8]

6 Kennedy, *The widening gulf*, p. 197.   7 Éamon Phoenix, 'Northern Nationalists, Ulster Unionists and the development of partition, 1900–21' in Peter Collins (ed.), *Nationalism and Unionism: conflict in Ireland, 1885–1921* (Belfast, 1994), p. 117.   8 CSJNI, *Northern Ireland: the plain truth*, p. 35.

In the private sector, largely dominated by Unionist employers, discrimination was also rife. The security apparatus was invariably aimed at Nationalists. Despite one third of police places being reserved for them, the number of Catholics in the RIC was fast diminishing, due in part to the retirement of former RIC officers. There was also widespread intimidation or hostility within the Catholic community to would-be recruits. Equally, the RUC was perceived as a 'cold house' for Catholics, given the attitude of many Protestant officers. Furthermore, Nationalists feared the B-Specials, regarding them as the paramilitary wing of Unionism.

With the overwhelming built-in Unionist majority, Nationalist politicians had never any electoral possibility of replacing the government. Led by Joseph Devlin MP, until his death in 1934, they had only entered the northern parliament, in 1925, at the behest of the hierarchy, to support Catholic education. Devlin and Cahir Healy were MPs in both Belfast and Westminster. Whenever they tried to raise Northern Ireland matters at Westminster they were ruled out of order. In the Belfast parliament, if they attempted to speak on matters reserved for Westminster, which accounted for £10 million out of the £11.5 million budget, the same happened. The only Nationalist bill ever to become law was the Wild Birds Act 1931. In 1932, after being silenced by the Stormont Speaker during the king's speech, Devlin reacted with bitterness:

> I believe this is the last time we shall meet in this House ... My colleagues and I who represent democracy here have no reason to rejoice at the years we have been here ... You had opponents willing to cooperate. We did not seek office. We sought service. We were willing to help. But you rejected all friendly offers. You refused to accept cooperation ... You went on, on the old political lines, fostering hatreds keeping one third of the population as if they were pariahs in the community, refusing to accept support from any class but your own and relying on those religious differences and difficulties so that you could remain in office for ever.[9]

On 11 May 1932, when Cahir Healy was again ruled out of order, all the Nationalist MPs walked out, leaving only Jack Beattie of Labour and two Independent Unionists, Tommy Henderson and J.W. Nixon. Having given up on Stormont, the Nationalists tried to persuade de Valera to admit northern MPs to Dáil Éireann, but to no avail. De Valera's sense of realpolitik appeared, for the time being, to rule out an active assault on partition. While this had a dispiriting

9 *Northern Ireland Parliamentary Debates*, vol. 14, cols 44–5.

effect on Nationalists, Unionists were not prepared to let down their guard concerning de Valera.

Catholic newspapers, the *Irish News*, the *Irish Independent* and the *Irish Press*, the latter founded in 1932 by de Valera, and a number of provincial weeklies, had a symbiotic relationship with the Nationalists. Radio Athlone, which began broadcasting in 1932, became the station of choice for many northern Nationalists, rekindling their faltering sense of national identity. They trusted the 'Athlone' news service over that of the BBC. Athlone broadcast live GAA matches, music and other aspects of Irish culture. Irish language broadcasts were a boon for enthusiasts, given their total blackout on BBC. The high point of the broadcasting year came in September with the All-Ireland GAA finals. The iconic commentator Micheál O'Hehir became a household name. In stark contrast, BBC Regional Director, George Marshall, suspended GAA results in 1934. This was because of 'numerous complaints ... Lord Craigavon, intervened and ... it was decided to give up broadcasting such results on the grounds that they were hurting the feelings of the large majority of people in Northern Ireland'.[10]

RELIGIOUS CONTROVERSY

Ancient and vituperative religious antipathy permeated all sections of Irish society. The Protestant and Catholic Churches had a very strong influence, reflecting the high rate of church attendance in both communities. A highly charged political campaign by Protestant clergy led to the 1930 Education Act. As Craigavon, who was largely its architect, announced in parliament, the act made schools 'safe for Protestant' children. Compulsory bible instruction was introduced into state schools and the Protestant Churches were given control of teacher appointments. Under the act, Catholic schools were given funding, though at a lower rate. On 24 March 1932, the Protestant Churches were given a major presence on the Board of Stranmillis Training College. At the Ulster Teachers' Union annual conference the following day, a delegate attacked the government's 'abject surrender' on Stranmillis: 'We are more clerical-ridden in the North than the people of the South, about whom we have been talking for years as priest-ridden.'[11]

The centenary of Catholic Emancipation in 1929 had been celebrated in the south with great circumstance and close identification of Church and State. This alienated Protestants, particularly in the north. Cardinal MacRory, a strong Nationalist and native of Ballygawley, Co. Tyrone, acerbically commented in his 1929 Lenten pastoral address, 'Some may regard the right then secured of sitting

10 Cathcart, *The most contrary region*, p. 67.   11 *Irish News*, 26 Mar. 1932.

in a foreign parliament as but another step towards our country's denationaliza-
tion ... while others again may maintain that especially here in the Six Counties,
we are not emancipated yet'.[12] 1932 had been fixed as the 1,500th anniversary of
the arrival of St Patrick as a missionary. Protestants generally were uncomfortable
with the fusion of Catholicism and Nationalism surrounding the patron saint. In
1931, Archdeacon W.S. Kerr published *The independence of the Celtic church in
Ireland*, which covered the period from St Patrick to *c.*1500. In this, he cogently
argued the claims of the Church of Ireland to the succession of Patrick and the
early Celtic church, which he described as independent of the See of Rome.
Catholics regarded this as a late-coming usurpation of their history and tradition.
A lecture was given in Armagh, by Revd S.J. Ryan SJ on 17 December 1931, to
refute the archdeacon's thesis. Ryan's thrust was that St Patrick had been sent to
Ireland under the auspices of Rome and that only the Catholic Church stood in
unbroken line to the Celtic Church. Cardinal McRory, chairing, in a vote of
thanks, stated in tendentious terms that the lecturer had given them

> abundant reasons for the belief of their forefathers that St Patrick founded
> in Ireland the Church in union with Rome ... I confess I find it very hard
> to treat seriously those of the separated brethren who are now trying to
> pose as the rightful heirs of St Patrick and the early Irish Church. I fear
> that what I have to say may give offence, but I cannot help that ... When
> they are not content to plod along quietly in comfortable enjoyment of the
> livings and other property of which the Catholic Church of Ireland was
> robbed, but to go on to pose as the rightful heirs of our ancient and
> glorious Church and the true representatives of Christ's Church in this
> island it becomes the clear if painful duty of me in my position as head of
> the Church here to speak out plainly. I say that the Protestant Church in
> Ireland – and the same is true of the Protestant Church anywhere else – is
> not only not the rightful representative of the early Irish Church, but it is
> not even a part of the Church of Christ ... It appeared in these islands in
> the sixteenth century, principally, through the action of a lustful monarch,
> who was also a cruel and heartless husband, but for ten centuries (from
> AD500 to 1500) there was not even a semblance of a Protestant Church to
> be found here or anywhere else on earth.[13]

Naturally, it fell to Archdeacon Kerr, a future Bishop of Down and Dromore, and
sometime Grand Chaplain of the Grand Orange Lodge of Ireland, to reply in the
newspapers:

---

**12** Oliver Rafferty, *Catholicism in Ulster, 1603–1983: an interpretive history* (London, 1994), pp 229–30. **13**
*Northern Whig*, 18 Dec. 1931.

the pitifully narrow and uncharitable bigotry of his Eminence ... (in) the
Christmas season ... His offence cannot be said to be an exceptional lapse.
In a Christmas message ... He writes that 'The Catholics of the Six
Counties cannot reasonably be expected to be enthusiastic about the
progress of the State or the success of its industries'. ... This gentleman's
*odium theologicum* evidently extends in a sinister way to non-theological
affairs ... All this puerile exclusiveness is only in keeping with the
medieval arrogance of his Church ... For any Christian body to claim the
exclusive presence of Christ and deny it to all others is intolerance carried
to the point of frantic absurdity. It is blasphemy against the Holy Spirit ...
To them, the machinery is all-important. Their religion centres on the
outward framework, whereas in the Gospel of Jesus it is the spirit that
matters ... The Greek Church, Coptic Church and Abyssinian Church
have continuity of organization from early ages. That can go with dead
formality and superstition of all kinds. Organization and so-called apos-
tolic succession may be preserved and the distinctive values of Christianity
lost and defaced.

The archdeacon went on a 'plain-speaking' offensive of his own:

The cardinal's church has invented new unscriptural dogmas ... such as
the Mass ... transubstantiation; ... purgatory; invocation of saints; vener-
ation of relics; obedience to the Roman pontiff ... Mariolatry; ... A new
dogma of the Immaculate Conception was manufactured in 1854 and one
of Infallibility of the Pope in 1870 ... how silly is Cardinal MacRory's
account of the Reformation and his dragging in of the name of Henry
VIII, who spent his life persecuting upholders of Protestant doctrines, and
who left money for masses to be said for his soul. At the Reformation, the
novel corruptions of Romanism were repudiated and a return made to the
primitive truth and practice of the Church of Christ.[14]

Kerr, in a second article, countering Ryan's lecture, denied that Patrick had been
commissioned by Rome and that the Celtic church he founded was in direct
communion with the Holy See. He stressed the independence of the Celtic
Church, evidencing its position at the Synod of Whitby in AD664, which he
argued was more about rejection of Rome's hegemony than simply disputation
of the Paschal controversy and the style of tonsure. No doubt relishing the
publicity that the controversy had generated, he exhorted his readers to consult
his book further.[15]

14 *Northern Whig*, 21 Dec. 1931.   15 *Northern Whig*, 23 Dec. 1931.

The controversy rumbled on into the summer. The Presbyterian Moderator, at the General Assembly, denounced the cardinal's statement as an 'astonishing piece of medievalism'.[16] The following resolution was placed before the Twelfth of July demonstrations:

> We emphatically protest against the arrogant, intolerant and un-Christian pretensions fulminated by Cardinal MacRory and the clerical and lay spokesmen of the Church of Rome against the Protestant Churches of Ireland, and we repudiate with all indignation his, and their, attacks on Protestantism, which we hold is the essence of civil and religious liberty. These attacks show the unchanging bigotry of Rome.[17]

This religious dichotomy took concrete shape with separate anniversary memorials to the patron saint at Saul, near Downpatrick. Patrick preached his first sermon there, using the shamrock as a simile for the Trinity. He also built his first church in the vicinity. The Church of Ireland erected a small church on the site in the Celtic-revival style with a round tower attached. The Catholic Church installed an imposingly large statue of the saint, attired as a bishop, on Sliabh Padraig above Saul. This national Catholic monument was unveiled by Cardinal MacRory.

## THE EUCHARISTIC CONGRESS

Against this ill-natured background, the 31st Eucharistic congress took place in Dublin, from 21 to 26 June 1932. Like the Olympics, they take place in a different city throughout the world, usually coinciding with an anniversary relevant to that venue. Eucharistic congresses are attended by leading churchmen and many thousands of international visitors and confer prestige on the host nation. The congress in Dublin, commemorating the 1,500th anniversary of Patrick's mission, was an enormous success even by international standards. De Valera, who had been excommunicated for earlier IRA activities, appeared throughout the proceedings in tune with leading churchmen. With ministers of state and the armed forces involved in the events, he used the congress to establish the Catholic nature of his government. Dublin was spruced up as never before, even in areas of extreme poverty where outdoor altars and shrines were lovingly erected by working-men. Cutting-edge technology was used in lighting, skywriting and sound amplification. The new Radio Athlone came on stream to broadcast the

**16** *Northern Whig*, 7 June 1932.  **17** *Northern Whig*, 2 July 1932.

proceedings to the over 30,000 radio licence-holders in the Irish Free State and
beyond. The pope's message to the congress, and the memorable rendition of
*Panis Angelicus* by John McCormack at the Pontifical High Mass in the Phoenix
Park, were relayed across Ireland and to the BBC and stations in Europe. The
memory of the congress and its impact on those present would take a long time
to recede. Although the north was directly out of the congress loop, an estimated
100,000 northern pilgrims attended. There were many street shrines throughout
Catholic working-class areas of Belfast, emulating those in Dublin. To mitigate
Catholic Belfast's sense of remoteness from the congress, the *Irish News* organized
a live relay of the Pontifical High Mass from Phoenix Park to Corrigan Park, in
the west of the city.[18] Cardinal Lauri, the special papal legate to the congress,
escorted by civic guards, visited Newry and Armagh, where he was mobbed by
vast crowds. In Armagh, he received an address from the Council.[19]

Eucharistic congresses by definition stress the doctrine of Transubstantiation.
The Reformation had largely been a refutation of this and it is still a main point
of rupture between Catholics and Protestants. Indeed, the spectacle of Ian Paisley
waving the Host at the Oxford Union caused a stir in 1967. Eucharistic congresses
are also professions of loyalty to the pope and his infallibility. In contrast,
Protestantism lays stress on the primacy of conscience and personal relationship
with God. The Protestant world could only ever manifest at best diffidence
towards the Eucharistic congress, though some Unionist papers did marvel at the
spectacle. Throughout the congress week, Catholic newspapers made constant
reference to 'the one true Church'. In council chambers, Unionists objected to
Nationalist councillors wearing robes at the congress. In Derry, the gerrymandered Unionist majority forbade it. With the already heightened tension of the
marching season, congress arches and flags were pulled down by Unionist extremists in Dungannon and Enniskillen.[20] Resolutions at the 1932 'Twelfth' railed
against 'Romish influences and Papal power' in the South, and 'the idolatry of
the Eucharistic congress'.[21] Special congress trains were stoned at Lurgan and
Portadown and passengers were attacked while alighting at Belfast, Larne and
Ballymena. In Larne, hymn-singing pilgrims were spat on and jeered and
attempts made to snatch their banners, while boarding a specially chartered ship
bound for Dublin.[22] Sir Edward Archdale, Unionist cabinet minister, speaking at
the 'Twelfth' demonstration, condemned 'the silly attacks on inoffensive people
going to a great religious festival [which have] done our cause great harm'.[23] Due
to pressure from Dawson Bates, magistrates were obliged to impose light
sentences or bail on convicted attackers. In a letter to Craigavon, Bates wrote 'I

**18** *Irish News*, 27 June 1932.   **19** *Irish News*, 29 June 1932.   **20** *Irish News*, 21 June 1932.   **21** Kennedy,
*The widening gulf*, p. 166.   **22** *Irish News*, 27 June 1932.   **23** Rafferty, *Catholicism in Ulster*, p. 235.

do not want when the new parliament house is opened … to have the government handicapped by having 70 or 80 young fellows in gaol'.[24] Thus, while the Congress was a great success for the Catholic Church and de Valera's government, it left relations in the north even more fractured. For Unionists, the closeness of church and state revealed during the congress was the fulfilment of 'Home Rule is Rome Rule', and this more than ever underlined the efficacy of partition.

## THE GOVERNMENT AND THE ECONOMIC CRISIS

In 1932, the Depression had reached crisis point across the world. That year Roosevelt was elected US President with a 'New Deal' to tackle the Depression. The British government eventually introduced the Special Areas Act to deal with unemployment in the regions. The Unionist government had no consistent remedial programme. They had hoped for favourable concessions at the Ottawa Economic Conference in 1932, but, being only part of the overall UK delegation, they got few concessions. Craigavon habitually dispensed patronage on journeys through Unionist areas in the north, more in the manner of an oriental potentate than a democratic leader. Thus, he would grant a local request, such as a new road, to the consternation of his Minister of Finance, Hugh Pollock, and Wilfred Spender, Head of the Civil Service, both advocates of severe retrenchment.[25]

In 1932, the government's economic lethargy led to challenges, from left and right, with the Outdoor Relief agitation and the rise of the Ulster Protestant League (UPL). The UPL, established in 1931, attacked the government both for inaction on employment and for being soft on Catholicism. The League proposed that, particularly during the recession, unemployed Protestants should be given priority in jobs. It also complained about Catholics in the RUC and the Civil Service. It opposed the Outdoor Relief Strike, claiming that it was a front for 'the communist Sinn Féin element to attempt to start a revolution in our province'.[26] The government, concerned at the growing challenge from the UPL, moved to shore up support among the Protestant working-class. It revitalized the Ulster Unionist Labour Association and ministers used Orange platforms to make increasingly hard-line speeches. In February 1932, Sir Basil Brooke proclaimed that 'The fight is only beginning and it will have to go on until Italy and the Church of Rome are submerged in the waters of the Mediterranean.'[27] At

24 Patrick Buckland, *The factory of grievances: devolved government in Northern Ireland, 1921–39* (Dublin, 1979), pp 219–20.  25 Paul Bew, Peter Gibbon and Henry Patterson, *Northern Ireland, 1921–1994: political forces and social classes* (London, 1995), p. 63.  26 Paddy Devlin, *Yes we have no bananas: outdoor relief in Belfast, 1920–39* (Belfast, 1981), p. 138.  27 Rafferty, *Catholicism in Ulster*, p. 232.

the 12 July demonstration at Poyntzpass, Craigavon made the statement: 'Ours is a Protestant government and I am an Orangeman.'[28] On 30 September, he further declared: 'I do not care a snap of my fingers so long as I have the staunch, loyal and Protestant majority at my back in the Ulster parliament and I will carry on as I have begun.'[29] Ministers began a campaign of scape-goating Catholics for high Protestant unemployment. They targeted cross-border migration both as a threat to jobs and the security of the state. For several years, this was to be the government's main response to the economic crisis. The most notorious of such speeches was made by Brooke at the 1933 'Twelfth' demonstration at Newtownbutler:

> a great number of Protestants employed Roman Catholics ... He ... had not a Roman Catholic about his own place ... He would point out that the Roman Catholics were endeavouring to get in everywhere and were out with all their force and might to destroy the power and constitution of Ulster. There was a definite plot to overpower the vote of Unionists in the north. He would appeal to Loyalists, therefore, wherever possible to employ Protestant lads and lassies ... Roman Catholics ... had got too many appointments for men who were really out to cut their throats if opportunity arose.[30]

Times had changed from his statement in 1922 that 'it does not matter what his religion was as long as he was a good man and knew his job'.[31] Brooke made several speeches, in a similar vein, and his career flourished. At Stormont, Craigavon gave unqualified support to Brooke. 'He spoke entirely on his own when he made the speech ... but there is not one of my colleagues who does not entirely agree with him, and I would not ask him to withdraw one word'.[32] Indeed, Craigavon himself went down this same road, saying that 'employment of disloyalists entering Northern Ireland is prejudicial not only to the interests of law and order but also to the prior claims of Ulster-born citizens seeking employment'.[33] Nationalists naturally saw in this as an economic boycott. Brooke was inevitably dubbed 'Captain Boycott' by the *Irish News*.[34] Investigations by Hugh Pollock showed that there was no pattern of mass infiltration by 'disloyalists' from the south. He conveyed this privately to Craigavon. Nevertheless, the assertions continued to be 'sedulously circulated', in Pollock's phrase, and the discrimination against Catholics continued.[35] The Ulster Protestant League had

**28** *Irish News*, 13 July 1932.   **29** *Irish News*, 17 Nov. 1932.   **30** Brian Barton, *Brookeborough: the making of a prime minister* (Belfast, 1988), p. 78.   **31** A.M. Kehoe, *History makers of 20th-century Ireland* (Dublin, 1989), p. 138.   **32** Barton, *Brookeborough*, p. 80.   **33** Ibid.   **34** Ibid., p. 79.   **35** Éamon Phoenix, *Northern Nationalism, Nationalist politics, partition and the Catholic minority in Northern Ireland, 1890–1940* in effect acted as a ginger group, pushing the government in a more extreme direction. As such, there was no longer a need for it. League members were heavily involved in the 1935 riots and in the same year they gained seats in local elections. By the end of the 1930s, the UPL had largely run out of steam. By then, the government to a great extent had stolen its clothes.

The bankruptcy of the government's economic policies was thrown into sharp relief in the ODR crisis in October 1932. It had displayed its lack of concern by having a six-month summer parliamentary recess. During this, the distress in the city reached crisis proportions. A special one-day sitting held on 30 September was solely to discuss arrangements for the opening of Stormont. Beattie and Henderson attempted to raise the unemployment crisis, only to be silenced by the Speaker. Beattie hurled the mace at the Speaker, shouting 'I absolutely refuse to sit in this house and indulge in hypocrisy while the people are starving outside.'[36] The two MPs walked out, leaving Nixon a one-man opposition. The Poor Law system in Belfast could no longer cope with the massive level of unemployment in the city. When the meagre unemployment benefit was exhausted, the choice for many was the workhouse or outdoor relief, in which men were assigned to 'task work' such as road-mending. Belfast paid the lowest rate in the UK at 12*s.* a week, whereas, for example, in Glasgow it was 25*s.* and in Bradford it was 26*s.* Not everyone qualified for outdoor relief, and those who did not were given food vouchers. They could not pay rent or gas bills with these. Relief was subject to humiliating means tests, forcing people to sell wedding rings or furniture before they could qualify.

With a few exceptions, the Board of Guardians, who administered the system, believed that poverty was largely self-inflicted and that the poor were out to swindle the rate-payers. Being mainly Unionists, they were also influenced in this opinion by the fact that 60 per cent of applicants were Catholic. In 1929, their chairwoman, Lily Coleman, made the statement that there 'was no poverty under the blankets'.[37] During the Eucharistic congress, while condemning 'dole-seekers and transitional benefits recipients', she claimed that 'there was not such distress in the city, judging from the street decorations this week'.[38]

Desperation made strange bedfellows of the unemployed Protestants and Catholics who united to demand reform, under the leadership of a Catholic, Tommy Geehan, of the Communist Revolutionary Workers Group. The relief workers went on strike on 3 October, but the guardians refused to make improvements. A protest march to the workhouse, planned for 11 October, went ahead although banned. The police attacked the marchers, while assembling in their

(Belfast, 1994), p. 376.   **36** *Irish News*, 1 Oct. 1932.   **37** Jonathan Bardon, *Belfast: an illustrated history* (Belfast, 1995), p. 215.   **38** *Irish News*, 23 June 1932.

separate districts. Riots ensued in all of the working-class areas and many were injured. The police moved strongly into the Falls area, where they opened fire, shooting two men dead. The funerals were attended by huge numbers from all the affected areas. Dawson Bates now feared losing control of the situation. Protestant clergy demanded positive action by the authorities. The government forced the guardians to greatly increase the rate of relief and remove the humiliating conditions. This was accepted by the men. It had been a great victory for solidarity across the sectarian divide. The euphoria and unity did not last long. The government and the Unionist media moved quickly to press Protestant workers back into their sectarian redoubt. Craigavon deliberately raised the bogey of Republicanism: 'if the mischief-makers who had come into Belfast had any plans ... towards obtaining a Republic: they were doomed to disappointment'.[39] The Catholic Church was scathing about communist influence. For a few years, some Belfast Protestant involvement with the RWG continued. In 1934, a Protestant group from Belfast marched at the annual Wolfe Tone commemoration at Bodenstown, Co. Kildare. However, they became involved in an undignified affray with Republican stewards over unauthorized banners. So much for Tone's 'Brotherhood of affection between Protestant, Catholic and Dissenter'. That the working-class remained as polarized as ever was abundantly clear during the July 1935 riots in Belfast.


## THE OPENING OF STORMONT


The opening of the new parliament building on 16 November 1932 was mired in controversy. Stormont was the gift of the Imperial government. Arnold Thornley, the architect, originally planned a domed building, with civil service offices on either side. This scenario, resembling the Capitol in Washington, was abandoned due to cut-backs in the Depression. The builders, Stewart and Partners Ltd, the family firm of W.J. Stewart, Unionist MP for South Belfast, also built the Royal Courts of Justice in Belfast, completed in 1933, and also a gift from the British government. Both buildings could equally fit E.M. Forster's description in 1936 of Belfast City Hall as 'a costly Renaissance pile which shouts "Dublin can't beat me" from all its pediments and domes'.[40] Stormont was the expression in stone of the northern conflict. For Hugh Pollock, Minister of Finance, it was 'the outward and visible proof of the permanence of our institutions; that for all time are we are bound indissolubly to the British crown'.[41] Nationalists had a very

**39** *Belfast Newsletter*, 13 Oct. 1932.   **40** *A guide to Belfast's literary landscape* (Belfast, 2007), p. 2.   **41** Bardon, *Belfast: an illustrated history*, p. 225.

different perspective. The Nationalist journalist, James Kelly, an eye-witness at the opening, described Stormont as the 'cornerstone on the partition of Ireland'.[42] The *Irish News* was particularly hostile to the extravagance and cost of the new building, at a time of economic distress. It brought out a supplement entitled 'The truth about Stormont' in January 1933. Craigavon countered this in parliament, stating that Stormont's construction was able to 'absorb as many as the out-of-work as possible, and especially those ex-Service men who are now in a very sad state'.[43] The Prince of Wales was anxious that 'not one penny more' than 'absolutely essential' was to be spent on his visit. In a letter to the Duke of Abercorn, he showed more sensibility than his hosts to the contrast between the festivities at Stormont and the dire straits of the working-class areas of Belfast:

> It is obvious that the fact of my going to Belfast to open the new parliament buildings must to a certain degree remind those thousands who are unfortunately unemployed and almost starving, that ... an enormous amount of money has been expended on bricks and mortar, and ... that this money would have been better spent on the great commercial enterprise which, in better times, provided these unfortunate people with a livelihood – as for instance in the great shipbuilding industry of Belfast.[44]

The *Irish News* published a Nationalist manifesto, signed by eleven MPs and three senators now in self-exile from the parliament. They issued this on the occasion to condemn partition and to appeal to the southern government to unite with them to undo it.[45] The paper also claimed that 10,000 Orangemen were to be recruited as special marshals to line the route of the Prince of Wales to Stormont, thus linking 'the English Royal House with an avowedly sectarian body'. This never materialized, possibly due to the *Irish News* exposé. The government prosecuted the editor, Sydney Redwood, under the Special Powers Act, and a fine of £100, plus costs, was imposed.[46] The Prince of Wales arrived at Stormont on 16 November to carry out the official opening, having passed along a route lined by B-Specials and Orangemen wearing blue rosettes and medals of the Prince.[47] Only the great and the good were at the parliament buildings. Other than Unionists, no opposition members were in attendance. This was the Unionist elite's unforgettable day of pomp and pageant. The security and future of Unionists was symbolized in the imposing dimensions of this iconic building,

42 James Kelly, *Bonfires on the hillside* (Belfast, 1995), p. 66.   43 *Parliament Buildings, Stormont* (Belfast, 1999), p. 19.   44 McIntosh, *The force of culture*, pp 38–9.   45 *Irish News*, 7 Nov. 1932.   46 Éamon Phoenix, 'The history of a newspaper: the *Irish News* 1855–1995' in Éamon Phoenix (ed.), *A century of northern life: the* Irish News *and 100 years of Ulster history, 1890s–1990s* (Belfast, 1995), pp 28–9.   47 *Irish News*, 17 Nov. 1932.

with its imperial statuary of Britannia and her lions astride its pediment. For Nationalists, Stormont was variously a 'Ruritanian white elephant', a 'cold house' and the seat of repression. The new building remained home to parliament until its replacement with Direct Rule in 1972. In the new dispensation, ushered in by the Good Friday and St Andrews Agreements, Stormont will hopefully in future serve as a parliament for all. This is very definitely a world away from what pertained in 1932.

# The significance of the 1935 Lancaster Street riots

## JIM McDERMOTT

The period of partition in Belfast from 1920 to 1922 was a bloody one. Jonathan
Bardon explains how from July 1920 until July 1922 the death toll for Belfast was
453. In addition to 35 members of the crown forces, 257 were Catholic civilians,
157 were Protestant civilians and 2 were of unknown religion. At the time,
Catholic relief organizations estimated that 11,000 Catholics lost their jobs and
23,000 Catholics were forced out of their homes.[1]

Thirteen years after this period, in 1935, a riot in Lancaster Street off York
Street in Belfast set off ethnic conflict which resulted in seven Protestants and
three Catholics being killed, fifty-five Catholics and twenty-eight Protestants seriously wounded and around 2,500 people put out of their houses.[2] Obviously,
many people who had witnessed the events in Belfast in 1920–2 were still alive in
1935, and parallels were drawn between the two sets of events. It was tempting for
some Nationalists to believe that the Lancaster Street riots were orchestrated by a
Unionist elite as a device to divide the Belfast working-class and thus retain
power. Some Unionists who had taken over the devolved administration of
Northern Ireland still held powerful positions in 1935. Among them was Lord
Craigavon, who had been Premier of Northern Ireland since 1921. In the Home
Office since 1921 was Sir Dawson Bates, while Sir Joseph Davidson was both a
Unionist MP and the Grand Master of the Orange Lodge.

This essay will examine how the 1935 riots affected these three Unionists as
opposed to its effects on three Republicans who were prominent in Belfast in
1921. Its impact on two socialists will also be considered. Davy Matthews was a
prominent IRA member at the period of state formation.[3] Dan Turley,[4] like Davy
Matthews, was a prominent Republican figure in early 1921 and, like Matthews,
took an anti-treaty position in Belfast in 1922. General Eoin O'Duffy became the
first Commissioner of the Garda Síochána (Civic Guard) in the twenty-six counties and had an important command position in the pro-treaty side of the Irish
Civil War. However, in the summer of 1921, O'Duffy had been the most senior
IRA man in Belfast as well as Chief Liaison Officer.[5] By 1935, he had become the

---

1 Jonathon Bardon, *Belfast: an illustrated history* (Belfast, 1982), p. 202. See also Jim McDermott, *Northern
divisions* (Belfast, 2002), pp 22–34.   2 A.C. Hepburn, *A place apart: studies in the history of Catholic
Belfast, 1850–1950* (Belfast, 1986), pp 183–6.   3 PRONI HA/5/526: file on Davy Matthews.   4 PRONI
HA/5/424: file on Dan Turley.   5 Fearghall McGarry, *Eoin O'Duffy: a self made hero* (Oxford, 2005), pp
78–83. See also McDermott, *Northern divisions*, pp 105–12.

leader of quasi-fascist groupings in the South and counted himself the 'third greatest man in Europe'.[6] While this was an absurd boast, how would this once powerful Republican have viewed the developments in Lancaster Street in 1935?

Two Belfast men of left-wing views were also to take a deep interest in events in York Street in 1935. Harry Midgley was an avowed Protestant socialist in 1921 who took a very brave stand against the expulsions of Catholics from their places of work in July 1920.[7] He was at that time anti-partitionist and stood for elections on a labour platform. By 1935, Midgley represented the Dock Ward adjoining Lancaster Street. Midgley strongly believed that the working-classes of Belfast should elect labour representatives to break the Unionist monolith. How did he feel then when Protestants and Catholics savagely attacked each other in his own constituency?

Tommy Geehan, who was relatively young in early 1921, was a leading member of the Communist Party of Ireland by 1935. In 1932, while a member of the precursor to the CPI, the Revolutionary Marxist Groups, Geehan was very prominent in leading the opposition to the Outdoor Relief schemes.[8] He was clearly non-sectarian, investing his hopes in the prospect of the working-classes of Belfast showing the same non-sectarian cooperation of the 'socialist summer' of 1932 in opposition to Unionist rule in Stormont.

In examining the careers of these individuals, I am largely leaving out the contributions of the constitutional Nationalist opposition of the time. Éamon Phoenix has chronicled the efforts of Joe Devlin and his colleagues very fully in his 1994 book, *Northern Nationalism*. The book explains that by 1929 the best efforts of the Northern Nationalist representatives were unable to stop Craigavon's government from abolishing proportional representation in elections for the Northern Ireland government.[9]

In February 1932, de Valera and the Fianna Fáil party formed their first government in the twenty-six counties. To Unionists in the North, this presented a fear of a Republican/Nationalist resurgence aided by the South. In the North, Republicans and Nationalists hoped for some dramatic initiatives from the Free State government. De Valera proved to be very conservative in his policy on a thirty-two-county Ireland, although he did distance the South of Ireland from continuing British rule.

Joseph Devlin and Cahir Healy met de Valera and his deputy Seán T. O'Kelly in February 1933 on behalf of Northern Nationalists. The Fianna Fáil leaders

---

**6** McGarry, *Eoin O'Duffy* (2005), ch. 10.  **7** Graham Walker, *The politics of frustration, Harry Midgley and the failure of the Labour Party in Northern Ireland* (Oxford, 1985), pp 19–22.  **8** Ronnie Munck and Bill Rolston, *Belfast in the Thirties: an oral history* (Belfast, 1987), pp 27–46.  **9** Éamon Phoenix, *Northern Nationalism: Nationalist politics, partition and the Catholic minority in Northern Ireland, 1890–1940* (Belfast, 1994), p. 363.

refused to countenance Northern minority representation in Dáil Éireann, and provided no advice on how Northern Nationalists should respond to Unionist rule.[10] On 18 January 1934, Devlin died, thus depriving the Northern minority of their most able representative and reducing his party to nine MPs, four senators and two Westminster MPs.[11] In real terms, this was not a viable opposition and in constitutional terms, Lord Craigavon and his Unionist colleagues looked to be in an electorally unassailable position so long as they retained the support of the Protestant voting bloc.

In reality, Craigavon and his cabinet were not as secure as they looked. The Unionist Party had secured their devolved powers from Westminster in 1921 as a consequence of the Government of Ireland Act, which was passed with the intention of pacifying Ireland. The Unionist lobby, which had included Walter Long and Lord Craigavon's brother Charles Craig, had been able to convince Westminster MPs that the six north-eastern counties of Ireland could be a viable economic unit that would administer the law fairly to all its citizens. By 1932, the economic underpinnings of the six counties looked much less secure and there was a clear partisanship toward the Protestant majority by the Unionist government. Two dangers therefore presented themselves to the Unionist Party. A failure to give adequate employment to the working-class could give rise to a non-sectarian labour or more extreme socialist party which could topple the Unionists. On the other hand, if the Unionist Party only were able to retain their interclass Protestant support at the cost of a Nationalist uprising and consequent repression, then Westminster might feel it incumbent upon them to rule directly or to reconsider the six counties' relationship to the United Kingdom.

In the first two decades of the twentieth century, Unionists had considerable economic arguments for the union with Britain. Belfast itself differed from other Irish cities and towns in having experienced exponential industrial and population growth in the nineteenth and early twentieth century. In 1907, Belfast was the twelfth largest city in the United Kingdom. It had grown from virtual obscurity at the start of the nineteenth century to increase its population to around 350,000 in 1901, making Belfast more populous than Dublin.

Belfast's industrial concerns had grown correspondingly large. It is estimated that Harland and Wolff and Workman and Clare's respectively were the first and sixth largest shipbuilding yards in the world. The rope works were the largest in the world and, on top of this, Belfast could boast of huge linen, tobacco and engineering factories.[12] In 1921, the Unionist cabinet were part of the business class which ran industry and agriculture in the six counties.[13] While theoretically this

**10** Ibid., p. 370. **11** Ibid., p. 373. **12** Booklet by ATGWU, *Belfast Lockout* (Belfast, 2007), p. 10. **13** Michael Farrell, *Northern Ireland: the orange state* (London, 1976), p. 68. Gives details on what individual

should have given the Unionist Party considerable powers of patronage, given their dominant political position, in fact, the Northern Ireland state was dogged by unemployment problems since its inception in 1921.

For example, in June 1921 there were 123,000 unemployed in Northern Ireland.[14] In 1925, a Labour Party member, Sam Patterson, was sentenced to six months imprisonment in Belfast for making a speech in which he said that 'While the people of Belfast are starving we have rogues, vagabonds, thieves and murderers in Sir James Craig and his government.' Patterson went on to advocate working-class unity and argued that the working-class could 'free ourselves in twelve months without the ballot box'.[15]

By 1932, the economic downturn continued so that each of the eight figures mentioned were in some way affected. Sir James Craig, now Lord Craigavon, and Sir Dawson Bates had good cause for alarm. They had shown in the past that they could be quite draconian in their treatment of opposition, with measures such as internment without trial and the Special Powers Act, but they could not afford to alienate their own Protestant working-class support. Yet, in 1932, no ships were launched in Harland and Wolff, only a skeleton workforce could be kept and 'grass grew on the slips'. By January 1935, Workman and Clarke's shipyard was to close forever and almost all of Belfast's industry was similarly blighted.[16] When the Poor Law Guardians of Belfast administered the Outdoor Relief Fund particularly parsimoniously, this led to the ODR riots of 1932, when large numbers of Protestant and Catholic workers united to successfully challenge the government.

While this had happened in the Carters and Dockers' strike of 1907 and the forty-four-hour strike of 1919, this had been the first time when a devolved Unionist administration was threatened by working-class unity. The scale of opposition to the ODR scheme was large enough to worry the Unionist cabinet. On 3 October 1932, 2,000 Outdoor Relief workers protested against their low rates of pay (the lowest in the British Isles) and other aspects of the scheme by downing tools and picketing ODR sites. There was a massive support march, which the organizers claimed was 60,000-strong, and even the *Newsletter*, which opposed the strike, conceded that there were 15,000 marchers.[17] On 6 October, Sir Dawson Bates met representatives of the Poor Law Guardians, who set the rate. Bates, presumably acting in agreement with Lord Craigavon, urged the Board of Guardians to give 50 per cent more time to task work for labourers on the ODR Scheme.[18] While this concession was rejected by the strike-leaders, it was a clear indication that the leaders of the Unionist Party were badly shaken by working-class unity.

Unionist cabinet ministers were.  **14** Ibid., p. 121.  **15** Ibid., p. 123.  **16** Munck and Rolson, *Belfast in the Thirties*, pp 19–20.  **17** Ibid., p. 27.  **18** Ibid., p. 29.

Other Unionist responses to the strike are very interesting. When the ODR protests led to violence it was noted that the police used batons on protesters in Protestant districts, whereas live rounds were fired on marches in Catholic districts.[19] Shooting around Albert Street on the Falls Road killed two men, Samuel Baxter and John Keegan, a Protestant and a Catholic. Fourteen other people were wounded on the same occasion. Ultimately, despite curfews and heavy-handed police tactics, the Poor Law Guardians and by implication the Unionist cabinet, were forced by the strikers to make concessions. Craigavon himself claimed that the riots were caused by 'troublemakers who wanted a Republic' who 'were doomed to disappointment. I am not a man to be intimidated'.[20] Despite the rhetoric, clearly the success of the ODR strike was a serious reverse for the Unionist government and the leaders of the opposition were euphoric.

James Kelly, who was a young journalist at the time of the ODR riots, gave great credit to Tommy Geehan for his leadership of the strike. Kelly claims that Geehan 'dominated the scene. A small thin-faced cadaverous figure, a kind of workers' Robespierre with a powerful voice and a commanding presence' who turned ODR workers from being 'an undisciplined mob' to 'an effective force to be reckoned with'.[21] Harry Midgley, who at that stage was an important leader of the Northern Ireland Labour Party, had little time for the tactics of Tommy Geehan and the other communist leaders of the strike, claiming that 'the truth is that had the workers half as much political intelligence as they have credulity for political knaves and adventurers they could have secured all they secured last week without the loss of a single life or one cracked skull'.[22] Geehan responded by calling Midgley a 'careerist' whose attitude to workers had been to let them 'starve another nine months', but there is no doubt that Midgley's reputation too had been enhanced by his more orthodox opposition to the ODR scheme.[23] On 30 November 1933, Harry Midgley won the Northern Ireland seat for Dock by 4,893 votes to 3,685.[24] There is no doubt then that the left seemed to be in the driving seat in 1932. The IRA in Belfast too was affected, if not directly. *An Phoblact* was ecstatic at the ODR strike, with headlines like 'Orange and Green United in Belfast',[25] yet the IRA, cautious as ever of being sidelined into social agitation, only took part as individuals rather than as the IRA per se. Both Davy Matthews and Dan Turley had turned their backs on the probable offers of commissions in the Free State Army, so both had an evidently highly idealistic side to their character which the ODR conflict would have excited. Matthews, who was OC of the IRA in Belfast, took part in stone-throwing with the strikers

19 Ibid., p. 32. Also *The Troubles: a history of the Northern Ireland conflict* (Belfast, 2001), pp 42–6. 20 Ibid. 21 James Kelly, *Bonfires on the hillside* (Belfast, 1995), p. 76. 22 Walker, *Politics of frustration*, p. 64. 23 Ibid., pp 61–7. 24 Ibid., p. 69. 25 Brian Hanley, *The IRA, 1926–1936* (Dublin 2002), p. 150.

in Sandy Row and encouraged others to do the same.[26] No doubt, many other
IRA men behaved in a similar manner, if only out of self interest. In 1934, out of
460 IRA men in Belfast, only 150 were employed.[27] However, Matthews and most
of the IRA there were far from communist and were not open to extreme left-
wing influence. While Matthews praised the ODR strike in the IRA Convention
of 1933, Belfast was not like Dublin in the 1930s. In Dublin, IRA men would mix
socially with left-wing figures such as Seán Murray, the Gilmore brothers and
Frank Ryan. This was less likely in Belfast. Matthews was never communist. Betty
Sinclair had no connection with IRA.[28]

It was accepted that the Belfast IRA could possess a dynamic for social and
economic change. In 1933, the Nationalist leader Joe Devlin told Davy Matthews
at a secret meeting that Craigavon and company did not fear constitutional resistance: 'It is you they fear, the man with the gun.'[29] Nonetheless, the Belfast IRA
in 1932 was slow to openly embrace a left-wing agenda, despite an upsurge in
recruitment in the wake of the ODR strike. Although Matthews supported the
ODR workers, he refused an order from Dublin which he considered to be
'communist propaganda'.[30] He opposed the materialism of Saor Éire in the IRA
Convention of 1932,[31] but remained staunchly non-sectarian, avoiding being
brought into conflict with the Protestant community in 1932 when there were
several serious attacks on Catholics.[32] However, Matthews did not hesitate to
mobilize sixty men to be on standby in Ardoyne of 12 July in case of Loyalist
attacks.[33] He also ordered his men to leave copies of the IRA 'Address to the
Orange Order' to be sent to Protestant districts. Written by Peader O'Donnell,
these 'Addresses' urged Protestant workers and small farmers to unite with their
Catholic counterparts in a struggle 'for the transfer of power over production,
distribution and exchange to the mass of the people'.[34]

While it is doubtful if many IRA men understood fully the implications of
O'Donnell's 'Address', copies were nonetheless left at hairdressers, boot repairers
and those 'who did all the talking' in Protestant districts. The 'Addresses' were of
course met with almost universal hostility in Loyalist districts. Yet, from 1932,
Republicans in Belfast for a time did take a more left-wing approach. Although
there was little Belfast IRA enthusiasm for the Republican congress of 1934, both
Matthews and Turley would have given approval to the direct intervention by the
IRA in the Railway Strike in 1933 on the strikers' behalf. In this strike, there is
even some evidence that the IRA crossed the sectarian divide with their cooperation with B-Specials.[35] Bob Bradshaw, an IRA man in 1933, recalls how Protestants

---

**26** Ibid., p. 151.  **27** Ibid., p. 255.  **28** Ibid., p. 151.  **29** Phoenix, *Northern Nationalism*, p. 376.  **30**
Hanley, *The IRA*, p. 151.  **31** Ibid., p. 146.  **32** Ibid., pp 146–7.  **33** Ibid., p. 147.  **34** Ibid.  **35** Ibid.,
p. 152.

called at Davy Matthews' home to ask for the IRA's help in blowing up trains in 'a harebrained scheme to bring Catholics and Protestants together'.[36]

One ex-IRA man who had no intention of embracing left-wing politics in 1932 was General Eoin O'Duffy. He was dismissed from his role as the first Commissioner of the Garda by de Valera. Although O'Duffy had been very effective in establishing the first unarmed police service in the history of the twenty-six counties, he had also shown more and more overt indications of egotism, was attracted to right-wing movements such as in Italy and Germany, and was intractably linked to Cumann na nGaedheal, who were bitter political rivals of Fianna Fáil.[37] O'Duffy was anti-communist, devoutly Catholic and attracted to the ideas of the corporate state. Despite his strong associations with Belfast in 1921, it is very doubtful if O'Duffy had any sympathies with the ODR strikes, although he remained an implacable opponent of the Unionist government in Northern Ireland.

We must ask if we look at the early 1930s objectively, was the Unionist government under threat from left-wing forces? To a limited extent only must be the answer. Despite Harry Midgley's victory in Dock in 1933, despite winning only ten seats out of sixteen in Belfast in 1935,[38] the Unionists remained in a strong position. The ODR strike was far from unique. There had been similar riots in Birkenhead, Liverpool, Westham, Clydeside, Croyden, North Shields, Paisley, Bristol and Central London. It was essentially a single issue victory.[39] Churches held great power independent of political parties. Harry Diamond, later to be a Republican Labour MP for West Belfast, had to approach Bishop Mageean to explain why he was opposing the policy of the Poor Law Guardians in case he was thought to have communist sympathies.[40]

The IRA's commitment to left-wing politics was sometimes more apparent than real. A prominent Belfast IRA man, Charlie McGlade, pointed out that 'there wasn't a great deal of sympathy' for social policy from most volunteers, 'it was too dry for them'.[41] Peader O'Donnell complained that James Connolly had not laid down any 'guidelines' for tackling the sectarian situation in the northeast,[42] and an indication of how safe the Unionists felt in 1932 was their opening of the Stormont parliament at the cost of £1,700,000 from the British Treasury, but also £30,000 from the local exchequer.

On top of this, while the social upheavals of the ODR strike were taking place, so too were the activities of the Ulster Protestant League. While the Unionist leadership in Northern Ireland was essentially middle class, an atavistic element of the Protestant working class existed, and organizations such as the

---

**36** Unseann MacEoin, *The IRA in the twilight years, 1923–1948* (Dublin, 1977).  **37** Hanley, *The IRA*, ch. 7 'red terror'.  **38** Hepburn, *Place apart*, p. 176.  **39** Munck and Rolston, *Belfast in the Thirties*, p. 21. **40** Ibid., p. 38.  **41** Ibid., p. 171.  **42** Ibid., p. 183.

UPL were useful in keeping such individuals within the Unionist family. The UPL was never a formal part of the Unionist Party, but rather a loose alliance of evangelical and very poor Protestants who encouraged Protestants to only employ Protestants.[43] Hepburn explains that their leadership was lower middle class, but they quickly showed that they could make dramatic, if sectarian, interventions in the every day life of Belfast. In 1932, they not only vocally opposed the Eucharistic congress in Dublin, but also successfully opposed the Catholic Truth Society using the Ulster Hall, a building which they claimed 'was sacred to every Protestant heart'.[44] Munck and Rolston have cautioned that the UPL may have been 'smaller and more fluid than supposed',[45] but they were a group who were seemingly indulged by the Unionist establishment.

While the UPL would deliberately set out to disrupt socialist or communist meetings by drowning out the opposition voices by beating Lambeg drums and so on, they rarely seem to have been cautioned by the RUC. On the contrary, oral testimony records that the police protected the Lambeg drummers and attacked the marchers: 'many a sore head was felt by the marchers and their supporters'.[46] While there may be some exaggeration here by an aggrieved socialist, there is no doubt that at times the UPL and the Unionist government could be in agreement. In the *Newsletter* in October 1932, the UPL were able to argue that poverty and hunger 'were used as a cloak by the Communist Sinn Féin element to start a revolution in our province'.[47] James Kelly noted that despite their proletarian make-up, the UPL appeared to have little difficulty in obtaining the Unionist Party headquarters in Glengall Street for UPL meetings and functions.[48]

It is significant that UPL activity was especially pronounced in the York Street district. Hepburn points out that Midgley's Dock Ward area was the most inter-mixed area in Belfast, a patchwork quilt of Protestant and Catholic mill workers, dock labourers and carters.[49] The problem of proximity to opposite religions was compounded by the competition of the two ethnic groups for finite economic resources. As already alluded to, the 1930s were marked by high male unemployment in the very industries on which the York Street area was dependent. Even for those who were working, wages tended to be lower than in Britain, and for those without work, unemployment insurance was only paid for six months. Matters were made much worse because traditionally in the York Street area, male wages were augmented by wives and daughters who worked in the local mills. In the 1930s, however, the linen industry, which, although low-waged, had a staff

**43** Hepburn, *Place apart*, p. 177.   **44** Ibid., p. 178.   **45** Munck and Rolston, *Belfast in the Thirties*, p. 11. Not one veteran of the UPL could be found to give an account of UPL activities in a Belfast in the thirties.   **46** Munck and Rolston, *Belfast in the Thirties*, pp 12–13.   **47** *Belfast Newsletter*, 15 Oct. 1932.   **48** Munck and Rolston, *Belfast in the Thirties*, p. 39.   **49** Hepburn, *Place apart*, p. 178.

make-up that was three-quarters female, went into serious decline and competition for jobs became more marked.[50]

From 1933 to 1935 the UPL's obsession with communist infiltration, the IRA threat and preference for Protestants over Catholics in employment were echoed by the upper echelons of the Unionist Party. An aside by G.C. Duggan, a former Northern Ireland Comptroller and Auditor General, noted that Sir Dawson Bates 'had such a prejudice against Catholics that he made it clear that he did not want his most juvenile clerk or typist if a Papist, assigned for duty to his ministry'.[51]

Sir Dawson Bates' views were reinforced by other senior Unionists such as Basil Brooke, who said on 12 July 1933 'I have not a Roman Catholic about my own place'. Lord Craigavon said in debate that 'the employment of disloyalists … is prejudicial to the state and takes jobs away from Loyalists'.[52] On top of Craigavon's statement that he was an Orangeman first and a politician second there was little to convince the working-class Catholics of the Dock Ward, that they could expect fair treatment. However, the most overt political expression of the UPL point of view came from Sir Joseph Davidson, Unionist MP and Grand Master of the Orange Order on 27 August 1932: 'when will the employers of Belfast recognize their duty to their Protestant brothers and sisters to employ them to the exclusion of Roman Catholics. I suggest the slogan be "Protestants employ Protestants"'.[53] This statement favouring Protestants over Catholics was to have serious implications in the York Street district from 1933 to 1935.

In November 1933, Dan Boyle, a Catholic publican, was shot dead in York Street. It was the first sectarian killing in Belfast since 1922 but it set in motion a series of armed attacks on Catholics and a chain of events which were to culminate in the Lancaster Street riots of 1935.[54] There is little doubt that economic circumstances, speeches by leading Unionist figures and the activities of the UPL had raised the political temperature to the extent that following the murder of Dan Boyle, in July 1934 shots were fired into the Catholic North Thomas Street. While these shots did not hit anyone, a Protestant crowd wrecked forty Catholic homes in New Dock Street and Marine Street. Following this attack, a Catholic young man, Andy McCombe died in hospital.[55]

From July 1934 until July 1935 there was an accumulation of incidents which were to heighten community tensions in the area. Before this, the Stormont representative for Dock, Harry Midgley, had made his maiden speech on 13 December 1933. It was acclaimed as a bold and impressive debut by the Northern Ireland Labour Party MP and it culminated with a call to end Northern Ireland's economic problems. He was congratulated on his speech by MPs Robert Lynn

**50** Ibid., p. 175.   **51** *Irish Times*, 4 May 1967, in Farrell, *The orange state*, p. 90.   **52** Farrell, *Orange state*, pp 136–7.   **53** Ibid.   **54** Ibid., pp 136–42; Munck and Rolston, *Belfast in the Thirties*, pp 45–60; Hepburn, *Place apart*, pp 137–43.   **55** Munck and Rolston, *Belfast in the Thirties*, p. 45.

and J.M. Andrews, but his biographer noted that 'It was one of the first of many compliments he was to receive from his Unionist opponents who obviously looked upon flattery as a way of taming the House's firebrands'.[56] By this stage in his career, Midgley had moved steadily from his anti-partitionist stance of the early 1920s and, while previously he had attracted attacks as a rogue Protestant, he now was attacked by Nationalists as well. On 9 May 1934, Midgley moved a writ for a by-election to contest the Belfast Central seat vacated by the death of Joe Devlin on 19 January of that year. The other prominent NILP representative in Stormont, Jack Beattie, who was strongly anti-partitionist, stayed away from the meeting. Nationalist anger focused on Midgley, who they accused of 'unprecedented interference'. The Nationalists believed that Midgley and Beattie both owed their seats to Catholic (Nationalist) votes. Some NILP members believed that the Nationalists were stalling to let the election coincide with the Catholic Truth Society Festival in June. In any case, Midgley was the object of Nationalist Party ire. His attempt to move the writ was defeated by the Nationalists, with the Unionists abstaining.[57]

When the election did take place on 4 June, the Nationalist candidate was the Catholic lawyer T.J. Campbell, while the NILP recalled the Protestant socialist William McMullan from Dublin. Whether in response to Midgley's moving the writ or not, the Nationalist election campaign was very sectarian, with Catholic votes being called upon to 'protect their religion' and being warned that a vote for McMullan was a vote for the Protestant Ascendency. McMullan still polled well for Labour,[58] but the signs were clear that, despite the socialist summer of 1932, religious atavism was extremely potent in Belfast, be it among Catholics or Protestants. By August 1935, Midgley was to find himself even more isolated from Nationalist opinion, particularly in his own Dock constituency.

Tommy Geehan and his communist comrades were also experiencing problems since their successes in 1932. The media were anti-communist, with the *Daily Mail* noting a 'husky Russian' among the ODR rioters in 1932. Frequent attacks from Catholic and Protestant pulpits were launched about pernicious communist influences. Peter Carleton commented that 'There wasn't a pulpit all over Belfast – Catholic [or] Protestant – that wasn't denouncing communism.'[59] In the 1933 elections, Tommy Geehan lost his deposit on standing in the Court Ward. Geehan was proactive in support of the Railway strikers in 1933 and was as unrepentant in 1935 as he was in October 1932, when he stated: 'I came into this fight as a communist and I am going out of it as a communist.'[60]

For the IRA in Belfast, their experience of the ODR dispute and the Railway

**56** Walker, *Politics of frustration*, p. 70.  **57** Ibid., pp 72–3.  **58** Ibid., p. 75.  **59** Munck and Rolston, *Belfast in the Thirties*, p. 38.  **60** Ibid., p. 39.

Strike had made them more radical on social issues and they had now some Protestants in their ranks. With their numbers increasing, they decided to contest the 1933 elections that November. The IRA was charged with communism and vote-splitting by the Nationalist Party. Cahir Healy had written in the *Irish News* that 'No Catholic could vote for the IRA'. Their director of elections, Davy Matthews, and forty-two other Republicans were put in jail and the IRA complained bitterly of RUC harassment.[61]

Yet, the IRA did remarkably well. Not only had P.J. MacLogan won a seat in South Armagh, but the Republican candidate in West Belfast, Patrick Thornbury, polled 4,650 votes to Joe Devlin's 7,411. The Republican vote was in fact 1,605 higher than de Valera had received in the constituency in 1918.[62] The IRA in Belfast now believed that there was a role for radical, non-sectarian politics in Belfast, but by January 1934 Davy Matthews was under court martial by the IRA[63] and by July 1935 the IRA was back to its traditional role of defenders of the Catholic minority.

In the Free State, de Valera's Fianna Fáil party showed considerably more interest in their own internal concerns than pursuing national reunification. Even the Republican congress of 1934 did not excite much activity in the North. However, Eoin O'Duffy's activities were headline-grabbing. His would-be fascist group, the Blueshirts, had for a time attracted considerable support from prominent Fine Gael members such as William Cosgrave, Richard Mulcahy and the Protestant Northerner Ernest Blythe. In fact, up until he resigned on 22 September 1934, Eoin O'Duffy had been President of Fine Gael as well as leader of the Blueshirts. His resignation was a tactic. The general was jumping before he was pushed, but although O'Duffy claimed 'I am glad to be out of politics', it was quickly evident that the unpredictable O'Duffy wished to retain a leadership role with his Blueshirts, with the result that a tug of war would soon commence between the two factions of the Blueshirts before both of them sank into oblivion together.[64] While O'Duffy had been very active as an IRA leader in Belfast in 1921, by 1934 his Blueshirt organization was fighting the IRA on the streets and the General himself was bitterly anti-communist. It is unlikely that O'Duffy would have had any sympathy for Midgley, Geehan, the Unionist cabinet or the radical politics of the IRA in Belfast.

Opposition to radical politics could also come from within the IRA itself. While support for the Republican congress was limited in Belfast, a small group of Protestant Republicans had travelled to Bodenstown on 17 June 1934 carrying a banner titled *Wolfe Tone Commemoration 1934 – Shankill Road Branch*. One

**61** Hanley, *The IRA*, p. 154. **62** Ibid., p. 155. **63** Ibid. Matthews had given an undertaking to the Northern Ireland Authorities to cease membership of the IRA. Hanley concludes that jail probably simply exhausted him after his long years of service. **64** MacEoin, *Twilight years*, p. 302.

contingent had printed 'Break the connection with capitalism'. On the grounds that no unauthorized banners were to be carried, the congress group found themselves involved in a scuffle with the East Tipperary Brigade under Mattie Ryan, who tried to seize the banners at the graveyard gates. While this group was able to return to the assembly point of Sallins Fields, where George Gilmore and Peadar O'Donnell addressed them, the damage was done.[65] The Republican movement too contained within it elements which were inimical to working-class unity.

By 1935 in Belfast, only three years from the 'socialist summer' of 1932, there were five distinct groups looking for the support of the Protestant working-class, each for different reasons. Some Republicans still hoped to convince working-class Protestants that their future interests would be best served in a thirty-two-county democratic Ireland. The behaviour of some elements of the Nationalist Party at election times and some Republicans at Bodenstown were hardly making the Belfast IRA's case very convincing. The Midgley element in the NILP had already been elected in Dock on the basis of Protestant and Catholic votes. Now, however, partly as a consequence of Midgley's own impatient style and partly because of his pro-union views, his support was under threat from both Catholics and Protestants.

Geehan had successfully led both Protestants and Catholics, but his politics were opposed by the main political parties, the media and the churches. He was not likely to be elected, even in corporation elections – O'Duffy's views on the corporate state had few takers in Belfast. Craigavon and Bates knew that they needed to keep the Protestant working-class vote from drifting, so they and some cabinet colleagues emphasized Protestant privilege and Catholic exclusion. However, in the York Street district in Belfast it was the UPL with their virulent anti-Catholicism that was attracting a lot of working-class support.

The UPL, with its lower middle-class leadership, could not of itself be a threat to the Unionist Party from 1934 to 1935, but it could push sectarian rhetoric and behaviour to extremes in light of some of the intolerant speeches by Unionist cabinet members of the time. There were certainly willing ears among some members of the Protestant working class of the York Street area. After all, the violence of 1920–2 led to a proliferation of official and non-official Loyalist groups who had been particularly active in that district. As well as the A, B and C Specials, the Imperial Guards and the Ulster Protestant Association had at one time very large memberships in and around this part of North Belfast and they had been particularly active in attacks on Catholics and their property.[66] UPL

---

**65** Raymond J. Quinn, *Rebel voices* (Belfast, 1998), pp 18–21. **66** More detail in Michael Farrell, *Arming the Protestants: the formation of the Ulster Special Constabulary and the Royal Ulster Constabulary, 1920–7* (Dingle, Co. Kerry, 1983); McDermott, *Northern division*; Patrick Buckland, *Factory of grievances: devolved*

activity promoted atavistic memories in a time of economic and territorial rivalry. As a newspaper article put it, 'there was land hunger and house hunger in Belfast'. Even some of the personnel of 1920–2 were once again involved in attacks on Catholics.[67]

Oddly, in April 1935, just as there was a ratchetting up of left-wing activity (a CPI-backed Tenants Defence League had concluded a successful rent strike) there was a simultaneous outbreak of shooting incidents in the York Street area, with Catholics as the targets. On 12 and 13 May, two Catholics were injured by gunshots. Also in May, as Loyalists celebrated the visit to Belfast of the Duke of Gloucester, the UPL went into action mostly against the CPI. They attacked and broke up CPI meetings at the Custom House Square on 5, 12 and 19 May and a party meeting in Library Street on 27 May. The UPL also warned the government to deal with the communist threat quickly and if they did not, then the UPL would. This activity seems to have alarmed the Trades Council and the NILP to the extent that they suspended the annual May Day march in the interests of peace.[68]

The UPL's activities in May 1935 were an alleged reaction to the boycott by Nationalists of the visit of the Duke of Gloucester in May, but they were to continue right through June. On 12 June, both the Socialist Party and the CPI headquarters in the York Street area were wrecked. During May, Catholic mill workers were often attacked on their way to or from work and two bombs were thrown into the Catholic area of Vere Street, while a young Catholic man received a gunshot wound in Nelson Street. On 10 May, a curfew was imposed on the area for the first time since 1932. In June, there was yet more gunfire against Catholics and in mid-June, Catholics had begun to fire back. When the CPI announced that it was going to form a workers defence league to combat these attacks, Dawson Bates banned all public meetings and demonstrations.[69]

The IRA condemned UPL activity but would not be drawn into sectarian violence. The CPI and NILP deplored the activities of the UPL as well, but urged that law and order be maintained. However, it was Sir Joseph Davidson, the Grand Master of the Orange Order, who took common cause with the UPL in the assertion that no curbs should be put on Protestant rights as expressed by the Orange Order. Flouting the authority of the Home Affairs Minister, an Orange parade was held in York Street on 28 June and the RUC did nothing. On the same day, Davidson said that

> You may be perfectly certain that on the 12th July the Orangemen will be marching through Northern Ireland. I do not acknowledge the right of

*government in Northern Ireland, 1921–39* (Dublin, 1979).   **67** PRONI HA/9/2/22: file on George Scott. **68** Munck and Rolston, *Belfast in the Thirties*, pp 46–7.   **69** Ibid., pp 47–8.

any government, Northern or Imperial, to impose conditions on our celebrations.[70]

As Farrell points out, the Unionist government was now in direct conflict with its main supporters,[71] largely as a result of their own miscalculated public utterances. On 27 June, Bates capitulated and lifted the ban. A steady occurrence of shootings and attacks on Catholic areas continued until 12 July.

The government had clearly misjudged the potential for violence. On 10 July, the Attorney General announced that Belfast was 'settled down once again to a state of tranquillity and peace'. After the speeches on 12 July, 40,000 Orangemen marched back from the field to the city in the early evening. A shot was fired on the marchers from the Markets district, for which a 24-year-old Catholic was arrested and sentenced to five years imprisonment. While news of this incident no doubt inflamed passions, it was while the North Belfast Lodges were passing along York Street at the bottom of Lancaster Street that the serious rioting broke out.[72] Henry S. Kennedy, who was a witness to the riots and an *Irish News* journalist, has left an excellent account of what he saw, while expressing amazement that Loyalist journalists appeared to have witnessed a different event. He noted the first fatality of the day:

> The space opposite Lancaster Street was quiet and almost empty except for a youth with his back against the wall of a public house with the innocent air of someone enjoying the evening sun ... I did not know it at the time but the youth, a follower of the Orange procession, was dying with a bullet through his chest.[73]

At the end of the night, four people (two Protestants and two Catholics) were shot dead and nineteen people were injured. The RUC brought prosecutions against ten Catholics and one Orange marcher. The Orange marcher was not convicted.[74]

The Catholic residents of Lancaster Street claimed that their houses were invaded by Orangemen and that they only acted in self defence, although there is evidence that stones were stockpiled by locals and 'firearms concealed in the district as in any "border" district in Belfast, and these were always likely to be used'.[75] While Kennedy forms an honest judgment that the residents of Lancaster Street acted in self-defence, and while the *Irish News* on 15 July claimed that 'the whole ghastly affray was the result of a trivial incident', the Orange Order and

70 Farrell, *Orange state*, p. 138. 71 Ibid. 72 Hepburn, *Place apart*, pp 179–80. 73 Henry S. Kennedy, *Riot at Lancaster Street* (1935), p. 101. 74 Hepburn, *Place apart*, p. 180. 75 Kennedy, *Lancaster Street*, p. 103.

Loyalist newspapers all insisted that the incident started because of a savage and unprovoked attack on an unoffending Orange parade.[76]

The following day, at a wreath-laying at the home of a Protestant casualty, 18-year-old Edward Withers, a Glasgow band, 'The Billy Boys', which police described as being composed of 'rather low-type Protestant youths' struck up with *Onward Christian Soldiers* as they marched through the Catholic Dock area, which was close to the Withers' home in Nelson Street. That night, fifty-six Catholic homes in six streets were wrecked or burned. Peace was not restored in the Docks district until 4am the next day, by which time two more Protestants (not locals) were shot dead and twenty-eight people were wounded, fifteen with gunshot wounds.[77]

The RUC were stretched badly and refused to interfere and the government called in the British troops. These troops did not endear themselves to Loyalists when they fired into a Loyalist mob attacking New Dock Street killing two men. The violence spread to the Short Strand, Sandy Row and the Peter's Hill district, and even to Portadown, where there were more attacks on Catholic property and a young Catholic was shot dead. On the Shankill Road, a young Catholic walking with his girlfriend was so badly beaten by a mob that he died a few weeks later.[78]

By 24 June, the British troops were withdrawn but the riots, on top of fatalities and woundings, comprised the worst violence in Northern Ireland from 1922 until 1969. At Jennymount Mill, employers could do little when Protestant workers refused to work with Catholics. At Harland and Wolff, 200 Catholic workers were kept out of their work by hostile Loyalist mobs. Community relations in the York Street area were as bad as they had been in the 1920s. Hepburn estimates that 2,500 people were put out of their homes, of whom 85 per cent were Catholic. The Catholics referred to the event as a pogrom. Graffiti appeared on a gable wall in a Catholic part of York Street, referring to the higher death-rate of Protestants in the riots: 'You can loot but we can shoot'.[79]

Many of those who evicted people were brought before the courts. Often, neighbours had evicted neighbours and the practice had spread to the Old Lodge Road and Village areas as well as the storm-centre of York Street itself. Many of the rioters came from outside the districts involved and they tended to be unskilled or semi-skilled. Hepburn explains that 191 people were charged with rioting; 125 Protestants and 41 Catholics, which roughly corresponds to Belfast's population in 1935.[80]

Clearly, the events around York Street were a severe blow to those who had hoped that the working-classes of Belfast would unite on a shared social

**76** Hepburn, *Place apart*, p. 180; Kennedy, *Lancaster Street*, pp 103–5.  **77** Hepburn, *Place apart*, pp 180–2.  **78** Farrell, *Orange state*, p. 139.  **79** Walker, *Politics of frustration*, p. 79.  **80** Hepburn, *Place apart*, pp 189–93.

programme. The MP for the Dock Ward, Harry Midgley, had devoted his political life to non-sectarian politics, although he had been increasingly opposed to
Jack Beattie over the issue of the primacy of the National Question in 1933–4.
While Beattie was anti-partitionist, Midgley had become increasingly pro-
partition. By 1934, Beattie had left the NILP and had become an independent
MP for Pottinger, leaving Midgley in effective control of the NILP. At the party
congress in 1934, Midgley asked the party to take a strong stand against the
growth of fascism in Europe.[81] Throughout the 1936–7 period, Midgley was to
take an increasingly adamant position in support of the Spanish Republic, while
forthrightly repudiating the pro-Franco stance taken by the Catholic Church
both in Spain and in Ireland. By 1938, many Nationalists in Dock had repudiated
Midgley to the extent that he lost his seat in 1938.[82]

One reason advanced for the dwindling Nationalist support for Midgley was
his lack of involvement on behalf of his Catholic constituents in July 1935 when
fifty-six houses in the Dock Ward were wrecked in a single night, the army was
called out, a curfew was imposed and hundreds of his constituents were expelled
from their workplaces.[83] Paddy Devlin noted that Midgley did not condemn
Loyalist violence in his ward because he could not afford to offend the Protestant
vote in Dock, yet his lack of condemnation cost him much of the Nationalist
vote.[84] Midgley's defenders point out that the Dock MP had led an NILP delegation to Dawson Bates before the troubles of July 1935, pointing out how
sectarian the situation had become in the York Street area.[85] Furthermore, they
could argue, Midgley was on holiday in July 1935 and anyway he was returned as
alderman for the Dock Ward in 1936 without Nationalist opposition. However,
his lack of support for his Nationalist constituents certainly contributed to his
electoral defeat of 1938 although his advocacy of the Spanish Republican cause
was also an important factor. In Midgley's attacks on Catholic support for
Nationalist Spain, he demanded to know if Catholics only supported liberty
when it applied to themselves.[86] Ultimately, Catholic trade Unionists turned
against Midgley (partly due to his arrogance), he was physically threatened and
in the 1938 election he had to abandon his platform as some Catholics called out
'We want Franco'.[87]

From 1933, Harry Midgley had been increasingly moving away from his position of the early 1920s. In 1942, he left the NILP and set up the pro-Unionist
Commonwealth Labour Party. In 1943, he was brought into Basil Brooke's
wartime cabinet as Minister of Public Security (1943–5), then he reverted back to

---

**81** Walker, *Politics of frustration*, pp 73–5. Jack Beattie went on to become National Organizer for INTO
from 1934. **82** Walker, *Politics of frustration*, pp 108–10. **83** Hepburn, *Place apart*, p. 197. **84** Walker,
*Politics of frustration*, p. 77. **85** Ibid., p. 78. **86** Ibid., p. 94. **87** Ibid., pp 105–10; Hepburn, *Place
apart*, p. 197.

the backbenches. Midgley joined the Unionist Party in 1947, was appointed Minister of Labour (1949–52) and Minister of Education (1952–7). Oddly, considering how badly treated he was by extreme Protestant groups in his early and middle career, Midgley later became a member of the Orange Order.[88] Ironically, it was Brooke's decision to take Midgley into his cabinet which led indirectly to promotion for Sir Joseph Davidson who had done so much to inflame passions in York Street in 1935. Brooke realized that the right wing of the Unionist Party would resent the elevation of a 'labourite' like Midgley. In order to placate this element, Sir Joseph Davidson was made leader of the Senate in 1943.[89] Unionism was as determined as ever to keep its power bloc united.

Tommy Geehan had already had an extremely busy career by 1935. He had been chairman of the Belfast ODR Workers' Committee and organizer of the ODR strike in 1932. From 1933 to 1936 he was the organizer of the Irish Unemployed Workers' Movement and was active in the Republican congress of 1934.[90] In the aftermath of the 1935 riots, Geehan involved himself greatly in re-housing Nationalists who had been put out of their homes. Evictions were not confined to the York Street district, and there were as many as twenty-one in the Village district, which were probably carried out to give houses in the district to Protestants.[91] Geehan helped homeless Nationalist families to squat in the new housing estate of Glenard, near Ardoyne. There were about 1,477 houses (of a superior working-class type) being built for Protestant families in Glenard, but about half of the evicted Catholic families squatted in these homes. Glenard, which had been the most ambitious housing project in Belfast between the wars, soon became known simply as the 'New Ardoyne'. This was not done without conflict. When the Catholic squatters had created a high enough bridgehead, sixty Protestant families fled, through actual or potential intimidation. Geehan himself served fourteen days in jail for resisting eviction.[92] After 1935, Geehan's political career lost momentum. He left the CPI following an argument and set about looking for work. The journalist James Kelly saw Tommy Geehan in 1942. He was wearing overalls and sipping a pint in the Monico bar in Rosemary Street. He was working in the shipyard: 'From the lofty heights of a "man of the moment", he slipped back into the ranks of the ordinary individual in the street, a forgotten man'.[93] This is probably exactly how Geehan would have wanted it.

By 1933 in Belfast, the IRA had started to recover from the setbacks of 1922. One veteran recalled that by that year there were 700 members.[94] Despite this, very few Belfast IRA men became involved with the Republican congress,[95] although they were socially progressive and very non-sectarian in the 1930s. Jack

---

**88** Farrell, *Orange state*, p. 345. **89** Ibid., p. 162. **90** Hepburn, *Place apart*, p. 193. **91** Ibid., p. 187. **92** Ibid., p. 189. **93** Kelly, *Bonfires*, p. 76. **94** Munck and Rolston, *Belfast in the Thirties*, p. 192. **95** Ibid., p. 176.

Brady recalled that although it was regarded as the IRA's duty to protect vulnerable Nationalist districts: 'you'd have got court martialled if you fired a shot on your own, if you fired at a Protestant area'.[96] Davy Matthews, who was once again in jail at this point, was unbending in his time as OC in enforcing this doctrine, yet he would have felt the irony that few IRA men were in Belfast on 12 July to defend Nationalists. Almost the whole IRA in Belfast, including A Company from York Street, were training at Giles Quay, near Dundalk. Only the Ballymacarrett Unit was left on standby in the city.[97] In fact, although the IRA was accused of being behind the trouble in Belfast, twelve of its leaders, mostly Belfast men, were arrested at Giles Quay on 14 July, making an IRA return to the city even more difficult.[98]

The Ballymacarrett Unit of the IRA did become involved, however. When Jack Brady was informed of the shooting in the York Street area, he rounded up thirty men with guns and set up a headquarters at Trainor's yard in Lancaster Street. For the next two days, the IRA men 'were in the thick of it' until they were relieved by returning IRA men under Jimmy Steele.[99] Although the IRA in Belfast was not responsible for the Lancaster Street riots, the hopes of Davy Matthews and company for working-class unity in Belfast based on Republican ideals had suffered yet another reverse. In fact, the fortunes of the IRA in general and the Belfast IRA in particular were to receive yet another setback with the Crown Entry raid at the *Craobh Ruadh* Club in Belfast city centre in December 1935, when twelve leading Republicans were arrested. The absence of senior experienced officers, the loss of a sense of direction in political matters and ambivalence over what position to take on the Spanish Civil War created problems for the Belfast IRA. As Farrell puts it

> The 1935 riots put an effective stop to the tentative alliance of radical Protestants and the IRA. The IRA was forced to defend the Catholic ghettos and turned its mind to more traditional activities.

The swing to the right in the IRA in the late 1930s meant a return to very strong internal discipline. It had long been stressed to incoming volunteers that the death penalty was mandatory for any member caught informing. The shooting of Dan Turley[100] in December 1937 as an informer was, however, one of the most

**96** Ibid., p. 182.  **97** Ibid., p. 182.  **98** Hepburn, *Place apart*, pp 193–4.  **99** Munck and Rolston, *Belfast in the Thirties*, p. 182.  **100** In this I feel I must declare an interest. Dan Turley's daughter Mary McNicholl (nee Turley), now deceased, was very kind to me in New York in 1970 and I said then I would look into the circumstances of her father's death. Over the years, I have spoken to veteran Republicans over this man's death and have found responses varied from agreement that he was an informer to more measured views. I can neither prove nor disprove Dan Turley's innocence or guilt, but I feel I can say that even at this remove of years his fate was tragic and unjustified.

controversial actions of the IRA in the 1930s. Few would dispute Turley's long record of service to the IRA. He had been involved in the mobilization of Volunteers at Coalisland in 1916. In the elections of 1918, Turley was director for elections in Belfast and he served numerous terms of imprisonment in Derry, Belfast, Larne and on the prison ship *Argenta* in 1922.[101] The file on Turley in the Public Records Office, which no one would see for seventy years, claimed that when his house was raided, one of Turley's wife's family (McPolin) claimed that this was the work of an informer, known to her but not named by her.[102] In 1932, Turley was arrested for bill-sticking and not paying a fine.[103] Despite being praised by *An Phoblacht* while serving time in 1932, by 1933 he was accused of informing and in 1933 he was exiled from Ireland and stayed for a time in Southampton. In 1945, an RUC raid on Turley's home in Dunmore Street revealed letters that he wrote from Southampton in which he described how he was taken to a house across the border by the IRA, where he alleged that he was beaten and tortured with pliers and a poker. It was after he returned home in 1936 that Turley was shot dead.[104]

From 1933, both Dan Turley himself and his family were adamant that he was not an informer.[105] Doubt is raised as to Turley's guilt in *IRA: the twilight years*,[106] and in Raymond Quinn's *Rebel voices*, wherein Quinn writes that

> There was some speculation (that) Dan Turley may have been 'set up'. The man who first threw Dan's name into the ring, eight years later in 1943, attempted to have a member of GHQ courtmartialled by saying he had informed on arms dump which had been moved from St Matthew's Parochial Hall.

It was a priest who found the dump who insisted that it be removed and the source of the accusation was more suspect than the accused.[107] At this remove, we can never know for sure if indeed Turley was an informant (and certainly there was division on the issue even then), but the question must be asked as in all common law, was there sufficient evidence to convict? Dan Turley's fate in 1937 has a sourness which is an obverse of the IRA's more optimistic outlook of the early 1930s.

In June 1935 at Dún Laoghaire, General O'Duffy, who in 1922 had been Deputy Chief of Staff of the pro-treaty forces, was in boastful mood about the number of Blueshirt Volunteers he had in Ireland. On paper, he claimed the support of 66,000 men, 40,000 women and 20,000 boys and girls.[108] O'Duffy

**101** Hanley, *The IRA*, p. 48. **102** PRONI HA/5/424: file on Dan Turley. **103** MacEoin, *Twilight years*, p. 427. **104** Hanley, *The IRA*, pp 48–9. **105** Ibid., p. 225. **106** MacEoin, *Twilight years*, p. 845. **107** Quinn, *Rebel voices*, pp 49–51. **108** MacEoin, *Twilight years*, p. 293.

had always been prone to exaggeration and self-aggrandisement, and he was in fact on the wane politically in the South of Ireland. He had been deposed as the President of the United Ireland Party in 1934 and formed his National Corporate Party on fascist lines in 1935.[109] The attempt to form a thirty-two-county club on Fascist lines in the Grand Central Hotel on 21 June 1935 proved to be farcical. Only ten people turned up, one of whom was Job Stott, who led the Ulster Fascists. By a vote of four to three they decided not to form a club, and one of those present at the meeting was described in a police report as 'a mental case'.[110]

It is unsurprising that O'Duffy should fail to get any significant support in Belfast in 1935, as he was opposed by the Unionist Party, the UPL, the NILP, the CPI and the IRA, yet the IRA's efforts to protect the Nationalist residents of York Street in July 1935 would have reminded some IRA veterans of O'Duffy's role in sending in the IRA to defend Nationalists in the summer of 1921, ironically in the York Street area. His biographer recalls

> Convinced that the police were conniving with the Orange mobs, O'Duffy retaliated with characteristic determination, ordering the IRA back on to the streets. 'We'll give them the lead', he told one journalist. His snipers, the *Manchester Guardian* reported, retaliated as effectively as Loyalist gunmen.

Ten Catholics and ten Protestants were killed in that particular round of ethnic violence, with victims including Protestant shipyard workers on their way to work,[111] but at that time, O'Duffy's stock as a Nationalist defender was high. By July 1935, O'Duffy's heavy drinking and extreme right-wing politics had alienated him from Belfast support, but the events in Spain in 1936 to 1939 meant that he enjoyed some resurgence in Nationalist support.

In 1936, O'Duffy led an Irish Brigade, the Bandera, to fight for Franco in the Spanish Civil War. The performance of the Bandera and O'Duffy is generally regarded as abysmal, and IRA men like Davy Matthews would have had far more sympathy for the International Brigades. Yet support for Franco was very high in Nationalist Belfast while the Unionists took no particular side. On 3 April 1938, an open-air meeting in favour of Republican Spain attracted 200 people,[112] but an application for a march by the Irish Christian Front up the Falls Road on 8 June 1937 anticipated 15,000 marchers and was to have four bands in attendance.[113] Optimism on working-class unity had been dented by the realities of tribal politics. O'Duffy himself vanished into political obscurity after the Spanish Civil War.

For Lord Craigavon and Sir Dawson Bates, tribal politics had always served

**109** Farrell, *Orange State*, p. 347. **110** PRONI HA/32/ /615. **111** McGarry, *Eoin O'Duffy*, pp 78–83. **112** PRONI HA/32/1/654. **113** PRONI HA/32/1/637.

well to hold the greater Unionist family together. The rebellious behaviour of the UPL and the Orange Order in 1935, however, had been very embarrassing for the Unionist Party. A confidential document from the party put a rather cynical spin on the events in York Street:

> Regrettable as the disturbances may have been, their bulk must not be exaggerated. The population of Belfast is about 450,000 and the population of the area affected about 4,500. Therefore not more than one per cent of the population has been affected.[114]

The argument was fatuous. There could have been severe censure from the mother parliament at Westminster. Dr Mageean, Catholic bishop of Down and Connor, protested to Craigavon on 17 July 'against the inadequacy of the measures taken by your government to protect my Catholic people'. Mageean received only a brief acknowledgment from the Cabinet Secretary.[115] Nationalist protest meetings were held and the British Liberal MP E.L. Mallelieu demanded that troops be withdrawn from Northern Ireland. Prime Minister Baldwin replied tersely that he was 'quite satisfied with the present position'.[116] Craigavon and his cabinet were fortunate that the Lancaster Street riots occurred when Westminster was in recess and they were very anxious to avoid an enquiry. On 2 August, the Northern Ireland Cabinet Secretary expressed relief to Craigavon, saying 'I do not think you will be troubled direct from London as they do not know your Scottish address'. Craigavon himself declared that he and his colleagues 'could not countenance any acts of oppression or tyranny against the (Catholic) minority'.[117]

In practise, the Westminster Convention held and there was no British government enquiry into the Lancaster Street Riots. Craigavon remained as Prime Minister of Northern Ireland until his death in 1940,[118] and Bates remained as Minister of Home Affairs until 1943 (he served until 1945 as a Unionist MP).[119] Unemployment remained high throughout the 1930s, reaching its highest point in 1938, when 28.3 per cent of the insured population were out or work,[120] but there were no significant indications of working-class discontent as there had been in the early 1930s. On the eve of the Second World War, the IRA was planning to take its war to England and the Unionist Party's position was still unassailable. In Belfast, the most substantial contribution that the left made in the late 1930s was to send volunteers to the International Brigades in Spain, where they served with some distinction. One of them was Liam Tumlinson, a Protestant socialist who was killed at the battle of Jarama in 1937.[121] Tumlinson was one of the Shankill Road Republicans at Bodenstown in 1934.

---

114 Munck and Rolston, *Belfast in the Thirties*, p. 56.  115 Hepburn, *Place apart*, p. 196.  116 Ibid.  117 Ibid., p. 197.  118 Farrell, *Orange state*, p. 339.  119 Ibid., p. 336.  120 Munck and Rolston, *Belfast in the Thirties*, p. 60.  121 Quinn, *Rebel voices*, pp 126–8.

# Cahir Healy (1877–1970),
# Northern Nationalist leader

## ÉAMON PHOENIX

Cahir Healy, poet and man of letters, Irish language revivalist, founder-member of Arthur Griffith's early Sinn Féin party and political internee, was for almost half a century one of the best-known leaders of the Nationalist movement in Northern Ireland.

He was born Charles Everard Healy on 2 December 1877 on the Doorin Peninsula near Mountcharles in south Donegal. His father, Patrick Everard Healy, was a small farmer and merchant. Irish was still spoken in the isolated district and the young Cahir recorded that he was reared in a 'bi-lingual house-hold'. He received a rudimentary education at the local national school, which was 'mixed' in a religious sense, with a Protestant teacher. This early interaction with members of the Protestant and Unionist tradition at a time when the Home Rule controversy was sharpening sectarian antagonism in Ulster, inculcated in the young Cahir a broad-minded tolerance which was to pervade a long involvement in northern political life. A 'monitor' at that school was Seumas MacManus, later to make his name as a writer of Irish legends and folklore.

From an early age, Healy exhibited an interest in reading and 'a preoccupation with men and affairs' which were to impel him inexorably towards a career in journalism. His ambition was temporarily thwarted by domestic circumstances, however: his mother, seeing no future for three sons on a tiny holding, decided that Cahir should train for a commercial career. He found employment with a drapery firm in Derry but began to contribute short articles and verse to the local press while attending Irish language classes in St Columb's Hall and classes in English and shorthand at Derry Technical School.[1]

His interest in journalism thus rekindled, he began his newspaper career in 1895 as a junior reporter with the *Fermanagh News* in Enniskillen. Two years later, on 2 January 1897, Healy married a local Church of Ireland girl, Catherine Cresswell, the daughter of a retired sergeant-major in the British army. Their marriage was solemnized in the Church of Ireland cathedral in Enniskillen.[2] Their union produced three children, two sons and a daughter.

The next few years were spent working on a number of local newspapers, including the *Roscommon Herald* – then under the editorship of the colourful

---

1 Public Record Office of N. Ireland (PRONI), D2991/C/1: Cahir Healy papers.

Jasper Tully, the anti-Parnellite MP – and the *Sligo Times*. Finally, at the turn of the century, Healy left journalism for a position with the Refuge Insurance Company in Enniskillen – a career which he was to follow until his retirement as district superintendent in 1937.[3]

Healy was clearly exceptional among the rural generation in which he grew up, and before the age of twenty-five, had made his mark as a capable journalist, writer and minor poet. His name appears prominently among the contributors to the *Shan Van Vocht*, a literary and political magazine of advanced Nationalist views which was published in Belfast in the late 1890s by Alice Milligan and Anna Johnston ('Ethna Carberry'). Through this journal, which in many ways prefigured the later Sinn Féin policy of Arthur Griffith, Healy was initiated into a select literary and cultural circle centred at 'Ard Righ', the Belfast residence of the historian and Protestant Nationalist, Francis Joseph Bigger.

Among the diverse figures who frequented the convivial 'Firelight' get-togethers in the cosy drawing-room of 'Ard Righ' – with its vast library, and its 'Ninety-Eight' museum – were Sir Roger Casement, Alice Stopford Green (the 'passionate historian'), Sir Shane Leslie, the Co. Monaghan-based writer and landlord, Cathal O'Byrne, the Belfast writer and ballad-singer, and Seumas MacManus, who had also been a contributor to the *Shan Van Vocht*. In 1904, Healy was invited to lecture to the National Literary Theatre in Dublin and in the following year he collaborated with Cathal O'Byrne to produce an anthology of Ulster love poems entitled *The lane of the thrushes*. The title poem captures the romantic, rustic flavour of much of his early verse:

> There is a crooning of wind through white drifts of briar bushes,
> The drowsy humming of bees where the bending fox-gloves gleam,
> A purple flame, and a green flame in a heart of gold, adream,
> And a riot of song that thrills through the dim woodland hushes,
> In the lane of the thrushes.[4]

The start of the new century witnessed the reunification of the Irish Home Rule Party, riven by the Parnell split, under the leadership of John Redmond. The young poet was keenly interested in their cause of 'Ireland a nation'. However, he was repelled by the crude sectarian image which the spread of Joseph Devlin's Ancient Order of Hibernians lent to the Home Rule Party in Ulster after 1904, and showed an early leaning towards the forces of the 'new Nationalism'. The Gaelic League, founded by Douglas Hyde and Eoin MacNeill in 1893, was the

---

**2** Church of Ireland Cathedral Records, Enniskillen: Register of Marriages; *Fermanagh Herald*, 14 Feb. 1970. **3** PRONI, D2991/D/2. **4** PRONI, D2991/B/1; Cahal O'Byrne and Cahir Healy, *The lane of the thrushes and other poems* (London, 1904).

harbinger of the new era and, significantly, it was Healy who launched the Enniskillen branch of the organization in November 1902. Revd Patrick McKenna, CC, later Bishop of Clogher, was chairman with the young Donegal man as secretary. In this capacity, he was one of those who invited the Gaelic revivalist and future revolutionary, Patrick Pearse, to open the Fermanagh Feis in 1906. By this time, Cahir Healy – as he now styled himself – had become chairman of the expanding Gaelic Athletic Association in Fermanagh.[5]

These years found him contributing articles and verse to Griffith's *United Irishman*, which became the organ for the propagation of its editor's novel policy of 'Dual Monarchy' after the Hungarian model. Politics beckoned, however, and in 1903 he campaigned for the Russellite candidate, Edward Mitchell, in the North Fermanagh by-election which saw Mitchell defeat the future Ulster Unionist leader, James Craig.

When, in November 1905, Griffith launched his non-violent Sinn Féin party, Healy was among the small group that attended the fateful meeting at the Rotunda, Dublin. He outlined his association with the new radical movement in a letter to Rory O'Connor in 1954: 'I was never connected with the Irish Party or any of its organizations. ... I was opposed to them. I represented Fermanagh at the convention in the Rotunda at which Sinn Féin was born.'[6] He has left us with a glimpse of that occasion in a memoir:

> Griffith's written speech read much better in his paper the week after than it did that day. Seumas MacManus and P.S. O'Hegarty talked a good deal ... Griffith had just published serially his 'Resurrection of Hungary' and everyone pretended to see the parallel (with Ireland). It was all over in a little while, and when we came into the street and mingled with the crowd, it seemed to me very much like the river that rushes to the ocean, to be instantly engulfed therein. The press took no notice. It was still hungering for the oratorical gold that fell from the lips of the 'leader of the Irish race at home and abroad'! (John Redmond).[7]

For the next few years, Healy devoted himself to the establishment of Sinn Féin branches in Ulster and it was at his own branch in Enniskillen in 1907 that Charles Dolan, a disillusioned Irish Party MP, first declared his disbelief in the methods of the Home Rule Party. When Healy drew Griffith's attention to Dolan's remarks, the Sinn Féin leader, 'with that intellectual conceit which made him often misunderstood' – as Healy later recalled – at first refused to publish

5 Peadar Livingstone, 'The Fermanagh story', *Clogher Record* (1969), pp 333–4; PRONI, D2991/C/1: Cahir Healy, *Notes on reminiscences* (1969). **6** PRONI, D2991/A/358A: Healy to O'Connor, 7 Mar. 1954. **7** PRONI, D2991/C/1: Healy, *Notes on reminiscences*.

them in his paper on the grounds that they were of 'little consequence'. In the upshot, however, Dolan resigned his seat in North Leitrim and re-contested it on a Sinn Féin programme. During the subsequent by-election campaign of February 1908, Healy accompanied Griffith from Enniskillen to Manorhamilton to address a meeting in support of the Sinn Féin candidate. The great theorist, he recalls in his memoirs, with his dull and monotonous recitation of statistics and facts, came as a damper to the 'fair-day' crowd, which quickly melted away towards a Redmondite orator who was dispensing 'the minimum of dead facts with the maximum of denunciation of the old enemy'.[8]

Sinn Féin's defeat in the North Leitrim by-election – its first parliamentary challenge – marked the beginning of Healy's involvement with the revolutionary IRB in Ulster. He would seem to have played no part in the 1916 Rising in the north or the mobilization of Irish Volunteers at Coalisland in April 1916. However, the universal tendency of the British authorities to regard the insurrection as 'a Sinn Féin Rebellion' led the local RIC in Fermanagh to suspect him of involvement and his home was raided on several occasions. Like his mentor, Griffith, Healy was quick to see the Rising and its crop of martyrs as having regenerated Ireland's national spirit and awakened the country to the compromising policy of the Irish Party leaders.

The readiness of the IPP leadership of Redmond, Dillon and Devlin to accept the 'temporary exclusion' of six Ulster counties from the third Home Rule Act in June 1916 split the Home Rule party in the north and confronted Fermanagh's Nationalist majority with the danger of permanent partition for the first time. As the mood of Nationalist Ireland turned against Redmond and towards the forces of revolutionary Nationalism, Healy's admiration for the executed insurgent leaders became increasingly more marked until in a poem, published in 1920, he could eulogize them as:

> Ye holy dead,
> Who died that we
> Might taste the sweet of liberty,
> Whose blood was shed
> That we from serfdom might arise,
> And like the morning star instead
> Hold God's glad freedom in our eyes.[9]

It was inevitable that Healy, as one of the founders of Griffith's original movement, should become one of the foremost personalities of the post-Rising Sinn

8 Ibid.   9 Poem by Cahir Healy in *Catholic Bulletin* (Dublin, 1920).

Féin party in the north. In September 1918, following the Nationalist campaign against conscription, he was prosecuted for posting anti-recruiting notices in Enniskillen and played a key role in the Sinn Féin election campaign of that December which witnessed the return of Griffith in North-West Tyrone and his party colleague, Seán O'Mahony in South Fermanagh.

The period 1919–21 witnessed the establishment of Dáil Éireann as the declared legislature of an all-Ireland republic and the outbreak of the Anglo-Irish War. As constitutionalism gave way to physical force, Healy became the leading Fermanagh Sinn Féiner. In June 1920, his profile was raised by his co-option as a Sinn Féin member of the county council.[10] During these formative years, Healy was able to turn his peripatetic mode of livelihood and his able penmanship to the advantage of the revolutionary organization over a large area of Fermanagh, Leitrim and Sligo, where he operated incognito as an organizer of Sinn Féin clubs. According to family sources, he may have occupied an intelligence role in the Irish Volunteers, now renamed the IRA.

An interesting aspect of his activities at this period was his involvement in the setting-up of Republican 'arbitration courts'. The latter attempted to supplant the normal petty sessions and county courts though in Ulster, outside Fermanagh, Cavan and Monaghan, their progress was slight and limited to 'a few raids by Sinn Féin volunteers on poitin-makers!'[11] Healy acted as 'county registrar' of these clandestine courts in Fermanagh. In his quasi-legal capacity, he was closely involved with a prominent Republican priest, Fr Lorcan Ó Ciaráin, whose parochial house at Magherameenagh Castle, near Belleek, was a frequent venue for secret judicial sessions. He was also an associate of the Omagh-born barrister Kevin O'Shiel, who acted as a Republican judge in Fermanagh during the Anglo-Irish War.

Healy's most enduring memory of these secret sessions was of one held in the village of Pettigo on the Donegal-Fermanagh border in the summer of 1920. The 'clients' and 'magistrates' had just assembled in the local Nationalist hall when a lorry-load of military, acting on a tip-off, suddenly arrived in the village. To the amazement of Healy and his associates, who had resigned themselves to arrest and imprisonment, the troops ignored the building where they had foregathered, and proceeded to surround an Orange Hall a few yards further down the street. They had misconstrued the date prominently displayed above the door of the latter: '1916'. Healy and company were able to complete the comic piece by making good their escape as part of the funeral procession which happened to be passing by.[12]

10 PRONI, D2991/E/24.  11 Livingstone, 'The Fermanagh story', p. 284.  12 PRONI, D2991/C/3: Cahir Healy, 'First Republican courts in North'. Healy's son, the late Pete Healy, related that his father had told him that he was 'an Intelligence Officer during the Troubles' (P. Healy to the author, 19 Feb 1982).

For Healy and his fellow Nationalists in Fermanagh and Tyrone – two counties with small but clear anti-partitionist majorities – the establishment of a Unionist parliament and government for Northern Ireland in June 1921 was offset by the intense – and ultimately forlorn – hope that in any subsequent negotiations between the Dáil representatives and Lloyd George, their territories would be transferred to the jurisdiction of a Dublin parliament. A deputation consisting of Cahir Healy, John McHugh of Pettigo, the Nationalist chairman of the county council, and Fr Ó Ciaráin met President de Valera in Dublin on 31 August 1921 to impress on him the urgency of the Fermanagh case. They reminded the Dáil cabinet that 'Fermanagh, by a large majority ... resolved that it would not submit to the partition parliament in Ulster'.[13]

When the treaty was signed in December 1921, however, with its formal recognition of partition, Healy supported it as containing the best terms that could be obtained in the circumstances and viewed de Valera's attack on it during the treaty debates as based merely on semantics. As a northerner, he was concerned pre-eminently with the partition issue, and shared the dubious optimism of northern Sinn Féiners – which was reinforced by the statements of Collins and Griffith – that Article 12 of the treaty, with its guarantee of a Boundary Commission to revise the territorial area of Northern Ireland, would result in the cession of Fermanagh, Tyrone, south Armagh, south Down and other preponderantly Nationalist areas to the south. Moreover, the long-term impact of such an excision, he argued, would be to render the residual northern area non-viable and so ensure the 'essential unity' of Ireland by a process of territorial contraction.

Healy was present at a meeting between a northern Nationalist delegation and the Dáil Speaker, Eoin MacNeill, in Dublin's Mansion House on 7 December 1921 to discuss the implications of the treaty for the northern minority. While the Mayor of Derry, H.C. O'Doherty, was contemptuous of the terms as 'handing over manacled the lives and liberties of Catholics' to the Unionist regime, Healy endorsed the 'non-recognition' policy towards the Belfast government advocated by MacNeill and later supported by Michael Collins. The Fermanagh activist rejected the principle of partition but felt convinced that the Boundary Commission would keep Fermanagh and Tyrone within the new Irish Free State.[14]

Like Collins and his successors, Healy could not possibly foresee that the final interpreter of the boundary clause – Judge Richard Feetham, the chairman of the Commission established in 1924 – would subjugate 'the wishes of the inhabitants' to 'economics and geographic conditions' in making its award, and so rob the

---

**13** Livingstone, 'The Fermanagh story', p. 298. **14** Minutes of *Conference of representatives of six-county Area*, 7 Dec. 1921, PRONI, D2991/82.

Free State of 'every scrap of her anticipated territorial gains'. As Healy saw the position of the north under the treaty,

> the principle of non-coercion was applied both to those who might not wish to remain under the Free State ... and to those who ardently desired to give it their allegiance. If the Belfast parliament decided to contract out, then the Nationalist majorities in the border area must be given an opportunity of being restored to the Free State. The principle of self-determination was applied all round.

In support of MacNeill's non-recognition policy, Fermanagh County Council declared its allegiance to the Dáil in December 1921 and was promptly dissolved by the fledgling Belfast government. Despite this serious blow, Healy publicly endorsed Collins' view of the treaty as the 'freedom to achieve freedom'. At a meeting of the Fermanagh Sinn Féin executive in Enniskillen on 30 December 1921, Healy's motion calling on the TDs for Fermanagh and Tyrone to support the ratification of the treaty in Dáil Éireann was passed by thirty-four votes to eight. Despite this pressure, however, the TD for South Fermanagh, Seán O'Mahony, vigorously opposed the settlement.[15]

In April 1922, Healy was selected by Collins to serve on the Provisional Government's 'North-Eastern Advisory Committee', established to formulate a definite northern policy following the breakdown of the Craig-Collins pact of 31 March. His membership of this body, together with his efforts to prepare the case of the Fermanagh Nationalists for the expected Boundary Commission, led to demands from border Unionists for his 'removal from circulation'. Thus, when in the wake of the murder of a Unionist MP in Belfast in May 1922, the Northern Ireland government ordered a round-up of some 500 suspected Sinn Féin sympathizers, Healy was among fifty men arrested in Fermanagh. For eighteen months from July 1922, he was interned with some 300 others on board the *Argenta*, a converted American cargo vessel which was moored, first in Belfast Lough, and later in Larne Bay, Co. Antrim.[16]

The Fermanagh Sinn Féin leader was particularly sensitive to the allegation, contained in an RUC 'Crime Special' report, and circulated by the Unionist regime, that he had been an 'intelligence officer in the IRA'. In a letter from the bleak hulk some months later, he sought to pinpoint a political motive for his incarceration:

> All my life, I have been a man of peace. It is not, therefore, because they feared that I would disturb the peace of Northern Ireland that they

15 Livingstone, 'The Fermanagh story', pp 298–9. 16 Ibid., pp 310–11.

dragged me away from my wife and family, but for political reasons. I have been engaged in preparing the case for the inclusion of these areas (Fermanagh and Tyrone) in the Free State. To get me out of the way, local politicians urged my arrest.[17]

Certainly, the public statements of Sir Charles Falls MP and the evidence of a confidential letter to Sir James Craig from a leading Fermanagh Unionist urging Healy's continued detention lend credence to his interpretation of events.[18] It seems likely, however, that he had provided intelligence to the local IRA during the War of Independence.

This phase of Cahir Healy's career is well-documented in a Northern Ireland cabinet file on his internment during 1922–4 and his own detailed unpublished narrative, 'Two Years on an Ulster Prison Ship'. Some impression of the harsh conditions on board the *Argenta* can be gleaned from a humorous ditty in his memoir:

> Such beds as we sleep on were ne'er seen before,
> They've downstairs and upstairs and were built to hold four.
> They're our chairs and our tables and writing desks too,
> Rotten cheese and sour milk, fat bacon and spuds,
> And tea that you'd think had been washing our duds.[19]

As he surveyed the rugged landscape of the Antrim coast from his floating cell, Healy harboured the increasing fear, as the months passed, that the fate of the 500 internees had been forgotten by the Dublin government, then embroiled in a civil war with the anti-treaty IRA. As early as September 1922, he had expressed the view in a letter to his friend, Kevin O'Shiel, now the Irish government's Assistant Legal Adviser, that the northern Nationalists had been abandoned to Craig's mercy: 'Personally, we must look after ourselves, I think'.[20] He was right. On 31 May 1923, as the civil war ended in the Free State, Healy confided to his diary:

> Today we distinctly heard the clarion-call of a blackbird on Island Magee. The lake lay sparkling like a bowl of silver. Two horses were grazing in a field; they came with heads erect and looked at us inquiringly. I daresay, after a day or two, they will have grown accustomed to our ugly hulk and take us for granted as so many of the wise humans now do outside.[21]

**17** Ibid.; PRONI CAB/9B/4: S. Watt to Private Secretary to PM, 12 Dec. 1923.  **18** PRONI CAB/9B/4: G.B. Liddy to Sir James Craig, 15 Jan. 1924.  **19** PRONI, D2991/C: Healy, typescript, *Two years on an Ulster prison ship*.  **20** Healy to O'Shiel, 30 Sept. 1922: University College, Dublin, R. Mulcahy papers, P7/B/287.  **21** Healy, *Two years on an Ulster prison ship*, PRONI, D2991/C.

His internment, however, was to acquire a new dimension when, in November 1922, he was returned in the British general election as one of the two pro-Free State candidates for the then joint-constituency of Fermanagh-Tyrone. The election of Healy and his colleague, the Nationalist T.J.S. Harbison, by majorities of over 6,000 over the Unionist candidates, was regarded in the two counties as a kind of plebiscite of 'the wishes of the inhabitants' in the face of the expected Commission.[22] Almost immediately, the Free State government began to press the British authorities for his release on the grounds that he was a supporter of the treaty. These pleas initially failed because of the Northern Ireland government's insistence that the Fermanagh MP had been active in the IRA. According to a minute by the Belfast Ministry of Home Affairs in Healy's internment file, the MP was 'an intelligence officer in IRA and ... a cunning and clever organizer'.[23] By December 1923, however, Healy's re-election to Westminster and the disappearance of the Conservative government's overall majority impelled the British Prime Minister, Stanley Baldwin, faced with impending defeat in the House of Commons, to ask Craig to consider releasing him. Baldwin told the Northern Ireland Prime Minister:

> I do not know the ground upon which he is interned but I understand that he is regarded by the Free State not as a Republican but as a supporter of the constitutional settlement ... The situation for the next few months is one of great difficulty and I am anxious that no unnecessary cause of embarrassment either to your government or to this country should be allowed to continue.[24]

In his reply, Craig was unbending in his conviction that Healy should remain in custody unless he was prepared to leave the northern area or provide guarantees as to his good behaviour. As public pressure for his release intensified, Healy denied that any charge could be brought against him, telling the Liberal MP, Frank Gray: 'I have always kept the law, and the northern authorities desire my being kept in custody until the Boundary matter is settled. They think they will, by holding 450-odd men ... have something to bargain over'. At the same time, Healy managed to smuggle out an article exposing the unsanitary conditions on board the prison ship. This was subsequently published in the *Sunday Express* and led to renewed questions in the British House of Commons.[25]

---

**22** F.W.S. Craig (ed.), *British parliamentary election results, 1918–49* (Glasgow, 1969), p. 600. The figures were: Harbison (N) 42,236; Healy (SF), 44,817; Pringle (U), 38,640; Allen (U), 38,589.  **23** PRONI, CAB 9B/4: Greer to Queckett, 22 Nov. 1922; memo by Queckett, 27 Nov. 1922; Watt (Ministry of Home Affairs) to Private Secretary to PM, 12 Dec. 1923.  **24** PRONI, CAB 9B/4: Baldwin to Craig, 19 Dec. 1923.  **25** *Irish News*, 22 Dec. 1923.

The upshot of the growing ferment was a frank letter from Baldwin – beset with the difficulties facing a minority administration – urging upon Craig the absolute necessity of dealing with the Healy issue:

> I think I see your difficulties but I want you ... to see some of mine. If we go into opposition ... my hands will be full of our own problems here. I do not want the Irish problem revived in the House of Commons in any shape or form ... But if Cahir Healy is still in confinement, the Labour Party is certain to fill the House and the press with it. The *Sunday Express* has already started a demand for a full enquiry. I should not find it easy to rally our men to support your policy of detaining Healy without trial.[26]

Indeed 'the troublesome agitation' which Baldwin foresaw in his letter to Craig was already underway and in January 1924, Pringle, a Liberal MP gave notice that he would be moving a motion for the appointment of a parliamentary committee into the MP's continued incarceration. It was not, however, until the appointment of the first Labour government in January 1924 that the Northern Ireland administration, 'on the general ground of not wishing to raise difficulties with the new government' reluctantly agreed to release the MP.[27]

Healy was finally released from Larne Workhouse on 11 February 1924, but this did not prevent the Minister of Home Affairs, Dawson Bates, from issuing a further order prohibiting him from entering that part of his constituency which included his home in Enniskillen.[28] The prediction of Sir Wilfred Spender, the Northern Ireland cabinet secretary, that Healy would 'have the chance of becoming a martyr again by refusing to obey the order' was soon fulfilled by his re-arrest.[29] In the end, it required a firm letter from the incoming British Prime Minister, Ramsay MacDonald, to Craig on 15 February 1924, warning him that the Belfast administration might become a 'direct issue' at Westminster to secure Healy's unconditional release in face of Bates' bitter opposition.[30] The Unionist government was clearly anxious not to foment an ugly quarrel with the new Labour Prime Minister in view of his responsibility for the setting up of the Boundary Commission.

The issue of Cahir Healy's detention stands out as one of the few examples of the Westminster government forcing its devolved Unionist administration to reverse a policy decision in the period 1921–68. The motivating factor was, of course, British government self-interest rather than the desire to ensure justice and fair play to the Nationalist minority.

**26** PRONI, CAB 9B/4: Baldwin to Craig, 14 Jan. 1924.  **27** PRONI, CAB 9B/4: Reid to Spender, 25 Jan. 1924.  **28** PRONI, CAB 9B/4: Watt to Speaker (Westminster), 8 Feb. 1924.  **29** PRONI, CAB 9B/4: Spender to Londonderry, 11 Feb. 1924.  **30** PRONI, CAB 9B/4: MacDonald to Craig, 15 Feb. 1924; Craig's reply, 16 Feb. 1924.

The existing evidence suggests that the Northern Ireland authorities feared that Healy, once released, would lend his journalistic skills to a sustained 'muck-raking' campaign against the Unionist government and, in particular, on behalf of the internees. In a letter to Lord Londonderry, the Minister of Education, Spender voiced his suspicion that 'Healy is going to make the most of his information about our internees and I expect a press campaign on the subject . . . I feel, however, that if the position is handled properly, anything of this nature will be greatly discounted by the fact that apparently he has no intention of attending the Imperial House'.[31]

In this assumption, Spender was a trifle precipitate. Healy, it was true, had been returned as a pro-treaty Sinn Féiner. However, it was the considered view of both the Free State government and the Nationalist convention which nominated him that he should abandon the traditional abstentionist policy towards Westminster and take his seat as a means of focusing attention on the boundary issue, the gerrymandering of local government and the plight of the internees. Healy duly took his seat in March 1924 but his entry to the House was directly responsible for the termination of his long friendship with Seumas MacManus, then plying his literary skill in the United States. In a splenetic letter, the latter vented his scorn that 'Cahir Healy, Sinn Féin advocate, had, amid the rapturous cheers of the English members, taken his seat in Britain's parliament'. He added 'That a Donegal man should be the betrayer is the poignant part'.[32] It was perhaps a reflection of the bitterness which the treaty and the Civil War had engendered among former comrades. In Healy's view, on the other hand, the real villains of the piece were de Valera's 'Irregulars', whose 'reckless actions' had split the independence movement, entrenched partition and forestalled the setting-up of the long-awaited Boundary Commission.

At Westminster, Healy sought at once the interest of the Labour Colonial Secretary, J.H. Thomas, in the plight of the *Argenta* internees. To his dismay, Thomas showed himself to be 'far from friendly' and affected to see the question as solely an internal one for the Northern Ireland government. The leader of the Labour Party, George Lansbury, was, however, more sympathetic and advised Healy to make the issue a 'live' one among the local branches of the party in areas with large Irish populations. When a few weeks' canvassing in this way produced an avalanche of resolutions on the Colonial Secretary's desk, an irate Thomas accused the MP of wantonly 'stirring up strife in the Labour ranks' at a critical juncture. However, he could not afford to ignore the feelings of a significant interest group within the party, and it was not long before large-scale releases of northern internees took place.[33]

**31** PRONI, CAB 9B/4: Spender to Londonderry, 18 Feb. 1924. **32** PRONI D2991/A/5A: McManus to Healy [1924]. **33** PRONI, D2991/C: Healy, *Two years on an Ulster prison ship*.

During this period also, Healy worked closely with the new Free State government's 'North-Eastern Boundary Bureau', set up under the direction of his old Sinn Féin associate, Kevin O'Shiel, to coordinate the preparation of the local cases of the northern Nationalists for conclusion in the Free State. A confidential Irish cabinet memorandum, written by O'Shiel in November 1923, described Healy as 'one of the sanest and far-seeing leaders of ... the Free State section of Nationalism in the six counties'.[34] From an early stage in the Commission's proceedings, he fully grasped the danger that the British-appointed chairman might impose a narrow interpretation on the ambiguous article in the treaty. 'If we cannot get the Commission to fix the terms of reference', he confided to a Free State official in December 1925, 'we are going to be diddled'.[35] If a debacle were to be averted, he argued, the Dublin government must insist upon a plebiscite of the electors in such areas as Fermanagh and Tyrone, where the Unionists' abolition of PR for local elections and re-drawing of the electoral areas had largely displaced the Nationalist local authorities. By December 1924, however, the chairman of the commission, Richard Feetham, had firmly ruled out the use of local plebiscites to ascertain the 'wishes of the inhabitants' along the border.

The Boundary Commission sat in Enniskillen from 22 April to 6 May 1925. The basis of the chairman's cross-examination of local Nationalist witnesses was the detailed case submitted by the now Unionist-controlled Fermanagh county council. This contended that the transfer of any part of the county to the Free State would 'not be an economic proposition'. In his evidence, Healy sought to rebut this by stressing 'the wishes of the inhabitants' as expressed in the return of Harbison and himself in two successive elections and 'the right that the people of the county had acquired under the treaty of remaining in the Free State'.[36] Despite the forcefulness of Healy's performance, E.M. Stephens, the secretary of the Irish government's North-Eastern Boundary Bureau, reported to Dublin that the thrust of Feetham's questions convinced the Nationalist witnesses, including the influential Archdeacon John Tierney of Enniskillen, that he was bent on mere 'rectification' of the border-line and 'intended using the gerrymandered electoral divisions to their disadvantage'. Many Fermanagh witnesses, Stephens noted, were interpreting a recent conference between Healy, Devlin and their respective supporters to discuss cooperation in the Northern Ireland election of March 1925, as a sign that no real change was expected from the Boundary Commission.[37]

Healy's worst fears were confirmed by the subsequent collapse of the Commission in December 1925, following the dramatic resignation of the Free

---

**34** National Archives (NA) S 5750/16: O'Shiel memo, 17 Nov. 1923.   **35** NA NEBB files: Healy to G. Murnaghan, 5 Dec. 1924.   **36** D2991/B/1/5C: Evidence of C. Healy to Boundary Commission.   **37** NA S 1801/M: Report by E.M. Stephens, 24 Apr. 1925.

State Commissioner, Eoin MacNeill, and a widespread belief that the body had merely recommended a minor 'rectification' of the border-line. The signature by the Free State government of the subsequent Tripartite Agreement of 3 December 1925, whereby they relinquished their rights under the boundary clause in favour of certain financial concessions, irrevocably alienated Healy and the mass of northern Nationalists from the Cumann na nGaedheal administration. It was 'amazing', he declared, 'that the liberties and rights guaranteed to the Nationalists by Article 12 should be scrapped, and the people sold into political servitude for all time.'[38]

Healy had already voiced his fears of a disappointing outcome in an article in George Russell's *Irish Statesman* on the eve of the first formal hearings in February 1925. He complained that the excessive delay in setting up the tribunal had greatly prejudiced the position of the northern Nationalist minority. More surprisingly, he launched a caustic attack on the policy of the Sinn Féin leadership towards the north in the years since 1916:

> The truth is that none of the Irish leaders understood the northern situation or the northern mind. Griffith, the sanest and best informed of them all, nursed a delusion for years – that the (solution) of the problem lay in London. Not even de Valera's non-recognition of it nor the rather jumpy efforts which, with Collins, passed for statecraft, could possibly bring us one day nearer peace.

But the former Sinn Féin advocate did not exculpate the northern Nationalists themselves from responsibility for their plight under the Unionist parliament. In Healy's view, they had failed to realize the danger of partition in 1918 and had failed to devise a united strategy to oppose it. 'If they have any policy today', he added, 'save the ostrich one of burying their heads in the sands of reality ... they manage to keep their secret only too well'.[39]

The shattering of their hopes with the collapse of the Commission confronted Healy and the border Nationalists with the reality of lasting partition for the first time. Since 1918, the northern Nationalists had been badly split between the adherents of Sinn Féin – strongest west of the Bann – and those who remained loyal to the constitutional Nationalism of Joseph Devlin. Devlin, always sceptical of the Collins' view of the Boundary Commission, had reversed his earlier policy of non-recognition of the northern parliament and taken his seat in April 1925. The Unionists had given notice of their intention to abolish Proportional

---

**38** D2991/B/1/10A: Healy letter in *Irish Independent*, 30 Nov. 1924.   **39** Cited in *Ulster Herald*, 21 Feb. 1925.

Representation (PR) for Northern Ireland parliamentary elections, and by 1927, Healy had come round to the view that only a *rapprochement* between the Devlinites (centred on Belfast and east Ulster) and his own border supporters would serve the clamant demand of the Catholic community for the constitutional redress of their grievances.

Throughout 1927, he sought to assuage the bitterness and petty jealousies dividing the incoherent remnants of Hibernianism and Sinn Féinism in the north as the prelude to a new united Nationalist Party. Unless the Nationalists 'did something for themselves', Healy told a Fermanagh gathering in May 1928, there was a real danger that 'partition would become an established thing'. His aim was to establish 'a virile and truly national organization' which would cooperate with any party in the south which was committed to Irish unity. He was careful to stress that a united Ireland might be based on a federal system with a subordinate northern assembly for the six counties.[40] Healy was already building bridges towards de Valera's new Fianna Fáil party, with its emphasis on Irish unity. In February 1928, his confidant, Fr Eugene Coyle, parish priest of Devenish West, Co. Fermanagh, and a member of the Fianna Fáil national executive, arranged a meeting in Belfast between Healy and Devlin and two emissaries of de Valera, Seán Lemass and Seán T. O'Kelly to discuss future cooperation on the 'national question'.[41]

The new united Nationalist movement finally emerged as the 'National League of the North' in May 1928 with the rehabilitated Devlin as president and Healy and Patrick O'Neill, the Nationalist MP for Down, as joint secretaries.[42] At first, Healy had high hopes that the growing difficulties which the Unionists were facing in the economic and social spheres might ultimately lead to a fissuring of the Unionist monolith and the emergence of a less 'frozen' political system in Northern Ireland.[43] At the same time, he established good relations with his old opponent, de Valera, and his new Fianna Fáil party and urged the need for them, once returned to power, to make the south as attractive as possible to the northern majority. But his hopes of a radical political re-alignment in the north were finally dashed with the abolition of PR in 1929. In 1932, dispirited by five years of barren opposition, Devlin and Healy led their followers out of the northern parliament. The Unionist government, they declared, was determined to 'rivet sectarianism' to Northern Ireland politics for the future.

Devlin died in January 1934, and for the next decade Healy assumed his mantle. However, his Sinn Féin background and Fianna Fáil orientation made him suspect among the Hibernian wing of the party identified with the Belfast

---

**40** *Ulster Herald*, 26 May 1926.   **41** D2991/B/9: Healy to Devlin, 8 Feb. 1928.   **42** *Irish News*, 29 May 1928.   **43** D2991/B/9: Healy to Coyle, 24 Dec. 1927.

Central MP, T.J. Campbell. Until the end of the Second World War, he and his fellow-Nationalists abstained for the most part from Stormont, preferring instead to enlist the support of de Valera – now in power in Dublin – and outside agencies in drawing the British government's attention to the treatment of the Nationalist minority. For example, in 1936, Healy was the driving force behind an important commission of enquiry into the allegations of gerrymandering and discrimination in Northern Ireland by the British National Council for Civil Liberties.[44] Moreover, during his two further spells at Westminster (1931–5 and 1950–5), he tried to use the House as a 'sounding-board' – as he put it – for his community's general sense of injustice. Following serious sectarian violence in Belfast in July 1935, Healy raised the issue at Westminster and in an interview with the Home Secretary, Sir John Simon. But while the Nationalist leader found Simon 'very sympathetic', he took the steady view of the British government that law and order in Northern Ireland was the exclusive prerogative of the devolved parliament at Stormont.[45] Until 1968, Westminster's attitude remained one of strict non-intervention in view of the oft-cited 'rights and privileges of the parliament of Northern Ireland.'

The failure of de Valera to obtain any concessions on either partition or the issue of civil rights for the northern minority in his negotiations with Neville Chamberlain in 1938 left Healy bitter and frustrated. Though consulted by de Valera in London during the Anglo-Irish conference, the 'Long Fellow's' failure to move the British on partition came as a crushing blow to the Nationalist leader. As he remarked to a leading northern Nationalist in February 1939, 'de Valera made a civil war about the differences between Documents 1 and 2 [during the treaty debates of 1922] but he is not prepared to say "boo" to Chamberlain over the loss of the six counties!'[46] Healy's disillusionment with de Valera was partly relieved a year later when the Taoiseach joined all shades of northern Nationalism and Catholic hierarchy in a successful campaign against the extension of conscription to the six counties.

During the Second World War, Healy shared the vague hope of many Irish Nationalists that the Allies' need for southern Irish ports (ceded by Neville Chamberlain in 1938) might somehow result in the removal of the border. In July 1941, he was arrested at his home in Enniskillen under the Defence of the Realm Act and interned by the British Home Secretary in Brixton Prison until the end of 1942. Healy's arrest followed earlier secret contacts between a section of northern Nationalists and the German Minister in Dublin, Edouard Hempel, in 1940. The reason for his eighteen-month detention was the interception of a

---

44 PRONI, CAB 9B/236/1.   45 P. O'Neill private papers: Healy to O'Neill, 24 July 1935.   46 Healy to Eamonn Donnelly, 18 Feb. 1939, E. Donnelly private papers.

letter from Healy to Revd Tom Maguire, the colourful parish priest of Newtownbutler, Co. Fermanagh, and an ardent anti-partitionist. According to Healy, the letter 'contained some loose sentences which could have been misunderstood' regarding the possibility of a German victory in the war.

The British Home Office file on Healy's detention shows the hand of the Unionist government in the affair. In June 1941, the head of the Royal Ulster Constabulary, Sir Charles Wickham, urged Healy's arrest following the interception of a letter from the politician to Maguire. Healy suggested that events might result in either peace or 'a long war' and asked the priest whether he thought the northern Nationalists should make an approach to the German legation in Dublin. While Wickham believed that this indicated Healy's preparedness to assist the Germans in the event of a Nazi invasion, Healy refuted this, informing a British official: 'I am not anti-British and have never had any liking for Nazism. I should like to see the peoples of Ireland and England living in peace and good fellowship'.[47] The Irish representative in London, John Dulanty, approached Herbert Morrison, the British Home Secretary, about the MP's release but was informed that this was 'somewhat remote in view of the extreme imprudence of his letter to Fr Maguire'. Healy's incarceration and the ensuing protest meetings were given wide publicity on Axis radio stations.

The Nationalist politician found conditions in Brixton more congenial than on board the *Argenta* two decades earlier. A bronchitis sufferer, he wrote from prison: 'My health is fine. ... My fellow-internees are very agreeable. Some are well-known public characters, authors, MPs, ex-officers ... so that life has every advantage which variety, intelligence and world experience can impart'. Among his prison acquaintances at Brixton was the Blackshirt leader, Sir Oswald Mosley, with whom he formed a lasting friendship, Admiral Sir Barry Domville and Gerald Hamilton, a member of an Ulster landed family and a Protestant Nationalist.

After the war, Healy, now almost 70, was involved in the launching of the broad-based Anti-Partition League (APL) which, for a short period in the late 1940s and early 1950s, caused serious anxiety at Stormont in its attempt to mobilize public and political opinion against partition in Britain and the United States. He was largely responsible, together with the Mid-Ulster MP, Anthony Mulvey, and the British Labour member, Hugh Delargey, in organizing the 100-strong parliamentary pressure-group, the 'Friends of Ireland' within the British Labour Party. He was, moreover, the author of the pamphlet, *The mutilation of a nation* (1945) which sold some 20,000 copies and became the 'bible' of every

**47** *News Review*, 17 Dec. 1942; Confidential Garda Report, NA GFA/A/23; C. Norton, 'The internment of Cahir Healy, MP, Brixton Prison, July 1941–Dec. 1942', *Twentieth-Century British History*, 18:2 (2007), 170–93.

League orator, including de Valera, who made an anti-partition tour of America in 1948.

The recrudescence of IRA violence in the late 1950s sounded the death-knell for the constitutional efforts of the League. The ageing Healy was unequivocal in his aversion to the use of violence to further the cause of Irish unity: 'Intrusions and physical force', he told the Bishop of Clogher, Eugene O'Callaghan, in August 1955, 'only further consolidate Unionist opinion against us, and result in injury to Catholics as a whole'.[48] Moreover, in his later years at Stormont, he became convinced of the futility of the policy of abstentionism, which he himself had espoused in the early decades of the state. It was anomalous, he argued, to refuse to recognize the parliament where laws were made, and at the same time have 'no objection to paying rates and taxes, nor to accepting grants and subsidies which issue from legislation enacted in that assembly'. Since a policy of civil disobedience was not feasible, he contended, abstention represented 'an insincere gesture'. As he told a critic in 1948, 'If we had continued to remain outside the two parliaments [Stormont and Westminster] ... our places would have been taken by Labour. ... That we take the oath (of allegiance) is just due to sheer necessity. ... We never profess that an enforced formula has changed our views'. He was scathing towards his inflexible Republican opponents, commenting: 'I wish Republicans could be more practical and face realities. They appear to live and thrive on a diet of theories. It will be tragic if they die on it.'[49]

Despite his loyalty to party policy, Healy was sceptical of Nationalist attempts in the post-War years to gain admission to the Dáil for the representatives of the northern minority. 'I never had any hope of sitting there', he wrote. 'We have no work to do in the Dáil – we are needed outside badly.'[50] Healy believed that the declaration of a twenty-six-county republic by the Fine Gael-led coalition in April 1949 was unhelpful to the cause of a united Ireland. In an effort to promote greater north-south understanding, however, he was instrumental in setting up a private meeting between Lord Brookeborough, the Stormont Prime Minister and the Irish Minister of External Affairs, Seán MacBride in the same year.

The Nationalist leader's desire for dialogue between the two traditions in the north by the end of the premiership of Lord Brookeborough was reflected in his support for the ill-fated 'Orange and Green Talks' of 1962–3. This initiative involving Healy's Nationalist colleague and vice-president of the Ancient Order of Hibernians, Senator J.G. Lennon, and the Grand Master of the Orange Order, Sir George Clark had sought to address such issues as discrimination in employment and housing and community relations. Unfortunately, the talks broke

**48** D2991/A/516E: Healy to Bishop E. O'Callaghan, 5 Aug. 1955. **49** D2991/A/166B: Healy to O'Kelly, 1 May 1948; *Irish Times*, 2 Jan. 1980. **50** D2991/B/4/11B: Healy to Canon T. Maguire, 5 Nov. 1950.

down on the Orange Order's insistence on prior Nationalist recognition of the 'constitutional position' as a precondition to further discussions.[51]

When Cahir Healy finally bowed out of the Stormont political scene in 1965 at the age of 87, Northern Ireland politics were undergoing an unprecedented process of flux: the O'Neill-Lemass meeting had ushered in the short-lived 'era of good feeling'; the Nationalists under Eddie McAteer's leadership had responded by accepting Official Opposition status for the first time, thereby conferring de facto recognition on the northern government; finally – and more significantly in the long-term – the traditional Nationalist party, with its essential rural base and its concentration on the single issue of partition, was coming under increasing criticism from a new educated and articulate middle-class – the beneficiaries of Stormont's 1947 Education Act – which demanded some refreshingly pragmatic strategy directed at the attainment of full equality of citizenship within Northern Ireland. As one who had given a lifetime of selfless and courageous service to the pursuit of the goal of Irish unity, it was perhaps natural that the respected veteran should be sensitive to such strictures. In one of his last public statements, in 1964, he sharply rebuked an academic critic who had asked in a journal, 'What is wrong with the Nationalist Party?': 'Speaking as one of the original party', Healy rejoined, 'I do not see that there is anything wrong with the Nationalists except that some splinter-groups would like to replace them.'[52]

He was spared just long enough to see the rise of the Civil Rights movement and the plunge into violence and chaos in 1969. His own thoughts on these events are not recorded, but he must have ruminated long and ruefully on the last political letter – dated 25 August 1969 – which he received from his friend and fellow Nationalist, Senator Patrick MacGill. The latter wrote that

> The present position is the outcome of Stormont's years of arrogant neglect. Time and again they were warned – not least by yourself – that their system of injustice could not endure. Today, desperately turning all ways at once in an effort to ward off their own dissolution, they must be thinking of the opportunities they missed, and the manner in which they turned an all-too-deaf ear.[53]

Healy had retired from his insurance post in 1937, but over the decades he had penned hundreds of literary and historical articles, broadcast scripts and plays for the Irish, British and United States media. He had a special interest in Irish history and folklore and was a founder of the Ulster Folk and Transport Museum

---

**51** *Irish Times*, 18 Oct. 1962; D2991/B/15/14: Lennon to Healy, 15 Jan. 1963.   **52** D2991: Healy draft.
**53** D2991, MacGill file: MacGill to Healy, 25 Aug. 1969.

in the 1960s. His personal friendships were eclectic and included the Unionist MP and historian, H. Montgomery Hyde, the left-wing socialist Republican, Desmond Greaves, the former Irish Minister for External Affairs Seán MacBride and Sir Shane Leslie, litterateur and cousin of Winston Churchill.

In many ways, the career of Cahir Healy provides a focus for the study of the political history of the Nationalist minority in Northern Ireland from the onset of partition until the late 1960s. He represented a distinctive strand within the northern Nationalist movement whose early associations had been with the original non-violent Sinn Féin movement of 1904 rather than with the Irish Party of Redmond and Devlin. In his last years, he had come to the conclusion that partition might have been averted had Irish Nationalists adopted a 'less aggressive attitude' towards the Ulster Unionist position. Pearse, he often asserted, had been prepared to accept the modest devolution measures contained in the Liberal government's Irish Council Bill of 1907. 'It was far less than the republic', he added, 'but it was for all Ireland. If we had accepted, it would have led by now to a united and free Ireland. There was some magic in the term "republic" for our countrymen in 1916.'[54] Partition, he reflected with hindsight, had been made almost inevitable by the Easter Rising.

Cahir Healy died at Enniskillen on 8 February 1970 (his wife pre-deceased him in 1948). His political and literary friendships spanned the politico-religious divide, while his considerable personal charm, breadth of learning and courageous advocacy of a tolerant non-sectarian view of Irish Nationalism earned him the respect and admiration of his political opponents. He deserves to be remembered both as a significant leader of northern Nationalist opinion and as a largely self-educated man who made a wide-ranging contribution to Ireland's literary and cultural heritage.

---

54 D2991/A/382B: Healy to Martin (New York), 4 May 1956.

# The Belfast blitz and its impact

## B.E. BARTON

The events in the history of twentieth-century Ulster which have proved most costly in terms of deaths have resulted not from internal political violence but from its involvement in two world wars. In World War I, the 36th Ulster Division sustained over 5,000 casualties during the first two days of the Somme. Arguably, this sacrifice measurably strengthened the Unionist position in the post-War Irish political settlement. In the Second World War, during the course of four Luftwaffe attacks on Belfast, lasting ten hours in total, c.1,100 of its citizens died. In Churchill's phrase, relations between Great Britain and Northern Ireland were 'tempered by fire'.[1] It was a factor in their much warmer relationship after the conflict; that this should have occurred could not have easily have been foreseen in 1939.

When the Second World War began, what most struck British visitors to Belfast was the uniquely casual atmosphere to be found there; the city and indeed the province seemed to be 'only half in the war'.[2] Symptoms of this lack of war urgency include: the consistently modest level of local voluntary recruitment to the armed forces; the initially low productivity of the region's major industries, aggravated by recurrent and disruptive labour disputes; and widespread popular apathy towards civil defence. Many factors account for this contrast with Britain, such as Northern Ireland's remoteness from the theatre of war and from Westminster, its deep sectarian divisions, and the absence of conscription, which helped sharpen public attitudes elsewhere. A further reason was the ineffectiveness of the leadership at Stormont. In 1938, the head the Northern Ireland civil service, Sir Wilfrid Spender, identified the Prime Minister, Sir James Craig, as the main source of weakness, describing him then as being 'too unwell to carry on'.[3] By 1940, Spender was convinced that Stormont's ineptitude would finally compel the British government to impose martial law.

When Craig died, on 24 November 1940, he was succeeded by his most experienced minister, John Andrews – an appointment greeted, even within his own party, with resignation rather than enthusiasm. Neither the confidence nor the prestige of his administration was enhanced by the German air raids on Northern Ireland during April–May 1941. Due in large part to earlier ministerial neglect

---

1 PRO PREM4/53/1: Churchill to Andrews, 6 May 1943.   2 PRONI CAB4/473: *Northern Ireland cabinet conclusions*, 15 May 1941. Also John W. Blake, *Northern Ireland in the Second World War* (HMSO, 1956), p. 368.   3 PRONI D715: Sir Wilfrid Spender, *Financial diary*, 2 Aug. 1938.

and prevarication, local defences were hopelessly inadequate, and the public was physically and psychologically unprepared for the blitz. By the spring of 1941, the strength of the anti-aircraft barrage around Belfast was just twenty-two guns. From 20 July 1940, an RAF squadron equipped with Hurricane fighters had been based at Aldergrove, but these could only operate fully under daylight conditions; yet experts had predicted that any substantial enemy raid would be at night. There were barrage balloons but no searchlights in the province until 10 April 1941. Nor was there any provision for a smoke screen to conceal Belfast's vulnerable and easily identified dock area. The government's schemes to evacuate women and children from Belfast had been a fiasco; a mere 4,000 had been relocated by April 1941. The shelters then available in the city could, if fully utilized, provide protection for just one quarter of its population. Its mortuary services had emergency plans to deal with 200 bodies; a civil servant at the time suggested that the figure was 'hardly enough'.[4]

Numerous factors account for this lack of preparation – the widespread conviction that enemy bombers were unlikely to risk crossing Britain, where there were more significant targets, in order to attack Belfast; the assumption that Éire's neutrality would most likely deter Luftwaffe attack; complacency bred by the fact that the city escaped attack for so long (by March 1941, 28,000 had already died as a result of German air-raids in Britain); lethargy on the part of local ministers, their belief that defence was a Westminster rather than a local responsibility, their lack of funds, and their increasing difficulty in acquiring defence materiel from Britain as the blitz there intensified. Too late, most ministers came to acquire a keener awareness of Northern Ireland's vulnerability. The fall of France (June 1940) accentuated the strategic significance of the United Kingdom's north-west ports, while leaving them more exposed. From late summer, these became the target of a major Luftwaffe offensive (Glasgow, Liverpool etc.). The likelihood that this might be extended to Belfast increased as more munitions contracts began to be awarded to local firms. Moreover, from September 1940 onwards, enemy reconnaissance aircraft were reported over the city with increasing frequency (Belfast's first red alert was on 1 October 1940; they averaged almost one per week over the next six months). Local newspapers reported that William Joyce, 'Lord Haw Haw', had announced in his broadcasts from Hamburg that there would be 'Easter eggs for Belfast'.[5]

It was in this context that a determined attempt was made to improve the province's defensive preparations. In mid-1940, John MacDermott was appointed Minister of Public Security and given this responsibility, but time was too short. Probably from his first day in office he was convinced that the region's

4 Brian Barton, *The Blitz: Belfast in the war years* (Belfast, 1989), p. 66.   5 *Northern Whig*, 12 Apr. 1941.

immunity hitherto would not last. On 29 March 1941, he wrote to Andrews and, highlighting the utter inadequacy of local defences, stated that it was 'doubtful whether Belfast was as well defended as any comparable city or port in ... the United Kingdom'. He finished with a chilling and eerily accurate prediction:

> Up to now, we have escaped attack ... Clydeside got its [first] blitz during the period of the last moon. There are certain technical reasons ... for thinking that at present the enemy could not easily reach Belfast in force except during a period of moonlight. The period of the next moon from, say, the 7 to the 16 of April, may well bring our turn.[6]

On the night of 7–8 April, Belfast did indeed experience its first raid, involving probably no more than eight aircraft, which over a three-and-a-half-hour period concentrated their attack mainly on the dock area, causing thirteen deaths. It was a light assault which entirely failed to shake public complacency. The city's first major attack came just one week later – on Easter Tuesday night, 15–16 April. An estimated 180 aircraft participated in a raid lasting five-and-a-half hours (11.30pm–4.55am). Bombs fell on average at a rate of two per minute. That there was little or no resistance from the ground was partly due to blast damage at the city's telephone exchange – as a consequence, what few anti-aircraft guns there were fell silent from 1.45am. By the time of the 'all clear', rung by hand-bells because of power failure, an official report stated that 'Quiet residential areas [were] enveloped by flames ... eating their way from street to street as quickly as a man could walk'.[7] Afterwards, the *Belfast Telegraph* reported 'bodies being recovered from heaps of rubble all over the place'.[8] Up to 900 people died, with 600 seriously injured. The death toll was so high because of the inadequacy of the city's defences, the dearth and under-use of shelters, the small numbers who had been evacuated, and the fact that so many bombs had fallen on densely popu-lated, working-class areas.

Major Seán O'Sullivan, an Air Raid Precautions observer from Dublin, arrived in Belfast hours after the raid, and subsequently produced a report for southern officials. It described the damage – the houses wrecked or damaged (the final total was *c*.35,000), and the fires still smouldering, some breaking out afresh. O'Sullivan considered that the warden service had 'functioned efficiently' – its members had 'remained at their posts and reported damage promptly'. However, his opinion was that the whole civil defence sector had been utterly overwhelmed, and that the 'greatest want' was 'the lack of hospital facilities... At 2.00pm, on the afternoon of the 16th ... the street leading to the Mater Hospital was [still]

---

**6** Blake, *Second World War*, p. 168.   **7** Barton, *Blitz*, p. 131.   **8** *Belfast Telegraph*, 18 Apr. 1941.

filled with ambulances waiting to set down their casualties'.[9] The city's mortuary services had been similarly overwhelmed. As a result, public baths (on the Falls Road and Peter's Hill) and a large fruit market (St George's) had to be improvised to cope with the dead. On 21 April, 163 bodies – those unclaimed and unidentified – were taken from St George's Market and given a public funeral.

The official history says of this attack: 'No other city in the United Kingdom, save London, had lost so many of her citizens in one night's raid. No other city, except possibly Liverpool, ever did ... [Its citizens] wondered how the life of the city could be revived'.[10] John Maffey, the British ambassador in Dublin, who passed through Belfast on the morning after the raid, stated that the scenes he witnessed there were 'more horrifying than London because of the numbers of small dwelling houses of poor people which were destroyed',[11] Early on 17 April, the German Minister in Dublin, Dr Eduard Hempel, felt constrained to call with the Irish Minister of External Affairs, J.P. Walshe, to offer sympathy. Walshe recorded that the German official was 'clearly distressed ... especially by the number of civilian casualties'. Hempel stated that 'he would once more tell his government how he felt ... and he would ask them to confine their operations to military objectives ... He believed that this was being done already'.[12]

After the attack, a leading civil servant advised Andrews that he should make a personal appeal, on the lines of Lincoln's Gettysburg Address, emphasizing that 'our best reply ... is redoubled effort'.[13] In fact, fear and panic had already reached epidemic proportions, especially in Belfast. Its most obvious symptom was a massive 'crash evacuation', which had been entirely unforeseen by the Stormont government. Even during the raid, people had begun to flee from the city – by car, on bicycles and on foot. O'Sullivan observed that

> From the early morning of the 16th and all throughout the day there was a continuous 'trek' to railway stations ... Any and every means of exit ... was availed of and the final destination appeared to be a matter of indifference ... On the 17th I heard that hundreds who either could not get away or could not leave for other reasons simply went out into the fields and remained in the open all night with whatever they could take in the way of covering.[14]

The latter were colloquially known as 'ditchers'; during the hours of darkness they went 'up the road' to take cover in hills, parks and fields, lying under hedges, and in dugouts and barns.

---

**9** NAD, D/T S 14993: Major Seán O'Sullivan, report on visit to Belfast on 16–17 Apr. 1941. **10** Blake, *Second World War*, pp 232–3. **11** NAD, D/FA A2: note by Walshe, 21 Apr. 1941. **12** NAD, D/T S 14993: note by Walshe, 17 Apr. 1941. **13** PRONI COM61/459: memo by W.D. Scott, 19 Apr. 1941. **14** NAD, D/T S 14993: O'Sullivan report.

Belfast experienced a further devastating bombardment on the night of 4–5 May – popularly referred to as the 'fire raid'. During the course of three hours, an estimated 200 bombers dropped *c.*100,000 incendiary bombs, followed by high explosives, mainly on the central, northern and eastern portions of the city. Unlike Easter Tuesday, when fifty aircraft had diverted owing to deteriorating weather, conditions for bombing were described as perfect. Afterwards, an official report stated that 'within one hour', the resulting fires were on a scale beyond the resources of local brigades.[15] Their best efforts were thwarted by shortages of appliances and hose, blast damage to water pipes, and falling water levels as the tide turned.

The explosions were audible in Bangor and Lisburn and, by dawn, the resulting inferno was visible from the Glenshane Pass, fifty miles away. Over 200 buildings were ablaze by the time of the 'all clear' at 4.25am (their still smouldering shells may have attracted three bombers who attacked the city shortly after midnight on the following night, killing fourteen people). The number of fatalities reached almost 200 and, once more, the unidentified bodies were brought to St George's Market. For several reasons, the death toll was lower than on Easter Tuesday – the attack had occurred on a Sunday night, had focused mainly on the docks and city centre, and had featured a high proportion of incendiary devices. In addition, the shelters available in Belfast had been more fully occupied, and a large proportion of its citizens had already fled into the immediate countryside and beyond. As on 15–16 April, help in fighting fires and in rescue work was provided by troops based locally, and more was requested from all over Northern Ireland, from Britain and also from Éire.

During the 'fire raid', Belfast's key strategic industries sustained heavy damage. Thus, for the first and only time in the entire war, the city made headline news in the German media. In graphic and detailed accounts, it repeated the claim that its industry had been devastated beyond recovery. Such reports would have been widely accepted within Belfast itself. In fact, unemployment throughout the north actually fell (by 30,000, January–June 1941) owing to: local firms attracting more British war contracts; military enlistment; and the increasing numbers employed building shelters, and servicing the expanding number of military personnel, British and later American, based in the province.

Meanwhile, public morale had all but collapsed; there was a widespread fear that the Luftwaffe was intent on pulverizing Belfast. A Ministry of Home Affairs report estimated that by late May up to 220,000 persons had fled from the city. They scattered throughout Ulster; 10,000 crossed the border. But, by August, most had returned. They had quickly become bored with country life and irri-

---

**15** Barton, *Blitz*, p. 183.

tated by the increased distances they had to travel to work. Moreover, they were encouraged to come back by the fact that Luftwaffe attacks on British cities had all but ceased from mid-May and the belief that, after the launch of Operation Barbarossa (26 June 1941), Germany's bombers would have been transferred to the Eastern Front. Meanwhile, police reports indicate that 'ditching' had also become a feature of contemporary life in many of the province's larger towns. The habit was spread by evacuees from Belfast. In addition, it was because on Easter Tuesday night (15–16 April) a number of bombing incidents had occurred at various locations scattered along the Luftwaffe's flight path. Londonderry, Newtownards and Bangor were the most seriously affected. In each of these, the features which had characterized Belfast's experience were replicated – most of the bombs fell on residential property, the public was unprotected and unprepared, the defences were inadequate, the blackout measures defective and the few shelters available under-utilized.

Regarding its political significance, the blitz undoubtedly exacerbated the Northern government's problems, diminishing still further its residual popularity. After the raids, one of MacDermott's prime concerns was the impact of the raids on the attitude of the general public. Thus, in late May, he raised with Spender the possibility that public anger over the lack of preparation for Luftwaffe attack might result in an assault by irate mobs on parliament buildings at Stormont.[16] It did not materialize. Nonetheless, owing to the deepening unpopularity of his government, Andrews was eventually forced to resign as Prime Minister in April 1943.

By then, Stormont's relations with Westminster had already begun to improve because of Northern Ireland's contribution to the war effort. It was as a consequence of the latter that Belfast had become a legitimate Luftwaffe target. At his meeting with Walshe, Hempel had justified the Easter Tuesday attack by stating that his government

> would not have ordered a raid on Belfast if it had not become absolutely essential for the prosecution of the war. [It] ... had become a very important port, especially for the transhipment of foodstuffs, and to abstain any longer from bombing the port, and the industrial area around it, would have greatly handicapped the German blockade of Great Britain.[17]

Its port had become an increasingly significant base for vessels engaged in the battle of the Atlantic, and was used for the import of war materiel especially from

**16** PRONI D715: Spender, *Financial diary*, 15, 31 May 1941. **17** NAD, D/FA A2: Note by Walshe, 17 Apr. 1941.

the US (airfields and other smaller ports in the six counties also made their contribution). After a slow beginning, war production in its industries had steadily accelerated, notwithstanding the destruction caused by the blitz. In addition, the province served as a wartime training ground for *c.*300,000 British and US troops; if required, these would have constituted a spearhead for the repulsion of any attempted German invasion of Ireland. Though enlistment levels remained modest, the six counties did provide *c.*38,000 personnel for Britain's armed forces, as well as a disproportionate share of its military leadership.

Overall, Northern Ireland's wartime role did win the gratitude of British ministers, and transformed their assessment of its strategic significance. Their response was closely related to their parallel sense of irritation with the policies adopted by the Dublin government. In fact, the latter's position was one of benevolent anti-German neutrality. This was illustrated, for example, by the liaison between British and Irish military authorities on plans for Ireland's defence, cooperation between their respective intelligence services, Éire's provision of meteorological reports, and of information about the movement of Axis planes, ships and submarines in the Irish Sea, and its granting of permission (January 1941) to over-fly a corridor over Co. Donegal, west of Lough Erne. Moreover, during the war, more than 100,000 Irish men and women worked without restriction in British munitions factories, upwards of 60,000 enlisted in crown forces, and the South provided Britain with its food surplus. However, in spite of allied pressure and powerful inducements – including the offer of Irish unity – de Valera pursued a policy of strict neutrality over a succession of vital issues. For instance, he denied the allies the use of Irish ports and airfields, refused entry to British troops, protested at the arrival of US troops in the North, and rejected American requests that Axis representatives in Ireland be expelled. His decision, on 2 May 1945, to visit the German legation in Dublin to offer his condolences on the death of Hitler caused much irritation.

Before the war was over, Stormont ministers had already reaped one reward for their supportive wartime role. They had become acutely anxious to begin catching up with social welfare provision elsewhere in the United Kingdom after the war, and to implement fully the terms of the Beveridge Report. But such a programme required a fundamental re-examination of the hitherto unsatisfactory financial relationship between Stormont and Westminster. By early 1944, the basis of a future agreement had been laid which guaranteed Northern Ireland ministers sufficient exchequer support to meet all of Ulster's reasonable expenditure.[18] The treasury's favourable response owed much to the sympathy generated

---

**18** See comments by Maynard Sinclair, Stormont Minister of Finance, on 16 Nov. 1943, in *Parl. Deb*, XXVI, col. 2090.

by the shared experience of war. It was a defining moment in the history of the province, as it formed the basis for the transformation of the region's social services after 1945.

Meanwhile, relations between the two governments within Ireland showed no comparable improvement. A 'cold war' had existed between Belfast and Dublin from the early 1920s. Subsequently, the political, economic and cultural gap had widened, especially after de Valera had become Taoiseach in 1932. Southern neutrality did much to reinforce partition, deepening the chasm in experience and identity between Northern Unionists and the South. However, this sterile relationship received a substantial jolt in the course of the conflict, when de Valera proved willing on two occasions to dispatch southern firemen to Belfast in response to requests from the Northern government after its two heaviest Luftwaffe bombardments. There had always been discreet inter-governmental cooperation (over such issues as fisheries, transport and land drainage), but the assistance provided during the blitz, along with obviously genuine expressions of sympathy by southern leaders and the hospitality shown to northern evacuees, made a deeply favourable impression on northern officials and people. It briefly raised the prospect of a new era of cross-border cooperation and friendship.

The decision to send assistance was taken by de Valera, possibly after discussion with J.P. Walshe. On the first occasion, the Taoiseach recalled receiving the request for help at about 1.50am on 16 April and that he 'spent a few minutes considering' it, before giving his consent.[19] His instructions to provide aid were passed on to the relevant fire authorities within twenty minutes of the contact being made. Sections of the English press claimed that this action elicited strong German protests. Certainly it caused some controversy in Éire. For example, Professor T.K. Rudmore Brown, of Trinity College, Dublin, wrote to de Valera, stating that it was 'insane to irritate the Germans' as he had done, that assisting the north was 'endangering our neutrality', a policy that should be persisted with 'even at the risk of starvation'.[20] In fact, Hempel's response appears to have been reassuring; a Ministry of External Affairs' minute states that 'Reports in the English papers that the German Minister protested strongly against our action as a breach of neutrality were completely false. In fact ... [Hempel] regarded it as only natural that we should send help to our own people'.[21]

Southern aid also generated controversy within the six counties. Opposition MPs at Stormont alleged that the Northern government failed adequately to acknowledge its debt or express publicly its gratitude for the help received. Undoubtedly, such open collaboration with the Dublin leadership had been

**19** NAD, D/T S 14993: memo on Easter Tuesday raid, initialled 'RF'.   **20** NAD, D/T S 14993: Rudmore Brown to de Valera, 5 May 1941.   **21** NAD, D/T S 14993: Note by Walshe, 17 Apr. 1941.

forced upon local ministers by the tragic and extreme circumstances of the blitz; they regarded the request for aid from de Valera as the 'only course available'.[22] Also, their sentiments of gratitude were diluted by a strong suspicion that the Éire government was, in Spender's phrase, 'utilizing the occasion to indulge in further propaganda for a united Ireland'. Irritation was caused by statements such as de Valera's (on 21 April) that 'they are all our people – we are one and the same people'.[23] This viewpoint was repeated in the southern media; the *Irish Times* commented that 'when all is said and done, the people of the six counties are our own folk'.[24]

In addition, Northern ministers contended that the un-blacked-out lights of southern cities and towns were routinely used by the Luftwaffe to help identify targets in the six counties. Such claims were not merely symptoms of paranoia. On 29 March 1941, Maffey had informed the Irish government that 'British air operational developments had made it clear that the lighting of ... main towns [in Éire] in the vicinity of the coast were a navigational help to the Germans'.[25] These findings in fact confirmed the views of W.P. Delamere, the Chief Officer in Éire's Air Defence Command; on 6 October 1940, he declared himself 'satisfied that unknown aircraft are making use of the lights of Dublin and other towns at night for navigational purposes'.[26] Likewise, a report produced by Éire's Ministry of Defence shortly after the blitz, concluded that

> the lighting in general, and that of Dublin city in particular, has been used consistently by aircraft for navigational purposes ... [The Luftwaffe] were apparently using the lights along the coast as an aid to navigation. The consistency with which they approached and touched at certain points made this obvious ... The lights on the south coast and of Dublin were used as points of arrival and departure.[27]

Earlier (on 8 April 1941), the Dublin government had agreed to impose a limited blackout; it applied to neon street adverts, shop window lighting and cinema exteriors, and came into effect on the evening of 15 April – hours before the catastrophic Easter Tuesday attack. But it was not in the South's own security interests to adopt a stricter blackout. In November 1941, Joseph Walshe stressed to Hempel that 'the present lighting of Dublin was a sufficient indication of identity' to the Luftwaffe, as also were the South's shipping lights; by implication, no air raids on southern territory or property could therefore be justified.[28]

**22** PRONI CAB4/469: cabinet conclusions. Also PRONI D3004: Sir Basil Brooke diary, 16 Apr. 1941. **23** NAD, D/T S 14993: text of de Valera's comments. **24** *Irish Times*, 17 Apr. 1941. **25** NAD, D/FA A2: Maffey to Walshe, 29 Mar. 1941. **26** NLI Ms 22152: report in J.J. O'Connell Papers. **27** NAD, D/FA A29: report by M.J. Deary, dated 16 July 1941. **28** NAD, D/FA A2: note of conversation between

In any case, during the war, Unionist leaders considered that they had every reason to treat the South with caution. In a number of ways, it seemed to represent a direct threat to Northern Ireland's survival; the pressure on Craig to enter into constitutional dialogue with de Valera in mid-1940 was merely the most overt instance. In May 1940, Sir Basil Brooke warned Craig of the danger that Germany might invade the South and exploit its endemic anti-British prejudices. In addition, Unionist leaders regarded the existence of the Axis legations in Dublin as a major security risk. They were likewise concerned at the growing number of Southern workers employed in the North (c.30,000 in November 1944), and the fact that a significant proportion was employed on highly sensitive construction sites, at quarries where explosives were available, and at the docks, the shipyard and aircraft factory. Tom Harrisson, a professional British observer, was equally convinced that they were involved in subversive activity, and in fomenting labour unrest. But there is little evidence to suggest that Germany did glean much information through spies or agents operating in Ireland, North or south. The Axis received no advance warning of either the North African expedition (1942) or the D-Day landings (1944), though it is almost certain that there was an unquantifiable Irish dimension to other security leaks (for instance, regarding the Dieppe raid (19 August 1942) and the Arnhem parachute drop (17 September 1944)).

A further cause of North-South friction was Éire's continuing intervention in what Stormont ministers regarded as their own internal affairs. For instance, de Valera unsuccessfully pleaded for clemency in the case of Tom Williams, an IRA man sentenced to death for his part in a police ambush in West Belfast in April 1942. The Taoiseach had earlier caused much Unionist resentment in opposing the introduction of conscription into the six counties, and in raising the issue with Westminster. When US troops arrived in Northern Ireland, he not only protested at their use of Irish territory – a technical breach of Irish neutrality under Articles 2 and 3 of the 1937 constitution – but reasserted Éire's claim to jurisdiction over the whole island, 'no matter what troops occupy the six counties'.[29] At times, it almost seemed to leading Unionists that de Valera played into their hands (for example, in refusing to trade Éire's neutrality policy for Irish unity, and in his response to Hitler's death). After the war, they sought to exploit the South's alleged perfidy during the conflict and to contrast it with the North's own record. This was projected as one of self-sacrificing devotion and undeviating loyalty to Britain and the allied cause.

This North-South polarization was paralleled within Northern Ireland by the persistence of deep sectarian tensions. War did cause some disruption of existing

Walshe and Hempel, dated 22 Nov. 1941.   **29** Quoted in *The Times*, 28 Jan. 1942.

trends; its unprecedented prosperity may have eased social tensions, while the relative retreat of the constitutional issue certainly contributed to growing support for the local Labour Party. Also, both communities did share some vital aspects of wartime experience. Civil defence activities provided increased opportunity for social integration – both persuasions could serve together as air-raid wardens, rescue workers and fire-fighters. Moreover, as the *Irish Times* observed, 'the bombs … made no question of religious or political difference. Orangemen and Fenians fell victims alike'.[30] In its aftermath, families from both traditions sought to identify the unclaimed bodies brought to St George's Market. Similarly, citizens from all parts of the city fled in terror from their homes, or 'ditched' during the hours of darkness in hedgerows, fields and barns. An enduring folk memory of the blitz is of women and children from the Shankill and Falls gathering in the vaults of Clonard monastery on the night of 5–6 May, while the Luftwaffe pulverized the streets outside. The Redemptorist priests had opened church property to the local community, whatever their religion, for want of alternative shelter in the area.

But even at the time of the blitz, there were limits to the shared nature of the experience. After the raids, the unclaimed dead were buried in separate graveyards, according to their presumed faith – a potent image of sectarian division. Police reports indicate that people preferred to 'ditch' in areas which they knew would attract those predominantly of their own faith. In general, Protestant evacuees billeted with Protestant householders and Catholic evacuees with Catholic householders. Even the geographical distribution of death and destruction caused by the Luftwaffe – Unionist East Belfast was hardest hit – reinforced Protestant suspicions that there was collusion between Nationalist areas of the city and the enemy, probably via spies operating from the Axis legations in Dublin.

Overall, wartime attitudes seem broadly to have split along traditional sectarian lines. No one could doubt that the Unionist Party supported the war effort, even though it lacked the sense of urgency found elsewhere in the United Kingdom. Thus, to Harrisson, Ulster seemed like 'a yelling spectator', rather than part of a country that was itself at war.[31] But among northern Nationalists, there is much evidence of hostility or indifference towards the war effort. One Éire minister stated categorically (on 22 April 1941) that most Nationalists 'were absolutely pro-German on account of their unjust treatment by the British government and its Belfast puppet'.[32] Such a response was encouraged by such factors as the operation of internment in the North, and the fact of Southern Irish neutrality. Garda reports, relating to the period when German invasion of Ireland

---

**30** *Irish Times*, 18 Apr. 1941.  **31** FR 1309: enquiry by Tom Harrisson, June 1942, in Tom Harrisson Mass Observation Archive, U Sussex.  **32** NAD, D/FA A2: comment made by F.H. Boland, in minute by J. Walshe, dated 22 Apr. 1941.

seemed imminent, detailed northern minority contacts with the legations in
Dublin. One refers to a meeting attended by Hempel, in August 1940, at which
three Nationalist politicians 'decided ... to place the Catholic minority in the
North under the protection of the Axis powers'.[33]

There is evidence that the two communities responded differently not just to
the war but to a number of key issues which arose during the conflict. It was the
expectation of minority opposition to conscription that effectively determined
Westminster's decision not to introduce the measure into Northern Ireland.
While it is far from clear that the Protestant population in general would have
welcomed its introduction either, committed Unionists would have done so
enthusiastically. The contrast in attitudes was possibly clearer in relation to civil
defence. Catholics were significantly under-represented in the various services.
The obligatory oath of allegiance was a deterrent, but, in addition, ARP
personnel in West Belfast experienced a degree of social ostracism; they received
threatening letters, and were on occasion physically attacked and subjected to
armed hold-ups. In June 1939, Republicans there held a mass demonstration, at
the end of which they 'built bonfires out of their government-issued gas-masks'.[34]
Religious identity also helped determine local reaction to the presence of US
servicemen in Northern Ireland. In Harrison's opinion (which is confirmed by
other sources), Protestants welcomed them for themselves, and for the war effort
and 'as a strengthening of the forces of order against the constant fear of Catholic
(Nationalist) trouble'. In his view, the Catholic population was generally antagonistic, suspecting that they were 'there to ensure partition and possibly even to
invade the South'.[35] At the time, this was of course a broadly accurate perception.

Employment matters remained highly sensitive despite wartime prosperity. A
recurring theme of the resolutions then being discussed by the Unionist Party was
concern at Catholics 'getting in all over the province' – purchasing houses or
farms, finding employment in the civil service, post office and local industry.[36] It
was alleged that they were exploiting the absence of Loyalists who had joined
crown forces or migrated to work in English munitions factories. British ministers recognized that some of the reluctance shown by Protestants to leave
permanent employment and enlist was due to fears that their positions would be
taken by someone of the opposing faith, as well as their assumption of substantial
long-term unemployment after the conflict was over. Andrews' view (March
1943) that the appointment of a single Catholic Permanent or Assistant Secretary

**33** NAD, D/FA P3: see Garda reports, 9, 18 Nov. 1940.   **34** Nigel West, *British secret service operations,*
*1909–45* (London, 1981), p. 312.   **35** FR 1306: enquiry by Harrisson, in Mass Observation Archive, U
Sussex. For more detailed discussion, see Brian Barton, *Northern Ireland in the Second World War* (Belfast,
1995), pp 124–5.   **36** PRONI D1327/7: minutes of Ulster Unionist Party standing committee, 11 Apr., 10
Nov. 1940, 9 Feb. 1945.

would 'end the government' indicates the strength of discriminatory forces among his supporters.[37]

Many Protestants shared a stereotypical view of the minority as a group whose grievances were not as great as they protested and were largely self-induced, and as a 'fifth column' – anti-British by instinct and tradition, and now pro-German. Though aspects of Northern Ireland government policy were influenced by such prejudices, it was not invariably determined by them. Andrews' successor, Sir Basil Brooke, broadly welcomed the Beveridge Report, was prepared to introduce far-reaching social reforms, and committed his government to full employment. In part, this programme reflected his hope that it might ultimately deflect northern Nationalists from their aspiration to Irish unity. It was his opinion that 'the only chance for the political future of Ulster' was if it became 'so prosperous that the traditional political attitudes [were] … broken down'.[38]

**37** PRONI D715: Spender, *Financial diary*, 30 Mar. 1943.   **38** PRONI D3004: Brooke diary, 5 Sept. 1944.

# The beleaguered left: the Northern Ireland Labour Party and its trials and dilemmas, 1924–79

## GRAHAM WALKER & AARON EDWARDS

### I

When it was decided to establish a Labour Party for the new political entity of Northern Ireland, in March 1924, conflict and division defined the context into which it emerged. The circumstances of Northern Ireland's birth had the effect of deepening the ethno-national divide between Protestants and Catholics, and providing for the 'zero sum' political culture which quickly developed. The first election for the new Northern Ireland parliament, in May 1921, had resulted in unambiguously tribal voting, and those candidates standing on a Labour plat-form had been roundly trounced. The victorious Unionist Party set about using the new devolved structures to bolster the position of Northern Ireland within the United Kingdom, while Irish Nationalists and Republicans refused to grant recognition to the new arrangements. Both mobilized their respective electorates around the national question and encouraged them to concentrate on it to the exclusion of all else. The prospects for a party advocating the politics of class rather than sectarian or national loyalties looked decidedly grim.

### II

Nevertheless, the Labour movement in the North had built up a presence through its embattled history since the late nineteenth century. Class issues had not been swept aside, even if Labour politics had struggled. The industrial economy of the Lagan Valley region had led to a significant growth of trades unionism, and episodes of industrial action such as the Dockers strike of 1907 and the Engineers strike of 1919 had demonstrated the Belfast workers' capacity for militancy. There had even been occasional electoral signs of hope: in 1920, for example, the Belfast Labour Party (BLP) won twelve local council seats. The BLP had been set up in 1917 by trade Unionists and activists of the Independent Labour Party (ILP), which had had a presence in the city since 1893.[1]

---

1 For the history of Northern Labour from its early days, see Henry Patterson, *Class conflict and sectarianism* (Belfast, 1989).

166

It was through the ILP that many prominent Northern Labour personalities of the 1920s and beyond cut their teeth. The Belfast ILP had also produced a major leadership figure, William Walker, a craft trade union official who served for a time on the Executive of the British Labour Party. Walker's political career, which ended in 1912 when he took up a post relating to the administration of health insurance, indicated the strength of the links between the North of Ireland and the British Labour movement during the late nineteenth and early twentieth centuries. Indeed, Walker's opposition to Irish Home Rule was based on the belief that it was in Ireland's interests to be part of the developing British labour movement and its quest for political power. He saw social progress for the country as lying in this direction.[2]

However, Walker's line of argument was vigorously challenged by the most capable Irish socialist of the day, James Connolly. Connolly's vision of working-class advance involved the independence of Ireland from Britain and the construction of an Irish Labour movement without any organic links to the British one. This, then, was Labour's version of the conflict caused by the national question in Ireland. Connolly's ideal of an Irish socialist workers' republic attracted many of the more doctrinal socialists of the North, and Walker's anti-Home Rule stance came to be a minority one in Northern Labour circles.[3] Nevertheless, the British Labour and ILP influences ran deep, and were evident in the commitment of many leading figures to issues such as municipalization of goods and services, the 'gas and water socialism' dismissed by Connolly and his followers.

The prevailing feeling in the Northern Labour movement in the early years of the Northern Ireland state was anti-partitionist; yet there emerged a pragmatic willingness to work within the six-county political structures. In addition, the strong ties with British Labour oriented the movement to British political issues and the increasingly class-based character of politics across the water since the end of the First World War.[4] A tight electoral contest for the Westminster parliament seat of West Belfast in 1923, in which the Labour candidate, Harry Midgley, lost to the Unionist by a slim margin, convinced enough activists that it was time to organize a proper party throughout the province. Hence, in March 1924, a conference involving delegates from the BLP and the Confederation of Shipbuilding and Engineering Unions resulted in the formation of what came to be known as the Northern Ireland Labour Party (NILP).[5] The worsening problem of unemployment also seemed to invite such political mobilization.

**2** See Henry Patterson, 'William Walker, labour, sectarianism and the Union' in Fintan Lane and Donal O'Drisceoil (eds), *Politics and the Irish working-class, 1830–1945* (Basingstoke, 2005). **3** See former Connolly acolyte William McMullen's introduction to Desmond Ryan (ed.), *The workers' republic* (Dublin, 1951). **4** See Graham Walker, 'The Northern Ireland Labour Party, 1924–45' in Lane and O'Drisceoil, *The Irish working-class.* **5** The party was actually known as the Labour Party (Northern Ireland) until the mid 1930s.

However, the party faced daunting obstacles. Organizationally, it was pretty much on its own, with little support, financial or otherwise, from the British Labour Party, and largely cosmetic associations with the Irish Labour Party. Northern Ireland's continuing membership of the UK in effect cut off Southern involvement; while the province's devolved status removed it from the mainstream of British politics, and from the British party system, and put it out of sight and mind where all the British parties were concerned. The NILP was squeezed between the Unionist and Nationalist blocs in Northern Ireland itself, and undermined by Southern Irish Labour weakness and British Labour indifference. The party was also overwhelmingly a Belfast one, although to its credit it managed to set up functioning branches in both Protestant and Catholic working-class districts.

From the start, the NILP had to battle to make itself and its brand of class politics relevant in the context of a society divided on ethno-religious terms by competing national identities. It faced two particular difficulties in this respect. First, the Unionist-Nationalist polarization of politics thrust the issue of loyalty to the state to the forefront. This was reinforced, at Northern Ireland parliamentary level, by the Unionist government's abolition of proportional representation in 1929 – it had earlier scrapped PR for local authority elections. This had the effect, as intended, of making it significantly harder for 'third parties' like Labour to be successful. Northern Ireland's first Prime Minister, Sir James Craig, desired a straight fight between Unionists and Nationalists which the electoral balance suggested that Unionists would always win. Both Unionists and Nationalists contrived to make every election essentially a referendum on the border. In 1925, the NILP actually won three seats in the Northern parliament, and these successes, along with those of Independents, alarmed Craig. In 1929, after PR's abolition, Labour was reduced to one seat, that of Jack Beattie in Belfast Pottinger.

Secondly, the way the Unionist government regarded devolution became a problem for Labour. Craig took the view that Northern Ireland was simply a subordinate regional assembly; his government had no wish to diverge significantly from Britain. Hence the policy of 'step-by-step' in relation to social welfare benefits. This had far-reaching consequences for the NILP's fortunes. The Unionists used 'step-by-step' to persuade working-class Protestants that they would benefit from British social legislation without having to vote on such issues in Northern Ireland. Thus, there was no incentive to ditch the Unionist Party, vote NILP and, from a Unionist perspective, send out ambiguous signals regarding the North's constitutional position. The Unionists *were* concerned about the potential threat posed by Labour politics, and they were not secure in urban working-class constituencies. Back in 1918, they had incorporated a Labour wing under the guise of the Ulster Unionist Labour Association (UULA),[6] and the party could not have preserved the cross-class alliance which gave it such electoral strength if it had been dismissive of workers' interests. Although the party was sectarian in outlook, its patrician concern for working-class interests led it to replicate legislation that was beneficial to Northern Ireland society as a whole, even if this was not obvious until the reproduction of the British welfare state measures following the Second World War.

However, even in the economically depressed 1930s, it was clear that the Unionists had effectively constricted Labour's room for electoral advance. At the Stormont parliament, the NILP leader in this era, Harry Midgley, protested about social injustices only to be given the stock answer that the Northern Ireland government did not have the power to do anything about them. Quite simply, the Unionists would not play the game of left-right politics.

Midgley's time as NILP leader was notable for his efforts to push the party towards a pro-Union position on the national question and to build more purposeful links with British Labour.[7] Midgley was elected for the seat of Belfast Dock in 1933 but his outspoken defence of the Spanish Republican government during the civil war in that country antagonized the Catholic Church and alienated many of the Catholic voters on whose support he depended. Midgley duly lost his seat in the Northern Ireland election of 1938 and assumed a bitter hostility towards the Church. This seems to have informed his subsequent attempts, after the outbreak of the war, to have the NILP plump clearly for the union with Britain and back the Unionist government's war effort. Midgley's thinking involved the prioritizing of Protestant working-class voters with the expectation that significant numbers of Catholics would in time prefer the NILP to the ineffective and largely abstentionist Nationalist Party.

However, the opposition to Midgley within the NILP was too strong for him. His main leadership rival, Jack Beattie, cultivated the Nationalists during the same period and was strongly anti-partitionist. Again, the Connolly-Walker lines of division were apparent. In addition, there were those in the mainstream of the party who did not wish the NILP to veer too far one way or another on the national question. Midgley could not get his way and, a year after sensationally winning a by-election for the NILP in Belfast Willowfield, he left to form his own pro-Union Commonwealth Labour Party (CLP) in early 1943. A cabinet-post as Minister of Public Security in the new Prime Minister Basil Brooke's government soon followed, and Midgley indeed was to take the final step into the Unionist Party in 1947. Beattie was expelled from the NILP in 1944 and spent the

---

**6** See Austen Morgan, *Labour and partition* (London, 1991), ch. 10.   **7** See Graham Walker, *The politics of frustration: Harry Midgley and the failure of labour in Northern Ireland* (Manchester, 1985), chs 5–7.

rest of his career as an anti-partitionist Labour MP at both Stormont and, for a time, Westminster. Thus, the conflict within Labour ranks over whether the party should build class-politics from a Unionist or a Nationalist orientation deprived the NILP in the end of both of its 'star players'; while, during the 1930s and early 40s, the same conflict undoubtedly prevented the party from pulling its weight in a united effort.

Notwithstanding the corrosive effects of such conflict, it should still be remembered that the NILP polled an impressive 66,000 votes in the 1945 Northern Ireland election. The vote for candidates of the left, whatever their orientation on the national question, came to some 125,000 at this contest, in comparison with the Unionists' 178,000. The first-past-the-post electoral system ensured that the Unionists again won a commanding majority, yet it was clear that a leftwards drift of opinion had occurred.[8] In response, the Unionists faced down internal party opposition to re-enact the post-War British Labour government's social legislation. It was a pragmatic political stroke which kept the 'Orange and Green' divisions out in front of those of class consciousness.

III

The NILP was represented in the post-War Stormont parliament by Robert Getgood (Belfast Oldpark) and Hugh Downey (Belfast Dock). Both men spent much time agitating on unemployment, housing and basic workers' rights. Unfortunately, the Parliamentary Labour Party (PLP) found itself handicapped by the Unionists, who consistently harried it for its ambiguous stance on the border.[9] Downey's frequent protestations that the NILP had a coherent policy on the issue looked hollow in light of Getgood's penchant for indulging in anti-imperialist rhetoric. Politically, the Unionist Parliamentary Party, by sheer weight of numbers, was largely successful in outmanoeuvring the tiny PLP, especially on legislation of a socio-economic hue. Equally dispiriting was the fact that the NILP was operating against a backdrop of a renewed irredentist campaign whipped up by the Anti-Partition League (APL), which ensured that public attention would drift away from material concerns towards the cardinal issue of partition.

The announcement by the Irish Taoiseach, John A. Costello, in September 1948 that Éire intended to leave the Commonwealth was greeted with suspicion and uncertainty by Unionists. In the week before Costello's announcement, the

---

**8** Walker, *Politics of frustration*, pp 167–9; Terry Cradden, *Trade Unionism, socialism and partition* (Belfast, 1993), pp 41–7.  **9** *Northern Ireland Parliamentary Debates*, vol. 29, col. 81, 24 July 1945.

NILP had held its annual conference, at which talk of the constitutional issue was deliberately avoided,[10] not because of any 'fence-sitting' on the matter, but rather because a special session had been convened earlier in the year with the express purpose of resolving the NILP's official stance on the border. It failed to placate anti-partitionists and internal disagreement remained considerably marked. The West Belfast Labour Party, for instance, saw partition as 'the greatest barrier to the political and economic development of both parts of the country' and called on the wider party 'to adopt all constitutional means to ensure its removal'.[11] Conversely, the South Antrim Labour Party thought that the party's interests would be better served by accepting 'the present constitutional position of Northern Ireland'; instead it pushed for the removal of 'abuses of the democratic expression of the will of the people and the liberty of the subject, at present in force in Northern Ireland'.[12] The dispute over partition spread to other key NILP branches across the province. In Derry, the Foyle Labour Party, under its chairman Stephen McGonagle, sought closer alignment with the Nationalist-orientated 'Friends of Ireland', a backbench British Labour Party (BrLP) pressure group led by Geoffrey Bing, the Ulster-born MP for Hornditch in Essex.[13] Nevertheless, key leadership figures in the NILP, initially ambivalent on national identity concerns, moved to maintain party unity by opting for a de facto acceptance of partition.

The consternation over the constitutional question shook the NILP to its very core.[14] Not only did individual members begin to leave the party from 1948, but whole branches disaffiliated or were expelled (like West Belfast) and soon switched their allegiance en masse to Republican parties and collectives, such as the Irish Labour Party (IrLP) and the APL. An immediate consequence of this acrimonious atmosphere was the defeat of the party's two MPs in the February 1949 election. Factional disputes had been a recurring nuisance for the NILP throughout the 1940s and had, arguably, contributed directly to the split along pro- and anti-partitionist lines.[15] The special party conference held on 9 April eventually affirmed the NILP's commitment to partition by a bloc-vote of 2,000 votes to 700.[16] This decisive result, combined with the party's decision to seek the closest possible alignment with the BrLP, heralded the beginning of the end for the 'broad church' and its replacement by an unequivocally pro-British ethos – an ethos, moreover, which envisaged Northern Ireland enjoying 'the benefits of

---

**10** *Belfast Telegraph*, 20 Sept. 1948. **11** Northern Ireland Political Collection, Linen Hall Library, NILP Box 1, *Special session of the 1947 annual conference: final agenda.* **12** Ibid. **13** Bob Purdie, 'The friends of Ireland: British Labour and Irish Nationalism, 1945–9' in Tom Gallagher and James O'Connell (eds), *Contemporary Irish studies* (Manchester, 1983), pp 81–94. **14** For a detailed analysis of the split, see Cradden, *Trade Unionism*, pp 170–213. **15** John Graham, *The consensus-forming strategy of the Northern Ireland Labour Party* (MSc., QUB, 1972), p. 4. **16** Labour Party Archives, GS12/NI/45ii: State of the Labour movement in Northern Ireland, June 1949.

the social and economic reforms promised by Labour for the new post-War Britain'.[17] However, opting for a greater British agenda did not absolve the NILP from its obligations to the working-class as a whole. The party continued to barrack its Unionist opponents on their attitude towards the minority. Furthermore, the breaking away of anti-partitionist activists ensured that party policy would now take precedence over the private consciences of individual members. From now on, the authority of annual conference resolutions would become a de rigueur feature of the NILP's discourse, as was the norm with the broader British Labour movement of which it was part.

The initial goal of the Protestant rump of the NILP in 1949 was to broaden its cross-sectarian appeal in order to reoccupy a political space comparable to that held prior to the split. In the short-term, party officers recognized that they could never fully hope to fulfil this ambition because of the changing socio-economic and political context of the early 1950s. At a time when the Unionist Party tried the patience of its bulky middle-class membership by implementing social welfarist measures emanating from Westminster on a step-by-step basis, the NILP had its room for manoeuvre constrained. Moreover, the decision by the IrLP to organize on a thirty-two-county basis from 1950 drastically reduced the NILP's scope for revitalizing its support-base in majority Catholic electoral wards. For much of the 1950s, working-class Catholics in Belfast would vote principally for candidates from an array of anti-partitionist parties, including the IrLP, Republican Labour and Independent Labour traditions. Nevertheless, by the late 1950s, the IrLP was entering a period of terminal retreat, making it easier for the NILP to win Catholics over to a non-sectarian programme and away from confessional-based choices.

That the NILP had benefitted from the changing socio-economic context by the end of the decade would soon become apparent in the Northern Ireland general election held in March 1958. Before polling had closed, there were signs that many working-class voters were making their decision based on calls from trade union leaders to vote on 'bread and butter' issues.[18] Of the eight Belfast constituencies contested by the NILP, half returned Labour MPs, notwithstanding the fact that the NILP's relatively small share of the vote (37,748) meant that its overall percentage was only slightly higher than its 1953 total. The *Belfast Telegraph* welcomed Labour's encroachment in Belfast industrial divisions as an indication that 'these are changing times, and the public has decided to give Labour a say, not in the main, we believe, for socialist purposes, but to see the effect of opposing constructive criticism at Stormont'.[19] The NILP's successes

---

17 Terry Cradden, 'The left in Northern Ireland and the national question: the "democratic alternative" in the 1940s', *Saothar*, 16 (Dublin, 1991), p. 36.  18 *Irish News*, 14 Feb. 1958.  19 *Belfast Telegraph*, 21 Mar. 1958.

were all the more important as they demonstrated that Labour could pool support in majority Protestant wards, as well as in those areas with a significant Catholic presence.[20]

The NILP's electoral triumph in 1958 – and its consolidation of these victories in 1962 – pointed towards the stabilization of a left-of-centre political tradition in Northern Ireland. Undeniably, Labour's successes in Belfast were by-and-large a result of the Unionist government's inept handling of a depressing economic situation.[21] Taking full advantage of Unionist misfortune, the NILP initiated a far-ranging propaganda drive to project it as a constructive non-sectarian opposition, strong on social justice and economic improvement. Of considerable importance too was the fraternal relationship with the BrLP. NILP candidates received the full backing of the BrLP in both the 1959 and 1964 Westminster elections and Hugh Gaitskell (BrLP leader, 1955–63) personally visited the province on the eve of the 1958 contest to wish the party well in the forthcoming poll. The following year, Herbert Morrison made a high-profile visit, on which he sensed 'a distinct improvement in the organization, coherence and outlook of the Northern Ireland Labour Party since I met the executive some years ago'. He reserved much criticism for the Westminster Unionists, 'stressing that it was damaging to Northern Ireland to have a solid block of right-wing Tory MPs'.[22] The BrLP gave considerable support to its 'sister party' once it looked likely that the NILP might return one of its number to Westminster.

With the advent of Terence O'Neill's administration in 1963, the NILP began to lose its raison d'être on economic policy. Despite some considerable legislative advances in the areas of the death penalty, criminal compensation schemes, legal aid and the Mater Hospital's continued exclusion from the NHS system,[23] O'Neill compounded the NILP's difficulties by openly challenging its monopolization of the moderate centre ground in Northern Irish politics – an indirect result of which was the acceleration of internal friction now prevalent among the front ranks of the party. Equally injurious was the decline in the unemployment rate – previously the centrepiece in the NILP's critique of the Unionist government's economic policy – and the bridging used to reach across the ethno-religious divide in Belfast. Nevertheless, for a brief period in the 1960s, the NILP presented an impressive political front, with four MPs, two senators and almost thirty local councillors.

**20** C.E.B. Brett, *Long shadows cast before: nine lives in Ulster, 1625–1977* (Edinburgh, 1978), p. 85.   **21** Paul Bew, Peter Gibbon and Henry Patterson, *Northern Ireland, 1921–2001: political forces and social classes* (London, 2002), pp 119–23; Graham Walker, *A history of the Ulster Unionist Party* (Manchester, 2004), pp 140–7.   **22** Labour Party Archives, GS12/NI/207i: Herbert Morrison to Morgan Phillips, 6 Oct. 1959.   **23** Aaron Edwards, 'Democratic socialism and sectarianism: the Northern Ireland Labour Party and Progressive Unionist Party compared', *Politics*, 27:1 (2007), pp 24–31.

Despite its successes as a parliamentary opposition, the NILP could not contain the extra-parliamentary momentum built-up around calls for 'British Rights for British Citizens', a campaign that it had instigated. The Northern Ireland Civil Rights Association (NICRA) was formed in Belfast in 1967 and among those elected to its first executive was Falls NILP activist Paddy Devlin.[24] Other party members like Erskine Holmes, Michael Farrell and Eamonn McCann also took leading roles in the organization. In his capacity as MP for Oldpark (1958–72), Vivian Simpson's consistent lobbying for the Mater Hospital to be admitted to the NHS system exemplified the NILP's attitude to minority community issues.[25] However, it was obvious that by the late 1960s, civil rights agitation had re-opened a Pandora's Box for the NILP hierarchy, leaving them with a considerable dilemma about how best to manage their Constituency Labour Parties: the cross-sectarian building blocks of the party's organizational structure. This was not a new problem for the NILP, as the division over partition in the late 1940s had previously demonstrated. What has probably led commentators of the period to overlook the NILP's progressive policies on civil rights was the inability of the party to lead from the front on the issue.

The late 1960s witnessed the emergence of a revitalized sectarian brinkmanship on the streets of Northern Ireland, as progressive and reactionary forces simultaneously mobilized and converged, with deadly consequences. Forcible demographic change and widespread sectarian segregation took root within these years. While one side, led from the front by middle-class Catholics, agitated for Civil Rights reforms, the other, Protestant followers of Ian Paisley and his allies among Unionist backbenchers, sought to entrench the traditional Unionist rhetoric of 'this we will maintain'. Perhaps the most significant generic feature of these conflicting trends was that they took place largely through the conduit of angry confrontations on the streets, not in the conventional arena of parliamentary politics. This made life extremely difficult for the NILP, which had hitherto based its style of political discourse on the British model of parliamentary socialism.

In the wake of the NILP's diminished performance at the so-called 'Crossroads Election' in 1969, the party retained only two Stormont seats in a contest that saw its share of the vote plummet from 20.4 per cent to 8.1 per cent. The NILP polled 45,113 votes and was knocked into third place by the anti-O'Neillite Unionists. The Nationalists had gained only 26,009 votes, retaining only six of their original eight seats, while a plethora of new civil rights linked parties returned such dominating personalities as John Hume, Paddy O'Hanlon

24 See Gerry Adams' description of NICRA's inaugural meeting in 'A Republican in the Civil Rights campaign' in Michael Farrell (ed.), *Twenty years on* (Dingle, Co. Kerry, 1988), pp 39–53.  25 See PRONI D/3233: *Vivian Simpson Papers.*

and Ivan Cooper, who would later go on to form the nucleus of the Social Democratic and Labour Party (SDLP) in August 1970.[26] Vivian Simpson (Belfast Oldpark) and Paddy Devlin (Belfast Falls) were returned to Stormont, but the departure of Senator Arnold Schofield left Norman Kennedy as the party's only member in the Upper House.

Notwithstanding the party's failure to loosen the grip of confessional-based parties, the return of Devlin to the Falls constituency signalled a turning point and indicated the temporary consolidation of the NILP's support among the Catholic working-class. His defeat of the sitting Republican Labour MP Harry Diamond was certainly a victory for the NILP's brand of non-sectarian demo-cratic socialism, though in overall strategic terms, the party had done quite badly in its bid to secure more seats, or even to win back those that it had lost in 1965. It was obvious that the main electoral issue centred on the future political direc-tion of Unionism, not on socio-economic issues. In the end, it was an unpropitious context for the NILP to promote a settlement based on shared communal grievances.

In 1970, the NILP's political profile peaked at an impressive 98,194 votes in that year's British general election, after which it entered a period of protracted electoral decline. Despite this decline, the party remained at the forefront of attempts to broker a truce between warring paramilitary factions at the height of the 'Troubles' in 1972. The facilitation of this 'bottom-up' peace initiative was greatly hampered by a lack of resources and by the fact that after 1973 the British government favoured a 'top-down' arbitration approach in which Official Unionists and the SDLP were pressured into embracing a power-sharing settle-ment. At a time when the newly formed Alliance Party was challenging the NILP for the cross-community vote, competition between these two centrist parties became inevitable.

IV

The outbreak of the 'Troubles' thus increased the NILP's political difficulties, yet the party remained a significant player in the early 1970s. British government files reveal that successive London administrations entertained hopes that the NILP could be an influence for peace and stability and might be an important part of a moderate 'centre ground' in Northern Ireland politics.[27] This is perhaps not so

**26** Gerard Murray and Jonathan Tonge, *Sinn Féin and the SDLP: from alienation to participation* (Dublin, 2005), pp 10–11. **27** See documents in National Archives, file CJ4/313. This is the source for what follows in this section.

surprising when the fact of the NILP's poll of almost 100,000 votes in the 1970 election is kept in mind.

After the introduction of internment by Brian Faulkner's Unionist government in August 1971, the NILP was left to champion the idea of a 'Community Government'. The party felt itself well placed to exert a moderating influence, and was anxious to appear willing to help in a situation where the recently formed SDLP was expressing the deeply felt sense of Catholic anger and injustice by withdrawing from dialogue over the future governance of the province. The NILP put itself forward as a party which could be trusted by both sides of the community, and offered to 'hold in trust' the cabinet office of Minister of Community Relations, since such a post could not be effectively held by either a Unionist or a Nationalist. However, this took insufficient notice of how little significance the Catholic community in particular had attached to this office as a conciliatory gesture by Faulkner; and if anything the NILP was viewed as having complied in the politics of cosmetic gestures by virtue of David Bleakley's time in the post from March until August 1971. Bleakley, who had been an NILP MP at Stormont between 1958 and 1965, resigned over internment, but this did not prevent the NILP being compromised in Nationalist eyes.[28] The NILP's alternative to internment, a Legal Security Commission, was rejected by the Northern Ireland and British governments as unworkable and had little appeal for Nationalists. In fact, the NILP was internally divided on the matter of internment, and no leading figure was in favour of the outright release of internees.

The NILP was well placed to advance ideas for reform, and it strove to do so. It advocated the re-introduction of a PR electoral system, which Faulkner personally supported but claimed his party would not accept;[29] and the NILP also called for periodic referenda on the border, changes to the senate, experiments in integrated housing and schools and a social reconstruction programme involving some 65,000 jobs and 150,000 houses. Yet the party was also anxious to demonstrate its support for Northern Ireland's place in the UK, and called upon the British government to draw up a treaty with its Dublin counterpart which would entail the latter's recognition of the North. It was felt, apparently by Catholic members of the NILP also, that the Catholic community did not want the border changed, simply the chance to participate in Northern Ireland political life and society on an equal basis. Party spokesmen in meetings with the British government in late 1971–early 1972 regularly voiced their fears of a Protestant reaction to the upsurge in IRA violence over internment. The NILP regarded with alarm, from the point of its own support base as well as the wider effects, the rise in

---

**28** For Bleakley's account of these events and his assessment of Faulkner, see David Bleakley, *Faulkner* (London, 1974), chs 7 and 8.  **29** Walker, *Ulster Unionist Party*, p. 193.

support for William Craig's hard-line Vanguard movement and the Loyalist Association of Workers. Following the suspension of Stormont in March 1972, the NILP counselled the British government to prioritize the calming of Protestant fears and to put a break on the release of internees.

Later in 1972, the NILP participated in the Darlington conference convened by Secretary of State William Whitelaw. By this time, the party had ditched the idea of a community government and instead supported voluntary coalition in a newly devolved Northern Ireland as the way forward. Much faith continued to be vested in PR to bring about a strengthening of the party's position, and fond thoughts were entertained about being a partner in a future government. At this point, the NILP clearly still believed that it could halt the rise of the SDLP, and that class politics could eclipse the liberal centre ground and appeal of that equally recent arrival to the party scene, Alliance. In this regard, it should be remembered that the NILP could legitimately point to areas of life such as trade Unionism, in which Protestants and Catholics still managed to work together. Moreover, as leading party figures stressed to British government officials and the Secretary of State, it could claim to be the second largest party in Northern Ireland on the basis of votes cast since the Northern Ireland election of 1958.

Nevertheless, communal violence drastically worsened over the course of 1972 and outright civil war seemed highly likely.[30] The NILP was eager for the British government to devise their future blueprint, and urged that the expected White Paper containing such arrangements be published in advance of the plebiscite on the border which Whitelaw had conceded to the Unionists. The NILP was also supportive of the plebiscite, seeing it as likely to reassure Protestants, but considered it crucial that Northern Ireland voters be encouraged to vote on changes in the structures and institutions of government as well as the single issue of the constitutional link with Britain. The NILP, in short, called on the government to try to 'de-sectarianize' the border poll. They saw an opportunity for the government to weaken the hand of the extremists on both sides, but only if both communities had the same incentive to vote.

As it turned out, the plebiscite preceded publication of the White Paper. The NILP's warnings about massive Catholic abstentions and the divisive effects of the poll were vindicated. The appearance of the White Paper then caused ruptures in the Unionist Party, with its clear indication of the requirement for a broad-based government representing the whole community. Fears intensified among Protestants over the future of the Union. In this connection, pro-united Ireland sentiments uttered by British Labour leader Harold Wilson undoubtedly damaged the NILP, and reflected the degree to which the party had lost the ear

---

**30** See Alan Parkinson, *1972 and the Ulster Troubles: 'a very bad year'* (Dublin, 2010).

of their British counterpart to the rival SDLP. At the same time, the British government was encouraging the NILP to draw closer to Alliance in a bid to stiffen the centre ground. The NILP, however, tended to see this as entailing the dilution of their social and economic programme and was resistant.

The Assembly election of June 1973 revealed the extent of the ground lost by the NILP in the context of deteriorating violence and communal polarization. The party won only one seat – Bleakley in East Belfast – and registered a disappointing 2.6 per cent of the vote. The NILP's attempts to influence the re-casting of the political framework after the imposition of Direct Rule in order to strengthen its role as a mediating force had failed utterly. The party later stood candidates at both British elections of 1974 and again at the Convention election in 1975, but its share of the vote declined each time, notwithstanding the fact that Bleakley kept the party on the map at the Convention. The party's last electoral foray, again in vain, came at the 1979 British general election.

V

The NILP always struggled to promote secular class-based politics in the unpropitious context of a society divided along ethno-religious lines over the national question. There were occasional electoral successes and short periods when the sectarian temperature cooled; however, in general, the party could not avoid being harmed by the tensions over the border in its own ranks and the way the issue was used against them by their opponents. The movement for civil rights took a form that prevented the party from playing a decisive leadership role; yet, it should be remembered that the NILP had argued for the civil rights demands over many years before the street demonstrations of the 1960s. Even with the onset of political violence, the party tried honourably to maintain political dialogue and keep doors open to both communities, in some contrast to the SDLP. Over the course of its problematic history, it was always a channel through which an alternative voice could be heard.

# Education and communal division
# in Northern Ireland, 1920–70

## SEÁN FARREN

The relationship between education and communal division in Northern Ireland in the period under review is essentially a story which continues a longer history enacted on the wider all-Ireland stage from at least the early decades of the nineteenth century, when educational structures in Ireland as a whole were being developed along lines that were still very evident well into the mid-twentieth century. Inevitably, those structures came to reflect fundamental characteristics of Irish society, most notably characteristics of a religious and political nature, especially of the former.

In a population where the overwhelming majority of people were Roman Catholic, the influence of that church was bound to assert itself in a sector in which it had a long history of involvement and concern. That influence was to be particularly coloured by the fact that as part of the United Kingdom of Great Britain and Ireland, the established church in Ireland was the Anglican Church, from 1870 the Church of Ireland. To a greater or lesser extent in the early nineteenth century, that church still regarded its mission as including the evangelization of the native Irish and their conversion from what were perceived to be the 'evils' of Roman Catholicism.[1] Education was obvious territory on which to pursue these goals. In doing so, this inevitably created the suspicion and hostility of the Catholic Church which at the same time was engaged in rebuilding its institutional life after a long period of attempted suppression.

As the nineteenth century progressed and the Catholic Church increased its influence in public life, one of its key concerns was to ensure that the National School system,[2] established in 1831 to provide elementary education throughout Ireland, would be acceptable for Catholic children and not be exploited for proselytizing purposes by Protestant churches and their various missionary associations.[3]

---

1 D.H. Akenson, *The Irish education experiment: the national system of education in the nineteenth century* (London, 1970).   2 See letter written in Oct. 1831 from Chief Secretary of Ireland, E.G. Stanley, to the Lord Lieutenant of Ireland, the Duke of Leinster, proposing the establishment of the National School system, whereby elementary education would be encouraged in schools funded in part by the state and operating according to common principles but managed by local interests, mainly local churches. Reproduced in Áine Hyland and Kenneth Milne (eds), *Irish educational documents*, vol. 1 (Dublin, 1987), pp 98–103.   3 A number of missionary organizations such as the Society for the Promotion Christian Knowledge founded schools in Ireland with the explicit aim of promoting conversions among the Catholic

Initially, the Catholic Church tolerated national schools as schools which Catholic children could attend no matter what church or organization controlled them. The critical understanding was that religious instruction would be provided separately from the teaching of 'secular' subjects.[4] A further safeguard was that since a majority of national schools were under the management of Catholic parish priests or of religious orders, most Catholic children were in effect attending Catholic schools. But the other churches, notably the Church of Ireland, Presbyterian and Methodist churches, also provided schools that to a greater or lesser extent were open to pupils of all denominations, and some did operate under an explicitly proselytizing policy, thereby justifying Catholic fears. Indeed, during the first half of the century, schools with a religiously mixed intake were common, especially in northern counties, where a majority of Protestants lived and where, in many areas, both Catholics and Protestants lived side-by-side.

In the second half of the century, however, the Catholic Church moved to a position where only exclusively Catholic schools staffed by teachers trained in Catholic colleges were regarded as suitable for Catholic children.[5] As the Catholic Church moved, so too did the other churches. The result was that by the early twentieth century the network of schools in Ireland, both at elementary and at the emerging secondary level, was characterized by its highly denominational nature.

This characteristic reflected not only the denominational balance in Irish society but also its general political allegiances. As the Catholic population became more enthused for some form of Home Rule and, ideologically, by an exclusive form of Nationalism, and the Protestant population resistant to either and, politically, staunchly Unionist, education found itself increasingly embroiled in controversies. What the Catholic Church favoured or opposed for its sector, Nationalist politicians also tended to favour and oppose, and what the Protestant churches favoured or opposed tended to be the line taken by most Unionist politicians.

The controversy over the MacPherson Bill in 1919, which sought to reform management structures in the National School system, mirrored precisely the wider political controversies of the same year.[6] Nationalists by and large sided with the Catholic Church in its vehement opposition to what was being

population. See *First report of the Commissioners of Irish Education inquiry*, 1825 (400) xii.   **4** The aims of the National Education system were summed up in the phrase 'combined literary and separate religious education'. See *Rules and regulations of the Board of Commissioners for national education in Ireland* (published annually, 1832–1921).   **5** The Archbishop of Dublin, Cardinal Paul Cullen (1852–78), was primarily identified with this move. See Peadar MacSuibhne, *Paul Cullen and his contemporaries*, vol. 1 (Naas, Co. Kildare, 1961).   **6** So named after the Chief Secretary for Ireland, Ian Mac Pherson, the Bill was entitled: *Education Ireland Bill*, 10 Geo.5. H.C. 1920.I, 563ff.

proposed. The argument was that the proposed legislation would mean encroachment by the state into the control and management of Catholic schools through
local authority representation on school management boards. Notwithstanding
the fact that already the funding for schools came to a significant degree from
public sources and that the bill proposed ways whereby additional and badly
needed funds could be raised by local authorities, a strong campaign of opposition was mounted by the Catholic Church throughout the country, with
considerable assistance from Nationalist politicians.

Unionists supported the bill, as did the main Protestant churches, which
accepted the case for greater public involvement in the supervision and management of schools. Indeed, Unionists had already taken a similar initiative aimed at
improving the financial situation for schools in Belfast where overcrowding had
become a major problem.[7] It was withdrawn following the introduction of the
more comprehensive MacPherson Bill. The latter was withdrawn, however, but
not before it had sharply revealed the tensions and challenges that an attempt to
change basic educational structures could provoke.

So, just as Ireland was being partitioned, education found itself caught in the
maelstrom of the crisis. What was clear was that in Northern Ireland, Unionists
were likely to pursue educational reform along lines of the ill-fated MacPherson
Bill and support a degree of public involvement in school management structures. Nationalists, however, as in the rest of the country, were just as unlikely to
do so and, instead, would tend to support the Catholic Church's insistence that
it maintain its exclusive and controlling role over its own schools. And so it
proved to be the case, with one unexpected twist that would reveal the Protestant
churches to be as determined as the Catholic Church to protect their influence,
if not control, over schools serving their community.

When Ireland was finally politically partitioned in 1921, the scene was, therefore, set, particularly in Northern Ireland, with its population balance of
one-third Catholic and two-thirds Protestant, for an intensification of tensions
between Unionists and Nationalists not only at a political level, but also in such
sensitive areas as education.

An early sign of these tensions was a minor revolt against the new education
authorities by some teachers in Catholic-managed schools. For several months in
1921–2, they refused to accept the legitimacy of the Northern Ireland Department
of Education. They were supported in their refusal by the government in Dublin
that, for several months, continued to pay their salaries.[8] The teachers' stand had
little or no effect and gradually fizzled out, finally ending when the Dublin

7  *Belfast Education Bill (1919)*: 'to make better provision for primary Education in the City of Belfast'.
8  Éamon Phoenix, 'Teachers rejected pay from Belfast', *Irish Times*, 2 Jan. 1988.

government stopped sanctioning salary payments.[9] What the 'revolt' foreshadowed, however, was the uneasy relationship that was to exist throughout the next fifty years between the Catholic school system and the various Unionist governments that held office during these years. This relationship reflected the general unease within the North's Nationalist community towards its new and unwelcome constitutional fate in partitioned Ireland. In the period under review, that unease varied from acquiescence, to reluctant cooperation, to phases of violent opposition.

On the broader issue of educational structures, Unionist politicians made no secret of the fact that they wanted no delay in having elementary education reformed essentially as proposed in the Macpherson Bill.[10] Lord Londonderry, the first Minister of Education in Northern Ireland in an exclusively Unionist administration, moved quickly to prepare the way for reform when he nominated a special committee, the Lynn Committee, to recommend how he should proceed. Despite several requests to the Catholic Primate, Cardinal Logue of Armagh, no representative of Catholic interests was nominated to the committee.[11] Indeed, the cardinal made known his church's strong opposition to the very principles upon which Londonderry seemed likely to proceed and that it would maintain its opposition to any proposals along the lines expected. In effect, this meant that the Catholic Church deliberately chose to keep its schools separate from the new system that emerged following the Lynn Committee's report and the legislation that followed in the Education Act of 1923. As expected, Nationalist politicians supported this stand.[12]

Since the act provided enhanced levels of funding for schools that accepted the new forms of management it proposed, Catholic schools found themselves unable to avail of the additional funds for building and equipment. Indeed, with less funding available to schools that chose not to join the new system than had been the case in the National School system, the Church claimed its principled opposition to the terms of the reforms meant that it was being deliberately denied funding.[13] This denial, it was also argued, amounted to a form of discrimination by a regime many of whose members were inherently inimical to its very existence. Education was, thereby, added to the list of grievances of which the Catholic-Nationalist community claimed it was victim, almost by virtue of the very nature of the northern state.

Central to the reforms proposed by Lord Londonderry and opposed by the Catholic Church was the creation of local education authorities and their nomi-

---

**9** Seán Farren, *The politics of Irish education, 1920–65* (Belfast, 1995), p. 44.   **10** *Education Ireland Bill, 10 Geo.5 H.C. 1920.*   **11** N.I. cabinet papers: Logue to Londonderry, 2 Sept. 1921.   **12** *Irish News*, 23 Sept. 1921.   **13** Cardinal McRory speaking at centenary celebrations to mark the Catholic Emancipation Act of 1829, reported in *Belfast Telegraph*, 22 June 1929.

nation of local political representatives to the boards of management of schools that would accept their authority. Local rate support would provide the additional funds, and it was this support that justified a local authority presence in school management structures in the form of two representatives on committees of six, the other four to be nominated by the trustees of a school (the church authorities themselves). This was essentially the kind of reform that had been proposed in the MacPherson Bill and opposed then by the Catholic Church on an all-Ireland basis on the grounds that outside 'interference', as public representation was described, in its schools was intolerable and, in any case, unnecessary.

In Northern Ireland, given Unionist control of a majority of local authorities, there was the added fear that such representation would be mainly Unionist. In other words, representatives with a Unionist and Protestant outlook would have a say in the running of Catholic schools, one of the fears that Catholic schools in Ireland had been developed to ensure against. Therefore, despite the financial difficulties that its stand imposed, the Catholic Church found it more acceptable to maintain its distance from the new system while also maintaining that it was being denied its rights to similar levels of funding as were available to schools catering for children from the North's Protestant community. It was a situation that was to persist with only some amelioration for more than forty years.

If Londonderry had to resign himself to the fact that Catholic schools would not become part of the reformed elementary system, he certainly did not expect that a second front would open, involving him in conflict with the Protestant churches whose schools he had anticipated would enthusiastically enter the system. After all, the Protestant churches had without hesitation nominated representatives to the Lynn Committee and had warmly welcomed the MacPherson Bill just three years previously.

The issue for the Protestant churches was the place to be afforded religious instruction in the curriculum. Within national schools, religious instruction, although delivered separately and on a denominational basis, was regarded as part of the curriculum. What the 1923 act provided was permission for religious instruction to be provided, but not as part of the curriculum and with no obligation on any teacher to make that provision. So, from a system that had included religious instruction and also allowed teachers to be obliged to provide it, the Protestant churches were faced with a new system that allowed religious instruction, but only outside of normal school hours, removed any obligation on teachers to provide that instruction and only provided a neutral form of 'Bible instruction' within the curriculum. As this realization spread, resistance to any transfer of Protestant schools to the new educational authorities grew.[14] Adding

---

**14** See *Education Amendment Act*, a pamphlet published jointly by the United Education Committee of the Protestant Churches and the Grand Orange Lodge of Ireland. Copy in N.I. cabinet papers, 9D/1/8.

to this resistance was a sense of betrayal by a Unionist government which the
Protestant churches had expected to be well disposed to their interests and certainly
not one that would take steps seen as undermining their role in education.

Londonderry was faced, therefore, with a new and politically more dangerous
threat, this time from a source that was seen as providing critically important
support to Unionism; the Protestant churches in Northern Ireland. Moreover,
Protestant opposition to his reforms threatened the whole package, since it was a
strong possibility that, without an acceptable resolution, the aims of the 1923 act
could not be achieved at all and his work would have been in vain.

Action by the government to address the crisis was judged essential.
Consequently, the first of two amending acts was rapidly passed by Londonderry
in 1925, and the second and more comprehensive act was passed by his successor,
Lord Charlemont, in 1930.[15] Both, but particularly the second, diffused the situation and ended the conflict with the Protestant churches, at least for a period.

While Londonderry argued that his reforms granted full protection for religious instruction within an education system with enhanced public funding, that
is not how the Protestant churches viewed them. They argued that they were
being asked to relinquish control of their schools and at the same time as having
to sacrifice the guaranteed provision of religious instruction available under the
previous system. They could also point to the fact that the Catholic Church,
notwithstanding lower levels of public funding, retained full control over its
schools, in terms of both management and curriculum. Extra funding and the
better facilities it bought meant nothing if control and influence were to be sacri-
ficed. On each side of Northern Ireland's communal divide, the latter counted
for much more than the former.

The 1930 amendments eased the situation somewhat. The new legislation
made religious education a full part of the curriculum in all schools and allowed
teachers to be required to provide that instruction. This provision satisfied the
Protestant churches and, relieved of the financial burden for their erection and
maintenance, enabled them to transfer their schools to the local authorities. The
Protestant churches were further reassured by their right, henceforth, to be represented on the management committees of schools which would essentially serve
local Protestant communities, notwithstanding the fact that, as local authority
establishments, such schools would no longer be church schools.

Additional financial support for voluntary (mainly Catholic) schools defused
some of the tension with that sector. By remaining apart from public authority
involvement in their management structures, Catholic schools were still less well
endowed financially than their Protestant counterparts. A grievance persisted to

15 Farren, *Politics of Irish education*, ch. 4.

add to others which the northern Catholic-Nationalist community voiced about their position in a partitioned Ireland.

Nonetheless, as a result of the 1930 arrangements, tensions abated somewhat, not to be raised to similar levels until a further set of reforms were proposed in the mid-1940s. The significance of the churches' revolts against the Londonderry reform package was that they underscored, though on different issues, the essential fragility of relationships within Northern Ireland and the risks inherent in being seen to change structures and/or to allocate resources in ways that could be claimed did not respect fundamental concerns of each community.

While the 1930 amending legislation addressed major concerns in each community, neither was fully satisfied. The danger remained that the outcome achieved could easily be upset in any future attempts to reform and restructure elements of the education system. Within a decade and a half, this is precisely what transpired.

The focus for renewed educational controversy involving the churches was the proposals for a further restructuring of the school system to extend access to second-level education in parallel with the far-reaching Butler reforms of 1944 in England and Wales. The basic thrust of the proposed legislation was widely welcomed as a progressive measure, but it was not long before it was gripped in familiar controversy. The Butler Act was an expression of the widespread conviction in developed countries that education to the highest levels should be made as available as possible to all who could benefit. Furthermore in the post-War world, doing so was essential to a country's economic wellbeing. Extending access for all to second-level schooling was a necessary first step. But taking that step in Northern Ireland would not be without controversy of a familiar kind.

The Protestant churches were the first to raise their concerns and, in doing so, they were once again able to rely on the support of many back-bench Unionist politicians. The concerns related to a new conscience clause intended to protect teachers against being contractually required to engage in religious education, the 1930 provision in this regard having been declared unconstitutional.[16] Such a clause, the churches argued, could, if widely invoked by teachers, seriously affect the provision of religious education for Protestant pupils. Anger on this issue was reinforced when another proposal would make additional funding available to Roman Catholic schools, still without any requirement to accept a public presence in their management structures. Furthermore, teachers in Catholic schools would be unlikely to invoke the conscience clause; there would be no risk to the provision of religious instruction in such schools.

While the Catholic Church welcomed any increase in funding, the fact that

---

16  The Attorney general so advised the N.I. cabinet. Cabinet papers, 4/586/11, 24 May 1944.

because of its refusal to accept local authority involvement in school management, its schools would still have to raise a proportion of its financial needs
directly from its own community, remained as a cause of annoyance and of
alleged discrimination. Nationalist politicians lost few opportunities to reinforce
this complaint.[17]

Once again, therefore, the needs of each community and the manner in which
it was proposed to meet those needs from public resources, were being jealously
measured against how the other community was seen to benefit, as well by the
alleged negative effects on one's own. Unlike when the earlier controversies raged,
however, the government did not waver on the main proposals for what became
the 1947 Education Act.[18] The conscience clause was retained and public funding
for Catholic schools was increased to 65 per cent. The Protestant churches had to
accept guarantees that religious education would be an essential part of the
second-level curriculum and the unwritten assurance that most teachers
requested to provide that education would be unlikely to refuse.

This was not the end of controversy, in particular controversy caused by
antagonism towards the increased funding awarded to Catholic schools while the
Catholic church continued its opposition to a direct relationship with local
education authorities. Unionist politicians, rather than the Protestant churches,
kept controversy on this matter alive, choosing issues like the payment of national
insurance for teachers in Catholic schools by the Department of Education, the
payment of clerical assistants in Catholic schools from public funds and the
payment of travel and fees for pupils attending Catholic boarding schools, to
question the legitimacy of such payments to schools that refused to accept public
representation on management boards.[19] Textbooks used for teaching Irish in
Catholic schools were singled out for criticism because, being published in the
Republic of Ireland, they contained illustrations of the Irish national flag, the
tricolour.[20] Not only were Catholic schools obtaining public funds that they were
not entitled to, but worse, in the eyes of some Unionist politicians, they were
guilty of promoting an Irish Nationalist outlook. In other words, subversion of
Northern Ireland was part of the curriculum!

Nationalist politicians strongly defended the Catholic system and vigorously
refuted allegations of non-entitlement, asserting in their responses that the underlying motive for these criticisms of the Catholic school system was one of deep
hostility to the Catholic Church and its community and its culture.[21] The
Catholic Church itself regarded such attacks, if acted upon, as likely

**17** Richard Byrne, a Nationalist MP, *Northern Ireland Parliamentary Debates*, vol. 23, col. 1306 (29 May
1940). **18** Farren, *Politics of Irish education*, pp 184–6. **19** Ibid., pp 211–15. **20** Letter from Minister
of Education reproduced in *Irish News*, 2 May 1952. **21** Harry Diamond MP, *Northern Ireland
Parliamentary Debates*, vol. 59, col. 1276 (2 Mar. 1965).

to confirm the opinion widely held not only among Catholics but among non-Catholics, that government policy is in the last resort being dictated by a body whose chief desire seems to be the resurgence of strife and disorder in this part of Ireland.[22]

While no change was effected in the arrangements made under the 1947 act, frequently raising the issue of payments to Catholic schools sustained a sense of grievance and discrimination within the Catholic community. Not until further legislation was enacted in 1968 was that sense of grievance finally removed.[23] The Education Act of that year saw the Catholic Church finally enter a direct relationship with local education authorities and accept public representation on school management committees.

Despite the various controversies which enveloped education in Northern Ireland during the years 1920–70, it was not educational issues that fuelled the disturbances that gripped the region in late 1960s and beyond. However, what the controversies underlined at one level was how deep-rooted the dual nature of northern society was and how essential it was for peace and good government that account be taken of demands that this be recognized and respected. Whenever this appeared not to be the case, controversy ensued. The various governments over this period had to work hard to arrive at an acceptable set of compromises to ensure that the education system functioned in an orderly manner within what effectively were two parallel sub-systems. Indeed, it could be said that this was achieved up to a point, though not without leaving, particularly within the Catholic community, a sense of having to campaign almost unceasingly for every advance made. Within the Protestant community, there was a general contentment with the educational system as it emerged post-1947. But the lesson was that despite rule by Unionist governments, vigilance was required lest developments be planned that were inimical to Protestant Church interests or that undue concessions be made with regard to Catholic Church influence over education. And so, despite the controversies that raged about them from time to time, successive cohorts of pupils passed peacefully through their schooling during these fifty years and increasingly more and more pupils from both communities benefitted from the gradual extension of educational opportunities.

What of course did not develop during most of this period was any significant thaw in communal relations generally. An education system that could have provided opportunities to promote cross-community relationships and so contribute to a thaw was not encouraged, indeed it was not allowed to do so.

**22** Circular letter from Cardinal D'Alton, Archbishop of Armagh, to Catholic school managers and quoted by H. Minford MP, *Northern Ireland Parliamentary Debates*, vol. 39, cols 1923–4 (12 June 1956). **23** *Education (Amendment) Act (Northern Ireland)*, 1968.

Contacts between schools from both communities were minimal, even in such traditional areas of contact as sport. Sporting traditions within each community were different – Gaelic games predominated in Catholic schools, rugby, soccer, hockey and cricket within schools serving the Protestant community.[24] Many other cultural activities marked differences and not commonalities – an emphasis on Irish language and music giving Catholic schools outlets for activities in which Protestant schools did not participate.

The educational and cultural reference points for each community had remained so exclusive for so long that the mild attempts at breaching the barriers undertaken in the early 1960s by some politicians and civic leaders in both communities lacked strategy, commitment and vision. Ultimately, these attempts came too late to positively influence events which, as that decade advanced, were hurtling towards a crisis, the scale of which had not been anticipated but whose seeds lay in the antagonisms informing relationships between two communities almost hermetically sealed from each other.

Whether education could have played a role in helping to mitigate the communal effects of that crisis is a question that is impossible to answer, but what is clear is that Northern Ireland's parallel systems of education remained potent symbols of two communities living apart while very uneasily sharing the same space.

---

**24** Don Batts, John Darby, Seamus Dunn, Seán Farren, Joseph Harris, Dominic Murray, *Schools together, schools apart?* (Coleraine, 1977).

# Education in a divided society

## DOMINIC MURRAY

Perhaps education, more than any other aspect of social activity in Northern Ireland, has been the most significant factor in determining, or at least perpetuating, the segregated nature of society there. This is in part because, as Wright has claimed, education is critical to the perpetuation and transmission of culture and identity within and across generations.[1] It is important therefore to be aware of the origin and growth of the segregated nature of schooling and the social factors which have influenced its growth.

Historically, schooling in Ireland had been shaped more by clerics than by educationalists. Religious issues have been dominant in the passing or rejection of every education bill since 1800. Indeed, long before the nineteenth century, religion and education were inextricably meshed and the resulting evolution was typified more by tension than by tolerance. In the sixteenth century, for example, Henry VIII instructed the Anglican clergy in Ireland to set up schools to promote both the English language and Protestantism among the Catholic masses. In fact, throughout the seventeenth century, successive repressive acts forbade Catholics to teach in Protestant schools, to keep their own schools, to employ tutors at home or to send their children abroad to be educated. Catholics were, however, encouraged to attend the Protestant establishments, but few accepted the invitation.

At that time, Catholic children got their education by means of illegal classes which took place in the open country, with lookouts posted to warn of any approaching authorities. These became known as 'hedge schools' and, by the end of the eighteenth century, the bulk of Catholic education was being achieved in this way. The hedge schools did in fact represent the first attempt by the Catholic population to have their own system of education, and it might be argued that the severe labour pains that were experienced then may well explain the antipathy of the Roman Catholic hierarchy towards later attempts at state intervention in their schools.

Interestingly, neither religious teaching nor Irish culture seems to have figured highly on the curricula of hedge schools. While some such schools were run by the local priest, the great majority were not, and reading, writing and arithmetic

---

1 Frank Wright, 'Integrated education and new beginning in Northern Ireland' in Frank Wright, *Understanding conflict and finding ways out of it (working paper six)* (Coleraine, 1988).

were the only subjects taught. This raises an interesting point with regard to more recent debates about the integration of Protestant and Catholic schools in Northern Ireland. Catholicism and the Celto-Catholic culture seem to have flourished in Ireland during this period in which little or no religious instruction was given in schools. This would appear to weaken the Roman Catholic segregationist point of view that the school must exist as a means of reproducing cultural and religious heritage. The claim that the Catholic school is essential for ensuring future generations of good Catholics also seems doubtful. It must be said, however, that hedge schools were never part of a mass educational system such as exists now, and perhaps therefore were not considered of the same importance by the Catholic hierarchy.

The year 1812 seems to represent a turning point in the approach to education in Ireland by the British government. According to Dowling, Protestant groups and societies, which were both overtly and covertly proselytizing bodies, abounded in Ireland at the time.[2] The Kildare Place Society was established in an attempt to 'afford the same educational advantages to all classes of professing Christians, without interfering with the peculiar religious opinions of any'. The stipulation that the Bible should be read daily 'without note or comment', while being perceived by Catholic clergy as an endowment of the Protestant position, was neatly dealt with. They simply used the school Bible readings as the texts for the following Sunday's mass. The mixed schools were therefore welcomed by the Irish bishops, and many Catholic parents sent their children to them. A point of interest, in terms of more recent objections, is that the Catholic Church in Ireland had accepted the principle of mixed/integrated schooling as long as there was no proselytizing taking place within it.

A government awareness of the acceptance of mixed schooling by the bishops may well have facilitated the establishment, in 1831, of a National School System, the first such system in Europe. The basic tenet of the commission was to provide mixed education for children of different creeds and to avoid even the suspicion of proselytizing. Three points, however, caused problems: Bible readings, although compulsory, were to be excluded from the secular day, all clergy were to have free access to the schools and children were to be excluded from religious instruction given by a person from another faith. Although the Catholic hierarchy grudgingly accepted the system, the Protestant clergy reacted vehemently against it. They saw it as an attempt to eventually exclude the Bible altogether, and allow the possibility of Catholic clergy having access to 'their' schools. This gave rise to a later assertion that 'the door is thrown open for a Bolshevist or an atheist or a Roman Catholic to become a teacher in a Protestant [sic] school'. It

2 P.J. Dowling, *A history of Irish education: a study in conflicting loyalties* (Dublin, 1971).

is not clear whether this represented a hierarchy of repugnance, but it leaves little doubt regarding the passions which schooling evoked at the time. In 1840, the government acceded to their demands and amended all three 'offensive' articles to the clergy's satisfaction.

Towards the end of the century, so many concessions had been granted by the commissioners to both sides that all National schools had become de facto denominational institutions and remained so until the establishment of the state of Northern Ireland in 1921. The historian, John Magee, sees this eventual denominationalism of schools in terms of each side getting what it wanted.[3] He contends that the Protestant churches had resented the initial National system mainly because it obstructed their work of evangelization among Irish children of all faiths. The Catholic bishops were equally concerned with the education of children of their own denomination in their own schools. It is important to note than at this stage both Catholic and Protestant representatives had fought for, and achieved, their own denominational schools and each received equal financial assistance from the government.

In 1921, responsibility for education in Northern Ireland was removed from Dublin and transferred to the new Ministry of Education in Belfast. The first Minister of Education, Lord Londonderry, appointed a committee under the leadership of Robert Lynn to plan the reform of the Northern Ireland educational system. The committee recommended that three classes of elementary schools be set up:

- *Class I* (latterly known as State/Controlled schools) were those built by local authorities or the ministry or those handed over to the ministry by the previous managers;
- *Class II* (maintained) those schools with special management committees composed of four representatives of the former managers and two of the local government authorities;
- *Class III* (voluntary) those schools whose managers wished to remain entirely independent of the local government authorities.

The Class I schools were to receive 100 per cent grants for both capital expenditure and maintenance. Class II ('maintained') were to receive about 82 per cent grants for capital expenditure and 50 per cent for maintenance, and Class III ('voluntary') schools were to receive a grant for heating and cleaning only.

By the 1940s, it was generally accepted that the conception of a state system of schooling would maintain the Protestant ethos of the State. As Joseph Morgan

---

**3** John Magee, 'The teaching of Irish history in Irish schools', *Irish National Teachers Organisation*, 10:1 (1971), passim.

claimed in a government debate, 'It is not too much to ask that a Protestant government, elected by a Protestant people, should maintain that we should have Protestant teachers for Protestant children'.[4]

The Voluntary sector was almost entirely comprised of schools under Roman Catholic control and, since it could be argued that each religious group had got what it wanted, this did in fact represent a form of discrimination. State schools which catered for the needs of Protestant children were receiving much more generous grants than were their Catholic counterparts. Under the subsequent 1947 Education Act, Voluntary schools were awarded grants of 65 per cent for maintenance and 65 per cent for capital expenditure. In the event, Catholic schools remained 'voluntarily' aloof until 1968, when an amendment act produced increased incentives for them to allow one third of their management committees to consist of government representatives (that is, become 'four and two', or maintained). Grants of 80 per cent towards capital expenditure were offered, together with a 100 per cent grant for maintenance. The less suspicious Catholic managers acquiesced quite soon after and by the late 1970s almost all Catholic primary schools had become 'maintained'. Currently, there is little difference in funding between the two sectors. Today, Catholic children generally attend 'maintained' schools and Protestant children attend 'controlled/state' schools.

Teachers in the Controlled sector often object to their schools being described as Protestant. They rightly claim that they are open to all, and are thus non-denominational. The reality is that controlled schools are de facto Protestant institutions, however, in composition at least. Data provided by Russell indicate that only 0.3 per cent of Roman Catholic teachers are employed in State primary schools.[5] They also suggest that 98.4 per cent of pupils within Catholic Maintained schools are nominally Catholic and in the controlled sector, 80.4 per cent of pupils are nominally Protestant.

It is generally accepted that in Northern Ireland, schooling is provided in Protestant and Catholic establishments which are perceived, and referred to, as such, by the local population. This is important in the arguments surrounding the extent to which segregated schools contribute to suspicion and perhaps the conflict in Northern Ireland. In fact, implicit in these debates is the assumption that there is a real difference in the experiences undergone by Catholic and Protestant children within their denominational schools. What is less clear is whether this should be seen in terms of cause or effect. That is, do segregated schools cause divisiveness or does the existence of different and sometimes conflicting, cultural groups in society dictate the existence of segregated

---

4 Joseph Morgan, 'Government Debate' (Stormont, Belfast, Nov. 1946).  5 David Russell, *Promoting shared education* (Paper read at the UNESCO Centre, University of Ulster, 2006).

schooling? My own research has attempted to shed some light on these questions and to increase a mutual awareness of what goes on inside the different establishments.[6] The data were gathered through full-time participant research over eighteen months in two primary schools; one Protestant, the other Catholic.

What was immediately apparent was that, at the level of the official curriculum, the practices within each school were almost identical. Both were subject to external scrutiny at various key stages and devoted the same time and effort to the preparation of their pupils for the same final (eleven-plus) examination. However, in the context of the relationship between the schools and the society in which they existed, differences were clearly observable both in terms of the perceptions of the schools by 'outsiders' and by the symbols and rituals displayed and practiced within them. For example, in any 'normal' society, it might seem perfectly natural for a Catholic school to display religious images and for a State school to fly the Union Jack. In Northern Ireland, things are slightly different. A Protestant teacher stated that when he saw all 'the statues and things' in a Catholic school he reckoned that a special show was being put on for his benefit and he wondered 'just what exactly went on inside'.

A Catholic teacher commented on a neighbouring Protestant school:

> They fly the (Union) flag down there to show that they are more British than the British themselves. It's also to let us know that they are the lords and masters and that we should be continually aware of it … What has the great Commonwealth ever done for us? They have milked Ireland dry for centuries and yet you still get people who applaud them for it.

On the other hand:

> I don't know why there is such a fuss about the flag. Why should we apologize for flying it? We are a State school and the flag is the emblem of the state. If they (Catholics) want to stay out (of the Union) that's fine with us. But how can they object to us showing that we want to stay in?

These, and many other examples, demonstrate the dangers of symbols in a segregated society. Individuals who are not aware of the meaning that symbols have for those most closely involved, must interpret their representations superficially. Symbols, by their very nature, must be clearly visible. In Northern

6 Dominic Murray, *Worlds apart: segregating schooling in Northern Ireland* (Belfast, 1985); Dominic Murray, 'Culture, religion and violence in Northern Ireland' in Seamus Dunn (ed.), *Facets of the conflict in Northern Ireland* (London, 1995), pp 215–30; Dominic Murray, 'School ethos: the Northern Irish experience' in Catherine Furlong, L. Monaghan and Noel Canavan (eds), *School culture and ethos: cracking the code* (Dublin, 2000).

Ireland, visibility is often seen as provocation. In this regard, it is possible that the separate schools themselves may serve as symbols of the segregated nature of society in Northern Ireland.

This separateness inevitably means a lack of mutual knowledge and thus, all emerging stereotypes emanate from this base of mutual ignorance. In an awareness of this, principals and teachers have, over the years, attempted to increase contact between the schools. Too often in the past, however, this contact actually reinforced stereotypes by focusing the attention of the participants on the differences between the schools rather than on what they had in common. This was all the more likely when such shared activities took place in a competitive milieu. On one occasion, I arrived at school playing fields during a football match just as a young child was leaving. I asked how the match was going and was greeted with the despondent reply that 'the Protestants are winning five-nil!' More ominously, at another football match between two primary schools – one Catholic, the other Protestant – one of the teachers was getting rather passionately involved in the action. When I teased him about it, he replied darkly that 'there is more to this than just football'.

The argument has often been advanced by critics of segregated schooling in Northern Ireland that they tend to foster different, and perhaps conflicting, notions of identity among their pupils. My work did suggest that Protestant schools did tend to identify closely with the administrative and policy-making sections of the educational system. These were deemed to be natural support structures, which, through contact and dissemination of information, moulded solidarity among all State schools. There seemed to be a sense of belonging to, and identity with, a kind of extended educational family. This resulted in bodies such as the Department of Education and the local Education and Library Boards being seen as natural extensions of the system to which State schools belonged: 'We take for granted the support of the Library Boards whose staff are so helpful when we ask for their expert advice'.

In the Catholic schools studied, these same legislative bodies tended to be seen more as necessities to be tolerated. One principal told me that when minor repairs such as fixing a broken window were needed, the school usually did it themselves, because 'it saves me getting in touch with the Board and have them crawling all over the place'.

Staff in another Catholic school, in order to demonstrate their lack of bias, gave the example of them actually allowing the police into the school to give a highway-code session! Again, some years ago, a principal in a Catholic school agreed that his pupils went on fewer trips to sites such as the fire station, local government offices, post office and police station than did their Protestant counterparts. He argued that it would be a waste of time, since 'my kids will never get a job in any of them'. This is disconcerting in that such negative perceptions may well curtail the occupational expectations and aspirations of the pupils. A kind of self-fulfilling prophecy may be operating. If pupils are given the impression that they are not likely to get a job in the areas because of their religion then it is hardly surprising that they may become underrepresented in these occupational sites. In the light of decreasing tensions and perhaps improved relationships in Northern Ireland, it should be a priority to determine the extent to which such negative perceptions still exist in Catholic schools. If they do, it can be validly claimed that the schools may be perpetuating community division by directing their pupils to or away from certain sections of it. Perhaps it is at the level of the fostering of different and conflicting perceptions of identity that the criticisms of segregated schools in Northern Ireland are most justified.

In this regard, much has been written about schools in Northern Ireland in terms of the role they might have played in continuing social divisions and, more recently, the function they may serve in social reconstruction. If schools are to be used for this reconstructionist purpose, it seems that there are two main ways in which it might be attempted. Firstly, we can try to change pupil attitudes within the existing segregated school system and hope that, if successful, there may be less resistance to future structural development in the form of increased collaboration and perhaps integration. I have termed this the attitudinal priority. Secondly, we can change the structures themselves by integrating schools with the conviction that pupil attitudes will be widened and moderated within them (the structural priority). The emphasis on civic and citizenship education as part of the curriculum in schools in England is an example of the former approach, while the bussing of pupils to previously all-white schools in America can be seen as an attempt to implement the latter strategy.

## THE ATTITUDINAL PRIORITY

There is a strong argument that such reconstuctionist efforts should be directed to areas where they are most likely to reach the majority of children; that is, within their segregated schools. In this regard, approximately 95 per cent of schoolchildren in Northern Ireland attend schools which are not integrated. More specifically, Department of Education figures (2004) show that from a total of 340,633 pupils, 144,575 attend State controlled schools, 157,166 attend Catholic-maintained schools, 16,494 attend integrated schools and 22,285 attend other (mainly voluntary grammar) schools.[7] Over the years, several reconstructionist

---

7 Dept. of Education, *Report of a survey of provision for education for mutual understanding (EMU) in post-primary schools* (Bangor, Co. Down, 2000).

programmes have been developed in an awareness, and perhaps acceptance, of the reality of educational segregation.

The first, and perhaps seminal, of these was the *Schools cultural studies programme*, which was introduced in the early 1970s. Robinson cites its main objectives as assisting pupils to cultivate and increase modes of sensitivity, tolerance and mutual understanding.[8] Controversial issues were tackled through a process of values clarification. The project was ground-breaking in its attempts to achieve these through a previously untried combination of curriculum provision (through the introduction of teaching resources) and cross-community contact (through joint field and classwork exercises). The project laid the foundation for almost all of the subsequent school-based approaches to social reconstruction. The project did not receive the necessary statutory government commitment, however, which would have been necessary for its long term success. It also tended to underestimate strong atavistic resistance, especially to the notion of values clarification. This strategy was seen by an uncomfortable number of both teachers and parents as an attempt to get children to reject the values of the home. In addition, it is difficult to overstate the problem of advocating tolerance to pupils, many of whom may have had close relatives killed by either paramilitaries or security forces.

Subsequent projects seem to have learned from both the successes and the shortcomings of SCSP. For example, in terms of the necessity of Statutory support, legislation to introduce the programme, *Education for mutual understanding* (EMU), was introduced as a cross-curricular theme in 1989, on the understanding that statutory requirement for its practice in schools would follow in 1992. In the context of the advisability or effectiveness of combining curriculum provision and community relations contact within the one project, it would appear that within EMU, cross-community contact was not seen as compulsory but rather as simply desirable and beyond the statutory obligations of other parts of the project's curriculum provisions. Smith and Robinson claim that this was despite the fact that teachers tended to perceive the project as cross-community contact in essence and very little else![9] The underlying objective was to foster self respect and respect for others and the improvement of relationships between people of differing cultural traditions. McCully argues that one deficiency was that too much emphasis was placed on personal relationships and not enough on structural considerations.[10] For example, teachers tended to define EMU in terms of what they were comfortable with. Sensitive issues such as values

**8** Alan Robinson, *The schools cultural studies project: a contribution to peace in Northern Ireland. Directors report* (Belfast, 1981).   **9** Alan Smith and Alan Robinson, *Education for mutual understanding: perceptions and policy* (Belfast, 1992).   **10** Alan McCully, 'Practitioners' perceptions of their role in facilitating the handling of controversial issues in contested societies: a Northern Irish experience', *Educational Review*, 58:1 (2006), 51–6.

and their clarification as attempted in the *Schools cultural studies project* seem to have been largely avoided.

Smith has claimed that while these school initiatives did aim to foster mutual respect, tolerance and positive attitudes towards the other community, objectives that were absent from these curricular initiatives were forgiveness and reconciliation.[11] Considering that forgiveness and reconciliation describe the processes that enable individuals and groups to move forward and to build new and positive relationships, their absence is all the more curious in the Northern Ireland context. This may be explained by the fact that according to a Departmental Report (2000), in the majority of schools, there was insufficient professional development for teachers, especially in handling sensitive, controversial issues in the classroom.[12]

By the mid 1990s, there seems to have been a growing awareness that, in order to achieve the desired development of mutual understanding and tolerance, it was vital to confront such issues in the classroom. At the same time, pressure was being exerted on the government's Community Relations Branch to put in place a more systematic cross-community contact scheme which had official support. This led to a demand for a more rigorous structure that was underpinned jointly by these key concerns and the provision of recognized timetable space for this type of work. Increasingly, the concept of Citizenship began to emerge as that most likely to satisfy these demands. The programmes developed corresponded with projects already existing in schools in the Republic of Ireland. They were also constructed in an awareness of moves towards citizenship programmes being implemented through the Council of Europe, especially in the eastern countries, where attempts were being made to come to terms with independence and the concept of democracy for the first time in many years.

If, however, the concept of citizenship is linked to relationships with the state (as it often is), it may well prove easier to introduce such programmes in those countries than in Northern Ireland. Here, not only are there conflicting perceptions of identity, but also of the state itself. The concept of *citizenship of where* remains debatable and debated. It is for this reason that a slightly different model of citizenship has evolved for schools in Northern Ireland. Smith has written about citizenship beyond national identity and the idea of hanging citizenship on key concepts like commitment to democracy, human rights and social justice.[13] So, part of the study of citizenship is not to accept citizenship's definition of these but rather for young people to engage in the process of understanding what the concepts actually mean. It was envisaged, therefore, that Local and Global

**11** A. Smith, 'Citizenship education in Northern Ireland: beyond national identity', *Cambridge Journal of Education*, 33:1 (2003), 15–31. **12** Department of Education, *Report of a survey of provision* (2000). **13** Smith, 'Citizenship'.

Citizenship would expand the remit of EMU and Cultural Heritage by focusing not simply on relations between Catholics and Protestants, but also on relations between all social groups in Northern Ireland and on individual and collective engagements in societies further afield.

The whole idea was to try to introduce controversial issues onto the curriculum (shades of SCSP thirty years before!). In the formal sector, the *Speak your piece* project was initiated.[14] It was a partnership between the University of Ulster, Channel 4 Learning, Ulster Television and the Youth Council for Northern Ireland. It sought to develop innovative approaches to the teaching of controversial issues in Northern Ireland based on themes such as identity, culture, religion and politics. For the first time, the project worked with both teachers and youth workers. Interestingly, at evaluation, it emerged that

> while their respective professional settings created differences in emphasis, the commonality of their professional values, competences and method-ological approaches is such that it is appropriate to refer to them collectively as practitioners in the handling of controversial issues.

The informal learning (the youth workers) proceeding to a project on diversity and interdependence which was an attempt to transform the youth work sector to a more social justice type of platform. In terms of the formal (curriculum) sector, it led eventually to a *Local and global citizenship*[15] approach to reconstruc-tionism in post-primary schools in Northern Ireland. The programme addresses four key concepts; Diversity and inclusion, Human Rights and Social responsi-bility, Equality and Justice, and Democracy and Active Participation. A statement of the minimum requirements of the project was given ministerial approval in 2004 and became a statutory requirement for all post-primary schools from September 2007. The current position is that, of all the subjects being offered currently in post-primary schools in Northern Ireland, the Local and Global Citizenship programme is the only one which must be included in the formal curriculum under this statutory requirement. The Department of Education has made it absolutely clear that there will be no tokenism in this regard.

## THE STRUCTURAL PRIORITY

Russell argues that the choice of education system in a divided society points in at least two directions, both to the protection of communities, culture and iden-

---

14 *Speak your piece: exploring controversial issues in Northern Ireland.* Final Report (Belfast, 2000).  15 Council for the curriculum examinations and assessment, *Local and global citizenship in Northern Ireland.* Preliminary evaluation (Belfast, 2006).

tity through segregation and to the promotion of inter-communal engagement by encouraging and facilitating integration.[16] The government's policy document, *A shared future*, sets out the need to establish a shared society defined by a culture of tolerance in which all individuals are considered equal and where differences are resolved through dialogue.[17] The document is unambiguous in claiming that 'separate but equal is not an option. Parallel living and the provision of parallel services are unsustainable both morally and economically'.

It should be remembered that, while most attention has been given to separation at the level of religion, schools in Northern Ireland are segregated at many other levels. Gallagher, Smith and Montgomery have shown that at age eleven, children undergo a 'Transfer Test', on the basis of which approximately one third are selected as more suitable for academic education in grammar schools, with the remainder attending secondary schools that are traditionally more vocational in focus.[18] In addition, some of these schools are also single sex, so there is segregation on the basis of gender and ability as well as religious denomination.

McGlynn argues that Northern Ireland is a society which not only has to deal with a history of ethno-political conflict but is also being faced with new challenges posed by globalization, such as increasing numbers of refugees and asylum-seekers.[19] In these circumstances, an inability to broaden the educational focus from the conflict to include other new minority groups could also threaten peace in the future. As Northern Ireland becomes a more multi-cultural society, it is essential that integrated, and indeed all schools reflect these changes by assuming a critical multi-cultural approach. Also explored was the extent to which exposure to members of the outgroup at school may influence perceptions of group memberships and encourage the emergence of new or alternative forms of self-identification. Generally, the research indicated that although integrated education was seen as an important socializing factor by the former pupils, the influences of maturation and family were considered to be more important. This corresponds with my own work, which suggested that children as young as six years had at least some idea of what it meant to be Irish or British.[20] In a study of integrated and desegregated schools, McClenahan suggested that cross-community friendships were increased by inter-group contact, but found no evidence of any change to national or socio-political identity as a result of co-education.[21]

---

**16** Russell, *Promoting shared education*.   **17** Office of the First Minister and Deputy First Minister, *A shared future: policy and strategic framework for good relations in Northern Ireland* (Belfast, 2005).   **18** Tony Gallagher, Alan Smith and Alison Montgomery, *Integrated education in Northern Ireland: participation, profile and performance* (Belfast, 2003).   **19** C.W. McGlynn, 'The impact of post primary education in Northern Ireland on past pupils: a study' (EdD, University of Ulster, 2001).   **20** Murray, *Worlds apart*, p. 64.   **21** C. McLenaghan, 'The impact and nature of intergroup contact in planned integrated and desegregated schools in Northern Ireland', *Journal of Social Psychology*, 136:5 (1995), 549–58.

Interestingly, the research indicated not only that the number of mixed friendships rose from 41 per cent prior to attending integrated school, to 67 per cent afterwards, but also that integration extended to the choice of partners. More than half of the past pupils of integrated schools with a partner had chosen one from a different background to themselves. In comparison, data from the Northern Ireland Life and Times Survey [NILT] (2000) indicated that only 8 per cent of marriages in Northern Ireland are inter-community. The significance of all of this must be considered in the context of residential segregation, which has been argued to make the continuance of such relationships a true test of friendship across the divide. Indeed, previous research on short-term cross-community projects has indicated that friendships often were not maintained because of the difficulties encountered when participants returned to their segregated communities.[22]

## CONCLUSION

Many studies of integrated education emphasize its potential for building social cohesion and for promoting forgiveness and reconciliation. Most claim that it is crucial that both the public and the governmental support required to enable integrated education to play its role in building a more peaceful and tolerant society in Northern Ireland are generated. Russell argues that there has been a tendency to view the choice between segregation and integration of schools as mutually exclusive.[23] But this does not have to be the case.

On the contrary, rather than engaging in laboured debate about which option is best, education can be conceived as a continuum, with segregated schools at one end of the spectrum and integrated schools at the opposite end. In between these poles are an indeterminate number of policy options.

A recent study by Montgomery, Fraser, McGlynn, Smith and Gallagher argued that, as Northern Ireland attempts to move out of conflict, it is crucial that the integrated education movement critically examines the achievements of the last twenty-two years and carefully charts the direction in which it now moves.[24] Research should also consider integrated education as part of the broader educational system in Northern Ireland, including comparisons with segregated schools, and also including a detailed investigation of different types of integrated schools and their approaches to education. This might be all the

22 Karen Trew, 'Catholic-Protestant contact in Northern Ireland' in Miles Hewstone and Rupert Brown (eds), *Contact and conflict in intergroup encounters* (Oxford, 1986), pp 123–43.  23 Russell, *Promoting shared education.*  24 Alison Montgomery, Grace Fraser, Claire McGlynn, Alan Smith and Anthony Gallagher, *Integrated schools in Northern Ireland: integration in practice* (Belfast, 2003).

more vital in view of the recent pronouncements of Secretary of State Peter Hain, who clearly views segregation of schools in Northern Ireland as coming at too a high price. He wants to see whether a new model of schooling, sharing across sectors, could help achieve higher standards, better facilities and a better use of resources. To reinforce his claim, he cites the fact that there are already 54,000 'empty desks' in our schools and this figure will rise to 80,000 over the next few years.

At a more specific level, the Bain Report highlighted the problems created by an educational system in a divided society where there are Catholic, Protestant and integrated schools existing at both primary and post-primary level.[25] The report recommended new minimum enrolments for all schools and found that currently one third of schools fail to reach these. Sir George offers the 'carrot' that 'schools should share more facilities and, if they do so, would get better buildings and their projects might get priority'.

He also suggests that the building of already approved schools should be stalled and future ones planned to cover the needs of a geographical area rather than the current situation, in which there may be Catholic, State, Integrated and Irish Language schools all within the same small area.

These utilitarian approaches may well sit uneasily with integrationists, who have tended to rest their case on the claim that the integration of schools can provide sites where difference, in identity for example, is celebrated as a valuable social resource. It is quite likely, however, that it will be economic factors rather than educational philosophies that prove to be the most powerful elements in future debates on collaboration between, or integration of, schools in Northern Ireland. Indeed, despite the fact that the Department of Education has a duty under the Education Reform (Northern Ireland) Order 1989 to 'encourage and facilitate integrated education', it would seem that government, after the first idealistic flush for social reform through educational integration, is now moving toward a 'shared future' through a combination of the structural initiatives of pragmatic (and perhaps enforced) collaboration and attitudinal strategies such as global citizenship programmes.

**25** Prof. Sir George Bain, *Report of the independent strategic review of education* (www.communityni.org) (2006).

# 'Ulsteria': the fortunes of the Irish language under Stormont, 1921–72[1]

## FIONNTÁN DE BRÚN

On a winter night in the early years of the First World War, Denis Ireland, the Belfast writer and future Protestant Nationalist, was walking round the walls of Derry. From an upper room beyond the parapet, a 'high insistent voice' was delivering a speech in Irish to frenzied applause. Feeling that this was no place for a newly-joined second lieutenant in a British greatcoat, the young officer stood back into the darkness, remarking:

> With me moved my maternal grandfather, invisible, but present in the frosty night. I never heard him discussed in the family, not with Carsonite rifles in the attic. If he figured at all, he figured as a sort of disreputable relative from the Australian outback, never to be mentioned in polite Belfast society.
>
> Actually, he was a Presbyterian minister, and somewhere about the middle of last century he preached from the pulpit of a small Presbyterian church in Co. Louth – in English one Sunday, in Irish the next. No wonder we kept quiet about him on the Malone Road. At the height of Carsonite 'Ulsteria', grandfathers who preached in Irish were pushed in behind the historical background, and kept there.[2]

Whereas another Irish Protestant writer, J.M. Synge, famously recorded a similar experience of exposure to and distance from the Irish language – through the floorboards of his room on the Aran Islands – the essential difference between them is the explicit political rejection of the Irish language by Ulster Unionist society in Denis Ireland's account.[3] Yet Ulster Protestants of the nineteenth century had been pioneers of the Irish language revival,[4] and so this political eschewal of Irish was, in Denis Ireland's experience, essentially the act of one generation of Unionists. Even then, the Carsonite generation was far from unanimous in its attitude towards Irish, as is evidenced in the membership of the

**1** Stormont is used here, as in popular usage, to refer to the life-span of the Northern Ireland government from 1921 to 1972, although the Northern Ireland parliament did not sit in the Stormont building until 1932, the year of the building's completion. **2** Denis Ireland, *From the jungle of Belfast* (Belfast, 1973), p. 43. **3** J.M. Synge, *The Aran Islands* (1907). See also Declan Kiberd, *Synge and the Irish language* (London, 1979). **4** See Roger Blaney, *Presbyterians and the Irish language* (Belfast, 1996); A.J. Hughes, *Robert Shipboy MacAdam: his life and Gaelic proverb collection* (Belfast, 1998).

Gaelic League in Ulster from the 1890s onwards, which included most famously, R.R. Kane, Orange Grandmaster and organizer of the Ulster Unionist Convention of 1892.[5] Nevertheless, the installation of a Unionist government in 1921 marked the beginning of an era in which Irish was rarely acknowledged by Unionists as anything other than a manifestation of Irish Nationalist, anti-partitionist sentiment. This attitude was reinforced by the new Free State's apparently wholesale adoption of the language through compulsory Irish in schools and the use of Irish by its civil service.

On the surface, the Irish language had an unambiguous political significance in the new Northern Ireland state. Nevertheless, a closer examination of the atti-tude of the Unionist government towards the language reveals some of the contradictions inherent in Unionism, both in terms of its own internal logic and in its efforts to curtail the use of Irish within the new state. Indeed, the antago-nism of the Unionist government towards Irish was often the thing that most sustained a passion for the language among Nationalists. In the absence of any relations with statutory authorities, Irish enthusiasts assumed a form of self-sufficient civil society. At the same time, and most ironically, the reality of partition encouraged the mostly Catholic, anti-partitionist Irish language move-ment in the North to develop a strong provincial ethos to the dismay of some of its southern counterparts. The purpose of this essay is to trace the outworking of these issues and in particular to examine the fortunes of the Irish language move-ment within the state of Northern Ireland from the state's inception in 1921 until the dissolution of the Northern parliament in 1972.

While it is difficult to give a precise date to the 'rejection' of the Irish language by Ulster Protestant society, Breandán Ó Buachalla points to a perceived change in attitudes from the 1860s onwards, citing Samuel Ferguson's conclusion after his failure to have a Chair of Celtic restored at Queen's College in 1875:

> We have done our endeavour to found such a chair here but all things Celtic are regarded by our educated classes as of questionable *ton* and an idea exists that it is inexpedient to encourage anything tending to foster Irish sentiment.[6]

Two decades later, the founding of the Gaelic League gave the Irish language a new national prominence and established a set of objectives for the revival of its

**5** See Aodán Mac Póilin, 'Irish in Belfast, 1892–1960: from the Gaelic League to Cumann Chluain Ard' in Fionntán de Brún (ed.), *Belfast and the Irish language* (Dublin, 2006), pp 114–17.   **6** Breandán Ó Buachalla, *I mBéal Feirste cois cuain* (Dublin, 1968), p. 272. See also Séamus Ó Casaide, *The Irish language in Belfast and County Down, AD1601–1850* (Dublin, 1930), p. 49, and A.J. Hughes, 'The Ulster Gaelic Society and the work of MacAdam's Irish scribes' in de Brún (ed.), *Belfast and the Irish language*, pp 65–100 at 96–7.

use throughout Ireland. As noted earlier, the multi-denominational membership
of the Belfast branch of the League demonstrates that, at least at this stage, in
1895, the Irish language movement and Unionism were not mutually exclusive
concerns. Nevertheless, the intervening period witnessed a consolidation among
Unionists of the antipathy towards the Irish language observed by Samuel
Ferguson in the 1870s. Gordon McCoy quotes from a 1904 article in the Unionist
*Belfast Newsletter*, 'the Gaelic League: its aims and methods', where the author
concedes the right of the League to pursue its aims but accuses the organization
of having deserted the non-sectarian and non-political aims of its founders.[7] The
adoption by the Gaelic League in 1915 of a motion supporting a Gaelic and free
Ireland is often characterized as the final stage in a process of positioning of the
League in direct opposition to Unionism, yet it is clear that Unionist aversions to
the language had been established well before that.

While the Gaelic League was initially successful in attracting the support of
some Unionists in the 1890s, it is clear that the time of Denis Ireland's anecdote,
the period immediately after the Home Rule crisis, was a period during which the
Unionists of Ulster, with few exceptions, held the aims of the Irish language
movement as antithetical to their own. In the years that followed, up until the
partition of Ireland in 1921, there is little to suggest anything other than a hard-
ening of Unionist opposition to the language. If the Irish sermons given by Denis
Ireland's grandfather were not to be mentioned during Carson's 'Ulsteria', the
Church of Ireland clerics who were members of *Cumann Gaodhalach na hEaglaise*
(the Irish Guild of the Church) found themselves equally at odds with their flock
in Ulster. In a letter to the Guild's publication, *the Gaelic Churchman (an t-
Eaglaiseach Gaodhalach)*, in 1919, an anonymous contributor from Belfast
described Irish-speaking Church of Ireland clergy in some districts as 'a sect
everywhere spoken against'.[8] A letter from Cork in another edition of *the Gaelic
Churchman* confirms the view from the south of the Ulster Protestant as naturally
ill-disposed to the Irish language. Referring to a report of the Church of Ireland
burial service of the Revd Patrick P. O'Sullivan at Templepatrick, Co. Antrim,
which was given in Irish by Canon F.B. O'Connell, the writer, 'A Cork R.C.',
remarked:

7 *Belfast Newsletter*, 28 May 1904, quoted by Gordon McCoy, 'Protestants and the Irish language in
Belfast' in *Belfast and the Irish language*, pp 147–8. The poet Alice Milligan gives a fascinating analysis of
the diverse groups that made up the membership of the Belfast Gaelic League in 1905, explaining that the
League should avoid 'the dangerous work of trying to force into a too close intimacy the boys who like to
wind up their meetings with "A nation once again" or "Duan na saoirse" and the people who are genuinely
delighted to hear that the Lord Lieutenant and Sir Horace Plunkett have commended the movement, and
that there is a version of "God save the king" in Gaelic' ('The Gaelic League in Belfast' in *An Claidheamh
Soluis*, 1 Apr. 1905, 8). **8** *The Gaelic Churchman*, 1:3 (1919), 16.

> Corkmen generally look upon Ulster as the home of black-hearted
> Protestantism and West-Britonism. The thought of the slightest spark of
> nationality or love of country and language in the heart of an Ulster
> Protestant of today, especially in that of a Protestant minister, and more
> especially within the walls of a Belfast University, would be looked upon
> as ridiculous; therefore you can understand why news of (Nationalist)
> Protestantism in north-east Ulster will be eagerly read by Corkmen.
>
> Ministers here try to be 'English', if possible, both in accent and
> manner, and they consider that Gaelic speech is 'vulgar'.[9]

The strident language of this letter, written in 1919, is itself indicative of an
ever-widening gap between Unionist Ulster and 'Irish-Ireland'. Within two years,
this gap had become the physical reality of the partition of Ireland and a new era
in which Ulster Unionism and Irish Nationalism would employ legislative power
to advance their opposing aspirations in two separate jurisdictions. Under the
Free State's 1922 constitution, Irish became the national language and steps were
taken to make the language compulsory for admission to the civil service.
Changes were also made to the school curricula, with Irish designated as a
compulsory subject in all standards in the national schools with effect from St
Patrick's Day 1922.[10] At the same time, the use of the Irish language in schools in
Northern Ireland was being questioned by Unionist representatives in the new
parliament. In December 1921, William Grant MP, a future cabinet minister, criticized the Ministry of Education's provision of an organizer of Irish language
instruction and was supported in this by a fellow Unionist MP, Thompson
Donald, who added: 'What do we want with the Irish language here? There is no
need for it at all.'[11]

While the issue of organizer of Irish language instruction was an important
signpost to future developments, a more serious affair was to follow in the shape
of the Catholic school teachers' campaign of non-recognition of the Northern
ministry of education. Some 800 teachers in 270 schools were involved in the
campaign from January to October 1922, during which time teachers participating in the campaign had their salaries paid by the Dublin government.[12] While
the non-recognition campaign was a response to the broader social and political
concerns of the Northern Catholic community, the head of the Dublin govern-

9 *The Gaelic Churchman*, 1:4 (1919), 13. The writer refers to a short account of the burial service of the Revd Patrick P. O'Sullivan by Francis Joseph Bigger in the first issue of *The Gaelic Churchman*, 1:1 (1919), 4. Canon F.B. O'Connell was a lecturer in Irish at Queen's University, Belfast. 10 Adrian Kelly, *Compulsory Irish: language and education in Ireland, 1870s to 1970s* (Dublin, 2002), pp 17–18. 11 *Northern Ireland Parliamentary Debates*, vol. 1 (1921), pp 520–1 (http://stormontpapers.ahds.ac.uk/index.html). 12 Éamon Phoenix, *Northern Nationalism* (Belfast, 1994), p. 190.

ment, Michael Collins, blamed the attitude of the Northern Minister of
Education towards the Irish language as the catalyst for a breakdown in relationships between the two respective education ministries.[13] The Northern minister,
Lord Londonderry, had earlier dismissed a request from the Dublin-based
Intermediate Board that examinations in subjects other than Irish might be
answered in Irish, referring, in his statement rejecting the proposal, to 'the so-
called Irish language'.[14] During the period of the Catholic teachers' boycott, Lord
Londonderry abolished the post of organizer of Irish language instruction and
shortly afterwards, in August 1922, funding and recognition of independent Irish
language colleges were withdrawn.[15]

When the campaign of non-recognition was ended in November 1922, the
guaranteed place of Irish as an optional subject within school hours, and an extra
subject after school hours, was an important part of the settlement agreed to by
the teachers' representatives and the Northern ministry for education.
Nevertheless, as Liam Andrews has shown, by April 1923 the position of the Irish
language in schools in the North had lost significant ground when one considers
that the post of organizer of Irish language instruction had been abolished; the
existence of bi-lingual districts such as those that pertained, albeit tenuously, in
parts of Tyrone and Antrim, had been denied; the teaching of Irish as an optional
subject had been reduced to ninety minutes per week in public elementary
schools; and recognition and funding had been withdrawn from the independent
Irish language colleges.[16]

Under continued Unionist pressure, and in the wake of the 1923 Lynn
Committee's report on education, the place of Irish in the public elementary
schools was further curtailed. Despite a submission from the Irish National
Teachers' Organization to retain Irish as an optional subject in all standards, Irish
was prohibited as an optional subject below the fifth standard with effect from
1924. Above the fifth standard, the possibility of Irish as an optional subject was
limited due to competition from other subjects. There were further restrictions,
with the removal of fees for the teaching of Irish as an extra subject in 1926 and
again in 1933.[17] Not surprisingly, the numbers of schools that taught Irish as an

---

13 Liam Andrews, 'The very dogs in Belfast will bark in Irish' in Aodán Mac Póilin (ed.), *The Irish
language in Northern Ireland* (Belfast, 1997), p. 60. The Intermediate Board was established in 1878 to institute and administer a system of public examinations (John Coolahan, *Irish education: history and structure*
(Dublin, 1981), pp 62–3).   14 Andrews, *Irish language*, p. 59.   15 The independent Irish colleges had
been established by the Gaelic League between 1904 and 1906 to give instruction and award certificates in
the teaching of Irish. There were three of these in Northern Ireland, the Belfast colleges, Coláiste
Chomhghaill and An Ardscoil Ultach and St Malachy's or the Rathlin College of Irish, Ballycastle.   16
Andrews, *Irish language*, p. 65. After partition it became impossible to gauge the extent of bilingualism
within Northern Ireland as the census question on ability to speak Irish was removed in the North until
1991.   17 Andrews, *Irish language*, pp 70–81.

optional or extra subject declined accordingly – between 1924–5 and 1927–8, the number of schools offering Irish as an optional subject was halved and the number offering Irish as an extra subject dropped by 70 per cent.[18] The rationale for the Unionist government's strictures on the Irish language is explained quite candidly in memoranda from its most senior figures, as Liam Andrews has demonstrated. The memoranda were written in response to demands from the extreme Loyalty League and William Grant MP that no public money be spent on what they considered to be the seditious business of teaching Irish. J.H. Robb, parliamentary secretary to the Minister of Education, explained the ministry's policy to Grant in 1928 saying that

> We found Irish teaching in being when we took over and so far from encouraging it, we have been reducing facilities, and as a result Irish is taught in only 149 schools as against 242 in 1922. I do not think that the Loyalty League would have felt any alarm if they had known the facts.[19]

The Prime Minister, Lord Craigavon, was equally frank about his government's policy in a letter to the Loyalty League in the same year:

> He [the Prime Minister] is by no means convinced that repressive measures would affect the object which both you and he desire. A prohibition of Irish teaching in the schools might have a result the very opposite to that intended. It would be proclaimed by interested parties as a provocative and arbitrary act on the part of the government and would be used as a potent means of arousing in many people an interest in a study to which there is good reason to believe they are gradually and steadily becoming indifferent. In the view of the government, it is better to keep a control by means of regulations over activities of this character than to drive them underground where they will undoubtedly tend to germinate and exert a baneful influence … You may rest assured that the government is watching the situation.[20]

While this patent hostility towards Irish can be largely attributed to the prevailing association of the language, in the eyes of Unionists, with both the aims of the 1916 Rising and the cultural and educational ethos of the new Free State, there are other important factors which pre-date partition or indeed the Easter Rising. The first of these is the issue of compulsory Irish and the second is the Unionist

---

**18** *Report of the Ministry of Education for the year 1927–8*, p. 20. See also *Northern Ireland Parliamentary Debates*, vol. 15 (1932, 33), p. 919.   **19** Andrews, *Irish language*, p. 74.   **20** Ibid., p. 76.

belief in their role and duties within the British Empire. In relation to compulsory Irish, it is clear, as Brian Ó Cuív pointed out, from the parliamentary debates
on the Home Rule Bill in 1912, that Unionists were then aware of the influence
of the Gaelic League and of the possibility of compulsion with regard to Irish.
Indeed, at its 1913 Ard-Fheis, the Gaelic League criticized John Dillon for
implying in a statement made in the House of Commons that if the question of
compulsory Irish arose, many Nationalists would join Unionists in opposing it.[21]
It is quite likely that Unionists viewed the introduction of compulsory Irish in
the new Free State, notwithstanding the modification of the original policy, as a
vindication of their concerns during the Home Rule crisis.[22] It was certainly a
common criticism of the southern state that Irish was being foisted on the population south of the border. Yet when viewed alongside the evidence of a vigorous
Unionist policy of stifling the Irish language, such accusations of a coercive Irish
language policy in the Free State appear somewhat disingenuous. Nevertheless,
Unionist concerns about compulsory Irish were evidently taken seriously by
Denis Ireland, who articulated a Nationalist Ulster Protestant perspective,
proposing a federal Ireland in which Ulster would take its place. In two important essays, written in the 1930s and 1940s, Denis Ireland highlighted the question
of compulsory Irish and warned against its inclusion in a future federal dispensation: 'Compulsory Gaelic ... would never be regarded by Protestant Ulster as
anything but retrograde, but the difficulty might be surmounted by reserving the
province of education in Northern Ireland to the northern legislature.'[23]

The second, and more ideologically based motive impelling Unionist
antipathy to the Irish language, is grounded in a perception of the language and
its revival as concerns which were at odds with the progress of the British Empire,
an empire to which their own good fortunes were resolutely bound. A very useful
insight into Unionist faith in the Empire is found in the reports of a mass
meeting held at the Ulster Hall in 1889 to express outrage at the killing of RIC
District Inspector Martin in Gweedore, Co. Donegal. Martin had been
attempting to arrest the local parish priest, Fr James MacFadden, after mass, over
activities relating to the campaign of land agitation, when he was attacked and
bludgeoned to death by parishioners in February of 1889.[24] The Ulster Hall
meeting, chaired by the shipping magnate, Sir Edward Harland, provided a
forum for expressing Unionist pride in their economic achievements as well as

**21** Brian Ó Cuív, 'Education and language' in Desmond Williams (ed.), *The Irish struggle, 1916–26*
(Dublin, 1966), p. 159.  **22** Where a majority of parents objected to either Irish or English as a compulsory subject, their wishes were to be respected. See Kelly, *Compulsory Irish*, pp 18–19.  **23** Denis Ireland,
*Ulster to-day and to-morrow: her part in a Gaelic civilization* (London, 1931), p. 40; see also: *Éamon de Valera
doesn't see it through: a study of Irish politics in the machine age* (Cork, 1941), p. 46.  **24** See Breandán Mac
Suibhne, 'Soggarth aroon and gombeen priest: Canon James MacFadden (1842–1917)' in Gerard Moran
(ed.), *Radical Irish priests* (Dublin 1998), pp 146–76.

consolidating their opposition to the political forces, both Irish Nationalist and English liberal, that would seek 'to thrust us out of the British Empire'.[25] Typical of the sentiments declared at the meeting were those expressed by Sir William Charley:

> Our soldiers and our sailors have contributed to build up that mighty empire on which the sun never sets, and what has made England what it is. We are members of an Imperial race and we are not likely to bow down in the dust before a parliament dominated by National Leaguers in Dublin. Just consider what a Dublin parliament, dominated by National Leaguers, means? The Nationalists hate with a cordial hatred the linen trade of Ulster, because in the honoured ranks of its merchants and of its industrious wage-earning classes, there is no time for the actions of screaming demagogues – there is no room for the principles of wholesale plunder.[26]

Much of the import of the Ulster hall meeting was to contrast two conflicting ways of life, the orderly and prosperous, industrial north-east with the anarchic and backward rural Ireland so starkly represented in the Irish-speaking peasantry of Gweedore. As the *Newsletter*'s editorial comment put it: 'Does anyone in his senses imagine that the Unionists of high and low degree assembled in the Ulster Hall would submit to the rule of yokels who are going about performing all manner of fantastic tricks?'[27]

This pre-eminence of imperial economic progress over the conservation of native rural traditions is evident in the critique of the Gaelic League, referred to earlier, which appeared in the *Newsletter* in 1904:

> Unionists have no objection to the Irish language, and they recognize the fact that Irishmen – and, for the matter of that, Englishmen and Scotchmen, too – have a perfect right to learn their language, and have their children taught to read and speak it, if they will. While they hold that from a business point of view the Irish language is altogether unnecessary, and that it is worse than useless when it occupies time that could be more profitably devoted to other subjects, still they are willing that where the parents desire it their children should have every facility for learning the language ... [Unionists] have no desire to force their convictions on those who differ from them, and, consequently, they are prepared to concede perfect freedom of opinion and action.[28]

25 Editorial column, *Belfast Newsletter*, 15 Feb. 1889.   26 *Belfast Newsletter*, 15 Feb. 1889, p. 9.   27 Editorial column, *Belfast Newsletter*, 15 Feb. 1889.   28 McCoy, 'Protestants and the Irish language', pp 147–8.

Where the *Newsletter* article contends that the study of Irish in schools is a waste of time and 'from a business point of view the Irish language is altogether unnec-essary', the author postulates an argument against the revival of the language which was to be frequently repeated by Unionist politicians in the debates of the future Northern Ireland parliament. McCoy summarizes this argument as 'an opposition between malign "traditions" and a benign process of "progress", manifested in increased industrialization, widespread literacy, market economies and democratization'.[29]

This view of the Irish language as essentially irrelevant in the modern age is one which is rooted in the dominance of utilitarianism in nineteenth-century British political discourse and it was a view vigorously disputed by nineteenth-century Irish cultural Nationalists such as Thomas Davis and John Mitchel. The latter despaired that 'the "nineteenth century" would not know itself, could not express itself in Irish'.[30] Ironically, Daniel O'Connell, a native speaker of Irish, declared himself 'sufficiently utilitarian not to regret its abandonment'.

The question 'what is the use of it?', favoured by the father of utilitarianism, Jeremy Bentham, as a summary of the central tenet of his ideology, was repeated almost verbatim by Unionist members of the Northern Ireland parliament in debates about the teaching of Irish in Catholic schools during the 1930s and 1940s. In response to Nationalist criticism of the withdrawal of grant-aid for the teaching of Irish as an optional subject in schools, Craigavon asked, 'What use is it to us here in this progressive, busy part of the empire to teach our children the Irish language? What use would it be to them?'[31] The Benthamite refrain featured prominently in an earlier debate on the same issue, where Major McCormick asked, 'Of what commercial value is Irish?'[32] and John Clarke Davison MP remarked that the teaching of Irish has been largely a matter of 'political propa-ganda, and of disloyal propaganda at that' before adding that 'I cannot see how it can be for the benefit of school children to teach them a subject which can be of no use whatever to them in after life.'[33]

Throughout the lifetime of the Northern Ireland parliament, Unionists clung to a policy of obdurately restricting or containing the Irish language in schools and other areas, such as broadcasting, where their influence could be exercised. Nationalists protested whenever matters came to a head, such as in 1942 when the principal of Strabane Technical School was dismissed by the regional educational committee for introducing Irish classes,[34] or when an Irish language reader, *Cosán an Óir*, was withdrawn in 1956 after an illustration of a child carrying a tricolour

**29** Ibid., p. 148.   **30** 'The Famine year' [reprinted as appendix to] *Jail Journal* (London, 1983), p. 415.
**31** *Northern Ireland Parliamentary Debates*, vol. 18 (1935, 36), pp 645–6.   **32** Ibid., vol. 15 (1932, 33), pp 1119–20.   **33** Ibid., vol. 15 (1932, 33), pp 1083–4.   **34** Ibid., vol. 25 (1942, 43), pp 2705–6.

flag was deemed unsuitable.[35] The parliamentary exchanges which surrounded such incidents bear witness to the language's association in Unionist minds with their polar opposites – Irish Republican separatism and the rival Irish Free State/ Republic.[36]

It is clear that, at the time of the creation of Northern Ireland, the Irish language was entirely a non-Unionist concern and the question of the language in the education system, thereafter, a political shibboleth in the Northern Ireland parliament. It is worth, at this stage, considering how that 'non-Unionist' concern developed under the hostile conditions of a Unionist administration which saw the promotion of Irish as the mission of its political nemesis in the Free State. If Unionists in Northern Ireland focused their energies on limiting the teaching of Irish in schools, there is no doubt that the efforts of the Gaelic League in Ulster had historically concentrated on the same area but with opposite intentions. In the early 1900s, the Gaelic League successfully lobbied the Catholic authorities to have Irish taught in the newly founded St Mary's Training College.[37] A report by the editor of *An Claidheamh Soluis*, Pádraig Pearse, describes an enthusiastic meeting: 'one of the vastest that has ever assembled under the auspices of the Gaelic League', held in Belfast in December 1904 and presided over by the Cardinal-Archbishop of Armagh, at which the Catholic Bishop of Down and Connor, Dr Henry, told those assembled that the teaching of Irish was flourishing at St Mary's and in the diocesan seminary, St Malachy's College.[38] The same edition carries the report of a deputation to St Mary's College sent by the League to enquire about the status of Irish there. The Mother Superioress assured the deputation that Irish was flourishing under the tutelage of Fr Gearóid Ó Nualláin and its report concludes by noting that 'the Mother Superioress is an Irish Irelander' and that 'the spirit of the College is, accordingly, what one would expect from such direction'.[39]

All of this presents a picture of Catholic social cohesion in which the Irish language movement was a unifying force bringing clergy and laity together in a common cause. Nevertheless, Catholic attitudes towards the Irish language appear more complex than this if one considers the testimony of the same Fr Ó Nualláin in his autobiography, *Beatha Dhuine a Thoil* (1950). Contrary to the impression recorded by the Gaelic League deputation, Prof. Ó Nualláin recalls how one of his colleagues at St Mary's had an aversion towards 'west-Britonism',

**35** Ibid., vol. 40 (1956, 57), pp 394–8. See also *Irish News*, 11 Feb. 2005, p. 1.  **36** In the debates that followed the withdrawal of *Cosán an Óir*, the Labour and Unionist-aligned Minister of Education, Harry Midgley, countered accusations of censorship with a critique of the censorship of books in the south of Ireland: 'The fundamental difference between this State with its principles of freedom and civil liberty and the State known as Éire is that there is a State censorship in Éire', *Northern Ireland Parliamentary Debates*, vol. 40 (1956, 57), p. 396.  **37** Founded in 1900, now St Mary's University College.  **38** *An Claidheamh Soluis*, 24 Dec. 1904, 6–7.  **39** Ibid., 8–9.

a trait which left some of her colleagues, who were 'not very Irish at all', ill-disposed towards her.[40] Just as Joyce's quintessential study of middle-class Dublin, 'The Dead', includes a clash between Gabriel Conroy and the Gaelic Leaguer, Molly Ivors, there is no doubt that support for the Gaelic League was far from unanimous among Catholics. P.T. McGinley, who in 1895 hosted the inaugural meeting of the Belfast Gaelic League in his home on the Beersbridge Road, recounts the attitudes of both Catholic clergy and politicians to the Irish language in the early years of the revival:

> Neither of these objected to the language or its resuscitation. They merely disliked the rise of an 'unauthorized' body which already assumed national proportions without being amenable to their control. Then many of the older clergy, and some of the bishops too, had a genuine dislike of Irish, and thought its revival a fantastic idea.[41]

It is likely that this reference to 'the older clergy' points to a residue of the controversy over Protestant evangelical groups' use of Irish texts in the mid-nineteenth century. McGinley makes the point earlier in his essay that his mother was 'fined in confession for the offence of reading Irish to earn fees – from a Protestant Society – at the bidding of a travelling teacher'.[42]

Whatever misgivings sections of the Catholic clergy and hierarchy may have had about the Gaelic League, the evidence of clerical participation in the League's organization and structures as it gathered momentum reflects a coincidence of strategic interests. Given the influence of the Catholic clergy over Irish society, their patronage of the League could only inspire popular confidence in the organization. Indeed, the issue of the clergy's endorsement of the League dominates Pádraig Pearse's personal account of a dinner he had with Bishop Henry and Cardinal Logue on the evening of the 1904 Belfast meeting.[43] Yet it is important to note that many clergy had discovered an interest in the Irish language without consideration to any of the church's strategic concerns but as individual enthusiasts. Indeed, many of the Gaelic League's original stalwarts, men such as Eugene O'Growney and Michael O'Hickey, happened also to be priests.

It is not surprising, therefore, to find that in the 1920s the key figure in the Northern Irish language movement was Fr Lorcán Ó Muireadhaigh (Fr Larry

**40** *Beatha dhuine a thoil* (Dublin, 1950), p. 47.   **41** P.T. Mac Fhionnlaoich, 'The language movement and the Gaelic soul' in William G. Fitzgerald (ed.), *The voice of Ireland: a survey of the race and nation from all angles by the foremost leaders at home and abroad* (Dublin, 1924), p. 449.   **42** Mac Fhionnlaoich, 'The language movement and the Gaelic soul', p. 445. For an account of the 'Bible war' in the Glens of Antrim, see Hughes, *Robert Shipboy MacAdam*, pp 73–6.   **43** Séamus Ó Buachalla, *The letters of P.H. Pearse* (Dublin, 1979), p. 88.

Murray) from Louth, for whom the Irish language was to become his life's work, both as a scholar and a revivalist. The demands of partition and the perceived neglect of Ulster Irish encouraged Ó Muireadhaigh to convince the Gaelic League in Ulster that its aims would be more effectively pursued in a new Northern organization consisting of the nine Ulster counties and Ó Muireadhaigh's native Co. Louth. Comhaltas Uladh (The Ulster Fellowship) was duly founded in 1926, its monthly publication *An tUltach* (The Ulsterman) having been founded two years previously, with Fr Ó Muireadhaigh as treasurer and editor respectively.[44] From the outset, Catholic clergy played a lead role in the new organization – of the twenty members of Comhaltas Uladh's first executive committee, twelve were priests.[45] Such high levels of clerical participation ensured that Comhaltas Uladh was an organization steeped in Catholic respectability and indeed the bishop of Down and Connor, Dr Mageean, was proud to note that the line of Irish-speaking bishops in Ulster had never been broken.[46] Aodán Mac Póilin positions Comhaltas Uladh at the heart of a phenomenon which he describes as 'Catholic communalism': 'an extremely effective form of passive resistance', according to which, 'cultural, social and sporting activities among the Catholic community in Northern Ireland were organized as an alternative society within the state, usually on the basis of parishes'.[47] Where the Irish language movement was concerned, there is no doubt that it gained considerably from its invocation as part of the official opposition to the Northern Ireland political establishment. Added to this was the important sense of historical and cultural definition which the Irish language lent to the Catholic community.

A seminal incident at the end of the 1920s demonstrates how this oppositional kudos was a constant bolster to the language movement. The Gaelic Athletic Association and the Gaelic League had planned a great fund-raising fair for February 1929 at which Eamon de Valera was to be the guest speaker. De Valera, who had been prohibited from crossing the border into the North, was arrested on the train near Newry and eventually sentenced to one month's imprisonment for having contravened the order. The fund-raising event went ahead in Belfast and, according to Seán Mac Maoláin, one of the organizers, the arrest of the guest speaker effectively created so much protest that donations far exceeded expectations, so much so that the Gaelic League was able to build a college and headquarters for *An Ardscoil Ultach* (the Ulster High School) in Divis St, where it remained until it was destroyed by fire in 1985.[48] By addressing the court in Irish

**44** Anraí Mac Giolla Chomhaill, *Lorcán Ó Muireadhaigh: sagart agus scoláire* (Dublin, 1983), p. 62.   **45** Aindrias Ó Muimhneacháin, *Dóchas agus Duainéis* (Cork [n.d.]), p. 150.   **46** In an address delivered to the national convention of the Gaelic League held for the first time in Belfast in 1932; *The Irish News*, 1 Apr. 1932.   **47** Mac Póilin, 'Irish in Belfast', p. 126.   **48** Seán Mac Maoláin, *Gleann Airbh go Glas Naíon* (Dublin, 1969).

at his trial, de Valera undoubtedly highlighted the Northern state's enmity towards Irish and accordingly increased the language's cachet as a badge of dissent. The tradition of Republican prisoners learning and speaking Irish in jail added to this, and *An tUltach*, Comhaltas Uladh's monthly publication, carried the prison diary of Tomás Ó Cormacáin of Belfast in 1933 and 1934.[49] Tarlach Ó hUid, a writer and internee in the 1940s, provided an extensive account of the Irish language society founded by inmates of Crumlin Road Jail at this time.[50] Also during the forties, the Curragh camp in Co. Kildare included some north-erners, such as Eddie Keenan, who shared cells with Brendan Behan. The Irish language was taught in the Curragh with remarkable success by the iconic Irish writer Máirtín Ó Cadhain.

In the context of majority rule, the Unionist administration's aversion to Irish ensured that any programme of political activism for the Irish language outside of education was practically impossible. This stasis ironically provided the circumstances in the North for the type of non-political Gaelic League originally envisaged by Douglas Hyde. For more than forty years after partition, the Irish language movement in Northern Ireland represented an often vibrant social, recreational movement which aspired to an alternative Gaelic Ulster based on an alliance with the Gaeltacht society of west Donegal, mostly through Irish colleges such as Coláiste Bhríde in Rannafast. A further irony was that, while overwhelm-ingly Nationalist and anti-partitionist in outlook, the Northern Irish language movement was underpinned by a robust sense of provincial loyalty to Ulster Irish which had its roots in an early split in the Belfast Gaelic League over Irish dialects, which led to the founding, in 1911, of *An Ardscoil Ultach* (the Ulster High School). The effects of partition were noted by members of the Gaelic League in the South who had ruefully observed a tendency among their Northern colleagues to lose interest in the national movement, in the wake of partition – a tendency which was of course translated into action by the establishment of Comhaltas Uladh in 1926. In his monograph on the history of the Gaelic League between 1922 and 1932, Aindrias Ó Muimhneacháin, himself a life-long Gaelic Leaguer, comments that the provincial concerns which led to the founding of Comhaltas Uladh had a profound legacy:

> This bisection of the Gaelic League would not matter so much if it were not for its legacy among the ordinary Irish speakers of the North ... They were cut off in their own minds, and unknown to themselves, from their Gaelic brothers in the rest of Ireland. Gradually, just as whinstone is worn

**49** 'Faoi ghlas ceannlá Thomáis Uí Chormacáin as Béal Feirste', *An tUltach*, 1933:10; 1934:1,2,3.  **50** Mac Póilin, 'Irish in Belfast', p. 133.

down by a constant trickle, over time a national calamity befell many Northerners, Irish-speakers and non-Irish speakers, in that Dublin, the capital of Ireland, was no longer their mental centre of gravity.[51]

Indeed, it often appears that places like Rannafast in the Donegal Gaeltacht, and not Dublin, were the alternative centre of gravity for the Northern Irish language movement – the celebrated Donegal writer, Seosamh Mac Grianna, describing how Belfast Irish speakers would treat his native Rannafast like a shrine.[52]

Here, one is struck by a converging set of contradictions afflicting both Nationalism and Unionism in Ireland. On the one hand, the Northern Irish language movement was seen as effectively partitionist, albeit that their partitioned entity included the entire province of Ulster as well as Co. Louth. The Irish language revival has always been hamstrung by the conflicting aspirations of each of its broad provincial dialects, something which became known as 'cogadh na gcanúintí' or the 'war of the dialects' in the early decades of the Gaelic League-led revival. Efforts to impose a national consensus on Irish speakers, most notably through the creation of a national standard for the written language, have consistently been harried by the opposing pull of loyalty to the provincial, or even local, dialect. On the other hand, Unionist MPs who disparaged the Irish language in the Northern parliament were often reminded of the contradiction of suppressing local regional culture in that it set them at odds with other constituent parts of the United Kingdom, namely Wales and Scotland, where Celtic languages were treated with respect.[53] One of those who frequently cited the example of Wales and Scotland was the Labour MP, Jack Beattie, who pointed out the disparity in the BBC's treatment of Irish, for which their were no programmes, against the treatment of Scottish Gaelic and Welsh, which enjoyed at least some broadcasts.[54] Despite representations by Comhaltas Uladh, the BBC continued to deny the Irish language any airtime until 1981 in the case of radio, and 1991 in the case of television.[55]

The sense, in the four decades after partition, of there being a hidden Ulster of Irish revivalism, entirely alienated from the culture of the state, is epitomized in an incident from the 1950s related in *An tUltach*. Included in a series of reports on Irish language events in Belfast throughout the 1950s is an account of the

---

**51** Ó Muimhneacháin, *Dóchas*, p. 158 (my translation).   **52** 'A thuilleadh scríbhneoireachta le Seosamh Mac Grianna in eagar ag Nollaig Mac Congáil, cuid 2' in *Feasta*, Iúil 2003:21.   **53** See, for example, *Northern Ireland Parliamentary Debates*, vol. 19 (1936, 37), pp 675–6; vol. 25 (1942, 43), pp 2711–12. **54** *Northern Ireland Parliamentary Debates*, vol. 25 (1942, 43), pp 2711–12.   **55** See Mac Póilin, 'Irish in Belfast', pp 129–30. Gearóid Stockman, former Professor of Celtic at Queen's University Belfast, recalls how, as a schoolboy in the early 1950s, he took part in a radio programme in which questions were put to BBC executives. When he explained to the producer that he intended to ask why the BBC had no programmes in Irish he was told 'sorry love you won't be able to ask that'.

reporter visiting the artist John Luke as he worked on his famous City Hall
mural, depicting the history of Belfast, commissioned for the Festival of Britain
in 1952.[56] Discussing Luke's work with him on top of thirty-foot-high scaffolding,
*An tUltach*'s reporter was astounded to be told that, while the imagery centred on
Arthur Chichester reading the Belfast Charter in 1613, the artist's style was
indebted to the artwork of the Irish monastic scribes. 'One wonders what the
Corporation would have to say if they could read what I have written here',
concludes the reporter, indicating that the artist's avowal of Irish monastic influences would have got him into trouble with the city fathers.

Such incidents affirm the impression of the Irish language movement occu-
pying a clearly defined space outside of the culture of the state and within an
alternative Catholic civil society. Nevertheless, it would be wrong to characterize
all the elements within that alternative society as being perfectly in accord where
the Irish language was concerned. In 1937, the Nationalist MP for South
Fermanagh, Cahir Healy, found it necessary to warn against Catholic complacency in the face of outside forces that were out to 'destroy their national
consciousness'.[57] While taking heart from the increased numbers of students
attending Gaeltacht summer colleges, Healy reminded his audience that 'Press,
wireless and government wanted them to forget the past' and that the government, in particular, was squeezing the Irish language and history out of the
schools. In such circumstances, Healy warned, it was natural that in time people
would begin to think that material prosperity was the only thing which mattered
and that, as they had to live in the state of Northern Ireland, it would be unwise
to question too much the policy of those placed over them. Another discordant
note, from a converse perspective, is heard in Max Caulfield's pessimistic novel
of early 1950s Belfast, *The Black City*, where he typifies Catholic education of the
time as taking place in 'rooms as dark as sea-caves' in which a pious regard for the
Irish language and Irish history was enforced:

> The man in the dock would have gone to a school like that. He would
> have learned Gaelic, as Flynn had. Gaelic? – even now, the thought of it
> caused a tension in Flynn's stomach. The strap stung; and you got it often
> and hard if you did not know your Gaelic. That and Christian doctrine ...
>
> Flynn could remember the chanting rhythms of the master's voice ...
> 'Language is the badge of nationality, boys, English for the English, Irish
> for the Irish ... and how musical it is, too, how poetical ... listen to it,
> *goidé mar atá tú?*' It used to be a great big pain in the arse.[58]

**56** 'Tuairisg na cathrach', *An tUltach*, 1953, 3:9–11. See also John Hewitt, *John Luke: 1906–1975* (Arts
Councils of Ireland, 1978), pp 80–2.  **57** Speech delivered at a Gaelic League aeraíocht (open-air enter-
tainment) in Lisnaskea, Co. Fermanagh; *The Irish News*, 7 Aug. 1937.  **58** Max Caufield, *The black city*

Interestingly, Caulfield's novel incorporates a sort of taxonomy of IRA recruits, including a schoolmaster who spends his summers learning Irish in Rannafast.

While the clerically dominated Comhaltas Uladh took a leadership role in the promotion of the Irish language, particularly through its close links with Catholic schools, support for the Irish language emanated from other sources. Denis Ireland's Ulster Union Club, a society of Nationalist and Republican Protestants founded in 1941, held Irish classes at its headquarters in Belfast and, through the essays of its founder, argued for the relevance of the language to Ulster Protestants while offering an incisive critique of de Valera's vision of a Gaelic Ireland.[59] For Denis Ireland, partition was a blessing in disguise, in that Ulster Unionists would have to experience the crumbling of their universe in order to realize that their future lay in 'turning back … to the *radicalism* and sturdy Protestant *Republicanism*' of their forefathers.[60] By the same token, what he considered to be the token Gaelic Ireland of de Valera was, in Denis Ireland's view, faced by a brick wall which could only be surmounted if replaced by 'a more real form of Nationalism than is involved in painting pillar-boxes green or beginning one's letters *A Chara*'.[61]

Besides the Protestant Nationalists of the Ulster Union Club, an enduring and very important strand of the Irish language movement was represented in those, often independent individuals, of a socialist bent. Perhaps the most vocal of these was Jack Beattie MP, mentioned above, who, while being distinguished for his vehement criticism of social injustice in the 1930s, famously casting the ceremonial mace on the floor in an act of defiance, consistently railed against the Unionist administration's disparagement of the Irish language. Beattie had been a teacher and later an organizer for the INTO, which may in some measure explain his frequent criticisms in parliamentary debates of the Ministry of Education's treatment of Irish in schools. His services to the Irish language move-ment are still commemorated by Comhaltas Uladh in 'Corn an Bhiataigh' (the Beattie Cup), a schools' competition for spoken Irish, as are those of another individual champion of Irish, the eccentric Lord Ashbourne, in 'Sciath Mhic Giolla Bhríde' (the Ashbourne Shield).

The chronic poverty of the 1930s was the background to the founding in 1936 of a radical branch of the Gaelic League, Cumann Chluain Ard (the Clonard Club), in Belfast, certainly one of the most portentous events in the history of the Irish language in the North of Ireland.[62] A booklet issued as part of the club's Thomas Davis Centenary celebrations in 1945 draws attention to its roots in the

(London, 1952), p. 13.  **59** See Risteard Ó Glaisne, *Denis Ireland* (Dublin, 2000), p. 123. Also Ireland, *Éamon de Valera doesn't see it through: a study of Irish politics in the machine age.*  **60** Ireland, *Ulster to-day*, pp 47–8.  **61** Ireland, *Éamon de Valera*, p. 25.  **62** Originally founded by the Peadar Ó Néill Crowley Gaelic Athletic Club.

'hungry thirties' and, significantly, places the cause of the Irish language within a Republican socialist discourse:

> Surely it must have seemed to the people of the Clonard district in 1936 that it was a most unsuitable occasion to attempt to awaken interest in such a futile project as the formation of 'another Gaelic Branch', because the times then were dark and gloomy for the workers of Belfast; poverty, hunger, mass unemployment were being accepted as something inevitable … People whose every thought was how they were to obtain work and food were in no mood to listen to what they must have thought was the empty idealism of a Gaelic-speaking Ireland.
>
> But yet it was two unemployed young men, Seamus Maxwell and Liam Rooney, who had the courage and foresight to attempt the impossible. They realized that the Gaelic League, that once virile organization that had been responsible for the revolution of 1916, was in 1936 only a social preserve for a group of Irish-speaking reactionaries, who, living in their own small circle, had no interest in those outside the movement.[63]

The writer of this piece, Seán Mag Aonghusa, goes on to explain how Cumann Chluain Ard aimed to reject the centralization of the Gaelic League in the Ardscoil and instead to localize the language movement so as to bring it 'into the homes of local people'. Most ominously, Mag Aonghusa claims the language movement as a socialist concern and anticipates a possible secession from the conservative Comhaltas Uladh:

> The language question must be aligned with the growing social and economic consciousness of the Irish Worker who should be made to understand that the revival of the language is not a subject of only academic interest but an essential part of the age-long struggle in Ireland for freedom.
>
> Although Cumann Chluain Ard is affiliated to Comhaltas Uladh and the Gaelic League, we are prepared to follow an independent path and if necessary, an unorthodox one, to achieve this end.

Such declarations of independence of a clerically sponsored organization were quite bold, particularly when they included references to the 'social and economic consciousness of the Irish Worker', at a time when socialism and

---

63 Seán Mag Aonghusa, '*Cumann Chluain Ard* … its history, its purpose' in Thomas Davis Centenary (1945) booklet published by Cumann Chluain Ard.

atheism were considered synonymous by many Catholics. Yet Cumann Chluain Ard was only able to assert this independence by dint of its financial independence. The club was quite rare in having purchased its own premises (still in use today) for the sum of £800, by way of voluntary subscriptions.[64]

Cumann Chluain Ard continued to forge a path of self-sufficiency throughout the 1940s and 1950s, becoming a rich centre of social and educational activity in Irish. Most significantly, perhaps, was the club's adoption, from 1953 onwards, of a no-English policy.[65] This move reflected the club's cherished affinity with the Gaeltacht, particularly Donegal and its desire to recreate the Gaeltacht in Belfast. It also marked a growing national alliance with radical language activists of which Máirtín Ó Cadhain of Connemara was to become leader. Ó Cadhain, the author of classic works of fiction such as *Cré na Cille* (1949) and *An tSraith ar Lár* (1967), is generally considered to have been the finest prose writer in Irish of the twentieth century. He was also an engagé, whose Republican socialist activism led to his dismissal from a teaching post in 1936 and his internment in the Curragh for the duration of the Second World War. Ó Cadhain was involved in political agitation to halt the decline of the Gaeltacht through Cumann na Gaeltachta and later Muintir na Gaeltachta, and in 1953 he was among those who founded Gael-Linn, a progressive, modernizing organization which went on to make an important contribution to the foundation of an Irish film industry with its feature films, *Mise Éire* (1959) and *Saoirse?* (1961), and the documentary series *Amharc Éireann* (1956–64).

The urgency and commitment which Ó Cadhain lent to groups had a tendency to lead to frustration, and so after leaving both Muintir na Gaeltachta and later Gael-linn after internal disputes, Ó Cadhain's energies were given a new outlet in the group 'Misneach' (courage), which he helped to form in 1963. Misneach appealed to a class of Irish speakers that refused to have English forced on them in their dealings with 'church or state',[66] and this appeal was enthusiastically received by those, such as the members of Belfast's Cumann Chluain Ard, who aspired to use Irish in every aspect of their lives. The name Misneach itself was a key to the group's philosophy and to its influence on radical Irish speakers in the North – *Misneach* had been the alternative title of the Gaelic League's newspaper *Fáinne an Lae* after it was banned in October 1919 by Dublin Castle.[67] Thus, Ó Cadhain's group sought to restore to the Irish language movement the spirit of national consciousness and underground opposition to the state which the original *Misneach* had embodied. In particular, Ó Cadhain's belief in the primacy of urban centres for the successful survival of the Irish language was

---

**64** Interview with the late Proinsias Ó Broin (8 Nov. 2006), who was a member of Cumann Chluain Ard from the 1940s onwards.  **65** Mac Póilin, 'Irish in Belfast', p. 131.  **66** Pádraig Ó Baoighill (ed.), *Ó Cadhain i dTír Chonaill* (Dublin, 2007), p. 338.  **67** Ó Muimhneacháin, *Dóchas*, p. 97.

shared by Belfast Irish speakers who eagerly responded to his challenge that not a single street outside of the Gaeltacht had been claimed by the Irish language.[68] After several years of fund-raising through cooperative schemes, a group of young couples met in Cumann Chluain Ard in 1965 to plan the building of houses for Ireland's first urban Gaeltacht on the Shaw's Road in West Belfast. The letter which announced this historic meeting reflected a new emphasis on the civil rights of Irish speakers within the state and argued that this could only be achieved when a community of Irish speakers was formed in one single area. The Shaw's Road houses were duly completed in 1969 and were soon complemented by the city's first Irish-medium school, *Scoil Ghaeilge Bhéal Feirste* (Belfast Irish Language School) in 1971.[69] The school was founded in defiance of a warning from the Ministry of Education, in the final years of the Stormont administration, that to proceed would be to incur legal action against the school's founders.[70]

This final note of conflict between the Irish language movement and the agencies of the state typifies much of the history that preceded it. The creation of Northern Ireland had left Ulster Unionists facing down a rival state and an irredentist minority. In such circumstances, the Irish language became synonymous for Unionists with the forces that sought to overthrow the state. Irish had become for Unionists, in the opinion of Andrew Boyd, a threat to the constitutional position of Northern Ireland.[71] Yet, as Denis Ireland maintained, the political and cultural values of Ulster Protestants had been transformed in the nineteenth century and as such were always troubled by a break with what he considered to be their proper roots in the radical tradition of the eighteenth century.[72] Clearly, before partition, and most certainly before the Home Rule crisis, Unionists were more able to express loyalty to the United Kingdom and at the same time to celebrate aspects of an Irish identity, including the Irish language. Yet the creation of a Northern Ireland parliament might be described as separatism by default in that it cut Ulster Unionists adrift from the United Kingdom parliament and thus disrupted that sense of coexisting national and United Kingdom loyalties. One occasionally discovers signs that even the most trenchant Unionists, while ostensibly declaring loyalty to the new provincial polity, were not entirely convinced that the Irish language or its attendant cultural identity were foreign to them. This attitude is memorably instanced in an emotional speech made just after the Second World War by the Shankill MP, Tommy Henderson, after a letter was addressed by an official of the British government to 'Northern Ireland, Éire':

---

**68** Seán Ó Laighin, *Ó Cadhain i bhFeasta* (Dublin, 1990), p. 442. **69** Now *Bunscoil Phobal Feirste* (Belfast Community Primary School). **70** PRONI, ED 13/2/123: Ministry of Education to James Browne (Séamus de Brún), 29 Nov. 1965. I am indebted to Bríd Mhic Sheáin, who supplied me with a photocopy of this correspondence, the original file being unavailable at PRONI. **71** *Irish Times*, 2 Apr. 1975. **72** Ireland, *Ulster to-day*, p. 48.

> I do not give way to anybody in this House in my pride in being an Irishman. I am as good an Irishman as they are, and sometimes when I hear some of them running down this part of Ireland I feel a better Irishman than they are. It is time the Minister of Finance drew the attention of the British government to where Northern Ireland is if they do not already know. They should be told that Northern Ireland played its part in this war.

Henderson added jokingly: 'Some of these days I will get up and speak in Irish – Shankill Road Irish'.[73]

Ironically, Nationalists faced with life within the new state of Northern Ireland were not immune to the same provincial outlook which partition and the devolution of power to a Northern Ireland parliament encouraged among Unionists. 'Ulsteria' might well have been a suitable soubriquet for the regional bias of the Irish language movement in the North, with its disproportionate attachment to all things that pertained to Ulster. This attitude became the object of satire in Myles na gCopaleen's (Flann O'Brien) famous comic novel *An Béal Bocht* (1942),[74] and indeed the author's uncle, Fr Gearóid Ó Nualláin, had been a party to the dispute over the Ulster and Munster dialects and consequent split in the Belfast Gaelic League in 1911. While it is tempting to ascribe a provincial mindset to Comhaltas Uladh and a more progressive nationally minded outlook to Cumann Chluain Ard, that would be to ignore Comhaltas' major achievement in ensuring, through partnership with Catholic schools, that the Irish language survived the unrelenting hostility of the Unionist ministry of education.

A discussion of the Irish language in the years of the old Stormont parliament inevitably leads one to speculate about the fate of Irish under the new Stormont assembly and to consider whether or not the language will be defined bluntly according to Unionist or Nationalist affiliations as it was within the old Northern Ireland parliament. Certainly, the 2007 Stormont debates on Irish language issues show that on the surface little has changed. The attitude experienced by Denis Ireland almost a century ago seemed to be reaffirmed by the Unionist MLA, Danny Kennedy, when he declared that his great-grandfather had been a fluent Irish speaker but that 'somewhere along the line, the family sorted that out – that tradition no longer exists'.[75] Yet while old positions appear to have been taken up within the new assembly, circumstances have changed considerably for the Irish language in Northern Ireland. Certain safeguards have been set in place for the

---

**73** *Northern Ireland Parliamentary Debates*, vol. 30 (1946, 47), pp 323–4.   **74** O'Brien's novel, translated as *The poor mouth*, includes a character from Donegal who steadfastly refuses to speak anything other than Ulster Irish.   **75** 'School openings and amalgamations', Northern Ireland Assembly Private Members' Business, 18 Sept. 2007.

language under the Good Friday Agreement which have the potential to presage a broader acceptance of the language and so allow it eventually to be freed of its association with political divisions in the North of Ireland. If the early revival movement, with its Nationalist and Unionist membership, was to some extent the product of a current of fin de siècle optimism, it is possible that the dynamic of a new era will allow people of diverse backgrounds to embrace the Irish language as a constituent part of a new cultural revival.

# The rise and fall of the Northern Ireland Civil Rights movement

INGER V. JOHANSEN

At the end of the 1960s, the Northern Ireland Civil Rights movement, the most consciously peaceful struggle of twentieth-century Ireland, triggered the violent conflict that continued through recent decades. The Civil Rights movement drew inspiration from the American Black Civil Rights movement and its tactics of non-violence and civil disobedience – and borrowed the term 'Civil Rights', which was new in a Northern Ireland context. So was its approach to work for democratic reform and equal rights, which meant putting aside the issue of the partition of Ireland, because Civil Rights campaigners hoped to be able to attract liberal Protestants to the struggle.

The Civil Rights movement was an extraordinary and innovatory movement of mass participation built up from the ground, which immediately and utterly transformed the situation. It took Northern Ireland into the modern era and generated international attention and support, coinciding with the worldwide upheaval, protests and struggles of the time.

The rise of the movement should be seen not only against the background of the repressive and discriminatory Northern state, but also in the context of a process of modernization of the Northern economy and society, including the introduction of welfare state reforms, which had begun after the Second World War under pressure from Britain as an attempt to regenerate a stalled economy. The Civil Rights campaign was part of the modernization of the whole of Ireland, where society and political life had been more or less at a standstill until the 1960s. It was when the Unionist and British governments failed to go through with the reform process in the North in the 1960s that the Civil Rights movement was initiated from below by political activists and grassroots. As a consequence, the movement became much more radical in its concept, espousing civil disobedience tactics and marching.

The Civil Rights movement was relatively short-lived as a mass movement – from the Civil Rights march in Derry on 5 October 1968, until the violent events of August 1969. The movement clashed with Unionist interests, and during 1969–70 it was swiftly superseded by violence. By 1972, there was a full-scale armed conflict.

This essay deals with the rise and fall of this movement and why – despite its aims – it seemed to generate increasing violence and polarization of the

communities, thus uncovering the divisions and conflicts of the past left unre-
solved by partition. Some have seen the Civil Rights movement as causing or
deliberately instigating violence and conflict. But they are simplistic explanations
of a very complex course of events.

## REFORM AND REACTION

The roots of conflict seem to originate in a clash between conflicting trends. On
one hand, the signs of a process of modernization of politics, the economy and
of society. Political developments in the 1960s also showed a surprising thaw in
relations between the North and the South of Ireland, reflecting as well a
rapprochement between Britain and the Republic of Ireland. Irish irredentism
was played down.

On the other hand, there were the stalled and discriminatory structures and
norms of the Northern Unionist state and society that the Civil Rights campaign
sought to redress: a society of inbuilt Unionist supremacy (de facto one-party
Unionist rule from 1921 to 1972) favouring those who supported Unionism
(Protestants) and excluding the Catholic community – a third of the population
– from power.

Already in the mid-1960s – a long time before there was any mobilization for
Civil Rights – there was a Unionist backlash against modernization and reforms,
and improved relations with the Irish Republic, initiated by the Free Presbyterian
minister, Revd Ian Paisley and his supporters, whose main target was the seemingly reformist-orientated Unionist government in Belfast led by Terence
O'Neill. A right-wing section of the official Ulster Unionist Party (UUP), the
government party, shared these fears. As early as 1966, there was a campaign of
murder and violent attacks on Catholics and Catholic property, for which three
members of the newly formed Loyalist paramilitary Ulster Volunteer Force
(UVF) were subsequently convicted.[1]

These right-wing currents promoted scare stories of an IRA plot, probably to
rally Protestants behind them. Later on, they promoted the idea of a Republican
or communist plot behind the Civil Rights campaign as part of an armed strategy
to destroy the Unionist government and state. The Civil Rights marches starting

---

1 These were the so-called Malvern Street murders. The UVF was named after the UVF of the 1912–22
period. There have been suspicions about possible links of Ian Paisley with the UVF. According to Steve
Bruce, *God save Ulster!: the religion and politics of Paisleyism* (Oxford, 1986), pp 80–1, Paisley did not seem
to have had any connection with the UVF. However, in *The edge of the Union: the Ulster Loyalist political
vision* (Oxford, 1994), pp 19–20, he confirms close links between the UVF and another quasi-military
organization, the Ulster Protestant Volunteers (UPV), which (according to Jim Cusack and Henry
McDonald, *UVF* (Dublin, 1997), pp 14–17), Paisley was closely linked to.

in 1968 contributed to strengthening the conspiracy theories of right-wing Unionists, traditional – Orange – marching being a Unionist prerogative in Northern Irish society.

Such convictions of a Republican plot behind Civil Rights have persisted among many Unionists, because they seemed to be confirmed by later events. But they also allowed the Unionist right wing at that time to treat the Civil Rights movement as an IRA insurrection, thereby increasing violent confrontation and conflict.

Others have pointed to 'hidden' Nationalist aspirations of the Civil Rights campaigners to explain violent escalation. But often these accusations have served as an excuse to disregard the causes of the rise of the Civil Rights movement originating in the discriminatory and repressive practices of Unionist authorities.

Although, traditionally, Northern Catholics have been opposed to the partition of Ireland, it is important to note that Nationalism did not seem to be an important issue or sentiment in the Catholic community just prior to and during the early Civil Rights struggle. The last aborted Irish Republican Army (IRA) border campaign of 1956–62 had failed mainly because there was hardly any popular support for it. The Civil Rights campaigners as well as many ordinary Catholics seemed to look to Britain to intervene in Northern Ireland for reforms in the mid- and late 1960s.[2] Ordinary Catholics welcomed British army intervention in August 1969. Irish Nationalism did not seem to gain a prominent role until the growing antagonism between the majority of Catholics and the British army during 1971–2. Other factors seemed to prompt increasing violence.

Nor is there any convincing evidence of a Republican conspiracy behind the Civil Rights struggle. The IRA had dumped its arms in 1962, and it is estimated that in 1967 there was hardly any military IRA organization capable of taking up arms again.[3] Republicans were numerically and politically weak. As a response to their devastating military defeat, and influenced by leftist intellectuals and communists, who they cooperated with in the Wolfe Tone Societies,[4] Republicans espoused left-wing politics and adopted gradualist tactics and strategy. This included support for and participation in a campaign for civil rights

---

2 Professor Richard Rose, the political scientist, carried out an opinion poll that showed significant trust among Northern Catholics in the link with Britain at the time. The opinion poll is published in Richard Rose, *Governing without consensus: an Irish perspective* (London, 1971), pp 188–9.  3 Brendan O'Leary and John McGarry, *The politics of antagonism: understanding Northern Ireland* (London, 1996), p. 161. This book describes the IRA as close to extinction as a military organization by 1967. See also John Bowyer Bell, *The secret army: the IRA*, 3rd ed. (Dublin, 1997), pp 346–7. The Republican leadership intended for the IRA to have a new political role (Henry Patterson, *The politics of illusion: a political history of the IRA* (London, 1997), p. 106).  4 The Wolfe Tone Societies (WTS) were discussion forums originating in ad hoc committees set up in 1963 to organize the bicentenary of the birth of Wolfe Tone, the leader of the United Irishmen in the 1790s. Some leading Republicans were members of the WTS.

and a reform of the Northern state by uniting Catholic and Protestant workers. The goal of Irish reunification was postponed to a future stage.

As a matter of fact, Republican support for civil rights constituted a switch away from their military strategy.[5] However, the new tactics and strategy also had serious flaws and the Republican leadership pursued it mechanically and persistently over the years, thus creating internal divisions in the Republican movement long before the rise of the Civil Rights movement. Many members defected, disillusioned or disaffected with the downgrading of militarism.

Whereas Republicans, as members of the Wolfe Tone Societies, had an important role in setting up the Northern Ireland Civil Rights Association – NICRA – in 1967,[6] they deliberately minimized their presence in the NICRA to avoid scaring off Protestants,[7] and did not begin to assert themselves in the Civil Rights movement until 1969.[8]

### THE MASS MOVEMENT

The NICRA was set up by a range of Northern civil liberties bodies, members of political parties and trade unions as a deliberate attempt to advance the struggle for reforms. The election of the British Labour government under Harold Wilson in 1964 had raised expectations of reform, and a number of scattered civil liberty groups in Northern Ireland and in Britain had spent years lobbying the Unionist and British governments to no avail. It is very doubtful how reform-orientated the O'Neill government really was, and it seems that the Labour government chose to keep at a minimum the pressure for reforms on the government, mainly because it feared intervening directly in Northern Ireland affairs, but also to avoid a Unionist backlash.[9]

A radicalization of tactics, including civil disobedience and protest marching, by Civil Rights campaigners took place during 1968, prompted by the continued lack of response by the authorities to their demands and by the popularity of civil disobedience and direct action tactics taken up by the Derry Housing Action

---

5 Vincent E. Feeney, 'The Civil Rights movement in Northern Ireland', *Éire-Ireland*, 9:2 (New Jersey, 1974), p. 40.  6 The ideological inspiration and input to create NICRA came from Roy Johnston and Anthony Coughlan in particular, who were the intellectual leaders of the Wolfe Tone Societies. They both had a past in the Connolly Association in Britain.  7 Feeney, 'Civil Rights movement', p. 38.  8 Niall Ó Dochartaigh, *From Civil Rights to Armalites: Derry and the birth of the Irish Troubles*, 2nd ed. (New York, 2005), pp 39–42; Gerry Adams, 'A Republican in the Civil Rights campaign' in Michael Farrell (ed.), *Twenty years on* (Dingle, Co. Kerry, 1988), pp 48–50.  9 Vincent E. Feeney, 'Westminster and the early Civil Rights struggle in Northern Ireland', *Éire-Ireland*, 11:4 (New Jersey, 1976), p. 12; Peter Rose, *How the Troubles came to Northern Ireland*, Contemporary history in context series (Hampshire, 2000/2001), pp 171–9.

Committee (DHAC) in Derry. By this time, Civil Rights was not yet a matter of popular focus. Without the years of government inaction on reforms during the 1960s, most likely a mass movement struggling for Civil Rights would not have emerged in Northern Ireland.

It was Unionist violence that sparked the Civil Rights movement, when the second Civil Rights march co-sponsored by NICRA, and taking place in Derry on 5 October 1968, was brutally attacked by the Royal Ulster Constabulary (RUC). The attack was widely covered by the media, television and radio, in Ireland, Britain and internationally, and served instantly to raise the popularity of the movement – among Northern Catholics in particular.

The students' movement, the People's Democracy (PD), was set up in October 1968 by Catholic and Protestant students at the Queen's University Belfast as an immediate reaction to the police response to the Derry march.

Up to the violent events of August 1969, the PD became very popular. Their daring non-violent actions fitted in well with the general mood of impatience among Northern working-class Catholics, who had been awakened from years of subdued passivity by the rise of the Civil Rights movement, and were now opting for change and equal rights.

This popular impetus, in combination with the PD's determination and militancy, pivoted the PD into a central role in the movement from the beginning of 1969, which was in fact also a sign of the weaknesses of the movement at large. It was not a strong unified movement. It was strong only because it had popular support. It was made up of different organizations: NICRA, which did not play a very prominent role during the first months after the Derry march; the PD, mobilizing 2,000–3,000 students in October 1968, Belfast-based but recruiting activists outside Belfast as well; and the broad-based Derry Citizens Action Committee (DCAC)[10] formed after the Derry march, which played the central role in the Civil Rights struggle in Derry, mobilizing a 15,000-strong peaceful demonstration on 16 November 1968 in Derry.

There were no real leaders of this movement capable of spearheading it and there was internal disagreement about tactics. The promises of reforms put forward in November 1968 by Prime Minster Terence O'Neill, under pressure from the British Labour government, when the movement was gaining pace, were not put into effect, increasing the frustration, disillusionment and divisions among Civil Rights campaigners. Had reforms materialized at this point, the movement would very probably have disintegrated.

---

**10** The Derry Citizens Action Committee (DCAC) was initiated mainly by local moderates such as John Hume and Ivan Cooper (a Protestant).

THE *PEOPLE'S DEMOCRACY*

To the PD, keeping up the pressure of their non-violent actions was the way to mobilize Catholic and Protestant workers and make the British and Belfast governments act on reform. But the more radical the tactics, the more violent was the response by extreme Unionism. The confrontational presence of Ian Paisley and his supporters from the very first Civil Rights march in August 1968 and their counter-demonstrations at the marches of the PD in October 1968 in Belfast were clear indications that the Civil Rights movement would be violently opposed by the Unionist right.

The PD long march from Belfast to Derry during the first days of 1969, modelled on the Selma-Montgomery march of the American Black Civil Rights movement a few years earlier, was a crucial turning point. On the third day of the march, it was ambushed and brutally attacked at the Burntollet Bridge by a few hundred Loyalists armed with stones, sticks and iron bars, many of whom later turned out to be local members of the part-time security force, the B-Specials. Young women and men were severely beaten and thirteen of them were taken to hospital in nearby Derry. The events provoked widespread rioting and sectarian clashes in Derry with the participation of local RUC men.

This also marked the time of awakening of the PD to the reality of the Unionist state and led to a further left-wing politicization of the PD.

PD numbers, which had dwindled before the Belfast–Derry march, started to rise again[11] at the same time as the popularity of the PD among Northern Catholics, working-class Catholics in particular, reached a new peak after the march.[12] The mass movement was recreated and radicalized, keeping up its own momentum during the coming months. PD members involved themselves in NICRA and stood in Stormont elections in February 1969, which were a huge success for the whole Civil Rights movement.[13] Subsequently, on 17 April, one of the prominent PD members, 21-year-old Bernadette Devlin,[14] was elected to Westminster in a by-election in Mid-Ulster with the largest ever majority of an anti-Unionist candidate in the constituency.[15]

---

[11] According to *Interview* with John McGuffin (1984), in unpublished interviews by Bill Rolston and Ronnie Munck. McGuffin was a PD member with a Protestant background. [12] This evaluation conflicts with that of the Cameron Report, *Disturbances in Northern Ireland: report of the Cameron commission*, HMSO Cmd 532 (London, 1969), p. 47. The report found that the march 'lost sympathy for the Civil Rights movement'. It is true that the authorities blamed the Burntollet violence on the marchers and the Civil Rights movement and that this may have influenced attitudes within the Protestant community. But the Stormont elections on February 1969 were a huge success for the Civil Rights movement. See also Bob Purdie, *Politics in the streets: the origins of the Civil Rights movement in Northern Ireland* (Belfast, 1990), pp 221–2. [13] Prominent DCAC leaders such as John Hume and Ivan Cooper were elected to Stormont. The PD polled well, an average of 26.4% of the votes in 9 constituencies. See Purdie, *Politics in the streets*, pp 219–20. [14] Bernadette McAliskey is her name today. [15] Michael Farrell, *Northern Ireland: the orange*

To explain the rashness of the PD, 1968 and the international context of revolutions and an upsurge of students, youth and anti-Vietnam war movements should be kept in mind,[16] although the PD was far more restrained. They adhered to the non-violent disobedience tactics of the American Civil Rights movement. Civil Rights had a strong appeal to them. But they and their supporters confronted the Unionist authorities in ways that had never been seen in Northern Ireland before. The PD clearly over-estimated the opportunities of the situation, but along with the vast majority of Civil Rights campaigners, they actually believed that they could attract the support of liberal Protestants and the more deprived sections of the Protestant community for Civil Rights and that reforms would be forthcoming.

However, the PD unwittingly contributed to exacerbating the tension and deepening the divisions in society because of their militancy, radicalism and continuing pressure on the authorities and by their mobilization of large numbers of working-class Catholics. Many Protestants saw the unification and determination of Catholics and feared the consequences. They were too tied up with Unionism and the Unionist state and many of them came to suspect and fear a Republican plot behind Civil Rights to subvert the state, as right-wing Unionists were arguing.

The involvement of PD members in NICRA in 1969 led to a radicalization of NICRA but also to deepening the internal divisions within the Civil Rights movement: between moderates and radicals, between the PD and the Republicans over the pushy tactics of the PD, and among the Republicans and within the PD. Concerns about Protestant alienation from Civil Rights underlay their disputes as well. Eventually this led to an increasing disintegration of the movement.

## THE UNIONIST AND PROTESTANT BACKLASH

There is no doubt that for far too long the Civil Rights movement was negligent or naive about Unionism. To a large extent, the reason for this was the 'innocence' of the broad mass of Civil Rights campaigners, most of them young people with no previous practical experience or even knowledge of how the Unionist system and state operated and the mindset of Unionists – let alone extreme right-wing Unionists.[17]

*state* (London, 1976/1980), p. 255.  **16** The Cameron report, p. 55. Also Purdie, *Politics in the streets*, pp 235–6, describes the impact on PD of revolutionary students' movements abroad, first of all the French 'Movement of March 22', a student alliance of Trotskyites, libertarians and independent leftists, who were at the centre of events in Paris in May and June 1968.  **17** The situation in Northern Ireland had been

Those who knew about Unionism and the sectarian clashes of the past were the older generation of Civil Rights campaigners, a handful of trade union people of Protestant and Communist Party background and the older Republicans. These more experienced people tried to hold back the movement, but still underestimated the full consequences of challenging Unionist supremacy.

The Civil Rights concept was perhaps more advanced than these activists were able to cope with in terms of facing the consequences of initiating a mass movement that so fundamentally challenged the existing political and social order, plus the factor of operating within a state with a sectarian set-up and divided working class. To ask for equal rights and democracy in such a state could very easily become a threat to the state as such, something which right-wing Unionists sensed at once. But it was not until the winter and spring of 1969, when broad sections of Protestants and Unionists rejected reform, that some kind of major clash became unavoidable.

There was a strengthening of right-wing Unionism and a Unionist and Protestant backlash against Civil Rights, directed as well against the moderate Unionist Prime Minister O'Neill. The Civil Rights movement was taken completely by surprise as communal clashes intensified during the spring and summer of 1969, ending with the violent Loyalist and Protestant attacks on the Catholic ghetto areas in West Belfast in August 1969.

The advance of right-wing Unionism within the Protestant community translated into a success for Unionist hardliners in the Stormont elections in February 1969 and a defeat of Terence O'Neill's moderate wing.[18] It forwarded the eclipse of O'Neillism and O'Neill's resignation as Prime Minister in April 1969. This was prompted by militant Loyalist explosions at electricity and gas pipelines in Belfast in March and April, which were deliberately and wrongly attributed to the IRA, the perpetrators turning out much later to be the UVF or militant Loyalists connected to Ian Paisley's organization.[19] They had clearly aimed at fuelling Protestant fears of a Republican plot and heightening the tension.

Whereas rioting and clashes had been commonplace in Derry for months, Belfast did not become embroiled in clashes until April. In Belfast – with its

one of relative calm since the Second World War, Catholics being 'used to' oppression as a norm. This also explains why the situation seemed to 'explode' with the Civil Rights movement.   **18** The election results weakened O'Neills' position, ending up with pro-O'Neill candidates winning only 11 seats, and anti-O'Neill candidates 12 seats.   **19** Scarman Report, *Report of the tribunal of inquiry into violence and Civil disturbances in Northern Ireland, 1969*, vols 1 and 2, Cmd 566, HMSO (Belfast, 1972), pp 7, 20–4. The report concluded that 'Protestant extremists' were behind the explosions, intending among other things to bring down the O'Neill government. Rose, *How the Troubles came*, p. 140; Peter Taylor, *Loyalists* (London, 1999), p. 61, quotes from an interview with Gusty Spence (UVF member convicted of the Malvern Street murders) in which he suggests that UVF men, as well as men from the UPV (Ulster Protestant Volunteers) and the UCDC (Ulster Constitution Defence Committee), the two latter organizations set up by Paisley, were involved in the explosions.

sectarian past and muddled Protestant and Catholic community divisions – this marked a serious deterioration of the situation, with young rioters gradually taking over the streets.

### DERRY – THE CRADLE OF CIVIL RIGHTS

Derry was the cradle and at the heart of the Civil Rights struggle from before October 1968 until the violent events of August 1969. In 1968, local radical left-wing activists in the DHAC had gained immense popular support by their civil disobedience actions and inspired NICRA. After the Civil Rights march on 5 October 1968, the formation of a broad alliance, the DCAC, was initiated by local moderates, which embraced nearly all anti-Unionist sections of the Derry community. All the first concessions of the Stormont government in November 1968 were directed at the demands of the Derry campaign, reflecting the strength of the Civil Rights movement there.

Derry was the most glaring example of the inequalities in Northern Ireland society, with its acute housing problems, job discrimination, unemployment and the social destitution of the Catholic ghettos, the obvious consequences of gerrymandering,[20] and other measures favouring Unionists and Protestants. Despite the fact that Derry's population was two-thirds Catholic, Unionists controlled the Londonderry Corporation. As local government had extensive powers with regard to the allocation of housing in particular, this had far-reaching consequences for Catholics.

The general social situation was bad in many parts of Northern Ireland, among large numbers of Protestants as well as probably a majority of Catholics.[21] The 1971 census figures show 'a marked tendency for Protestants to dominate the upper occupational classes'[22] and a majority of Catholic men belonging to the section of semi- or unskilled workers or the unemployed. This is a decisive growth at the lower end of the Catholic social scale since the census figures of 1911 – before partition – demonstrating that there had been a general deterioration of the social position and conditions of Catholics during the existence of the Northern state. This explains to a considerable extent the enormous appeal of the Civil Rights movement to ordinary working-class Catholics.[23] The violent

**20** Gerrymandering realigned constituency boundaries to favour Unionists and Protestants. **21** In *Interview* with Michael and Orla Farrell (1984), in unpublished interviews by Bill Rolston and Ronnie Munck, Michael Farrell describes Protestant and Catholic families living in houses with no electricity, running water or toilets and with dirt floors in the Bannside constituency, which he was contesting in the Stormont elections in February 1969. Bannside was also the constituency of the prime minister. **22** E.A. Aunger, 'Religion and class: an analysis of the 1971 census data' in R.J. Cormack and R.D. Osborne (eds), *Religion, education and employment: aspects of equal opportunity in Northern Ireland* (Belfast, 1983), p. 33. **23** Paul Bew, Peter Gibbon and Henry Patterson, *Northern Ireland, 1921–96: political forces and social classes*

conflict that finally developed may have had ethnic/national/religious dividing lines, but the causes underlying and igniting the conflict (and the Civil Rights movement) were clearly social.

A number of academics have argued that there was no widespread discrimination and repression of Catholics to explain the rise of the Civil Rights movement.[24] Such claims can be refuted by the findings of the Cameron Commission, which show a systematic pattern of electoral distortion and discrimination in housing policy and jobs in localities in the western part of Northern Ireland (west of the River Bann), where Catholics were often over half of the population.[25] In the eastern parts, local Protestant majorities made it more irrelevant to resort to such measures. There are good reasons why the early Civil Rights campaign began in the western area.

The Cameron and Hunt Reports,[26] published in September and October 1969, reversed the British quiescence with discrimination and repression of Catholics in Northern Ireland, recognizing that major grievances had caused the events of 5 October 1968 and the 'consequent disorders'.[27]

The Civil Rights movement raised a number of demands closely linked to the aim of reducing the effects of Unionist supremacy, such as discrimination and the use of the 1922 Special Powers Act. These demands were also very modest, as they only addressed a limited number of issues. For example, it was not until 1976 that the first anti-discrimination legislation was introduced to prohibit direct discrimination in the labour market.[28]

The following demands were put forward by NICRA in the spring of 1969 to put pressure on the Unionist government to act on its promises:[29]

> – One man, one vote (a demand for universal suffrage, the British franchise, which also meant votes at eighteen for all in both Stormont and local government elections);
> – Fair boundaries (the end of gerrymandering);

(London, 1996), pp 149–51, put forward this explanation and disagree with the view of the Cameron Commission that Catholic mobilization was mainly due to an increase in the numbers of the Catholic middle class.   **24** See, for example, a discussion between Christopher Hewitt (who claimed that there was no widespread discrimination etc.) and Denis O'Hearn in the 1980s in the *British Journal of Sociology*, 32:3 (1981), pp 362–80; 34:3 (1983), pp 446–51; 36:1 (1985), pp 94–101, 102–5; 38:1 (1987), pp 77–87, 88–93. **25** The Cameron Report, Conclusion §134.   **26** The Hunt Report, *Report of the advisory committee on police in Northern Ireland*, HMSO Cmd 535 (London, 1969).   **27** The Cameron Report (p. 55) concluded that 'The weight and extent of the evidence which was presented to us concerned with social and economic grievances or abuses of political power was such that we are compelled to conclude that they had substantial foundation in fact and were in a very real sense an immediate and operative cause of the demonstrations and consequent disorders after 5 October 1968.'   **28** The Fair Employment Act 1976. Indirect discrimination was not prohibited until The Fair Employment Act 1990.   **29** From a leaflet put out by NICRA in June 1969. NICRA archives, Linen Hall Library, Belfast.

– Houses on need (the introduction of a compulsory points scheme for the allocation of houses);
– Anti-discrimination laws (a demand for the law to control religious discrimination);
– Civil liberties (an end to the repressive laws of the Stormont government): the repeal of the Specials Powers Act, the withdrawal of the Public Order Bill, the repeal or amendment of the Public Order Act, 1951;
– The disbandment of the B-Specials.

Reforms were generally too few or came too late to make a difference to Catholics. Frustrations built up within the Catholic community and fuelled the discontent already there. In April 1969, a few days before his resignation as Prime Minister, Terence O'Neill conceded in principle the introduction of one man, one vote.[30] But it was not put into effect until the local government elections in 1973. Some reforms made no change at all: for example, the disbandment of the B-Specials in October 1969, which was part of a parcel of security-related reforms.[31] In their place, a part-time force was set up, the Ulster Defence Regiment (UDR), very often comprising the same men that had been in the B-Specials or even worse, they were also infiltrated by Loyalist paramilitaries.[32]

## AUGUST 1969

The violent clashes and Protestant attacks on the Catholic ghettos of August 1969 marked the end of the Civil Rights movement as a mass movement, prompting a change in the preoccupation of Catholics from a focus on Civil Rights to one of defence. This, along with a number of other factors, led to a growing fragmentation of the movement and marginalization of NICRA and the Civil Rights campaign in 1970. Although NICRA kept on playing a significant role at least until after the British army attack on the NICRA march in Derry on 30 January 1972 – Bloody Sunday – there was a slow descent into violent confrontation between the British army and Catholic youths, eventually between Republicans and British forces.

The events of August 1969 were the culmination of a period since the spring of 1969 of intensified rioting and communal clashes, but also a consequence of

---

**30** It was confirmed by the British Prime Minister Wilson after a meeting with the new Northern Prime Minister James Chichester-Clark on 21 May that the next local government elections in the North would be held under the 'One man, one vote' principle. **31** These reforms were the recommendations of the Hunt Report. **32** Mike Tomlinson, 'Reforming repression' in Liam O'Dowd, Bill Rolston and Mike Tomlinson, *Northern Ireland: between civil rights and civil war* (London, 1980), pp 185–6.

the deep political antagonism that had evolved between the two communities which were locked in conflicting aims with regard to a reform of the Unionist system and state.

Ultimately, the August violence was a culmination of a power struggle, which ended in a stalemate situation when the British government sent in the British army but chose to keep the Stormont government intact. This was a recipe for a further widening of the conflict, as Catholics quickly came to see this policy as one of Britain upholding and protecting the repressive Unionist regime and state.

A number of factors seem to have played a significant role in unleashing the escalating violence during the days from 12 to 16 August, when rioting and clashes ended in devastating Protestant attacks on some of the Catholic ghettos next to Protestant areas in West Belfast. Despite the fact that the British government sent in the army, British troops were too late, too few or too ignorant of the geography of West Belfast to make a difference. The Catholic ghettos in Belfast were left largely defenceless in this situation. Whole streets were set alight and homes burnt down. 1,800 families had to flee their homes, of these 1,500 were Catholic.

The decision by the British Labour cabinet to let the annual parade of the Protestant Apprentice Boys[33] go ahead in Derry on 12 August 1969, despite a very tense situation in Derry and Northern Ireland, was decisive.[34] A crucial factor seems to have been the fact that both communities were consumed with fear and convinced of extreme violent intentions and actions by the other side, which in itself contributed to an important degree to the escalation of violence.

On the Civil Rights/Catholic side, this belief seemed to originate in the attack by the RUC in cooperation with Loyalists on Catholic youths after a clash between the youths and Protestant marchers on 12 August. This was instinctively interpreted by even moderate Catholics as a concerted RUC/Loyalist attack on the Bogside and it led to a genuine popular uprising and defence of the area, the 'Battle of the Bogside'.[35] Civil Rights spokespersons telephoned Civil Rights campaigners all over the North to make them organize diversionary demonstrations to relieve the Bogsiders of the RUC. This contributed to a spread of demonstrations, rioting and clashes all over the North on the night of 14 August and the following days, but these were also spontaneous reactions to the events in Derry. Indeed the Protestant attacks in Belfast – seen by many Catholics and anti-Unionists as a pogrom – were interpreted by many of them as sponsored by

---

33 The Apprentice Boys parade on 12 Aug. usually attracted thousands of Orangemen from all over the North. The parade passed the walls alongside the Bogside in Derry.   34 Rose, *How the Troubles came*, pp 155–64, on British cabinet deliberations.   35 The television broadcast of the speech by the Irish prime minister Jack Lynch in the evening of 13 Aug. was an important incentive to the Bogsiders, but did not initiate their uprising. In the speech, he said that field hospitals would be set up and troops moved to the border. The Irish government had made a request to Britain to ask for a UN peacekeeping force, but this was also a form of pressure on the British government to intervene, which it did on 14 Aug.

the state, especially as B-Specials were seen operating together with Protestant mobs.[36]

On the Unionist/Protestant side, fear of an IRA armed uprising to topple the Unionist government and state seems to have led to attacks by Protestant mobs on the Catholic areas in West Belfast. In the light of later developments, an IRA conspiracy was also seen to use these events to pave the way for a resumption of a Republican armed campaign.[37]

Most damaging is probably the fact that these conspiratorial fantasies engulfed the Unionist government and the forces of law and order and induced the government to use excessive force, which could easily have resulted in more casualties and deaths – with the RUC using Shorland armoured cars armed with Browning machine guns in Belfast against rioting Catholic youngsters, shooting down the streets and killing a 9-year-old boy in his bed when a bullet crossed the walls of the high-rise Divis Flats. Months of right-wing Unionist propaganda had had the effect of convincing the Protestant community and the forces of the state of the existence of an IRA uprising.[38] Nonetheless, it demonstrates the total incompetence of the Unionist government, all the more serious in a situation of communal confrontation and violent escalation, which might have led to civil war.

REPUBLICANS

No one has yet been able to substantiate the beliefs in conspiracies.[39] As to the Republicans, the IRA existed as an inactive formation at the time and had not been re-armed. They had a very limited number of old guns at their disposal. A number of IRA veterans tried to respond to the attacks in West Belfast by using old guns to defend the Lower Falls area.[40] The Scarman Tribunal in its examination of the August 1969 events ascribed the few deaths – ten in all – of these days of violence to the very limited use of guns by civilians.[41] This in itself should hardly have convinced anyone of an IRA rebellion.

**36** B-Specials were used in Derry as well on 14 Aug., before British troops were sent in, increasing the fears of the Bogsiders.   **37** The Aug. violence has also been referred to as the 'birth of the Provisionals' – meaning that the events laid the groundworks for the later establishment of the 'Provisional' Republican movement.   **38** It is difficult to ascertain if there was any direct manipulation by Paisley and Loyalist organizations in advance of the attacks in Belfast to make local Protestants believe that there was a Republican rebellion. The Scarman tribunal rejected this assumption, pp 13–14.   **39** The Scarman tribunal refutes the beliefs in violent intentions on both sides, pp 13–14.   **40** With the RUC and the B-Specials heavily armed any organized widespread IRA armed response could very easily have increased the violence and the deaths dramatically – and would have resulted in total defeat for the IRA. This was an important reason why the IRA had not been rearmed. Their limited armed response seemed to be a last-minute decision among some local Republicans.   **41** The Scarman report, p. 14. The report underlines that there was no sustained shooting by civilians except for the shooting from St Comgall's School in the

Neither was there any immediate strengthening of Republicans as a consequence of August 1969. To many Catholics, Republicans in particular, the inability of the IRA to defend Catholic areas meant a total loss of credibility. Local Catholics set up defence committees. August 1969 actually deepened and blew open the internal divisions among Republicans and led to a split in the movement in December 1969/January 1970 – with the formation of an 'Official' and a 'Provisional' wing. The Republican leadership became the 'Official Republicans', whereas the Republicans who built up the Provisional Republican movement, promoted Nationalism and came to lead the armed campaign, had mostly been out of the movement in the 1960s or were not in leadership positions.

Developing out of the divisions and competition among Republicans as well as between different Civil Rights forces after the events of August 1969, NICRA seemed to be taken over and controlled by the Official Republicans and the small Communist Party by 1970. Somehow, Unionist and Loyalist beliefs in a Republican conspiracy masquerading as Civil Rights could be seen to materialize, but not with any premeditated intention of destroying the Unionist state. On the contrary, despite embarking on a limited armed campaign encouraged by popular sentiment, the Official Republicans stuck to their gradualist strategy of gaining Civil Rights through a reform of the Northern state. They defended the existence of the Stormont parliament during this period, in the face of other anti-Unionist forces and the Catholic community at large, who by this time favoured a suspension or abolition of Stormont.

The split meant a further weakening of Republicans. It could have undermined the entire movement decisively, had Unionist repression and British army tough tactics against young Catholic rioters, as well as concrete events (such as internment without trial and Bloody Sunday) and confrontations, not helped to attract new recruits to the two wings of the IRA and popular support. There were no particular efforts by Republicans to recruit other than to demonstrate Republican willingness for defence and to engage in armed action.[42]

Neither of the Republican factions was very capable at the time; the Provisionals to an even lesser degree than the Officials. When during 1971–2 the Provisionals seemed to gain the upper hand, a primary reason was that, unlike the Official IRA, they were determined to fight the Unionist state, and they were there promoting the national question when Northern Catholics became strongly anti-British and anti-partitionist.

There is no doubt that Republicans played an important role in forwarding an armed campaign from 1970, when the two factions competed to attract new

---

Lower Falls (the IRA veterans). **42** Eamonn McCann writes that ordinary Catholics in Derry and Belfast 'created' the Provisional IRA, because 'there was no existing organization for them to turn to naturally' (in Eamonn McCann, *War and an Irish town* (London, 1974/1993), pp 293–5).

volunteers. But they would not have succeeded with this, had they had less popular support. The Unionist Prime Minister, James Chichester-Clark, declared Northern Ireland to be 'at war with the IRA Provisionals' in February 1971.[43]

Nationalism seems to have developed from a process of alienation of Catholics, compounded by escalating violence: first from the Northern Unionist state (August 1969), and subsequently from the British army, a process more or less completed by the time of the Falls Road Curfew in July 1970, when the whole Lower Falls area was sealed off from the outside for thirty-four hours for the British army to conduct a brutal house-to-house search for the IRA, in which three people were killed. And finally, through an increasing rejection of the British state.

## BRITISH POLICIES

British government policies during these years convey a general impression of British mismanagement in relation to Northern Ireland, largely because the British cabinet was determined 'not to get sucked into the Irish bog'.[44] The Labour government did increase pressure on the Unionist government from October 1968, but it attempted consistently to minimize British intervention and involvement. This being said, most reforms were promised or accorded by the Unionist authorities mainly to prevent British intervention.

The same British policy continued even after the violent events of August 1969, when the Wilson government chose not to introduce direct rule from London, keeping the Unionist government and state in place despite the regional government's obvious incompetence during the violent events, and a total loss of legitimacy in the Catholic community. After some months of limited reforms, the British government – from June 1970 a Conservative government – left the situation largely to the then even more repressive Unionist government and the British army, enhancing the conflict considerably.

It seems that starting with the introduction of internment without trial in August 1971 and at the latest with the shooting dead by the British army of thirteen unarmed civilians at the Bloody Sunday march organized by NICRA in Derry on 30 January 1972, it was no longer possible to reverse the slide towards full-scale armed conflict. In March 1972, after nearly three years of escalating violence, the British government suspended Stormont and introduced direct rule from London.

**43** Farrell, *Orange state*, p. 276. Peter Taylor, *Brits: the war against the IRA* (London, 2001), pp 57–8.
**44** Rose, *How the Troubles came*, pp 171–9. Rose mentions Harold Wilson, Roy Jenkins and James Callaghan (Home Secretary after Jenkins) behind this non-intervention policy. The quotation is from James Callaghan, *A house divided* (London, 1973), p. 15.

# 'The first item on the agenda': splits in Republicanism, 1970–2000

## JIM McDERMOTT

### INTRODUCTION

This short essay is limited in scope and structure. It seeks only to ask why divisions within Sinn Féin and the IRA in 1970 led to a bitter split but similar divisions in Sinn Féin since 1986 have not caused anything approaching the same outcome? Of necessity, then, it will not involve other Republican splits, nor will it encompass the role of constitutional Nationalists or other political groups since 1969. It makes no value judgment on the rights or wrongs of the protagonists' views. Rather, it works on the assumption that all parties acted with integrity at the time that decisions were taken, regardless of unforeseen outcomes. It quotes some commentators of the period as a means of illuminating how events were seen by various writers, but accepts that many other interpretations can be placed on these events. The essay concludes with a distillation of the views of some contemporary observers who have given their various views on why the new departure of Sinn Féin has been relatively successful.

### THE DIVISIONS

On 11 January 1970, a group of Irish Republicans split from the then mainstream Sinn Féin organization at the Ard Fheis held in the Intercontinental Hotel in Dublin. Having left the hall, this group of people went to Kevin Barry Hall at 44 Parnell Square. Seán Ó Brádaigh released a statement on 17 January 1970 on behalf of the Caretaker Executive of Sinn Féin,[1] which was soon to be the nucleus of Provisional Sinn Féin and the ideological and moral imperative behind the campaign of arms by the emergent Provisional IRA which was to provide the most significant attempt at militant separatism since the 1916–22 period. Although there had already been an embryonic Republican army formed in Belfast that refused to follow the Gardiner Street leadership, the general public, for the most part, became aware of a Republican split at the 1970 Ard Fheis.

It is interesting to note the five main areas of dissent which caused the split in

---

1 Statement on behalf of the Caretaker Executive of Sinn Féin, Jan. 1970; Linen Hall Library, Belfast.

1970. The traditionalists objected to the willingness of the 1970s Ard Fheis to recognize the parliaments at Westminster, Stormont and Leinster House. The document claimed that 'sitting and participating in the affairs of these assemblies constitutes recognition of them, all reasonable people will agree without hesitation'. The statement further claims that the then Sinn Féin leadership was prepared to use sleight of hand to manipulate the Ard Fheis:

> Having failed to secure the necessary two-thirds majority to effect these changes, they then pressed on the Ard Fheis a resolution requiring a simple majority, viz 'expresses allegiance to an IRA leadership' which had prior to the Ard Fheis adopted recognition of Westminster, Stormont and Leinster House.

The statement continues, 'Thus the delegates loyal to a thirty-two-county parliament could not tolerate this and since the resolution seemed likely to be carried they took the only action open to them if they were not to be compromised – they walked out and resumed the Ard Fheis elsewhere'.[2]

The first page of the 1970 statement reveals a contemporary tone. There are strong resonances today, in the post-Good Friday Agreement situation, when more hard-line Republicans bitterly castigate Gerry Adams, Martin McGuinness and the rest of the present Sinn Féin organization for having sold the dream of a republic for short-term gain and individual advancement. Indeed, page one the 1970 statement accuses what was to become official Sinn Féin and later the Workers' Party of being 'yet another political party seeking votes at all costs'. Both members of the Workers' Party and dissident Republicans could point to the irony of how the Provisional movement was set up at least partially to oppose participation in 'illegal' assemblies, only for some of its founders to become central to the existence of these institutions, despite nearly three decades of armed struggle and immense suffering.

The counter to this from the present Sinn Féin is that the situation in 2007 is very different from 1969. They could claim that all the decades of insurrection and suffering, while certainly terrible, had changed the political landscape in the North of Ireland. The demands of the Civil Rights movement had been met, by and large. Sinn Féin is not the small marginalized group it was in 1969, but a vibrant, confident, modern political party with a firm policy on reaching a thirty-two-county democratic socialist republic. That they are now the largest Nationalist party in the North, they could claim, is a direct consequence of their proven willingness to oppose unfair administration, be it from the Unionists or

2 Ibid., p. 1.

the British government. Certainly, many of their personnel can point to great personal hardship in the past as a consequence of their participation in either the Provisional IRA or Provisional Sinn Féin.

Despite this, many historians and journalists have expressed great surprise that there had not been more defections from the present Sinn Féin or even a more cohesive Republican opposition to it, given the historical precedent of January 1970 when, as Bowyer Bell has pointed out, 'in the 1960s the IRA was too small and ineffectual for a split, although traditional Republicans could always make almost a government in waiting'.[3] It says much for the management skills of the current leadership of Sinn Féin that they were able not only to retain members and support in their acceptance of Stormont and Leinster House, but also to increase their representation at the ballot box. Certainly, Sinn Féin in 2010 are free from the accusation levelled at the Sinn Féin leadership of 1969 that they had allowed themselves to be infiltrated by 'other radical groups' involving cooperation for limited objectives 'to be brought a stage further, that it is formalized into an alliance to be known for the sake of convenience as the National Liberation Front'.[4]

In the late 1960s, Republican traditionalists were certainly alarmed at the influence of left-wingers from outside mainstream Republicanism. The influence of Roy Johnston, a scientist from a Protestant radical tradition, was seen as particularly sinister. As Bell points out,

> Traditional Republicans live by certain rituals which reinforce their faith. It is therefore easy to identify heretics through Republican funerals, collections, commemorations, Bodenstown, attitudes to hunger strikes etc.[5]

Alien influences were evident to traditional Republicans in January 1970 when their statement claims that

> some of those who came into the movement from the Irish Workers' Party were prominent in both the 'Conference' of 1965 and the Commission of 1968–9. In point of fact, by 1969 they had, with the aid of a few long-standing members, become the 'masterminds' and policymakers of the Republican movement. One of them in particular had been in charge of an 'education department' for the stated purpose of educating new members and re-educating older members into certain social and economic policies.[6]

---

3 John Bowyer Bell, *The IRA, 1968–2000: analysis of a secret army* (London, 2000), p. 59.   4 Statement on behalf of the Caretaker Executive, p. 2.   5 Bowyer Bell, *The IRA*, p. 60.   6 Statement on behalf of the

The individual referred to was Roy Johnston and by an irony, he himself left the
Official Republican movement in 1972 as he felt that the Republican left had
become marginalized, that the Official IRA was in competition with the
Provisional IRA and that the Officials remained victims of their own military
illusions.[7] So then, we have the strange situation of the Provisional movement
splitting from the Official Republican movement because Johnston was not traditional enough and Johnston splitting two years later because the Officials were
too traditional.

Clearly, however, the traditionalists in 1969 were very worried about extreme
socialist influences on Sinn Féin. In fact, they were convinced 'that the ultimate
objective of the leadership which remained at the Intercontinental Hotel is
nothing but a totalitarian dictatorship of the left'. Great distrust was expressed at
the joint education classes between Sinn Féin, the Irish Workers' Party and the
Communist Party of Northern Ireland. There were fears of mergers and amalgamations. It was noted with alarm that the role of the Republican Youth
Organization and the Republican 'Clann na hÉireann' were being played down
in favour of the less Republican but more socially militant Connolly Youth movement and Connolly Association in England. Even more alarming for
traditionalists was the banning of the entire Cumann na mBan organization
(Women's Movement), as they had objected to the banners of 'radical groups'
taking part in the Bodenstown Parade of 1968.[8] Equally pernicious to traditionalists, the Sligo town Cumann of Sinn Féin, which included the mayor, the late
councillor Norbert Ferguson, was disbanded in 1969 because he objected to the
local Connolly Youth movement marching as a body in uniform in the Annual
Easter Commemoration Parade. After the Republicans were thrown out without
their side of the case being heard, a new Cumann was formed, consisting almost
entirely of the Connolly Youth movement.[9]

As the Connolly Youth movement was comprised of avowed communists, it
is small wonder that traditional Republicans were angry and upset. They disliked
change intensely and, for Bowyer Bell, 'what many saw as a split in 1969 was, for
the Provisionals, merely the faithful drawing back from the wrong road. Dublin
GHQ had chosen seeming advantage over principle, [and] were in the process of
discarding the ideal for less gain'.[10] Why then was there not a more substantial
reaction to radicalization in Sinn Féin more recently? Apart from decommissioning, there have been serious changes which traditionalists within Sinn Féin
had either to accept or else quit the movement. The IRA as a body has been stood
down. There is no longer a Cumann na mBan or Fianna Éireann to support the

Caretaker Executive, p. 2.   **7** Roy Johnston, *A century of endeavour* (Dublin, 2006), p. 261.   **8** Statement
on behalf of the Caretaker Executive, p. 3.   **9** Ibid., p. 3.   **10** Bowyer Bell, *The IRA*, p. 58.

current Sinn Féin strategy. Sinn Féin members take their seats in Stormont and Leinster House. They take salaries from the British exchequer, although much of this is channelled back to Sinn Féin. They support the rule of law and ask their supporters to assist the PSNI in trying to stop crime. They share administrative duties with Unionists who are in utter loyalty to Britain and Sinn Féin have now joined the Police Board.

Clearly, the current Sinn Féin stance is in many ways far more anti-traditional than the attitudes the Official Republican movement of 1970. Why then have the current Sinn Féin policies not been more comprehensively opposed by more traditional Republicans?

The Provisional movement helped answer this conundrum in 1979. A lecture entitled 'The Split' dismisses the simplistic view of the early 1970s that the 'Provos are Nationalistic militarists, while the Sticks are much more politically conscious radicals, or, even more simplistically, the Provos are prepared to fight while the Sticks are not'. It goes on:

> The Republican movement has had three tendencies: a militarist and fairly apolitical tendency; a revolutionary tendency; and a constitutional tendency. The terms as used here are relative to conditions, the circum- stances and the historical background against which the movement functions.[11]

This statement shows an appreciation of realpolitik. Bowyer Bell's view of Republican sacrifice is essentially at odds with the pragmatist of 'The Split'. Bell writes:

> To be a Republican one must deny the easy emotions of anger, hatred, the worldly emotions and so enter a secular world where the dangers are tangible, the sacrifices all too real and the personal returns rare.[12]

While Bowyer Bell's prose reflects the experiences of many Volunteers, in effect militant actions were not of themselves advancing the Republican project. The leadership of Sinn Féin were aware of a large untapped source of electoral support which could be used to political advantage while stopping unnecessary violence and emptying the jails of Republican prisoners. If traditional Republican ideas (and weapons) had to be dumped for the greater good, so be it. It was an internal decision unlike the early Official Republican movement, Provisional Sinn Féin remained 'Ourselves alone', with ideas emanating from within a broad church

---

**11** The split (1979) 3035743: Linen Hall Library, p. 1.   **12** Ibid., p. 57.

which had been created by the circumstances of the 1970s and 1980s (particularly by the hunger strikes) and the way was clear for new directions. People were getting war weary, parents feared the next generation would repeat the same tactics with the same tragic results and a constituency for change was created. 1986 and 1994 were quantitatively different from 1970. However, internal house-clearing was still felt to be needed.

Between 2006 and 2008, the Sinn Féin leadership was accused in the media of taking almost a Stalinist line on internal discipline. Ed Maloney's book, *The secret history of the IRA*, makes a strong case that Gerry Adams and his closest supporters are arch-conspirators who manipulated the Provisional Republican movement to their particular vision while ruthlessly sidelining all opposition on their way. While certainly not as rigidly leftist as the Official Republican movement in 1970, there are at least some similarities in the ways that the Sinn Féin leaderships of the late 1960s and late 1990s conducted their treatment of internal dissenters.

The caretaker statement of January 1970 cites the internal methods of discipline used by the Sinn Féin leadership of 1969 as one of five reasons for the split. They cited in particular the ousting from the Republican Organization in 1966 of the entire North Kerry Comhairle Ceantair of Sinn Féin,

> embracing thirteen Cumainn and 250 members including three local councillors and leading figures such as Miss May Daly (sister of Charlie Daly executed at Drumbo, Donegal, in 1923), John Joe Rice, Sinn Féin TD (1957–61), and John Joe Sheehy, veteran Republican and Kerry footballer.

The statement claims that the underlying reason for their dismissal was the 'uncompromising stand of Kerry in refusing recognition to Westminster, Leinster House and Stormont'.[13] Why then did more recent resignations from Sinn Féin on issues relating to moving away from traditional Republicanism and internal methods not have greater effect? Central to this must be the charged atmosphere of the late 1960s, when the potential for a Loyalist backlash in the North of Ireland constantly loomed. The Caretaker Sinn Féin statement of 1970 lashed the Gardiner Street leadership for the manner of dismissal of Seán Keenan of Derry, a militant northerner soon to become a leader of the Provisional movement, and it had this to say of the dismissal of Jimmy Steele:

---

**13** Statement on behalf of the Caretaker Executive, p. 4.

Jimmy Steele of Belfast, who had suffered almost twenty years actual imprisonment in Crumlin Road Jail for the Republican cause, was expelled last July because he dared to criticize ultra-left policies in his oration at the re-internment of Peter Barnes and John McCormack in Mullingar.[14]

This was certainly at odds with how the soon-to-be Official Sinn Féin viewed matters. Roy Johnston claimed that Jimmy Steele's speech was a 'Provisional call to arms'. A serious disagreement had emerged in the late 1960s over which tactics were most appropriate to use to try to oppose Unionist rule in the North and end partition. The traditional Republicans favoured a military campaign and regarded the defence of the minority population as axiomatic. The reforming leadership of 1969 in Sinn Féin were well aware of the traditionalist view, having as a rule come from the same background, and were impatient to get on with political methods, even if that meant a split. Roy Johnston explained that

> It is evident in retrospect that the repeated postponed sanctioning of the politicization process had been initiated too late and was too indecisive and uncertain to enable a strong, principled and united movement to face with political weapons the armed B-Special counter-attack of August 1969.[15]

This view was endorsed by Cathal Goulding, the Chief of Staff in 1969 of the still undivided IRA. 'We couldn't match the Free State Army and we certainly couldn't match the British army'[16] was Goulding's view, strongly influenced by the failure of the IRA's 1956–62 campaign in which Goulding himself had actively participated. Notwithstanding the failure of the previous Republican campaign, traditionalists such as Belfast's Billy McKee were disgusted at the over-emphasis on politics and said of himself and others at the time:

> We realized that if Goulding and this new leadership were allowed to carry on, Republicanism would die a natural death … They had the reins. Anyone who wanted to join the IRA went to them. They took them in and schooled them for a while and the next thing was they joined Sinn Féin and went fishing.[17]

Fish-ins were an important part of agitation for Sinn Féin in the late 1960s and, used in isolation, they gained the contempt of Republicans like Billy McKee who,

**14** Ibid.  **15** Johnston, *A century of endeavour*, p. 262.  **16** Ibid., p. 222.  **17** Peter Taylor, *Provos* (London, 1977), p. 22.

although liberal in social policy, was fiercely anti-communist, and was and was a daily communicant. In 1969, Goulding regarded McKee and those like him as living in 'a fantasy world'.[18] Cathal Goulding is now dead but he would, I imagine, have at least applauded Billy McKee's consistency, as McKee is implacably opposed to the new direction and methods used by Gerry Adams and the present Sinn Féin. However, despite Billy McKee's high status in the pantheon of Republican heroes, relatively few Republicans are inclined to support his views today. This is a telling reflection of the Nationalist community's desire for peace in the past decade or so, as opposed to at least a toleration of conflict following the events of August 1969. Internal methods by Sinn Féin are largely tolerated and indeed sometimes defended as tactically necessary.

Before dealing with the events of August 1969 and how they led to a sea-change in Republican fortunes, let us look at the Caretaker Sinn Féin of the 1970s' fifth reason for splitting from Gardiner Street influence. The Sinn Féin leadership of pre-split 1969 wished to retain the Stormont parliament as part of its stages theory of revolution. This was anathema to most traditionalists, who believed that

> surely it was preferable to have a direct confrontation with the British government on Irish soil without the Stormont junta being interposed. In any event, the taking away of the Orange Order's power block would surely be a step forward rather than backward.[19]

A later Provisional Sinn Féin paper could see the theoretical logic of the Sinn Féin leadership's position on Stormont in 1969, but still felt that they were seriously in error:

> The Republican movement, fairly weak numerically, became deeply involved in NICRA (Northern Ireland Civil Rights Association). There were two different attitudes between those who were involved. One attitude was that of the leadership, which felt that the struggle for Civil Rights was a process by which the six-county state could be democratized. Given the 'democratization of the state', the movement could then freely and legally engage in the social and economic struggles which affected both the Unionist and the anti-Unionist working class. From Republican involvement in these struggles would emerge a united working class supportive of the Republican position.[20]

---

**18** Ibid., p. 24. **19** Statement on behalf of the Caretaker Executive, p. 5. **20** The split, p. 2.

There is little doubt that the Sinn Féin leadership prior to the split believed that reunification was inevitable and believed that the 'far-seeing leaders of British Imperialism saw that the bright young men of Fianna Fáil might prove a better bet for preserving British influence in Ireland in the long run than the bigoted fanatics of the North'.[21] The events of August 1969 were to destroy any trust that Northern Nationalists might have had about the reformability of political Ulster, but one tends to agree with Bowyer Bell's view that in the early 1970s

> the Officials were still run as a conspiracy by those trained in Republican practice, divided on means rather than ideas, even as all concerned offered a highly detailed analysis to disguise a largely traditional split, a matter of personality and tactical priority.[22]

This injects a note of realism to what really caused the split in 1970 and why its divisions were felt so deeply by all protagonists. One consequence of the Sinn Féin approach of the late 1960s had been to place less emphasis on the role of defence of the Nationalist minority traditionally adopted by the Belfast IRA since around the period of partition:

> In pursuance of this objective and in the process of democratization, the Republican position on the national question would, however, have to become subordinate to the feelings of the Unionist working class and, furthermore, in order to allay Unionist fears and because the process was necessarily a lengthy one, the movement had to be demilitarized.[23]

To most Nationalists living in working-class areas, the left-wing theories of Roy Johnston or the espousal of traditional Republicanism by Seán Ó Brádaigh would have been unimportant. Relatively few Republican Volunteers in the early 1970s generally would have paid too close attention to the debates which split them so irrevocably. However, after 1969, most Nationalists would have felt that something had gone amiss in August 1969 when Loyalist mobs assisted by members of the RUC and B-Specials had attacked Nationalist areas. The IRA was largely absent from their traditional role as Nationalist defenders, a role they had held since 1920. This fact was the main catalyst for support for the newly emerging Provisional IRA, most of the other reasons for the split being seen as mere politicking.

Yet, few if any members of the Provisional IRA or Provisional Sinn Féin in

**21** Ways and means, Feb. 1970. Sinn Féin Gardiner Street (Linen Hall Library P.1373), p. 25. **22** Bowyer Bell, *The IRA*, p. 75. **23** The split, p. 2.

1970 could have anticipated the situation where an ex-IRA leader like Martin McGuinness would be Deputy Minister to Ian Paisley as First Minister in an administration emphasising conciliation rather than conflict. Not only does this situation exist, but indeed it is electorally popular. International statesmen have applauded this new development. The political memoir of Bill Clinton, for example, shows that he regards his contributions to the present peace in Northern Ireland as one of his finest political achievements.[24] Not everyone shares this view, Ruairí Ó Brádaigh, like his brother Seán, was as consistent in 1996 as he was in 1969 in claiming that '1918 was the last time the Irish people as a whole voted as a single unit and they voted for a republic',[25] yet the public on both sides of the border have determined that historical circumstance has made the constitutional path a more popular option for progress. Time alone will tell if the current peace process will be a success, but the question remains as to why the recent sea change in Republican tactics is now popular, whereas from 1970 an arguably more traditional Official Sinn Féin was becoming increasingly marginalized.

The answer, I feel, has several interacting elements. The concerted campaign by the Provisionals had shown a remarkable tenacity and capacity to improvise, but they had ultimately not succeeded in their primary goal of bringing the British government to the stage where they wanted to withdraw from the six counties. On top of this, Loyalist paramilitaries, often with the active cooperation of state security forces, were waging a terror campaign of their own, to which effective defence was quite impossible. While these two factors acted upon each other, there was still a pool of young Republican volunteers who were willing to engage in a military campaign. However, by 1986 the veterans, some of whom had known twenty-five years of service in the Provisional IRA, were aware that generation after generation might risk death, wounding or imprisonment for no foreseeable tangible outcome, and realism required more divergent thinking.

Certain other developments since 1969 might have suggested that a move from military to constitutional methods might prove more fruitful. In the period after 1981, with a Northern leadership firmly in the ascendancy, electoral success indicated that Sinn Féin could gain hegemony within the Nationalist community in the six counties. Arguably the only other time that Republicans had enjoyed such dominance was in the short period between truce and treaty from July to December 1921. The Nationalist community was furthermore proportionately larger than it had been in 1969 and indeed looked as if it could be a majority community in the near future. It was also a community that was modern in outlook, far different in essence, from the other, more devoutly Catholic body of

---

**24** Bill Clinton, *My life* (London, 2004), pp 784–5. **25** Ruairí Ó Brádaigh, 'The evil fruit has ripened once more', *The Irish Reporter* (Dublin, 1996), p. 19.

1969. A more pliant pluralist electorate had developed, as acknowledged in 1996 by Ruairí Ó Brádaigh, a founder member of the Provisionals in 1970. He claimed that 90 per cent of the southern state was Catholic and Confessional, whereas the Northern state remained sectarian. Ó Brádaigh said there needed to be separate church and state to create a pluralist society.[26] This was not the type of idea favoured by the Caretaker Executive in 1970. Yet Ó Brádaigh remained surprised that there was so much support for Sinn Féin's new approaches. He claimed in 1996 that the

> most that will come of such a new Stormont will be cross-border boards, when such is finally seen to be the case. Support for the Provisionals will fall away – just as it did for the Officials when they were absorbed into the established system in the early 1970s.[27]

As yet, there is no significant indication that Sinn Féin's fortunes are in decline, although it is a matter of historical fact that the fortunes of the Old Official Republican movement were to deteriorate steadily from 1970.

To understand why the Official Republican movement went into such steep decline, we need to look at the poor defence of Nationalist areas by the then IRA in Belfast in August 1969 and how the reactions to this lack of preparedness led to the formation and early popularity of the Provisionals. Since the early 1920s, the IRA had adopted the role of protectors of the minority community against state and paramilitary Loyalist aggression. In 1969, the then leadership of the Republican movement seemed unaware of or were certainly unprepared for the scale of attack by armed Loyalists in Belfast.

In Belfast's Nationalist districts, reeling from recent attacks, the lack of defence was certainly a heady factor in galvanizing support for the emergent Provisionals, and in Belfast and other parts of the north it was the promise of weapons that was to give them dominance, rather than political disagreements with the Officials. Matters played further into the Provisionals' hands by an unapologetic, uncompromising approach by some senior Officials. Roy Johnston felt that a political response was the best way to deal with the pogrom. He believed that to get guns was a trap: 'the Provisionals fell for it completely and the Officials half fell for it.'[28]

Around this time, the people in the Nationalist ghettos in Belfast would have been unlikely to have shared his views. Even among the Officials themselves, there were clearly those who wished for a more militant strategy, and Johnston records that although he and Anthony Coughlan held out for a purely political

26 Ibid., p. 20.   27 Ibid., p. 21.   28 Ibid.

response, 'no-one was listening'.[29] While there is an argument advanced, for example, by Bew and Patterson in *The politics of illusion*,[30] that a more concerted military defence by the IRA would have led to far more Nationalist casualties, the IRA's lack of preparedness helped lead to the creation of a constituency for the Provisional movement. The Official movement, in their determination to retain a left-wing identity, were thereafter often characterized as anti-Republicans, while R.F. Foster claims that the Officials' left-wing odyssey led them eventually to repudiate thirty-two-county Republicanism.[31] In fact, it could be argued that the Official Republican movement remained a broad church with many convinced Republicans within the ranks all through the name changes, policy reverses and internal splits of its subsequent existence. What is historical fact is that even after its ceasefire of 1972, there was no decommissioning of weapons. It is doubtful if such an action could have been sold to its supporters at that stage. This is in marked contrast to the relatively passive acceptance of the later decommissioning of the obviously more active Provisional IRA's arsenal. Again, however, the Provisional IRA's campaign had been longer, fiercer and more determined than any similar engagement in Irish history. As an illustration of this, the Official campaign, regarded with contemptuous disdain by the Provisionals, was almost as long as the IRA's War of Independence, 1919–21. The Officials in turn, of course, were contemptuous of the way they claimed that the early Provisionals had permitted Fianna Fáil to finance them.

For traditional Republicans in 1969, the 'failure of the Republican movement to give the maximum possible protection to our people in the North last August' was, according to the Caretaker Executive's document, the main reason for the split.[32] This was an underlying reason for the 'Walk-out': 'despite repeated warnings from last May on, sufficient priority was not given to this matter with results too well known to require enumeration ... we might add we feel particularly strongly on this point'.[33] This they certainly meant. While the rest of the document lays down some social and economic policy, the reader is left in little doubt as to the legacy of bitterness left from August 1969. It writes of the attempts of the already compromised Army Council to smear the Caretaker Executive as 'divisive malcontents' and notes how it

> spoke in typically hard-line terms of the Provisional Army Council and the supporters, saying that 'if they persisted in error', then all sentiment would be put aside in dealing with them. This dogmatist attitude is surely worthy of the Inquisition of many years ago in its dealings with heretics.[34]

**29** Ibid. **30** Paul Bew and Henry Patterson, *The politics of illusion* (London, 1989). **31** R.F. Foster, *Modern Ireland, 1600–1972* (London, 1988), p. 589. **32** Statement on behalf of the Caretaker Executive, p. 5. **33** Ibid. **34** Ibid., p. 7.

The Caretaker document goes on to claim that they are the true Sinn Féin with the 'support of almost all the country outside of sections of Dublin and Wicklow and a small number of scattered individuals elsewhere'.[35] That the split is irrevocable is made very clear, and an almost comradely warning is given 'to those who would follow a leadership which flies in the face of all reason ... the road to Westminster, Stormont and Leinster House is paved with the good intentions of such erstwhile Republicans'.[36] Some twenty-five years later, many of the figures who originally formed the Provisional movement found that they would not command the same numbers to repudiate the Sinn Féin of Gerry Adams and company. Partly, this was because change was managed much more carefully. Bell claimed that 'the arguments of 1969 resurfaced a generation later, but this time (1986) a majority accepted the decision as it did not affect the armed struggle'.[37] This particular dispute was about the validity of electoral politics and the taking of seats but, unlike the Caretaker Provisional movement of 1970, 'Republican Sinn Féin could not control an army or have sufficient influence in Irish America'. Indeed, so long as the Provisional movement substantially remained intact, they were impervious since 1986, as 'those who leave the faith do not threaten the faith – it is those who threaten the faith from within who are the greater danger'.[38]

The fact that the Official Republican movement remained intact and from March 1971 was largely non-combatant often made relations between Provisionals and Officials very strained on the ground. Whereas by the late 1970s, Bell could claim that the 'Officials had gone their Marxist way and became irrelevant to the Provisionals',[39] this was not the case in the early years when Officials claimed to be the true inheritors of the Republican Mantle: 'after 1970, these Official units, especially in the North, not only claimed to be Republicans but even pursued an armed struggle'.[40]

Surprisingly, when I conducted a number of interviews with key figures in both organizations in the early 1970s, I discovered a remarkable degree of understanding at Officer level of the positions taken by some key players. While, for example, a leading Republican from Ardoyne was bitter about the way his area was left undefended in 1969, he retained a genuine respect and affection for some leading Official Republicans, despite nailing his colours firmly to a Provisional mast.[41] The same could be said of the views of some Official leaders of the time of their Provisional counterparts.[42]

From the start of the split in Belfast, there was no doubting the numerical superiority of the Provisionals and it is likely that bitterness between Provisionals

---

**35** Ibid., p. 8.   **36** Bowyer Bell, *The IRA*, p. 58.   **37** Ibid., p. 67.   **38** Ibid., p. 69.   **39** Ibid., p. 70.   **40** Ibid., p. 66.   **41** Private interview.   **42** Private interview.

and Officials was more pronounced at Volunteer level. The split itself was often manifested in political geography, family relationships and personal loyalties, yet a survivor of the time recalls that at an IRA meeting in 1970 when most of Belfast's city units went Provisional (as high perhaps as eleven out of thirteen),[43] the mantra was repeated by the Official leader Billy McMillen's adjutant, Jim Sullivan, that at least they had D-Company, to which Billy McKee responded 'What is D-Company? A Panzer division?' All laughed, he recalled, including, to his credit, McMillen himself.[44] There was little laughing in later years, particularly 1971, 1975 and 1977, when rivalry led to murderous feuding, an aspect of Republicanism mercifully absent from more recent divisions. Therefore, although opponents of the current Sinn Féin strategy can call upon historical precedent to attack that organization, there has not really been enough support for the dissidents to create a significant threat to the new approaches taken. If anything, this short article warns us to be careful in making assumptions about the future. Comparing two different eras can be very misleading. The events of the middle-to-late 1960s were to produce radical changes in the thinking of the Republican leadership of the period. On top of the failure of militarism from 1956 to 1962 was the Republican movement's apparent lack of relevance to the lives of the mass of the people in Ireland. With interest focused on the Vietnam War, trade union militancy and student protests, a left-wing drift to interest in the demand for greater democratic accountability by the Civil Rights movement in Northern Ireland was unsurprising.

### VIEWS ON THE SPLITS

The views which follow are the results of correspondence or conversations which I had with a number of people who have watched political developments with interest and advanced their opinions on why opposition to the new departure of Sinn Féin has not met as much opposition as may have been expected. The views given represent essentially layman opinion, and a different set of perspectives would emerge from a different sample of people, but they reflect the interest of some intelligent observers and I have tried to present their views as coherently as possible, even at the expense of some overlap of views previously given by myself in this essay.

The attempts of the Republican movement of 1966 to the 1970s to redefine itself in contemporary terms led inevitably to conflict with Republicans who took what has been called a more 'traditional' outlook, but in effect covered a larger

---

**43** Private interview.  **44** Private interview.

group of individuals (north and south working class and middle class, young and middle-aged) who had in common a belief in an armed insurrection in the north but often little else. By 1986, the insurrection had been going on for over a quarter of a century, so that, unlike in 1969, a serious insurrection had been enacted. It had not succeeded and the overall alliance had started to fracture. Undoubtedly, the Provisionals could have pursued the armed struggle for a considerable time after this, but casualties had already been high, the jails were full of activists and questions were now being asked as to whether war was still the best policy, as there seemed to be no prospect of an imminent withdrawal of British forces.

The hunger strikes had largely politicized the Nationalist population in the six counties, and certain observations were fairly obvious. Unlike in 1970, there was now a northern leadership in Republicanism which found itself in an influential position with a largely northern membership. There was now a strong argument that the democratic struggle of the Civil Rights movement had largely come to a successful conclusion (although critics of the Provisionals could point out that some of them had opposed it at the time). There was also clear evidence of electoral success and that success was apparently linked to low levels of violence. Sinn Féin was an all-Ireland organization, so there was a possibility of Sinn Féin holding cabinet positions in the North and South at the same time. This remains an interesting prospect, despite the Sinn Féin setbacks at the Dáil election in 2007.

Ever since Secretary of State Peter Brooke's announcement that Britain had no selfish or strategic interest in remaining in Northern Ireland against the wishes of the people, the possibility of bringing the armed struggle to a conclusion was made more attractive. Since 1981, Sinn Féin had also harnessed a large membership, generally of the younger generation, but they tended to join a political party rather than a secret army. Some commentators have pointed to the fact that those imprisoned in the early 1990s for IRA activity were people in their late thirties and early forties who had been in jail before. While this is a generalization, and the IRA had confounded critics who had written them off before, it indicates either personnel problems or fear of security force infiltration or both. The later revelations of informers within the organization certainly worried Republicans and, no doubt, they were aware of grave problems by the early 1980s. However, this problem should not be overstated because, although General Sir Michael Jackson called Operation Banner 'one of the very few (military operations) brought to a successful conclusion by the armed forces of a developed nation against an irregular force',[45] this understates the professionalism and indefatigability of the IRA campaign. It also occludes the fact that Operation Banner tied

45 *Sunday Times*, 5 Aug. 2007.

down 28,000 troops for more than a generation in an area 120 miles by 80 miles and then only with the help of thousands of locally recruited forces in the Ulster Defence Regiment and the Royal Ulster Constabulary.[46] Clearly, the British government too had a vested interest in promoting a peace process in both military and economic terms, and it was therefore unsurprising that they favoured the deal-making element in Sinn Féin to the exclusion of others, and hence the efforts put into the Downing Street Declaration and the Good Friday Agreement.

Republican critics of the current process would bitterly denounce Adams and company as being to a greater or lesser extent in the control of British or Irish security forces, but there was undoubtedly a ground-swell of support for the current situation. Loyalist paramilitaries, often with the connivance of state forces, were conducting a fairly indiscriminate murder campaign for which the IRA could find no truly adequate response, short of being drawn into a sectarian conflict that was anathema to then. While Loyalist paramilitary activity alone or logistical problems in the IRA itself would not have led to a ceasefire, the considerations of the larger global context of the late 1980s to 1990s, as against the late 1960s and early 1970s, were further pressures for a ceasefire and new tactics.

In the last two decades of the twentieth century, radical changes came about which would have been unforeseen in the early 1970s. Who then would have predicted the breaking of the Soviet bloc, the fall of the Berlin Wall, peace in South Africa and attempts at peace in the Middle East? Old certainties began to collapse, among them the possibility of the type of republic envisioned in the early 1970s. Social and economic decisions on Irish matters were now being taken by the European Economic Union rather than the Dáil, with Connolly's contention that Ireland would still be ruled through foreign financiers, banks and other institutions having much validity. A new, more monolithic economic status quo was forming in the latest manifestation of international capital which would simply move finance elsewhere if there was a problem. Irish economic isolation could prove too difficult an opponent for traditional IRA tactics, although some Republicans could argue that physical force to remove the British presence in the north is a moral imperative. In real terms, however, there was a clear majority in favour of a peace policy.

There were still great difficulties facing Gerry Adams, Martin McGuinness and company as they steered in new directions, but they had certain advantages. They had learned lessons from the Republican split of 1969/70 and had advanced their own project very slowly and carefully, having a lot of patience with those who opposed the embracing of constitutional politics. In this regard, Brian Feeny gives great credit to Adams: 'In the last analysis, since the peace process meant

**46** Ibid.

bringing the Republican movement into the political mainstream, the central figure in achieving the aim was Gerry Adams.'[47] Any comprehensive account of the peace process could only be written with a full explication of the roles of John Hume, Albert Reynolds, George Mitchell, Fr Alec Reid, Denis Bradley, Bill Clinton, Tony Blair and many others, but it would be fair to say that Gerry Adams risked his political and actual life in changing Republican tactics so dramatically.

While this is undoubtedly true, it is also the case that the peace process has made many of Adams' former comrades his current enemies. Nonetheless, the standing of Adams and company within in the Republican movement was an undoubted asset in selling the New Departure to many of the Republican faithful. As Desi Murray put it to me, it was back to Michael Collins' 'What's good enough for Gerry (or Martin, or whoever) is good enough for me'.[48] The dissidents on the other hand, whether from the Real IRA or the Continuity IRA, never had the popular support or momentum of the Provisional IRA in the early 1970s. Many of their early operations were ineffective and the Omagh bombing proved to be an albatross around their necks, whereas the early Provisionals were able to capitalize on Catholic anger at the events of August 1969, including the burning of Bombay Street by loyalist mobs.

Moreover, whereas the early officials were accused of infiltration by communist organizations from the late 1960s, Sinn Féin has kept its own decisions largely internal, regardless of any outside advice it may have sought. The network of relationships of the marriage, friendship, work, job schemes and so on within Sinn Féin and the IRA forged over a long and dangerous period of time created its own unity, while dissident groups were very often compromised by informers. Many political dissidents simply walked away rather than join either the Continuity or the Real IRA, often also torn between conviction and old personal loyalty.

Irish America, which traditionally gave great financial and moral support to armed insurrection and certainly helped sustain the Provisional campaign, wholeheartedly endorsed the policy of Gerry Adams (even moreso after 9/11), which effectively isolated the dissidents from that most important sphere of influence. Time had moved on since 1969, and a new, younger membership of Sinn Féin did not carry many of the attitudes prevalent in Republicanism in 1970. Only time will tell where the present Republican process will finally arrive at.

---

**47** Brian Feeney, *Sinn Féin: a hundred turbulent years* (Dublin, 2002), p. 383.  **48** Information from Desi Murray. Here too I must also acknowledge the help of Brian Campfield, Dermot Campfield, Noel O'Reilly, Seán O'Hare, Frank Glenholmes, Seán McErlean, Kieran Stewart and many others to whom I spoke about the latter section of the essay.

# The Poppy-Day bombing: Enniskillen, 1987

## ALAN F. PARKINSON

### SMASHED WREATHS AND POPPIES

The Enniskillen bombing in 1987, although it did not claim the greatest number of fatalities in the modern Troubles, was undoubtedly the single incident of terrorism within the province which made, for a sustained period, the greatest impact upon the British public and politicians. I have chosen it as a case study of the modern Northern Irish conflict for this reason and would like to pose a number of questions. Why did the Enniskillen bombing arouse so much interest in Britain, particularly when other attacks in Northern Ireland had not? What were the main features of the national media's coverage of the attack, and how did these reflect existing views about the conflict in general and about the Unionist position in particular?

What lay behind the IRA's choice of Enniskillen for the Poppy Day bombing? Obviously it is difficult to fathom the logic behind the justification of such an attack, particularly when the bombing divided the Republican community itself. However, it can be argued that a number of factors influenced the decision to bomb the Remembrance Day ceremony in the Fermanagh town. Provisional IRA strength and the existence of a 'maverick' fringe within the area's Republican community, the need to revive morale during an especially difficult year (apart from a recent arms interception on board the *Eksund*, eight Republicans had been killed in an army undercover operation earlier in 1987), and the town's military connections, combined to make Enniskillen's Remembrance Day parade a potential target for an IRA attack.

Enniskillen, the county town of Fermanagh, with its 'mixed' population and its close proximity to the border, had experienced considerable suffering in the conflict before November 1987. However, this had, in the main, been restricted to attacks on security personnel, notably 'easy' targets, such as off-duty members of the RUC and UDR.[1] Despite this earlier focus on off-duty security force personnel, the IRA was well aware of Enniskillen's wider significance and its history as a military base. Enniskillen had been a garrison town since the seventeenth century and its mainly Protestant regiments, such as the Royal

---

[1] Local MP Ken Maginnis pointed out in parliament that there had been 169 killings in his constituency and that there had been a mere 14 resulting convictions; quoted in the *Guardian*, 10 Nov. 1987.

Inniskillings, had a distinguished record in earlier overseas campaigns. Indeed, the military significance of the town was highlighted by the BBC in their early coverage of the bombing.[2]

Clearly the IRA appreciated the symbolic significance of an attack on what they perceived to be a military target, a 'triumphalist' British commemoration of their dead in two previous military campaigns. What they seemingly failed to grasp was that the British, and more importantly from the Republican perspective, American and European audiences, differentiated between British soldiers carrying out their duties in Ulster and British forces remembering their fallen comrades from previous campaigns. Indeed, from a practical perspective, it had been rather more than a designed attack on British soldiers, as both the operationally successful Enniskillen bomb and the unsuccessful 150-pound landmine at Tullyhannon near the Irish border (which had been scheduled to explode at a time when a Boys' Brigade band would have been playing at another Remembrance Day parade), were inevitably going to involve large numbers of civilian casualties.

Despite the clear risk to civilian life, the IRA was obviously prepared to take a gamble with such a device. While the British media were clearly unaware of the sectarian nuances implicit in attendance or participation in a Remembrance Day parade (and indeed, the distinction between 'our' civilians and 'theirs'), the local brigade of the IRA was not. Therefore, while a small number of Catholics might have been involved in the parade, the vast majority of participants and observers were likely to have been Protestants. With the recent setback, in both military and propaganda terms, of the *Eksund* arms interception, a Republican counter-attack, or 'spectacular', was clearly needed to raise Republican morale, and Enniskillen was perceived, at least by local Republicans, to form a likely and appropriate response.

It is believed that IRA personnel planted the bomb in the Reading Rooms of St Michael's Catholic Church late on Saturday 7 November. This hall, situated a mere twenty yards from the town's war memorial, had proved to be a popular vantage point on the procession route for many local people. Thus, as the service was due to commence the following morning, a small crowd of less than a hundred, were standing outside the Catholic Memorial Hall. The bystanders would have been idling away the few minutes before the start of the parade, making casual conversation with friends about the chances of rain falling later in the morning, or perhaps estimating the likely size of the parade, or fondly remembering ex-servicemen who might have passed away since the previous year. The vast majority of them were Protestants – a mixture of Presbyterians,

2 An iconic image of Enniskillen was the bowed figure of the town's cenotaph 'Tommy'.

Methodists and members of the Church of Ireland – and they would have been looking forward to hearing the familiar war tunes of the military bands, as well as watching the procession of youngsters from the various youth organizations. That morning, many of the youthful parade members (later estimated by police as constituting over 200 boys and girls) had been delayed and were due to start their approach to the memorial about the same time as the bomb was primed to go off. Fifteen minutes before the nation remembered the dead of two world wars, a thirty-five-pound device, small by Ulster standards, exploded, blasting out the gable end of the Reading Rooms, trapping many bystanders between a solid wall and the security barriers on the pavement.

While the device was not a large one, the effects of falling masonry and collapsing buildings proved to be devastating. Many eye-witnesses reported that their first recollections following the blast had been those of rising dust, a short eerie silence, followed by the horrendous screams and moans of the injured. A report of the immediate aftermath of the blast highlighted the inevitable confusion:

> For a few seconds, it looked as if the town had suddenly been plunged into a thick fog. But the fog was dust settling on a scene of carnage. Children screamed for their parents and the injured screamed for help. Those who were still on their feet began to pull frantically at the rubble to free bodies.[3]

In the shroud of 'fog', it was the different sounds which stayed in the memories of those caught up in the blast. Local councillor Sammy Foster recalled 'a deathly silence' followed by 'all hell breaking loose'.[4] Teenager Stephen Ross, who was seriously injured in the blast, recalled the 'horrendous' noise of the bomb and his spontaneous recognition of what had just happened. He blanked out, only to come round when people were pulling him out of the rubble. He recalled:

> I couldn't see a thing. I couldn't feel my left leg at all below my knee and I just remember tasting dust and blood in my mouth and putting my hand in my mouth and finding that most of my front teeth had gone. I tried to open my eyes but I just couldn't see anything ... all I could hear was people screaming and shouting.[5]

Although the holocaust which would have undoubtedly occurred had the bomb exploded when the full parade had assembled, was avoided, the toll of civilian

---

3 David Hearst in the *Guardian*, 9 Nov. 1987.   4 In Denzil McDaniel, *Enniskillen: the Remembrance Sunday bombing* (Dublin, 1999), p. 11.   5 Ibid., p. 15.

casualties was the worst to occur since the Droppin Well bomb five years previously. Eleven people died and sixty-three were injured (nineteen seriously) in the Enniskillen blast. *Daily Mirror* photographer Michael Martin, an eye-witness, wrote about 'desperate rescuers clawing at the rubble' and utilized a range of images to describe the carnage:

> Smashed wreaths were trampled under foot, old soldiers were helping rescuers in the rubble and children were wandering in a daze looking for friends or parents. They'd all been spruced up in their smartest Scouts, Guides and Brownies uniforms. Now they were covered with dust and blood. The dust coated everything like shroud and through it all the cries of the wounded drifted like some terrible nightmare.[6]

### THE POLITICAL RESPONSE

The reaction of British political and religious leaders to the events in Co. Fermanagh was unparalleled. They recognized that Enniskillen was different, not just in terms of the number of casualties, but also on account of its sacrilegious dimension and the belief that it appeared to break the 'ground rules' of the conflict. The volume of rebuke was unprecedented, with the 'groundswell of outrage' quickly becoming 'an avalanche of damnation'.[7] English politicians, devoid of any real answers, were united in their condemnation of the attack. Yet with Enniskillen, the tenor of the condemnation, its degree of harshness, and the manner in which politicians of every hue vied with one another in their condemnation, was unique. The Prime Minister, clearly moved by the bombing, emphasized its sacrilegious nature. She said: 'Every nation should honour its dead – and we should all be able to stand and honour them in peace.'[8] In stressing that her government would actively pursue the terrorists, she maintained there would be 'no hiding place' for them and appealed directly to Republican sympathizers in North America, trusting that anyone 'who ever had sympathies for the terrorists, will not have any more now'.[9]

There was cross-party condemnation of the attack. Labour leader Neil Kinnock described the bombing as 'an atrocity against ordinary people', while the Liberals' Ulster spokesman David Alton called for Catholics to 'end their

---

**6** *Daily Mirror*, 9 Nov. 1987.  **7** Padraig O'Malley, *Biting at the grave: the Irish hunger strike and the politics of despair* (Belfast, 1990), p. 251.  **8** Margaret Thatcher on BBC1, 'Late evening news', 8 Nov. 1987.  **9** Ibid. Thatcher was later to observe that 'of all the atrocities inflicted on the people of Ulster, the act of merciless savagery against the people of Enniskillen stands out in its infamy'; quoted in McDaniel, *Enniskillen*, pp 90–1.

ambivalence and join the RUC'.[10] However, Labour's front bench was embarrassed by the involvement of National Executive member Ken Livingstone and Shadow Employment spokesperson Claire Short in a Troops Out meeting barely a week after the blast. Although Short was to pull out of the meeting, it obviously caused the Labour Party considerable embarrassment.

Despite their vehement condemnation of the IRA, the government offered little immediate hope to the beleaguered Ulster Protestant border community. Secretary of State Tom King conceded that there was no 'easy solution' to such security breaches, and far from reassuring the Protestant community, cautioned them to ensure that 'anger mustn't take the form of retaliation and people taking the law into their own hands'.[11] Tory critics of the Prime Minister lambasted her government's reluctance to alter its Ulster policy. Writing in the *Standard*, Enoch Powell condemned English politicians and public alike for their 'surprise' at what had happened in Enniskillen, suggesting that such a tragedy was 'the almost inevitable result of recent government policy'.[12] Powell pinpointed the significance of the Anglo-Irish Agreement and maintained 'there has to be an end to the differential treatment of Ulster and a reassessment of English political interpretation of the problem' which had culminated in 'an Anglo-Irish Agreement as shameful to Britain as it was injurious to Northern Ireland'.[13] Unionists were also furious with the government, linking its breaches in security with the Hillsborough Agreement. The local MP, Ken Maginnis, had expressed his scepticism about his political counterparts' determination to eradicate such acts of terrorism that Sunday evening:

> When I go to Westminster tomorrow my colleagues will be gracious and sympathetic. But when they go home to their constituencies next week they will have forgotten Ken Maginnis and the people of Fermanagh and South Tyrone.[14]

Church leaders united in their condemnation of the attack. Most significantly, it was the clear response of Catholic clerics which made most impact. A Catholic bishops' statement immediately after the blast argued that there was 'no room for ambivalence' and verbalized the 'sense of disgust' in their community. Their statement ended:

> In face of the present campaign of Republican violence, the choice of all Catholics is clear. It is a choice between good and evil. It is sinful to join

---

**10** In O'Malley, *Biting*, p. 252 and in the *Guardian*, 10 Nov. 1987. **11** *Guardian*, 10 Nov. 1987. **12** *London Evening Standard*, 10 Nov. 1987. **13** Ibid. **14** *Guardian*, 9 Nov. 1987.

organizations committed to violence, or remain in them. It is sinful to support such organizations or to call on others to support them.[15]

Local Catholics felt both anguish at the plight of their Protestant neighbours and growing concern for both themselves and their families. An Enniskillen priest, Seán Farren, felt that there was 'a sense of guilt attached to us and we had to convince our Protestant neighbours that we didn't want this'.[16]

BRITISH MEDIA COVERAGE OF THE ENNISKILLEN BOMB

Enniskillen certainly had a great impact on the national audience. The story not only dominated the news bulletins for most of the week leading up to the victims' funerals, but it also encroached into other news areas, including programmes such as 'Question Time' and 'Kilroy'. Enniskillen was also different in the sense that it was not allowed to 'evaporate' like other Ulster tragedies. Thus, television used new angles on the original story to rekindle interest in the event. In the days just after the attack, attention was drawn to the forgiving, dignified figure of Gordon Wilson. After the funerals of the victims, the wit of the Prince and Princess of Wales on 17 November and the suffering and stoicism of some of the town's injured, continued to claim the headlines. Indeed, the story appeared regularly in the national bulletins until the rearranged Remembrance Day service on 22 November, and programmes relating to the event were transmitted nearly two years after the explosion. The Enniskillen tragedy was featured in over fifty BBC television national broadcasts, including studio audience discussions, religious programmes, and interviews with victims and political and security features, as well as news bulletins. The media's initial assessment was that here was an Irish story which, although it had emanated from the same violent backdrop as countless other Ulster news stories, was 'different' on account of the community's response to the violence, and which provided new hopes for a more peaceful future. Most of the early news bulletins featured not only extracts from an amateur video recording, but interviews with eye-witnesses and political reaction. The available film footage was indisputably stark and raw in its nature. A local shopkeeper, Raymond McCartney, who had intended to take a film of the parade on his VHS video camera, hastily switched on his camera to the drama unfolding right in front of him. His eleven minutes of videotape were used by the BBC, ITV and RTE – on account of there being no TV personnel on the ground in Enniskillen – and consequently, McCartney's tape was used by television

15 McDaniel, *Enniskillen*, p. 73.   16 Ibid., p. 71.

companies all round the world. This video brought home the horrors of the bombing in a way that previous post-bombing coverage had failed to capture. Although the BBC thought it prudent to cut the soundtrack from Mr McCartney's video and ITV omitted some of the more harrowing images from its earlier bulletins, the edited use of a live recording of a catastrophic event had a profound effect, particularly on external audiences, whose experience of such an event would have been minimal.

The national media were quick to exploit the image of one individual's extraordinary capacity to forgive as being symbolic of Ireland's growing mood of atonement. By concentrating on this aspect of Enniskillen, the media avoided considering the underlying cause of the attack, namely the government's apparent inability to protect its citizens. Although it seemed slightly bizarre for an increasingly secular society to be advocating the essentially Christian virtue of forgiveness, this was the predominant feature of British coverage of the bombing: a forgiving response of a provincial society, one which surmounted political and religious barriers and which promised fruitful change emanating from below, rather than being devised and implemented by those from above.

The personification of this willingness to forgive and the torch-carrier for future peace hopes was Enniskillen draper Gordon Wilson who, apart from his own blast injuries, had lost his daughter Marie, a trainee nurse at Belfast's Royal Victoria Hospital, in the blast. For the national and international audience, Wilson quickly became the 'voice' of Enniskillen. An honest, dignified man, he was perceived to be the antithesis of the perpetrators of the bombing and the local politicians who appeared either unwilling or unable to stem the flow of violence. Television cameras focused on his remarkable capacity to forgive those who had taken the life of his daughter and fellow citizens. On 9 November, he told the nation that he had 'prayed for the bombers last night'.[17] He gave an emotional account of Marie's last moments, ending with the words, 'Daddy, I love you very much', and added that he and his wife had 'no ill feeling towards the IRA'.[18] The *Daily Express* also highlighted Gordon Wilson's propensity towards forgiveness. The paper's headline, 'Marie's father mourns with dignity and a remarkable lack of bitterness', concentrated on this apparently new Irish angle. John Burns' centre-page report highlighted the feelings of the Wilsons, but gave the impression that they represented the mood of other grieving families in the town. Burns wrote with passion about how Wilson 'prayed for the bomber' who 'would have to face his Maker' and wondered in amazement at the 'unselfishness' of the local community:

---

**17** BBC1, 'Six o'clock evening news', 9 Nov. 1987. **18** Ibid.

In other homes (apart from the Wilsons) in this backwater town, there are tears for the victims. Yet no one talks of bloody vengeance against the killers and all strive to hide you from their tears. Time and again you are rocked by the unfailing niceness of the bereaved. Whenever their self-control slips, they quickly apologize for their tears, yet you want to weep with them.[19]

Gordon Wilson was often cited by the national media as an example of how Christian charity and forgiveness could conquer those agents of sectarian division in the province and hold out hopes for a better future. The *Sunday Times* noted that 'what local bitterness there has been has been limited and held in check', and praised the contribution of a 'remarkable' man, whose 'display of simple Christian faith' promised to 'cut the ground from beneath the extremists who prefer conflict to compromise'.[20] The same paper was just one of the journals which grabbed the opportunity of lashing out at the familiar target of Unionist politicians. Although Ian Paisley had restricted his Enniskillen comments to a renunciation of IRA violence and a renewed call for tighter security measures, some journalists could not resist the chance of contrasting Paisley's belligerent persona with the tolerance of Gordon Wilson:

If Mr Wilson can forgive, what right have others to call for revenge? Not for the first time, it's the Revd Ian Paisley who is out of touch with the public yearn for peace, not Mr Wilson.[21]

A few days later, it was Marie's funeral which was highlighted by the media, with *Today* devoting its front and centre pages in a six-photo treatment of the funeral under the headline, 'Enniskillen says farewell to Saint Marie'.[22] The *Independent* described the great cross-community sympathy for the Wilson family, quoting the Methodist minister's description of the nurse who was 'like a whirlwind breathing life and vitality' into Enniskillen.[23]

Many papers concentrated on the clear contrast between the destruction of Marie's own life and her obvious care for the lives of others. To some, particularly the tabloids, it was this angelic quality which, along with the statue of the soldier bowing his head in front of the blast damage, was to become the potent symbols of Enniskillen. The *Daily Mirror*, besides singling out Marie as the embodiment of the tragedy, also decided that her vocation – caring for the sick – would make an appropriate vehicle for a fund appeal. In a page feature article, 'Front-line

**19** *Daily Express*, 10 Nov. 1987. **20** *Sunday Times*, 15 Nov. 1987. **21** Ibid. **22** *Today*, 11 Nov. 1987. **23** *Independent*, 11 Nov. 1987.

angels', Mary Riddell spotlighted the Royal Victoria Hospital in West Belfast, where Marie had been a student nurse. Describing the scene in the maternity unit 'where smiling nurses masked their grief as they worked', the *Mirror* appealed to its readers for 'donations which would help alleviate the burden of an over-stretched hospital staff'.[24]

Although the national media was to maximize the forgiveness theme – this response, with its stress on avoiding a backlash, was obviously in accordance with British policy in Northern Ireland – the local press also investigated the degree of suffering experienced by Enniskillen victims long after the explosion, and questioned the extent of forgiveness in the wider Protestant community. Jane Bell's *Belfast Telegraph* report – 'Head Ronnie Hill retired on Monday, but he doesn't know ... he's in a coma'– graphically illustrated the extent of suffering of blast victims long after the actual incident.[25] Bell informed her readers that Ronnie Hill 'needs round the clock care as he lies and sits in his hospital room. Tubes feed him and help his breathing. The only independent movement he can make is to open and close his eyes.'[26] His wife Noreen felt that the Poppy Day bombing had 'sadly made no difference' and attacked the gunmen, arguing that if they were human, they could not do it: 'I don't know how anyone could support them.'[27] A decade later, a seriously injured victim of the blast, Jim Dixon, remembered that his anger about Gordon Wilson's statements was shared by many in the town.[28] Dixon said: 'It annoyed me badly to hear that he forgave the IRA. What right had he? It was obnoxious. They had committed a sin against humanity, not against him.'[29]

On account of the bombing occurring at a 'typically British' ceremony in a garrison town, the external audience was more prepared to pay attention, as they were more familiar with the occasion and ceremony. Therefore, the tabloid press in particular focused their wrath on what they regarded as an act of sacrilege. The *Sun* led with three pages of the attack, including one with the caption, 'Death in the Debris' and its headline the day after the bomb was 'Poppy Day massacre – 11 dead and 63 maimed by the IRA'.[30] The reporter noted the 'merciless savagery' of the IRA and concluded:

> Eleven men and women, wearing their Remembrance Day poppies with pride. Red poppies that became bathed in the blood they symbolize. They were cut down at a service for heroes – with a bomb planted by IRA cowards.[31]

---

**24** *Daily Mirror*, 13 Nov. 1987. **25** *Belfast Telegraph*, 3 Nov. 1988. **26** Ibid. **27** Ibid. **28** Several papers referred to Dixon verbally attacking Secretary of State Tom King as he visited the injured in Enniskillen Hospital. Mr Dixon rebuked the minister for 'having his hands dripping with the blood of the Protestants of Ulster'. **29** In McDaniel, *Enniskillen*, pp 131–2. **30** *Sun*, 9 Nov. 1987. **31** Ibid.

The *Daily Mirror* also picked out the sacrilegious aspect of the Remembrance Day attack. Leading with the headline 'Poppy Day of blood – a blot on mankind', the *Mirror* stressed the 'role-reversal' of bandsmen and marchers with medals from world wars who 'ran from the parade in a desperate attempt to rescue victims'.[32]

Allied to the forgiveness theme of media coverage was that of community cohesion in the explosion's aftermath. The idea that 'total community horror' at the attack promised optimism for the future was featured in several television reports. Thus, 'Newsnight' and the main BBC 'Evening News' bulletin concentrated on Enniskillen 'looking to the future', and another BBC report observed how teachers were trying to prevent their children from becoming insular in their attitudes as a result of the bombing.[33] Another report looked at 'the after-effects of the Remembrance Day bomb on the community'.[34] Special emphasis was placed in several reports on the explosion's repercussions on local schoolchildren. Carmel McQuaid noted that, despite local schools' attempts to ensure a speedy return to normality, there were many cases of pupils suffering 'delayed reaction', with several instances of 'insomnia, nightmares, depression, unsettled behaviour and outbursts of weeping' being reported.[35]

Enniskillen was portrayed by the media as an attack on the wider community and not simply one aimed at the Protestant section of that community. The joint involvement of local Catholics and Protestants who had fought 'shoulder to shoulder' and 'with heroism' in previous conflicts was noted by Ted Oliver in the *Daily Mirror*.[36] The *Sun*, too, emphasized that, despite the exclusively Protestant fatality count, parades in the town were not perceived by many, including the RUC, to be solely Protestant occasions. The reactions of a police officer witness to the blast, who had noted that the march had 'not been just a Protestant parade' and that 'Catholics too were paying their respects to the dead', were recorded.[37] Indeed, this perception that the bomb, rather than being a blatantly sectarian 'anti-Protestant' act, was a crime against the wider community and indeed, humanity, was of crucial significance in ensuring that Unionists were unable to turn the Enniskillen outrage to their political advantage. It could be argued that this perception was one largely constructed by the national media which did not desire the outrage to be given a 'political' dimension. In other words, by restricting coverage of Enniskillen to an attack on the wider community, the national media was not providing Unionist politicians with sufficient leverage to turn the Enniskillen bombing into propaganda 'fodder' for their anti-Anglo Irish Agreement campaign. Therefore, as has been noted, coverage of the explosion

**32** *Daily Mirror*, 9 Nov. 1987. **33** BBC2, 'Newsnight' and BBC1, 'Evening news', 13 Nov. 1987. **34** BBC1, 'Breakfast time', 10 Nov. 1987. **35** *Times Educational Supplement*, 11 Mar. 1988. **36** *Daily Mirror*, 9 Nov. 1987. **37** *Sun*, 9 Nov. 1987.

concentrated on the scale of human loss, the unusually large measure of Christian forgiveness to emerge from Enniskillen and the sacrilegious nature of the IRA's attack on the 'war dead'. It was these facets which made Enniskillen 'different' in the eyes of the British media, and not the belief that one section of the Northern Irish community was being specifically targeted by terrorists emanating from another section of that same community.

Consequently, the religious composition of Enniskillen's victims was rarely referred to. When it was, reference was indirect, such as where the victims worshipped or were buried. Papers like *Today* reported the names of the churches in their descriptions of the funerals and the *Express* mentioned 'the Armstrong couple who sang together in the town's Darling Street Methodist Church Choir', and also observed that 'six devoted members of the same church' (Enniskillen Presbyterian) were victims of the blast.[38] However, few papers deemed it necessary to analyze why the suffering was exclusively Protestant, nor was the issue of Protestants being targeted by the IRA covered in depth in the press (for instance, in the form of a leading article). Fleet Street chose rather to contextualize Enniskillen as a Republican response to the *Eksund* arms find, thereby ignoring its position in the framework of an IRA 'genocide' policy in a border area.

Ironically, the external audience's only awareness that the bombing had a sectarian dimension emanated from the statements of individuals, principally from Catholic spokesmen. The *Standard* was one of a number of papers to print John Hume's statement regarding the magnitude of Enniskillen, which he described as 'the worst act of provocation against the Protestant community in the whole seventeen years of the conflict'.[39] In a similar vein, the *Times*, on its front page, reported a statement from Irish Catholic bishops (without actually commenting on their implications), where they 'called on the Irish people to attend Sunday Mass in large numbers to show their collective solidarity or sympathy with the Protestant community'.[40]

'Suffering children' was another powerful media image of the Enniskillen bombing. Apart from focusing on the tragic fate of a young adult (Marie Wilson), the *Sunday Times* presented an in-depth, illustrated life-story of the student nurse, 'Born into strife; the life and death of Marie Wilson'.[41] Much of the national media also highlighted the physical and psychological suffering of those injured in the blast, like Stephen Ross and Lisa Cathcart, as well as those who had lost parents and other relatives in the bombing, most notably Julian Armstrong (who had been injured in the bomb) and that of his older sisters. The *Express* wrote about how 'orphaned Julian Armstrong was yesterday struggling to come to terms with the loss of his parents'.[42]

---

**38** *Today*, 11 Nov. 1987 and *Daily Express*, 10 Nov. 1987.  **39** *London Evening Standard*, 9 Nov. 1987.  **40** *Times*, 14 Nov. 1987.  **41** *Sunday Times*, 15 Nov. 1987.  **42** *Daily Express*, 10 Nov. 1987.

Another example of Enniskillen's youth personifying the resilient spirit of the town was provided by 6-year-old Lisa Cathcart, the youngest casualty. A photograph of her playing with a typewriter presented by NIO Minister Richard Needham, under the caption, 'Lisa's keys to recovery', was featured in the *Express*.[43] The media also concentrated on youngsters like Stephen Ross, who had been badly injured in the blast but who showed bravery and determination in overcoming many of the problems caused by his serious injuries. The horrific facial injuries suffered by an otherwise normal teenager were given special treatment by the media. The *Daily Mirror* combined its reporting of the horrible injuries suffered by Stephen, a 15-year-old Enniskillen schoolboy, with an appropriate condemnation of the IRA's account of the event. In a front-page report dominated by a photo of Stephen clearly in pain – 'The IRA regrets'– reporter Joe Gorrod told his *Mirror* readers that Stephen was 'so badly injured in the blast that he needs a cage to keep the bones of his face together'.[44]

Stephen Ross was one of the many Enniskillen survivors to receive the interest and sympathy of the Royal Family, an interest which, especially as it involved the Princess of Wales, inevitably captured media attention. Papers commented on the 'healing' effect of the royal visit to Enniskillen Hospital and how this had resulted in 'bringing the smiles back' to the townsfolk. A *Times* report noted how the injured had been 'cheered up by the royal visitors' and it was accompanied by three photos of the royal couple meeting some of the injured.[45] One featured Princess Diana sympathizing with an injured policeman by his hospital bed, another showed her signing an autograph for an injured teenager and the third photographed her with Gordon Wilson, who later told the press: 'The visit has helped me – Princess Di is a lovely girl.'[46] Even the queen, who rarely visited the province or made statements on the situation there, was sufficiently moved by both the timing and the nature of the Enniskillen bombing to issue a message shortly afterwards:

> I was deeply shocked to hear of the atrocity which took place at Enniskillen today and of the innocent victims who were sharing in the nation's Remembrance. My heartfelt sympathy goes to the bereaved and injured in their distress.[47]

**43** Ibid.  **44** *Daily Mirror*, 12 Nov. 1987.  **45** *Times*, 18 Nov. 1987.  **46** Ibid.  **47** The Queen, reported in *Guardian*, 9 Nov. 1987.

## ENNISKILLEN – APPORTIONING THE BLAME

It was not long before attention turned to apportioning the blame for the outrage. It is my contention that, despite the increase in the volume of sympathy for bomb victims and a definite, if short-lived, upward shift in support for the presence of British troops in the province, British analysis of the explosion concentrated more on the faults and weaknesses of Irish parties than delivering an in-depth investigation of British policy and attitudes to Northern Ireland. A significant amount of attention was paid to analyzing the effects of the incident on the Catholic hierarchy, and the response of Sinn Féin and of politicians and the general public in the south of Ireland.

A lot of coverage was given to the muted reaction of the political representatives of the IRA. Paul Kerrigan, Sinn Féin leader of Enniskillen Council, was followed by a large media contingent, who had been waiting, in vain, for his reactions to the bomb, and allegations of disagreement within the Republican movement were raised in a BBC evening news bulletin.[48] Although some observers reminded their audiences that the IRA had not strictly adhered to their own 'code' in the past, there was a general feeling that the Republican organization had 'broken their own ground rules', and by making 'no attempt to phone a warning', it was clearly 'impossible to see how such an operation could have been planned without envisaging civilian casualties and Protestant ones at that'.[49]

Criticism was averted from the British authorities for failing to deal adequately with breaches in security preceding the Cenotaph blast and hoisted instead onto the Irish government. In a front-page report, the *Express* announced that the RUC were 'naming' the bomber responsible for the blast and that the Irish premier would 'soon face an extradition test.' Its reporting team located the whereabouts of the alleged bomber who was 'lying low in his Donegal bolthole, just thirty minutes drive from Enniskillen', and drew attention to the 'sanctuary' afforded by the south:

> Now Irish premier Charles Haughey will have to show whether he has the political will to show IRA killers that there is no hiding place for them in the Republic and that they will be extradited to face British justice.[50]

The *Times* differentiated between Haughey's sympathies with the Republican cause and the position adopted by Garret Fitzgerald, Fine Gael leader and signatory of the Hillsborough Agreement. The paper maintained that 'the government

---

**48** BBC1, 'Nine o'clock news', 10 Nov. 1987. **49** *Spectator*, 14 Nov. 1987. **50** *Daily Express*, 12 Nov. 1987.

of the Republic wriggles uneasily to rid itself of its predecessor's commitment to tighter extradition laws'.[51] Only whenever they fitted into the existing media agenda did the British press and television stations select other Irish dimensions, notably the visit of the Mayor of Dublin to the town and the holding of a minute's silence for the victims of Enniskillen.

Unlike the British press' open condemnation of the behaviour of the IRA and the apparent inactivity of the Irish government, their criticism of the British government's security failures was veiled. The *Standard* argued that the Enniskillen bombing had highlighted the need for Northern Ireland to be placed higher on the political agenda and urged the Prime Minister to exert more influence on Irish policy:

> For too long, Anglo-Irish affairs have been dealt with in a low-level at the London end. This is an opportunity for Mrs Thatcher, who was largely responsible for getting the Agreement through and weathering the antagonisms in Ulster and in her own party, to take the reins back into her own hands.[52]

Predictably, the *Daily Mirror*'s criticism of Thatcher's Northern Ireland Secretary was more virulent, with a leader demanding that the 'ineffectual' Tom King 'should go'.[53] Elements of the Tory press condemned security arrangements, even questioning the accuracy of army and police statements. The *Express* reported Ian Paisley's television claim that police had admitted that the Catholic hall opposite the war memorial had not been searched because there could have been 'a serious reaction' from sections of the Catholic community.[54] The *Standard* also reported this story, noting Paisley's 'amazement' that a search of the building had not been made and reported his call for a full-scale debate on the security situation, 'which had seriously deteriorated'.[55]

The political representatives of the Protestant community were not to enjoy a sympathetic response from the British press after the bombing. Many commentators agreed with British politicians in their belief that, by refusing to accept the Anglo-Irish Agreement gracefully, Unionists were guilty of stalling the political process and were consequently guilty by default of prolonging the terror campaign. The *Sunday Times* was perhaps the most specific in its criticism. In its leader, 'Out of tragedy – hope', it maintained that both governments 'must continue to shoulder their responsibility' and that an essential task was 'to strive to make the Anglo-Irish Agreement more productive'.[56] Apart from its noticeable

51 *Times*, 9 Nov. 1987.   52 *London Evening Standard*, 9 Nov. 1987.   53 *Daily Mirror*, 9 Nov. 1987.
54 *Daily Express*, 10 Nov. 1987.   55 *London Standard*, 9 Nov. 1987.   56 *Sunday Times*, 15 Nov. 1987.

restraint in sympathizing with the Enniskillen victims, the *Guardian* made little reference in its leading articles to the frustration, anger and problems faced by the Unionist community in trying to cope with the direct loss of individuals and also the threat posed by their own paramilitaries. The *Guardian*'s advice was, as they admitted themselves, 'sanctimonious'. By offering a psychological interpretation of terrorists' motives, by offering a theoretical rather than a practical, basic analysis of the province's problems, the paper seemed to agree with Conor Cruise O'Brien's condemnation of 'politics against the last atrocity'.[57] By stressing the 'only hope' formula of defeating the IRA by 'pulling the rug from under their feet by cooperation between peoples and governments', the *Guardian* also argued that, in effect, the British were powerless in political and military terms , with only the Northern Ireland people having access to the key to a permanent solution of their problems.[58]

In their reporting of the understandably emotional response of Unionist representatives, the British press sympathized more with British political leaders 'who have beaten their heads against Ulster's brick wall of hate', than they did with the leaders of the Protestant community, whose 'megaphonic, incandescent incoherence overshadowed the stifled, small voice' of moderation in the area (as represented, the *Guardian* argued, by John Hume). Criticizing Unionist parliamentary condemnation of the attack, Andrew Rawnsley noted their 'frightening determination to build more funeral pyres in Ulster from the bodies of their own dead'.[59]

On the rare occasion where a British paper did sympathize with the Unionist position, it could usually be attributed to the recognition of the special place held by the writers on the far right of British and Irish politics. Thus, voices such as O'Brien and Enoch Powell were drowned out by those in the British media which portrayed Loyalists as incorrigible bigots. This latter, negative interpretation of what appeared to the writers as a hopeless and illogical situation, where 'hardly anything that has happened in the past nineteen years makes any sense at all', dominated a report in the *Express* by a veteran commentator on the Ulster conflict. Lamenting the demise of the notion of Ulster as an independent republic, Jon Akass bemoaned that 'it was not to be', adding that 'we are stuck forever with the gleeful gunmen and roaring bigots like the Revd Ian Paisley'.[60]

Subsequent media coverage looked more fully at Unionist reaction to the bombing. Peter Taylor's 'Newsnight' report observed the attitudes of several Unionists at local level.[61] Although it was clearly important to gauge the local Protestant response, it was inevitable that this would be, in the heat of the

---

**57** *Guardian*, 9 Nov. 1987. **58** Ibid. **59** *Guardian*, 10 Nov. 1987. **60** *Daily Express*, 10 Nov. 1987. **61** BBC2, 'Newsnight', 9 Nov. 1987.

moment, more emotional than logical, and that a broader, more rational response from the wider Unionist community in the province, would have been more insightful. A former Ulster Unionist councillor in Fermanagh, Bertie Kerr, filmed driving his tractor, maintained that, on account of the bomb, there could be 'no possibility of Catholics in government, while voting for the IRA', and other prominent local Unionist figures, including Ken Maginnis and Raymond Ferguson, dismissed any possibility of power-sharing.[62] Other Unionists called for a complete review of the government's security policy and this formed the substance of Unionist Party leader Jim Molyneaux's case when he met Margaret Thatcher.

The bombing also coincided with the second anniversary of the signing of the Anglo-Irish Agreement. Indeed, Unionists were to use the emotional backdrop of Enniskillen to highlight their opposition to the Hillsborough Accord. The BBC featured a Loyalist demonstration in London protesting against the Agreement. The short news item contained film of a group of Loyalists marching behind a pipe-band on their way to Downing Street, where they delivered a message to Thatcher. In an interview, Ian Paisley claimed that the Enniskillen tragedy had 'brought home to the [English] people what is happening in Northern Ireland'.[63] Unionists' responses to the Enniskillen bombing and their continued resistance to the 1985 Agreement, therefore, appeared to be uncompromising and diehard to the British public, and might well have resulted in Loyalists conceding some of the moral high ground which they had briefly gained as a result of the attack.

Public opinion in Britain has rarely been highly sympathetic to the Unionist case. However, for a brief period after the Enniskillen bombing, opinion within Great Britain became noticeably more sensitive to the need for maintaining a military presence in the province. In a Marplan poll conducted for Channel 4's 'A Week in Politics', there was a sharp reduction both in the number of Britons who wanted the troops withdrawn from Northern Ireland and also in the proportion of those who supported the creation of a united Ireland.[64]

The drop in support for troop withdrawal from Northern Ireland illustrates a softening in British attitudes towards Unionist protest. Of 1,185 people interviewed between 20 and 24 November, 46 per cent wanted troops to stay in the province as long as violence continued, an increase of 12 per cent since a similar Marplan poll that January.[65]

It would be unwise to underestimate the unique effect which the coverage of the Enniskillen bombing had on the British public. For perhaps the first and only time, they were able to fully empathize with the civilian population of Northern

**62** Ibid.   **63** BBC1, 'Six o'clock news', 12 Nov. 1987.   **64** Channel 4, 'A week in politics', Nov. 1987.
**65** Ibid.

Ireland. The event was seen as catastrophic by the media in Britain as well as many politicians and was regarded as a possible watershed in the Troubles, in which the decency of the ordinary people would overcome the evil forces of terrorism. However, as David McKittrick reminded his *Independent* readers, there had been 'a great many false dawns' in Ireland over the previous twenty years. He added:

> The IRA could yet salvage something from the wreckage. A retaliatory Loyalist outrage or even a recklessly fired plastic bullet could begin to dull the impact of Enniskillen in the Nationalist ghettos.[66]

Despite the unprecedented degree of empathy in Great Britain with the predicament of ordinary people in Northern Ireland, and some evidence of a short-term increase in support for both troop involvement in the province and the constitutional guarantee, the 'Poppy Day' bombing was not to lead to a closer awareness of, or identification with, the Unionist position. Unionists were unable to capitalize on the tragic events of that November morning and their ostensibly just claims for resisting the Hillsborough Agreement continued to be ignored in Great Britain and further afield. What was more apparent in the national media's coverage of Enniskillen was its condemnation of the IRA and, indeed, its apportioning of blame to the various groups in Ireland. By interpreting the story in this manner – that is, within the traditional framework of Britain having to act as a peacemaker between two 'unreasonable' and 'irrational' forces in Ireland – Enniskillen became depoliticized and was confined in its significance to an, albeit major, terrorist incident.

What, then, was the true significance of Enniskillen? At a local level, the task of community rebuilding proved to be generally (but not universally) successful. A writer noted a year on:

> On a wider front, the ability to adjust following a disaster is also about community self-confidence and its ability to transform what has been a tragedy into an opportunity for growth. Enniskillen has shown much evidence of this, with the town itself being the subject of many new commercial and architectural developments.[67]

The dashed hopes of those longing for a 'turning point' in the conflict bore testimony to the claim of hard-nosed realists that the extreme polarization of

---

**66** *Independent*, 17 Nov. 1987.   **67** David Bolton, 'The threat to belonging in Enniskillen' (1988), quoted in McDaniel, *Enniskillen*, p. 208.

Northern Irish society by the late 1980s inevitably meant that a 'Damascus-style' conversion to a peaceful society would be doomed. Thus, Enniskillen did not prove to be, like numerous atrocities before and afterwards, a turning point.[68] However, it did lead to continued soul-searching, reflection and endeavours to foster cross-community developments.[69] Finally, it succeeded in relaying the brutal horrors of sectarian violence to the external audience and resulted in a genuine outpouring of sympathy and understanding for Northern Ireland's long-suffering people. At its core, Remembrance Sunday is a 'British' occasion and on that fateful November morning in 1987, the British and indeed international audience was rocked into a realization of how low the protagonists in Ulster's mucky war were prepared to stoop. The dignity of Gordon Wilson and his willingness to forgive were largely behind this increased willingness of the Great British public to empathize with Ulster's suffering majority. Few would have been unmoved by Mr Wilson's statement the day after his daughter Marie had been killed in the blast:

> I have lost my daughter and we shall miss her. But I bear no ill will. I bear no grudge. Dirty sort of talk is not going to bring her back to life. She was a great wee lassie. She was a pet and she's dead. She's in Heaven and we'll meet again.[70]

---

**68** As in many other terrorist cases, this was not helped by the lack of a successful prosecution. Despite hundreds of statements and follow-ups to enquiries, as well as media speculation on likely suspects, those responsible for the blast have not been brought to justice. **69** See McDaniel, *Enniskillen*, p. 201. **70** Ibid., p. 64.

# Index